WITHDRAWN

Thirty Years of
The American Neptune

Thirty Years of

The American Neptune

Ernest S. Dodge, editor

Harvard University Press
Cambridge, Massachusetts
1972

© Copyright 1972 by the President and Fellows of Harvard College
All rights reserved
Library of Congress Catalog Card Number 72-82988
SBN 674-88465-5
Printed in the United States of America

Contents

	Introduction	vii
I	Life at Sea	1
II	New England Grab Bag	35
III	Some Distinctive Coastal Craft	91
IV	Perils at Sea	151
V	The Nineteenth-Century Navy	193
VI	Varied Fare	237
	Appendix	293

Introduction

The American Neptune

THE evening of October 23, 1939, Lincoln Colcord was scheduled to speak to the Peabody Museum Marine Associates in Salem, Massachusetts, on "The Last Forty Years of American Sail, 1865–1905." The monthly meeting of this group of maritime enthusiasts was preceded by a convivial dinner at the Hawthorne Hotel in the course of which there was animated discussion about the possibility of founding a journal of maritime history as an American counterpart of England's *The Mariner's Mirror*. Afterward, when the party assembled around the big table in the workroom of the Peabody Museum, Linc Colcord was so fired up that he never got around to talking about his announced subject, but instead made an impassioned plea, urging the assemblage to establish a maritime historical publication. Before the evening was over the Peabody Museum Marine Associates, without any authority whatsoever to do so or any funds, had voted enthusiastically to found the journal now known as *The American Neptune*.

It was then left to Walter Muir Whitehill, Assistant Director of the Peabody Museum, to carry the ball. The Museum Trustees did not choose to be responsible for the publication of a journal which they were reasonably convinced would be a failure; after all, the Depression was still with us. Therefore, a new and separate corporation was established, with Samuel Eliot Morison, the country's most distinguished maritime historian, elected president, and Walter Muir Whitehill, secretary and treasurer. Legal problems were to be solved by Augustus Peabody Loring, Jr., then a trustee of the Peabody Museum, later its president. The new corporation received a grant of $1,500 from the Carnegie Corporation to pay for the printing of a brochure and the first number of the journal.

The first four editors of the newly established journal were Walter Muir Whitehill, Lincoln Colcord, M. V. Brewington, a Philadelphia banker, and Howard I. Chapelle, a naval architect. Whitehill in effect served as Managing Editor, and his office at the Peabody became headquarters for all correspondence connected with editorial work as well as subscriptions. The editorial advisory board appointed was a well-selected group of the most active people in the principal American maritime museums, plus representative historians, librarians, collectors, naval officers, sailors, lawyers, printers, and pure amateurs, working in the maritime field in the United States and Canada. Ten years later Whitehill commented that only four of the forty advisory board members were engaged in college teaching of American history, and that only half of the group had any formal connection with learned institutions.

The first meeting of the Editorial Board was held in Walter Whitehill's brick-floored barn in North Andover on May 5, 1940. The selection of a name brought forth many suggestions, but John Philips Cranwell, thinking of *The Mariner's Mirror*, named after the famous English Coast pilot, came up with *The American Neptune*, paraphrasing the great *Atlantic Neptune*, a collection of charts issued by the Admiralty in the eighteenth century. This title was unanimously approved and the journal was so christened, with the subtitle *A Quarterly Journal of Maritime History*.

Volume I, Number 1, appeared in January 1941, and Walter Whitehill's editorial laid out the wide field of action. Articles of many and divergent subjects would be welcome: those dealing with the design, construction, and operation of various types of vessels at different periods, the results of technical nautical and marine historical research; histories of merchants and shipping lines, and of individual vessels and voyages; studies of ports; naval, privateering, steamship, and yachting history; the history of scientific navigation, nautical instruments, charts and maps; sealore, including eyewitness accounts of sea serpents, disasters, and sea chanteys; biographical accounts of captains, merchants, and shipbuilders; regional studies (though not genealogical accounts or works of local piety). Maritime art, paintings, prints, ship carving, the historic decoration of water craft, and scrimshaw would play an important part; accounts of historical ship models or collections, and data or plans that could be used for the construction of ship models would be included. Maritime museums and institutions with maritime collections were encouraged to submit accounts of their material. A section on significant unpublished documents and reprints of very rare tracts, including early photographs, was planned. There were to be book reviews, listings and notes on old and new maritime publications, and sections of queries and answers. (Vernon D. Tate became first and only book review editor, an office that was soon dropped.) Plans altered over the years. A detailed bibliography of maritime material published in American magazines and journals and books was prepared by Robert G. Albion until it became too expensive. A popular feature for the last dozen years has been an annual Pictorial Supplement, consisting of pictures on a given maritime subject published in the four issues and then offered for sale as a separate pamphlet.

The first masthead showed Neptune rising from the waves, trident in hand, with Benjamin Franklin lecturing him severely from the shore. It was replaced in the third issue by the full-face portrait of Neptune (drawn by Rudolph Ruzicka from a carving owned by Count Pehr Sparre) who has gazed benevolently ever since. The format, which has never changed, was designed by Fred Anthoensen.

Nor has the manner of conducting business changed. From the beginning the acceptance and rejection of articles submitted for publication has rested in the hands of the editors, assisted by the Editorial Advisory Board. In substance, this has been the responsibility of the Managing Editor or the most active editor, although various editors and Board members have rendered valuable assistance by reading and advising upon manuscripts.

The contents of the first number are typical of what they have been ever since. Samuel Eliot Morison led off with an article on "Columbus and Polaris," a by-product of his work on the Columbus voyages. The late William Bell Clark submitted an article on "American Naval Policy, 1775–1776." Robert G. Albion wrote on "Inspection Comments on American Ships and Barks," and Cedric Ridgely-Nevitt published an account, complete with drawings suitable for a model maker, on "Auxiliary Steamships and R. B. Forbes." William B. Sturtevant reminisced on "A Boy's First Day at Sea in the Bark *Belle of Oregon*—1886," and Frank A. Taylor gave an account of "The Historic American Merchant Marine Survey." The volume concluded with a section on documents, a number of queries, and some news items and book reviews.

When Whitehill went off to Washington to serve under Commodore Dudley W. Knox in the Office of Naval Records and Library of the Navy Department during World War II, he took *Neptune's* editorial work with him. Since M. V. Brewington was in that office throughout the war, and John Haskell Kemble, John W. McElroy, and Charles G. Summersell were there for shorter periods, rump sessions of the Board frequently convened. Moreover, Samuel Eliot Morison often worked there while writing his monumental history, as did his assistant Alexander C. Brown, another *Neptune* editor. Thus, through Commodore Knox's understanding tolerance the journal weathered the war under the roof of the Navy Department.

In 1946 Walter M. Whitehill, about to return to the Peabody, accepted the directorship of the Boston Athenæum instead. He continued editing *The American Neptune* there through 1950, thus seeing the first ten volumes of the journal through the press. I became Director of the Peabody Museum of Salem that same year, and in 1951 was named *Neptune's* first official Managing Editor. For eighteen years I continued on the course set by Whitehill. Consequently, the editorial work of the *Neptune*, after migrating to Washington and Boston, returned to the Peabody, where the subscription business had always remained. I completed my tour of duty with the October 1968 number. With the January 1969 issue, Philip C. F. Smith, Curator of Maritime History at the Peabody Museum, became Managing Editor, a post he holds at the present time.

The first loss in what might be called *Neptune's* founding family was the death, on November 16, 1947, of Lincoln Colcord, whose inspirational talk had stimulated its founding. Walter Whitehill, writing feelingly in the January 1948 editorial, said that Linc's death had "broken for the first time, the small group of friends who have been responsible for the editing of this journal."

The first decade of the *Neptune's* existence concluded, as it began, with a variety of contents. With the beginning of the second, in my first editorial (April 1951), I paid tribute to Walter Whitehill's ten years as Editor. In the next issue I mentioned that before the war it had been the custom of the Editorial Advisory Board to meet once a year, eat fish, drink rum, and discuss problems concerning the magazine. During the war we had gotten out of the habit; now it was time to resume the pleasant custom.

The meeting was held in September 1951, and I reported in January 1952 that, as *The American Neptune* was "Launched at an inauspicious time upon a sea of troubles, it was meet that we take the now aging craft into drydock to see how she had weathered ten stormy years of war and economic instability. Was the rigging getting frayed? Was she opening at the seams? Or was the cost of keeping her afloat becoming more than the stable freight rate would bear?

"After some five hours of stimulating discussion, broken only by a brief respite for refreshment and fish chowder, one unanimous agreement stood out above all others; no one wanted to change the format of *The Neptune* as a measure of economy. We like the cut of her jib. A discussion of some of the changes which might mean economies showed that the savings would be so slight that they would not offset the cheapened appearance of the magazine. So much for the rigging.

"The seams were tightened by the following changes, additions, and reaffirmations. Readers apparently like to know something about the authors so in the future, as will be noticed in the present number, there will appear a few lines of brief biographical data about each author at the end of his article. Another unanimous decision was that the *Neptune* would better serve the interests of maritime history if we discontinued our reviews and substituted a comprehensive descriptive bibliography of all writings in the field which come to our attention."

American subjects are dominant in the *Neptune*, as its name implies, but the journal is by no means restricted to them. Beginning with an article in the first volume, entitled "Present-Day Craft and Rigs of the Mediterranean," throughout three decades there have been numerous articles on European, Asiatic, and Oceanic subjects. One such series, well remembered for the vigorous differences of opinion by its authors, Richard LeBaron Bowen and Carroll Quigley, was on the diffusion and distribution of oculi. There have been several articles on outrigger canoes and sail types in Pacific and Asian waters. E. Kenneth Haviland's series on steamships and steamship companies of the China coast is a notable contribution to the history of that area. Naval and merchant activities of Western Europe have shared space with rafts and other craft of South America. In fact, there is hardly a maritime nook of the world that has not received some treatment.

For the active editor—and I think both Whitehill and Smith would agree with me—one of the great rewards of editing the journal has been the deep and lasting friendships developed, notably with authors and those who manufacture the magazine, such as the late Fred Anthoensen, amiable and talented head of The Anthoensen Press of Portland, Maine, and his successor, Warren F. Skillings, as well as the present manager, Harry Milliken. In the editorial for January 1965 I wrote: "During the fourteen years that I have been editing this magazine the person I have worked with most closely at The Anthoensen Press was Ruth Chaplin. It was her expert knowledge that straightened out many a sticky makeup problem. Her suggestions, comments, correspondence were always looked forward to because they shone with her own grace, sensitivity and wit." We have worked just as closely with Harold Hugo at The Meriden Gravure Company, Meriden, Connecticut, which has continued to make the illustrations; the journal has benefited from his interest, advice, and willingness to help.

Philip C. F. Smith wrote his first editorial as Managing Editor in the January 1969 number. It was gracefully done.

"Readers of *The American Neptune* are well aware of the scholarly standards and the editorial competency with which Ernest S. Dodge has steered its course during the past eighteen years. As the journal's catalytic agent he has contributed significantly to its present reputation, having seen more than 6,000 pages through the press during his term as Managing Editor. As a reviewer, author of its popular editorials, and himself a contributor of articles, he has set the professional tone that has encouraged the talents and the support of many people."

Although at no time in thirty years has any author or anyone connected with the journal been remunerated, most of the work has been done by the Peabody Museum staff. Without the support of the Museum trustees it would have been impossible for the journal to survive, and in 1966 the *Neptune* Board and the Museum trustees mutually agreed to dissolve the *Neptune* corporation and have the journal published by the Peabody Museum of Salem. Subscriptions are now handled by the Sales Department of the Museum.

The October 1970 issue, Volume XXX, Number 4, closing three decades of *The American Neptune*'s existence, dealt appropriately with the announced Peabody Museum expansion program, but there was no chance to mention in it the most momentous event which happened in the magazine's history. On November 5, 1970, the Anthoensen Press sustained a serious fire which destroyed practically the entire building. The October number had just been mailed out to subscribers, but all back issues of *The American Neptune* were destroyed without insurance coverage, leaving only the small stock stored at the Museum. The entire remaining stock of the first five volumes had been moved to the Museum some years before, but it is not large and several numbers are out-of-print. It is impossible to fill orders for complete sets at the present time, although an agreement has been made with the Johnson Reprint Company to produce out-of-print volumes. The long association of the magazine and the Press, however, will continue. Because of the holocaust the fourth decade of *The American Neptune* started out tardy, but soon will be well on its way to a half-century of existence.

Although maritime history is not a formalized academic study, it has been a branch of history that over the years has attracted young men in great numbers, and those who, no longer young in years, are young in spirit. It is a rare subject that bridges the wide spaces between the academic world, sport, and industry. Nearly everyone who sails for recreation seems also to have some interest in the history of maritime activities. Many of those active in the field are, or have been, yachtsmen, fishermen, or sailors, either in the navy or the merchant marine. One cannot be engaged with the sea without, apparently, being interested in its past. This is not always true with the land, for a man can race automobiles without being interested in the history of race tracks or the evolution of the gasoline engine. But one cannot race yachts without learning something of the history of yachting or the development of the boat that one owns.

The articles I have chosen for this book by no means represent the broad interests of the journal. They were selected for general reader interest, and, with one exception, are restricted to American subjects. This volume commemorates the thirtieth anniversary of the most distinguished journal in North America dedicated to the study of maritime history. The subject is one of increasing popularity. Several colleges and universities now have courses and professorships in the subject; Harvard, for example, has a chair of Oceanic History. As it enters the decade ahead, *The American Neptune* will play an increasingly useful role as an outlet for publication for a growing number of students, while continuing to be, as it traditionally has been, a catalyst for all those who love the sea.

Salem, Massachusetts
May 1972

Ernest S. Dodge

I

Life at Sea

A Boy's First Day at Sea in the Bark *Belle of Oregon—1886* by William B. Sturtevant	2
Domestic Life on American Sailing Ships by Joanna C. Colcord	8
The Meeting of the Ships *Dauntless* and *Thomas Dana* off Cape Horn by Dr. William Allen Wilbur	19
Reminiscences of a Voyage in the Bark *William H. Besse*, Including the Java Earthquake of 1883 by Mrs. B. C. Baker	23

Life at sea was hard and uncertain in the days of sailing vessels. Many a young man's career was cut short by a fall from aloft. Sometimes a wave swept a deck clean, taking overboard an unfortunate sailor who could not find a hand for himself as well as one for the ship. But some went to sea all their lives, never encountered a real hazard, and died peacefully in retirement.

Bark *Belle of Orgeon* entering Hong Kong
Oil painting by Chinese artist

A Boy's First Day at Sea in the Bark Belle of Oregon - 1886

BY WILLIAM B. STURTEVANT

East Boston, Massachusetts

AS a boy my greatest desire was that some day I would follow the sea. Possibly I may have inherited some of this from my family but at that time many of the people of East Boston were sea minded. Most of the men I knew were engaged in the shipping business.

Donald McKay left East Boston when I was about eight years old and retired to Hamilton but a portion of his yard on Border Street was taken by the firm of Smith & Townsend and another part by Campbell & Brooks. D. D. Kelley's yard was still in existence. Of the ships built by Smith & Townsend I remember three: ship *Independence*, ship *Luzon*, and bark *John D. Brewer*. At Campbell & Brooks I remember the ship *Governor Goodwin*, and bark *Freeman*. There were three mast and spar yards operating, two rigging lofts, with the forges of Kennison and Edward Preble, ship smiths. There was also the block factory of Bagnall & Loud. Besides these there were ship-joiners and old workers, those who made repairs on ships, sail-makers and caulkers.

A short distance from Donald McKay's old home was a small basement cobbler shop where each night you could see 'old Cal' and his man, each with a mouth full of wooden pegs, busily engaged in putting taps on boots. Around the room there would gather, after they had their supper, men who would come in to smoke their pipes and talk about the different ships they were working on. I remember hearing George Young, a ship-joiner, tell how it was necessary in order to finish his work to continue down to Boston Light in the ship, and how the mates had been obliged to use knock down arguments in order to get the sail on her. I liked to go into the mast yard where a friend of mine was working on spars. His father made spars for Donald McKay and he went to work in the spar yard when he was only ten years old. I liked to sit astride the big mast facing him and watch the long shavings that would curl from his plane. They had such a salty smell. We boys spent most of our time playing around the wharves. There was one old bark called the *Moonbeam* slowly rotting away, and it is a wonder that we did not meet with a serious accident as we ran all over her rigging.

I am afraid I didn't try to please the teachers at school and consequently was often sent home. My idea was that I would be allowed to go to sea, but my mother seemed to have a faculty of straightening things out, so I would be obliged to return!

While in the graduating class of the grammar school, a large ship anchored between the East Boston ferries, waiting for her crew. Her hull, mast-heads and bowsprit were pure white, her spars were scraped bright and on her stern in large gold-leafed block letters was her name, *Paul Jones* of Portsmouth, New Hampshire. She also carried a figurehead of Paul Jones in uniform. It was no use, however, as I was told I must finish school, but I was promised that after that I would be allowed to make a voyage.

There was a newspaper published in Chatham Row, Boston, near the Custom House, called the *Shipping List* and in it was the list of all vessels bound for Boston from different ports. I was watching for the bark *Belle of Oregon*[1] which was on her way from Illoilo. My parents knew the mate and thought it would be better for me to go with someone I was acquainted with. I afterwards discovered that it would have been easier for me perhaps to have gone with a stranger. However, I began to make my preparations. With another boy to help me, I went over to McQuarrie and Chisholm, outfitters on North Street, and bought a blue tumble-in chest, for, of course, I couldn't think of going to sea without a sailors' chest. We carried it home and my mother attended to the packing. Another thing which I have thought since was a mistake were letters from relatives and friends smuggled in and placed between the clothing.[2] In due time the bark came in, discharged her cargo and went to New York to load case oil for Saigon, Indo-China. I was given directions just how to get to New York, and also some post cards which I promised to send back as soon as I arrived.

Dodd's Express Company took my dunnage to the bark, which was lay-

[1] For an account of the *Belle of Oregon* (built at Bath, Maine, in 1876), see Frederick C. Matthews, *American Merchant Ships*, 1850-1900 (Salem: Marine Research Society, 1930), pp. 44-47. The figurehead of this vessel is preserved on the grounds of the Webb Institute of Naval Architecture, New York City.

[2] Perhaps I should explain my reference to the letters smuggled into my chest before leaving home. While I was seasick I naturally was homesick and I would have given anything to be able to walk ashore, but as the sickness wore off I began to feel more at home until I had occasion to get something out of my sea chest. Then I would find a letter addressed to me 'Somewhere, don't know where.' All the homesickness would return and this was repeated two or three times until I dragged the chest out on deck, turned it upside down and shook everything out. Then I repacked it, finding several more letters, which I read all at once and then recovered for good.

ing at Java Street, Greenpoint, Brooklyn. My things were soon on board, and I found my berth in the half deck-house, which I shared with a boy from Maine.[3] We were put to work at once, and didn't I feel important as I swept the deck with a big Chinese broom! I was already half way to the captain's job. How was I to know what changes would take place in the next forty-eight hours. It reminds me now of that once popular song *Ain't It Funny What A Difference Just A Few Hours Makes*. The crew came on board the next morning before daybreak and after their 'shore duty' was over they were about half alive. Several of them had to have their noses tickled before they came to. We were all given black coffee, which after several attempts I managed to swallow, and then came a loud order to 'turn to.' I pulled and hauled with the others but I worked so hard that soon my hands were full of blisters, and when they broke the salt water made them very sore. When it came time for breakfast I could only drink some coffee. The salt beef I couldn't swallow; it smelt bad. I think we were allowed about fifteen minutes and then were hustled out to make sail, the tow boat having got us by Bedloes Island, which, by the way, did not have the Statue of Liberty completed.

The wind was quite cold and the sea choppy, so that I began to be seasick. When it came time for dinner I didn't care if I never had anything to eat. After dinner I was given the job of stowing the holystones that had been dumped in the carpenter shop. Some of these stones were about the size of six bricks. A square iron band fitted over the top and a wooden handle was set in a socket so that when in use they were hauled back and forth, athwartship on the deck, the sand and water cleaning the planks and planing them level. The small ones were about the size of one brick and were used to get into the corners: these were called 'prayer books.' Weak and sick, I had to double up and crawl under the carpenters' bench dragging in and piling the stones so that they wouldn't come down until wanted. There was no let up, and one thing after another followed until supper time. At this meal I was introduced to hard tack, but it was so filled with weevils that the tack, which was usually hard enough to break with a hammer, would fall to pieces at the slightest shake. However, it made no difference to me, for I couldn't eat anything.

Just before dark the watches were picked and I found myself in the mate's watch. We went below until eight bells (8:00 o'clock) and then came on deck until midnight. Just before midnight it was decided to furl

---

[3] The half deck-house had a tier of barrels of beef and pork, as there wasn't room for them in the fore peak. These barrels would leak more or less and as they were not a first class product you can imagine that, mixed with the smell of bilge water, it was a poor sanitarium for a boy in my condition.

the main skysail and I was sent up aloft with a sailor. I was given to understand in no uncertain language 'to look sharp' because next time I would have to go alone. I certainly wasn't in first class condition to go aloft; seasick, tired out, hands so sore that it was painful to close them, and I had eaten nothing since we started, but I started up the main rigging. It was pitch dark, very cold (February) and the bark was pitching and rolling considerably. The sailor was soon out of sight but I climbed as fast as I could. When I got to the futtock shrouds, which is the only sailor-like way of getting over the main-top, I felt for a moment that I couldn't do it. But I reasoned that if the sailor had done it I must. Well, I got over it after a struggle, but I felt as though I had a handful of knife blades. As long as there were ratlines to step on I managed, but, when I arrived at the eyes of the topgallant rigging, I found no more ratlines. To get up to the royal and skysail I must shin on a backstay or anything I could find.

While I was considering the best way to get there a hoarse shout came up from the deck to 'get to hell out on that yard.' No reply was expected, so I laid hold of some gear and started to shin. The sailor on the yard was having trouble because the buntlines had been hauled up too high and needed to be slacked. He was cursing and dancing around on the footrope trying to make them hear him on deck. He finally got what he wanted and then the sail was furled. I watched very carefully, for I realized that it wouldn't be very healthy for me not to know what to do next time. Well, it was finished and we started down the rigging. He was soon out of sight, but I had to be careful. My watch had gone below and as it was about 1:00 A.M. I knew I had lost one out of my four hours.

This was not the end of a perfect day but it was the end of my first day at sea — 3:00 A.M. to 1:00 A.M. — 22 hours. Not exactly banking hours, and all for the munificent wage of $5.00 per month and found. Wages of an 'AB' at that time were $14.00 a month out of New York and £2/10/- out of Liverpool.

The pleasant weather of the next few days revived my spirits and I found myself enjoying the second dog watch very much. One of the songs that caught my fancy was 'The Oxford' and as it seems appropriate to use it at the commencement of any voyage I will include two verses and chorus. This crew as a whole had fairly good voices and in a chorus they sounded well.

A BOY'S FIRST DAY AT SEA

1. 'Twas in London in the cold month of December
   That I found that all my money it was spent.
   How I got there I don't just remember,
   But I down to the shipping office went.
   On that day there was a great demand for sailors,
   For India, China, Java and for France,
   So I shipped before the mast on the *Oxford*
   And we went away to booze all our advance.

   Chorus:

   Then its get back, give in the slack,
   Bear away your capstan heave a paul.
   'Bout ship staysails boys be handy,
   Then its raise tacks sheets and mainsail haul.

2. We all came on board a Sunday morning,
   And everyone was heavy on the booze,
   So I sat down on my chest aquietly thinking
   Whether I'd turn in my bunk and have a snooze.
   When I heard a voice loudly calling,
   I listened and I heard that voice again.
   It was the chief mate at the forecastle door a-howling!
   Come lay aft boys and answer to your names.

   Chorus: etc.

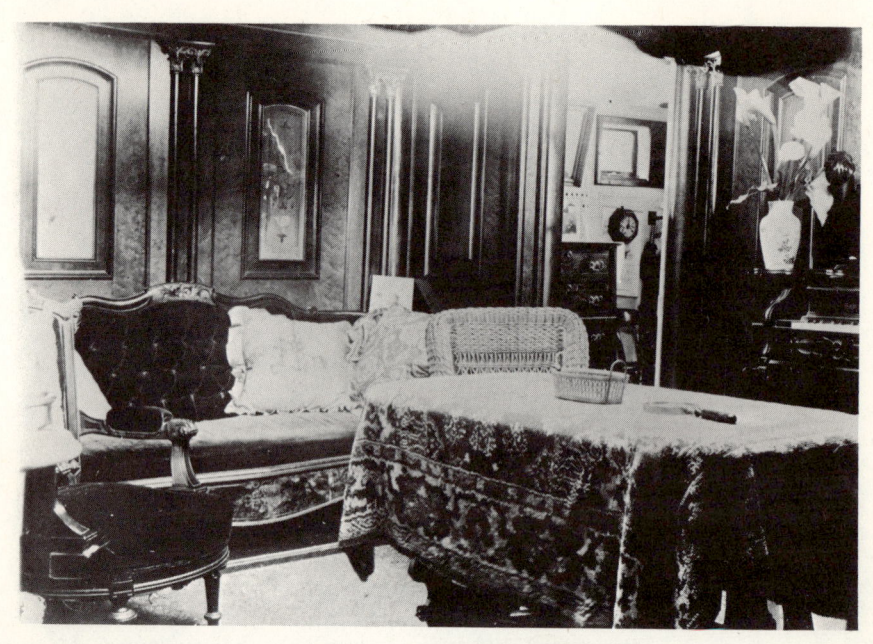

Cabin of bark *Guy C. Goss*, built at Bath, Maine, 1879:
1,430 tons, 213.8 x 39.8 x 24.4 feet

Photograph by Captain Walter M. Mallett, about 1900, showing the starboard side of cabin, with the captain's state-room seen through the open door. The windows over the built-in sofa were of ground and figured glass. The forward window had light from the starboard state-room; the other was backed by a clothespress.

Cabin of ship *A. J. Fuller*, built at Bath, Maine, 1881:
1,782 tons, 229.3 x 41.5 x 26 feet

Photograph, showing Captain and Mrs. Theodore P. Colcord seated in the cabin, by Mrs. George C. Lockwood of Norwalk, Connecticut, who made a voyage as passenger with Captain and Mrs. Colcord in 1888.

Domestic Life on American Sailing Ships

BY JOANNA C. COLCORD

RECENT literature, fiction and otherwise, has to some degree familiarized the reading public with the fact that masters of American sailing vessels of the last century customarily took their wives and families to sea with them on at least some voyages. My purpose here (since I was one of those children born and partly reared at sea) is to give a picture of what all this meant in the lives of New England seacoast families.

Family life at sea was made possible by the peculiar co-operative nature of the business of ship ownership and management as it used to be conducted. A vessel was customarily built for a certain man who was to be her master, and he and his friends took shares in the enterprise, each agreeing to pay so many eighths, sixteenths, or whatever, the rest being sold to general investors. Their joint shares usually added up to a controlling interest in the vessel. A master-builder contracted to build, launch, and rig the vessel ready for sea. A managing owner would be chosen to attend to the banking, insurance, and other shore features of the ship's business, to keep the absent master informed of conditions of world trade, and to secure domestic charters when the vessel was homeward bound. But the main burden of ship's business was carried by the captain, who, in addition to his knowledge of navigation and seamanship, had to be well up on business methods and admiralty law.

Under these conditions, if the master wished to take his family with him, no question was ever raised by the other owners. But when the time came, at the beginning of the present century, that shipmasters who were not ready to retire 'went into steam,' not the least of the unpleasant evidences of their changed status in the eyes of owners and managers was the flat prohibition by practically all steamship lines against the presence on board, even as passengers for a single trip, of wives and children of the masters.

In the old days, however, family life at sea was the rule rather than the exception. Many women accompanied their husbands constantly, not even staying ashore when they were anticipating a child. An incomplete list which has been compiled of those born at sea to families from the small town of Searsport, Maine, contains over seventy names. Only one fatality in childbirth is remembered to have taken place among them. They tell a tale of Captain William Blanchard and his wife, all of whose six children were born on shipboard. Their vessel, the *Wealthy Pendleton*, entered Kobe, Japan, during a typhoon and anchored beside the bark *Willard Mudgett,* which was flying a signal for a doctor; but on account of the weather, no boat came from shore. Ascertaining by signals that the captain's wife was in labor, and the young couple distracted with anxiety, Captain Blanchard got his own boat over, and he and his wife delivered the child successfully.

One woman who lived to grow up and tell the tale, was born in an open boat at sea, after her father's ship had been destroyed by fire.

The accompanying plan (Fig. 1), shows the lay-out of the accommodations provided. There were slight differences between ships, but in their main features, American ship cabins were pretty much alike.

The after cabin, in which seagoing families lived, was sunk part way below the quarter-deck and entered by a companionway—a short flight of stairs in front and slightly to port of the wheel. Small square windows, protected by heavy shutters, opened upon the deck and alleyways near the top of the cabin, and there was a large raised skylight in the center of the main saloon. At night, light was furnished by kerosene lamps swinging in concentric rings called gimbals, which kept them always upright.

The captain's state-room occupied the starboard corner aft; across the companionway from it lay the bathroom and toilet, served by two large salt and fresh water tanks above the ceiling. The ship's medicine chest was built into the bathroom. Two state-rooms occupied the forward corners of the after cabin. The space left for the main saloon was thus roughly in the form of a cross with blunt arms.

Two doors in the forward bulkhead led to the forward cabin where meals were usually taken. This room was long and narrow, with state-rooms and pantry opening off both sides. It was lighted by a skylight, under which was sometimes a swinging rack for glass and condiments. The table, provided with 'fiddles' to prevent the dishes sliding off in rough weather, was flanked by two long fixed settees of mahogany or teak; the captain sat at the head in a revolving arm-chair, also screwed down. The captain and family, together with the chief mate, had their meals first; the other officers were served at a second sitting. The mates and steward occupied state-rooms opening from the forward cabin; the cook bunked off his galley, in the forward house occupied by the sailors. Exit from the forward cabin to the deck was through a coach-house with doors to starboard and port. If the poop deck ended at the forward end of the cabin, exit was directly to the main deck; otherwise a flight of steps—the forward companionway—led up to the coach-house.

Both cabins were handsomely decorated, the cabinet makers of the shipyards expending their best skill on their beautification. Some of them were painted white, the panels being separated by pilasters with carved capitals embellished with gold leaf; other cabins were finished in various hard woods. The cabin of the Bath-built bark *Guy C. Goss* (page 8) is described as follows: 'The lights back of the made-in sofas were of ground, figured glass... The finish of the cabin was all veneer—bird's eye maple, satin-wood and mahogany. Each panel had a small trim of ebony.'

Two built-in sofas, carved and handsomely upholstered, occupied the port and starboard alcoves of the main cabin, and a built-in sideboard stood between the doors leading to the forward cabin. Easy chairs, and a table used as a chart-table at sea, but covered and bearing ornaments in port, completed the furnishing of the main saloon (page 8). Storage space was provided under the couches and bunks, and in the alleyways under the decks. In port, the rooms were full of the knick-knacks beloved in the last century; when the ship sailed, carpets came up, pictures and ornaments were stowed away, furniture was screwed to the floor, and every movable object was chocked off against the motion of the ship.

In pleasant weather, when the skylights could be opened and the rooms ventilated, the cabins were pleasant living rooms; but during heavy weather, they were necessarily dark and gloomy. The all-pervading odor from the ship's bilges crept into them, and in spite of the protection of shutters, battens, and coamings at the doorways, some of the salt water washing about decks inevitably found its way down into the cabins. The steward was kept busy mopping it up; but after a good wetting down with salt water, the cabin was damp and clammy till the weather cleared.

All the housework in the after cabin—sweeping, cleaning, polishing the brass thresholds—was done by the steward. He also did the heavy washing, brought the food from the galley, served the meals, and washed the dishes. There was little for the captain's wife to do but oversee his work, make the beds, and wash out handkerchiefs and stockings. Chinese were preferred as cooks and stewards, because they were more cleanly and efficient than whites who would take such jobs.

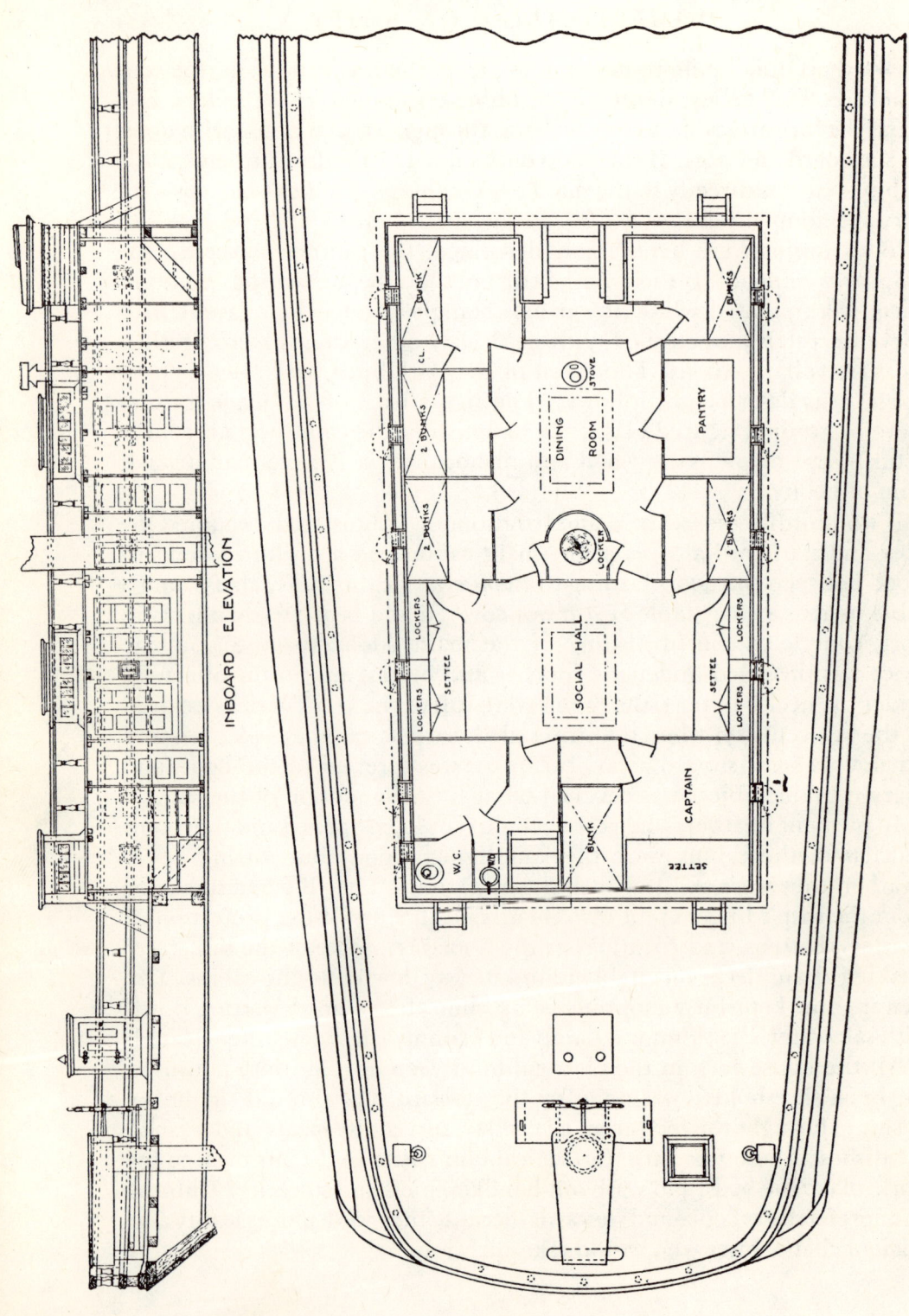

Figure 1. Cabin plan of ship *Emily F. Whitney*, 1,249 tons, built at East Boston, 1879. *Drawing produced by Historic American Merchant Marine Survey. U.S. National Museum.*

The food on American ships was as good as the current methods of food preservation permitted, and far better than in any other merchant service. The only milk was the treacly condensed variety in cans; evaporated milk and cream had not yet come on the market. Tinned Danish butter was always fresh, although it got pretty soft and oily in the tropics. A large variety of canned fruit and vegetables, fish and meat, was carried. The meat was mostly the staple corned beef, and this was supplemented by frequent dishes of the good old salt beef used in the forecastle. The cook would select the best pieces of this for the cabin, and it was delicious; I still recollect the taste of it with pleasure. Fresh potatoes and onions did not long survive the first crossing of the equator. The quality of bread, cakes, and puddings varied with the cook, but Chinese cooks were clever and capable to an extraordinary degree.

In general our meals were excellent, even in heavy weather. We always had a dinner of three courses, soup, meat or fish, and dessert. Split pea or bean soup was a meal in itself, and vegetable soup turned up long after the fresh vegetables were gone. Monday, not Friday, was fish day, the staple for dinner being salt cod and pork scraps, with boiled potatoes. Breakfast also was a hearty meal, with cereal and possibly salt mackerel or tongues and sounds, or a cold meat. For supper we would have hash or some form of hearty food, topped off with canned peaches or pears and cake. Always there were plenty of biscuits, in which infrequently a weevil appeared, startlingly black against the whiteness of the bread. One remembers, too, certain occasions when a long black hair of coarse texture, unmistakably Chinese, would be removed from the bread, at which my mother would be apt to leave the table.

These were hearty men's meals, it will be seen, arranged for the appetite of the captain and the mates; they offered plenty of variety for the children aboard. Occasionally a dolphin or bonito would be caught, or a porpoise grained, and any flying fish that landed aboard were by custom sent aft to the captain's wife, unless the ship's cat got them first. Porpoise was especially delicious, the steaks a sort of half-meat and half-fish, the liver like the finest of calf's liver. Some masters carried hens, rabbits, or even pigs, and I have heard of vessels equipped with milch goats when there were young children aboard.

On a long voyage some food-stuffs would spoil; cook and steward waged incessant battle with mice, rats, weevils, and cockroaches. Toward the end of the trip, the fancy stores ran low. Coming on the coast one winter, we were reduced to little more than flour, beef, and pork. The mate, who could not look black coffee in the face, ground up some chalk to make its color bearable to him. The cook outdid himself to vary the menu; he contrived a sauce of vinegar, Worcestershire, and chopped pickle thickened with cornstarch which made slices of salt beef taste like a new dish.

But these shortages were usually temporary; the occasions when an American ship ran out of basic provisions were so rare as to be extraordinary. Shortages were preliminary to regular food binges in the first port reached. Milk, fresh meat and vegetables would come off by boatloads before the anchor was fairly down, together with fruit in profusion—cocoanuts and whole bunches of bananas at the islands of the Pacific, grapes and peaches in Chile, pink-fleshed pomeloes and mangosteens in Singapore, lychees and green-skinned sweet oranges in the China ports. Sailing children knew and revelled in them all, though better than the lot of them was the first red-cheeked apple into which one bit when the homeward-bound voyage ended.

Daily life in the after cabin was conditioned by two things: the weather, and the ship's routine. The system of watches meant that at all times except at meal times and in the early evening dogwatch some one of the officers would be sleeping in his room at the forward end of the after house. Piano-playing by the captain's lady, noisy romping by the children, were taboo except for those evening hours. The children played quietly, on the starboard side of the deck if it was the mate's watch below and to port if it was the second mate's. On our ship, we became quite ingenious in developing quiet games. With dominoes for ships, we would charter, load, and sail them on a chart spread on the cabin floor. Boys learned to splice and tie knots, girls learned to sew and do fancy-work, and both, so soon as they were old enough, learned from their fathers some of the processes of navigation. Regular lessons went on at sea; our parents consulted with the teachers at home, and we learned and recited the same lessons from the same books—this was before the days of progressive education—as did our schoolmates at home. There was a ship's library, in a yellow wooden case, changed each voyage by the American Seamen's Friend Society, and the family's own books and periodicals were swapped with other shipmasters' families in every port. Our family was fond of reading aloud, and many pleasant evenings passed with this and with cards, authors and dominoes. I still have a folding table with the scores entered on the bottom, of a cribbage tournament that was kept up for an entire voyage.

Many shipmasters, particularly those who made long voyages alone, developed hobbies, some singularly feminine for men who were surely

DOMESTIC LIFE ON SHIPS

not sissies! Captain Andrew S. Pendleton[1] was a master hand at making net lace; he finished a bedspread each voyage. Captain David A. Scribner's[2] specialty was macrémé lace. Captain Joseph P. Sweetser[3] became more than an amateur painter of marines. Captain Walter M. Mallett[4] was a camera fan away back in the gelatin-negative days. Captain Edward Payson Nichols[5] carried a printing press, and he and his family got out a periodical called *Ocean Chronicle*[6] which is a graphic and interesting record. The hobby of Captain John Drew of the *Sea Witch*[7] also was writing—he was a regular contributor to Maine papers under the pseudonym of 'The Kennebecker.' Captain H. A. Starrett, in command of the first ship *Frank N. Thayer*,[8] during a period of seven years labored over a large rigged model of the vessel which he kept set up in the cabin. This beautiful model is still in the Starrett home in Belfast, Maine, and has been exhibited at the Penobscot Marine Museum. The list of shipmasters' avocations might well be extended. Isabel Hopestill Carter was writing fact, not fancy, when in her fine book *Shipmates* she presents her shipmaster hero as expert in tapestry needlework.

Not only the crew, but everyone on board a ship was subject to discipline. Wives and children, on board by sufferance and carrying no part of the ship's duties, had to learn to keep out of the way when there was men's work afoot. In good weather, they might be on deck as they pleased, so long as they were unobtrusive and quiet; in bad weather their place was below and out of the way. Nerves wore short after thirty-six hours of sleepless vigilance, and the less heard from children while father was trying to catch a few winks between squalls the better for the children! We read, or played games in complete silence, inventing grimaced signals to take the place of words.

The curious hierachy of ship's discipline made the family aft completely isolated from the rest of the ship's company. Women and girls

[1] Captain Pendleton was master of the ship *Emily F. Whitney* (Fig. 1), and the barks *Thomas Fletcher, Trovatore,* and *Emma T. Crowell.* His last command was the ship *Aryan,* built in 1893 in Phippsburg, Maine; the last wooden full-rigged ship to be built in the United States.

[2] Captain Scribner was commander of the ships *St. David, St. Francis,* and *Henry B. Hyde.*

[3] Captain Sweetser's commands were the ships *Premier, Zephyr,* and *John Watt.* His son, Captain Joseph D. Sweetser, who was master only in steam, was also a marine painter and a model-maker.

[4] Captain Mallett commanded the bark *Guy C. Goss* (page 8) and the ship *Hawaiian Isles* (now the Swedish training-ship *Abraham Rydberg*).

[5] Captain Nichols's best-known command was the ship *Frank Pendleton.*

[6] Reprinted in 1941 by the Penobscot Marine Museum.

[7] Not the famous clipper of the name, but the second *Sea Witch,* built by R. F. Jackson in East Boston in 1872.

[8] Not the second ill-starred vessel of the same name, on board of which in 1885 the famous mutiny took place in which two Malays in the crew ran amok, killed the first and second mates and severely wounded the captain, and took charge of the ship for two days before they leaped overboard.

were supposed to behave as if the sailors did not exist. With the officers, some conversation was possible at meals, but not frequently on deck when the mates were on duty. Children might chat with the officers, though not with the men, as long as they did not bother them when busy. The family group was thus thrown upon itself for society as no shore family could possibly be. This should have had bad psychological results, but I cannot discover that it did. Seagoing families continued to be singularly united families in spite of the enforced close association.

But prolonged separation was also familiar to them. Bertrand Russell has remarked that the family was never a suitable institution for seafaring peoples, because 'when one member of the family went on a long voyage while the rest stayed at home, he was inevitably emancipated from family control, and the family was proportionately weakened.' Since the author comes from one of the greatest seafaring peoples the world has ever seen, he ought to know whereof he speaks, but I do not think he does. Something in the alternation of close association and prolonged separation, during which unaccustomed pens learned the art of holding each other close by long journal-letters, seemed to work quite the other way. Seafaring families have remained among the most close-knit of any in the world.

My recollection of the long days at sea is that they were never monotonous. The small incidents of the day, the changes of weather, wind, and the look of the sea, which all had significance to us, made no two days alike. A landfall absorbed us for days before and after; a ship met and signalled at sea was a high peak of excitement. Under favorable conditions, sailing on the same course in the trades, there would sometimes be visiting back and forth between vessels. A British captain came to dinner at sea with us once, and as he stepped over the rail of the American vessel, he asked, 'Do you by any chance know Captain Carver from Searsport, Maine?' That happened to be our home town, and Captain Carver a relative.

A boy's letter in my possession, dated in 1874, which came home on a whaler and bears a 'New Bedford-Ship Letter' postmark, tells of such a visit, and of the mutual treasure which he and the boy on the whaler exchanged. And my own grandmother, wife of Captain Jeremiah Sweetser of the *Mary Goodell*, writing to her eldest son from Rotterdam in 1877 tells of a meeting with neighbors, inward bound from a long voyage, who lived 'just up the road' in Searsport:

We had the pleasure of speaking Capt. [George] McClure in the English Channel. One morning when Father came on deck and was spying at the ships around, he saw one a little bit ahead of us that he said looked some like the [*John C. Potter*]. We gained on her and before long he could read the name. . . . They signalled, and before long we came up with them so that they could speak. We kept along together so that they got all the home news we could give them, and two or three times we were so near that Mrs. McClure and I could speak. Father threw a line with a lead on it on board their ship, and sent a nice new ham (one that he got in Queenstown), a late newspaper, a bag of walnuts, and some candy that Bert happened to have for the children. They were all on deck, and Charles [later Captain Charles McClure of the *Iolani*] was kiting around. He seemed quite pleased to see Bert, and wanted him to come down to London while they were there. It was very pleasant meeting them so.

The long periods spent in foreign ports while discharging and loading cargo were holidays from schooling. Social life went on at a great rate among the fleet and with people engaged in shipping industries ashore. The ladies made joint shopping, calling, and sightseeing trips, meeting their husbands at night at the favored ship chandler's store, where all foregathered once a day before going off aboard their respective ships. Several times a week, the masters and their families would all spend an evening aboard one of the vessels, sitting on the broad awning-covered quarterdeck if the weather permitted. (Plate 28.) The white-jacketed steward would pass about with drinks—lemonade for the ladies and children, something a bit stronger for the men—the cigar-tips would glimmer through the soft darkness, and the talk went on, all of ships and of mischances and adventures at sea.

Often picnics would be organized, or excursions to neighboring points of interest. National holidays were the occasion of joint celebrations, participated in by masters of other countries as well. I remember a Thanksgiving dinner at a Buenos Aires hotel at which not more than half the company were Americans; and an English captain gave himself a nasty burn on our poop deck once, when trying to set off a rocket in celebration of America's independence from Great Britain.

But when the fleet was large enough, the different nationalities tended to flock by themselves. 'This is a dreadfully lonely place,' wrote my grandfather from Iquique, 'there is not *another American ship in port!*'

One of the largest gatherings of sailing ships the world has ever seen took place during the 1860's and 1870's when the guano islands of Peru were being feverishly stripped of their vast accumulations of bird-dung to fertilize the worn-out soil of Europe. Hundreds of ships of all nations lay there for months at a time, waiting their turn at the chutes. The islets were rocky deserts with no resident population. There was nothing to go ashore for, until one enterprising captain's wife discovered a wealth of beautiful fine seaweed of all colors which could be floated on paper and arranged in designs which, owing to the surface gelatin of the weeds, were permanent when dry. A craze ensued, to see which could develop the prettiest designs; and many a lacquered cabinet in New England coast towns still harbors wreaths and pictures made of Chincha Island sea mosses.

I am so fortunate as to possess a series of letters written home from sea by members of my family over a period of nearly one hundred years. Except in time of great national emergency, the writers show no particular interest in social and political developments. My father, arriving in Dunedin, New Zealand, in 1881, was hailed by the pilot who came out to meet him with the news 'Garfield's been shot!' The last thing my father was thinking of was political developments at home; and he told it on himself ever after that he sung out in reply, 'Garfield *who?*' Politics were the concern of shore folks, whom sailors by tradition dislike and even fear. Economics, as they affected world-trade, were of prime importance to them, however; they spent their lives in guessing where to pick up advantageous charters. The vicissitudes of seafaring are discussed in these letters with sailorly brevity; the wives at home are expected to understand the significance of the terms used. But the outstanding characteristic of all is interest in and longing for the seacoast village whence the writers hailed. My grandmother writes wistfully from Java (with all the fruit of the tropics at her disposal), 'It must be just about strawberry time at home now. How I wish I might have a dish before me this minute.' My grandfather, on a long voyage alone, tells his wife that she had better 'sell the pretty cow and keep the homely one—but do as you think best.' He enjoins her, 'Don't suffer for the want of good things, for it gives me far greater pleasure to know that my family has them than to have them myself.' In the next port, she must 'be sure and have lots of letters. Write me all the little local news; it may look small to you, but it interests me.'

The writers of these letters were not rollicking adventurers, swashbuckling carelessly through life; they were cautious New Englanders doing a hard job which some of them even disliked, because by its means they could provide a better livelihood for their families than in any other way open to them. But home was where they always longed to be; and at home most of them now lie, in the cemetery facing south across Penobscot Bay.

The Meeting of the Ships Dauntless and Thomas Dana off Cape Horn

BY DR. WILLIAM ALLEN WILBUR

A MARINE painting of 1874, done in Liverpool, shows two clipper ships under shortened sail meeting somewhere south of Cape Horn. The sea is shadowed by lifting clouds, and a gray morning light is on the picture. Against the northern horizon — a vast shadow like an iceberg — is the rock of Cape Horn, and the northeast is streaked with the pale brightness of the dawn.

Two Noank men, brothers and masters of ships, wrote the story separately.

The ship *Thomas Dana*, Captain John P. Wilbur, from San Francisco towards Liverpool, 47 days out on Thursday, 20 August 1874, was 7000 miles from San Francisco. The log-book of this date vividly portrays Cape Horn weather. The sea day begins at noon:

> First part strong gales from the northwest, fearful sea running, rainy, dark-looking weather. Ship scudding under foresail and lower fore-topsail and lower main-topsail. Seems to me I never saw such a sea before. Have had to watch the steering close; it seems risky running, but am loth to come to. Ship fills herself even with the rail two or three times this afternoon. At 6 P.M., barometer 28.82, wind lulls somewhat, and it becomes clear overhead. Barometer also commences to rise. At 10 P.M. sea becomes more smooth, made topsails and reefed mainsail. Midnight barometer 29.12. Latter part, strong breeze from northwest with fine weather; at noon nearly calm. Diego Ramirez bears about west-north-west twelve miles: very fortunate to make such a landfall. Barometer had gone down about one-tenth at noon.

Cape Horn, latitude 55° 58' 40" south, longitude 67° 16' 10" west, the southernmost point of the Hermite Islands, 500 feet above the sea, is the turning-point of ships going around South America. Friday, 21 August, at noon, begins in latitude 56° 30', longitude 60° 20', with entries as follows:

Commences light airs from northeast. Cloudy weather at 4 P.M., barometer 28.98, black-looking squall in the northwest, clewed up all the light sails before it struck. At 9.30 P.M. Cape Horn bears about north five miles. Strong breeze from west, fine moon and clear. Midnight, moderate breeze.

About 5.30 this morning, just before daylight, lookout reported ship ahead. I was on deck just in time to answer his hail as he passed by to leeward. Soon after passing, he rounded to and came after us on the port tack. I thought it might be my brother when he went by. And this maneuver confirmed me in thinking it was my brother [in] the ship *Dauntless*. I wore ship and came to on the starboard tack, main and mizzen-topsails aback, waiting for the coming of the welcome ship, which proved to be the *Dauntless* — my only and very dear brother. We had both hoped and prayed that we might come together on this voyage. But how strange that we should thus meet on this great and wide sea, both steering for each other, and knowing nothing of it. Only one-half (perhaps one-quarter) of a mile apart, and neither of the ships would have been recognized.

My heart softens, the eyes of faith look upward: I see the guiding hand of a loving Heavenly Father. It is all clear now; nothing comes by chance. The same watchful eye that marks the sparrows when they fall, marks the progress of two ships, and steers them together on this great ocean amid the darkness of night. The weather was such that it was not prudent that either of us should board the other, but we had time to see and pass a few kind words of greeting; found all well. There we separate — he sails one way, we the other. So we meet on life's voyage, and so we part. I trust that by and by we shall all safely reach that haven of rest from which there shall be no more going out, no more parting in the great home on high — for there shall be no more sea.

My wife and little boy both on deck to greet my brother this morning.

The ship *Dauntless*, Captain Robert P. Wilbur, from New York towards San Francisco, has the following entry in the captain's log-book:

This has been one of the days of my life in which I have plainly seen the working of a kind Providence in answer to prayer. At 6 A.M. my first officer, Mr. Nelson, who had charge of the morning watch, saw a light on the starboard bow coming for us; then, in a shorter time than it takes to tell it, he saw it was a large ship with a heavy press of canvas bearing down on us. We were by the wind on the starboard tack; she was running free with the wind on the port side. To avoid a collision Mr. Nelson gave orders to starboard the wheel, lowered our spanker so our ship swung off quickly, giving the other ship the right of way that belonged to us. As she was passing us, Mr. Nelson hailed her, 'What ship is that?'

The answer came back, '*Thomas Dana*.' Then a voice from the *Dana*, 'What ship is that?'

We answered '*Dauntless*,' and sung out 'Heave to!' And we wore our ship around and put after her.

As it was getting light in the east we could see that they were shortening sail, and they wore around, heaving to on the starboard tack with the main yard aback. We ran down to and around her, coming up under her lee. We backed the main yard and thus slowed down, and had a good chance to talk together. It was a pleasure indeed to talk to them and see my brother, his wife and little Rossie, face to face.

At 8 A.M. we parted, they for Liverpool, we for San Francisco. God only knows when and where we shall meet again. We hope to meet again on earth, but if it is ordained otherwise, I pray we may all meet an unbroken family in Heaven.

One strange thing about this providential meeting: at 4 A.M. this morning I woke out of a sound sleep, notwithstanding I was up late last night passing through the Straits of Le Maire. It seemed to me something was going to happen. I got up, dressed, put on my coat and boots, lay down on the side of the bed, but not to sleep — waiting for something, I know not what. I got up again, went to the companionway, told Mr. Nelson to look for Barnevelt Island, although I did not think the ship was up to it; went back and lay down on the outside of the bed — waiting for something, I knew not what. About 5.30 the steward brought me coffee, and I had just finished when the meeting-time came.

My brother and I had both prayed for this meeting.

This is the story of the ships, as written separately in the two log-books. The course by the chart that each ship sailed is about 13,000 miles; these two lines intersect at only one point — off Cape Horn. The ships reached the intersection at the same time; they were actually in danger of collision, and they did not pass in the night. One incident not in the log my uncle, the captain of the *Dauntless*, told me. The *Dauntless* sailed around the *Dana* three times, and the third time around, the topping-lift of the spanker boom broke and dropped the boom down upon the wheel, so that for a time the ship was without control, as she drifted by the *Dana* so close that the yard-arms just cleared. It was a moment of great anxiety until they drifted clear. So close were they that they could easily speak with one another.

The meeting of the ships occurred on the morning of 22 August 1874. Captain John Wilbur died in a foreign port two years later, and this was the brothers' last meeting on earth.

Reminiscences of a Voyage in the Bark William H. Besse
Including the Java Earthquake of 1883

BY MRS. B. C. BAKER

Edited by Harold Bowditch

LOOKING backward through fifteen years of continuous going, and turning the leaves of memory,[1] there seems to have been condensed into eight months a lifetime, in contrast to which all other experiences are as nothing.

After weeks of delightful tarry in Hong Kong we were chartered to load sugar at Manila for Boston.

Any port with a Boston or New York terminus makes a Cape Cod man's heart rejoice. With Boston this time there were thoughts so far reaching we dared not speak them.

Steamer after steamer came into Hong Kong from Manila with rumors of cholera which was raging fearfully there. We held many a congress as to whether my son and I should continue on or turn our faces upon the plague and come to America by steam. We were a little family and it was harder to go than to stay, but as we bade our comrades good-bye and went out from the harbor, we felt with every dip of the ensign that we were sailing into the future as never before.

It is a dangrous way, as many of you know, that which has to be taken—full of islands, shoals and currents. We travelled it, however, without incident of any note and had begun to hope that the plague had passed when we made Manila and came to anchor. It was just at nightfall when we rested. A hush was over the Bay which seemed heavy with foreboding.

---

[1] These reminiscences were written for presentation before a club by the widow of Captain Baker, master of the bark *William H. Besse,* who died within two years after his return from the 1883 voyage here described. The text is derived from a manuscript copy made many years ago by Miss Helena Shaw, who at that time was a resident of Middleborough, Massachusetts, who knew Mrs. Baker, and borrowed her account in order to copy it. Miss Shaw tells me that on returning from this voyage Captain Baker left the sea and went into the coal business, but died shortly thereafter. The text is true to the original with a minimum of editing—such as omitting capital letters, of which the author was over fond—and the omission of a few sentences which refer to an earlier talk given by Mrs. Baker or bear solely upon this paper's presentation as a lecture.

The bark *William H. Besse,* 1027 tons, 179.9 x 36.2 x 20.6, was built at Bath, Maine, in 1873. In 1883 she hailed from Wareham, and was owned by William H. Besse and others.

However, with the morning came the usual business men. Each had his account of how one and another of our brethren had fallen, yielding to the scourge. Our great wish was to load and leave as quickly as possible. Vessels of deep draught anchor in the Bay and load from lighters, reaching the town by small boats, and up a narrow river into which every ripe matter is thrown, such as dead animals and filth of all description.

Of course the odor to delicate nostrils is distressing, for the tide seldom clears the stream. It is no wonder that under that tropical sun germs of deadly disease thrive and find a home.

Everything was made comfortable and the hours brightened, until after a few days the mate came to me saying, such a man seems very sick, I think we must do something for him. Hearing the description of his symptoms I said, 'It is the cholera — wait a bit — I'll see.' Taking our Medical Guide I read every symptom in that description. The captain being on shore I said, 'Go to yonder ship, ask the captain to come and stay with us while you go to town for our captain and medical assistance. In the meantime I will mix drugs as the book directs and send to the man.' A man was placed to tend the sick and Captain Slocum came on board. Just here let me tell you, that captain took off his coat, went into the forecastle and tended that sick man as he would a brother, notwithstanding danger lurked in every kind act. Could a man do that for strangers and abuse his sailors? Yet of such indeed his men accused him when later he came to New York, and it took a goodly slice from his hard earnings to clear himself from the charge.

After a time came our own boat with captain, mate, doctor and interpreter. It was a brief visit. Cholera in its worst form was pronounced. Our faces whitened and a deep silence fell.

At ten that evening the mate rapped at our door with 'the man is dead, Sir.' Just then the vessel gave a tip, and crash went a large vase sending a chill through every nerve of our bodies. A boat was sent to get a permit to bury our dead. You that have Christian burial know little of the horror that death brings on board ship. To the mate fell all the arrangement of the box and into a boat were carried the remains. There they stayed until late in the afternoon in the broiling sun before the authorities would allow them to be moved.

From that time on for six weeks we lived in mortal fear. The harbor was filled with the groans of the dying — like sheep they were falling right and left. Scarcely a tobanger passed us without its dead.

Business only called our captain from the ship. We were told never to sit on deck after nightfall. Our food was of the simplest — never a drink of water. Tea was frequently made and kept hot under the cosy. Gungy water made from rice, toast water and oatmeal gruel, with now and then a chicken, was all we dared take.

Shortly after the first man's death came the mate again with the same old story. As before our captain had gone on shore. Not seeing the mate as he left, he told me to tell him that if any more men were ill to take them on shore at once. I gave the message and the boat came alongside. Mr. Gibbs had not gotten into it when aft came another man. His face told his story ere he spoke and said, 'Missus, I am awful sick.' No one was near to hail our boat, so I signalled to the mate and told him he must take another.

It is needless to say that they never came back. We then had to fumigate, and, with Sidney, I went for a week to our sister ship the *Bourne*,[2] which had shortly before arrived, making only three of our countrymen then at Manila.

The *Bourne* coming later escaped the scourge. After a time our captain found a remedy which, taken at once, never failed to do its work. From that time we did not have a case. You can not know how terrible it is to live even six weeks in such an atmosphere. A friend called Manila the Port of Desolation.

I shall never forget the day the *Bourne* weighed anchor and left us alone in that stricken port. We never turned our backs upon land with more thankfulness than when the *Besse* took her anchors and sailed out into purer air.

One morning as we made the headland at the entrance of Macassar Straits way to leeward we discovered the *Bourne*, and soon the *Northern Light*.[3] We made merry by signalling through the day and burning torches at night. Thus passed several days until one Sunday morning there came a dead calm, and from the *Bourne's* signals we read, 'I'll come on board.' We watched the little dinghy skim along under the *Bourne's* bow, and rejoiced to meet our old friend where every breath was not a groan. That Sunday at sea was a benediction; it gave us rest and hope. The day was soon spent, and back to his home went the *Bourne's* captain.

Shortly after a light breeze sprang up, and every sail was pulling for the home coast. We thought that our paths parted, but we met her again and yet again. Of her wandering after leaving us at Manila it may interest you to hear a little, and better words than the captain's own I can not give.

[2] The bark *Jonathan Bourne*, 1472 tons, 203.3 x 39.8 x 24, was built at Bath, Maine, in 1877 by Goss and Sawyer. In 1883 she hailed from Boston, and was owned by William H. Besse and others.

[3] The ship *Northern Light*, 1859 tons, 219.7 x 43.1 x 28, was built at Quincy, Massachusetts, in 1872 by G. Thomas. In 1883 she hailed from New York, was owned by Benner and Pinckney, and commanded by Captain Joshua Slocum (who assisted Mrs. Baker at Manila in tending cholera victims).

Captain Doane's Letter.

Bark *Jonathan Bourne,*
Sulu Sea, May 30th 1883.

My dear Capt. and Mrs. Baker,

Two long and tedious weeks have elapsed since I bid you good night on the eve of leaving the port of desolation for our welcome homeward bound passage, and daily do I hold you in remembrance and long to know if all is well with you and if the gentle zephyrs have wafted you even ahead of us. For I find that at noon we are only 514 miles S. by East from Manila and that our log shows our sailing to have been 874. This leaves 360 miles that we may call yachting, although there has been no fun attached to it, but a full measure of care and anxiety.

Perhaps a brief review of our progress may comfort you if you have had better luck. You were doubtless surprised to find that we had not taken our departure on the night of the 15th. But the *Jonathan* performed an evolution on getting under weigh that has astonished my weak nerves ever since. At midnight the wind was N.N.E., hove short, made sail, hauled in the starboard fore braces to pay off to N.W. and clear the *Tancook*[4] on starboard tack. Hove up anchor and *J. B.* fell off to North, when to my utter astonishment she began to go to the Eastward in spite of all we could do. Then tried to fill the other way, but in the mean time the old *Jonathan* was going stern first for the old *Tancook* in a way that would have made match-wood of him had we collided. Our best bower with all our sails hard full, brought us up about 20 feet from his jib boom.

Soon after hove short again as I thought we could drift clear, but when short the Old D . . . l pointed straight for the *Tancook* again and I was forced to wait for daylight and steam.

At noon we passed out by Corregidore and as the weather looked nasty and barometer falling I ran W.S.W. During the night it set in thick and rainy, wind increasing to a moderate gale from N.E. After daylight wind increased rapidly, and gradually hauled to Northward. At 9 A.M. took in lower topsails and scud before the typhoon under bare poles. At 2 P.M. wind N.W. and blowing violently with a very irregular sea. We broached to and things were rather moist for a time. Got two canvas bags with oakum saturated with lamp oil, and put them over the side, but the wind blew the top of the water off so I fancy they did not much good. At 4 P.M. moderating and hauling to S.W. and finally to South.

When the storm abated we had 19 inches of molasses to pump out, which took our steam pumps 8 hours to accomplish. Thereby hangs a long yarn which I will tell you if I have paper enough and you don't already begin to cry Hold, enough!

Now, friend Baker, you know my weakness for China Sea, having had such good luck on two former passages in May. When the storm was over I found myself 150 miles S.W. of Corregidore, and as the wind had got around to South I would still keep on, which I did for another day, making however only 60 miles. I was just congratulating myself on how I was going to astonish all you fellows that took the Mendora passage, when my attention was called to something coming up from the Gulf of Siam.

[4] Presumably the British bark *Tancook*, 876 tons, 170.5 x 34.3 x 21.3, built at Mahone Bay, Nova Scotia in 1873, which in 1883 hailed from Quebec.

Well, to make a long story short it was an argument that proved most conclusively to my mind, as I saw topsail halyards going, and both leaches off our best mainsail, not to mention the terrible state of flutter and excitement our smaller sails were in, that China Sea route was *impracticable* just at this time.

So we up helm and run for poor despised Mendora. And didn't I address pet names to myself for all this folly?

I was ready to bet all the straw hats on board that before we could reach the straits all the Manila fleet would be through and that we should bring up the rear as we did on *entering Manila*. What a yarn I'm spinning. So here goes 'solid facts.' Passed through Northumberland Straits into Mindoro Sea on the 20th, fifth day out. On the 28th off the Western entrance of St. Basilan, wind light from nowhere, and strong current setting us to the Westward, the *Belle of Bath*[5] & German Barkentine in company — sometimes one gets a puff and spurts ahead and then another will be favored. On the 29th the German and ourselves were over on the Basilan shore when we were favored with the first of a southeast breeze that took us through into Sulu Sea at midnight. The *Belle of Bath* was nearly out of sight astern at sunset.

After getting safe into the Sea with a moderate breeze from S.S.W. I lay me down and had the first good sleep since we left port, and this morning when my eyes swept the horizon and I saw neither land or the *B. of B.* I was ready to sing all the Sankey and Moody hymns in the double ender....

It is said that people wearing cholera bands never have cholera. How true this is I can not state. Bands however were made for both our captain and mate. The following may show how effective they proved in this case, for the captain of the *Bourne* says:

Mr. Stone is a genius. A few days after leaving Manila I passed his room, and there he sat in his bunk, a picture of patience and contentment. One leg was thrown promiscuous like over the edge of the berth showing the calf well tied up with the cholera band Mrs. Baker so kindly made. He explained that having worn the belt, and never feeling an ache or pain in the region of the diaphragm, and discovering a small boil on his leg he thought it advisable to move the band nearer the seat of disease, and was happy to say that the result was proving the wisdom of his judgment, and his gratitude to Mrs. Baker for her thoughtful favor will be everlasting.

Of Manila you all know as a Spanish port, capital of the Philippine Islands, and full of sweetness in all its stages. It consists of the old and new Manila; the old is a walled city within which I am told foreigners are not allowed to sleep. The streets are narrow and dirty. On every side is shown how times without number the heart has been shaken by many an eruption, nature covering as well as it can the ruins by luxurious growth of vines. The Cathedral alone has withstood all the convulsions. It is a gloomy structure, bare and horrid inside. New Manila has its poor shops and narrow streets with a little hum of life about them.

---

[5] The ship *Belle of Bath*, 1418 tons, 203 x 39 x 24.3, was built at Bath, Maine, in 1877 by Goss and Sawyer. In 1883 she hailed from Bath and was owned by P. M. Whitmore and others.

After winding in and around numerous islands, straits and seas which look so small on the map, we had 600 miles of Sulu Sea and Macassar Straits before we entered Java Sea with its one thousand islands.

June 24th, ship *Northern Light* ahead, we made the South Watcher, the first of the southern portion of the Thousand Islands. The day was beautiful; the Easterly Monsoon was gentle and soft as a zephyr; every sail was full, and our hearts were as light as the air we breathed. We passed one and another island until at 5 P.M. our captain judged we were clear of danger. The *Bourne* was near us, her white wings making a pretty picture which we never tired of watching. The second mate from aloft had just made his report of the position of Babia when the bell rang for dinner. As I arose from my chair I felt a terrible shock which threw me off my feet in an instant. We knew we were hard and fast on some coral reef which doubtless had been thrown up during some of Nature's numerous convulsions. Our first thought was to save the *Bourne* whose captain we knew was at dinner, and felt, like ourselves, that all danger had passed. We shouted, all to no purpose. On came the noble ship until it seemed that both would find a burial there. Our captain and men were using every means in their power to call attention to our position, when for the first time in our lives our Stars and Stripes went up union down. 'Twas a hard pull, it meant so much.

The *Bourne* was scarcely fifty yards from us when at the lee rail came the captain's head, just in time to hear our captain shout 'For God's sake port your helm!' He sprang for the wheel, shouting 'All hands aft!' He had heard the cry, seen the coral, felt it graze his ship's side, and sprang to save her. One moment longer and the two would have lain there with trembling hulls and flapping sails.

As the *Bourne* dipped into deeper water our captain shouted 'I'm ashore, come on board.' The reply came across that sunlit water, 'I will, as soon as I can deepen my water.' Silently save for the dip, dip of the oars came the *Bourne's* captain. Over our fallen ship's side he climbed and grasping our captain's hand said, 'Baker, you've saved me.' The reply came in low tones—'This is the last of the *W. H. Besse* and the last of me; take my wife and child to Angier with you; I must know they are safe, and I will come to them as soon as I can.'

But again we stayed, our presence more than ever necessary. All night we worked to clear ourselves from the coral clutches, while the *Bourne* went to Angier to telegraph for assistance from Batavia.

A fearful sea began to rise; with it our poor home bumped, bumped, and all effort could not save her. Water was gaining on the pumps. Boats were made ready, provisioned and watered, with trunks containing just the most needful, so that at a moment's warning we could take them.

Much to our surprise one morning as we labored we discovered that the vessel floated. Our men were much exhausted, not having taken food for many hours, and all seemed favorable for a half hour's much needed rest. As there was hard work yet to do our captain gave the order, and we waited. But not long—for snap went one hawser. The sea lent its strength and threatened to snap the other. Then our captain called his men, stationed them, gave his orders, and said, 'Let every man do his duty faithfully without a *moment's* delay; all depends on your promptness when I give the word.' All was excitement. At the given signal off glided the *Besse* with a bound, but the treacherous tide took her like a plaything and piled her broadside on the coral from which she sprang. Out went the big anchor to keep her from going on more, but oh! how she bumped. Her masts shook like reeds; we thought every moment they would go overboard. The last resort, of cargo overboard, was taken, with no improvement. All had been done that could be and every man was spent. Rest was taken anywhere, our captain alone watching for we knew not what. Early the following morning a steamer was sighted coming to our assistance. We took her hawser and turned for Batavia, a ship in distress, a prey for every land vulture that could in any capacity swoop down upon us.

Divers went down and reported us badly damaged, bringing up pieces of wood as large as your arm all chewed up. Docks were inspected, and finally a floating one on the island of Amsterdam was selected because of lower terms and a warehouse nearby in which to store our sweetness. Of all that weariness you will not care to hear.

This little island abounds in gum Arabic trees which we often tapped, and from which we gathered the gum. Fever lurked in every corner of that island, so that Sidney and I were ordered by a good old Dutch doctor to be sent up among the mountains in the interior of Java to a place called Buitenrorg, the seat of the Dutch Government. Batavia had too much cholera for us to stay there in safety. Buitenrorg is a pretty place. The Governor's house is there. There are lovely drives and good air. It is Dutch to the backbone—an official at every turn. Low German only is spoken with Malay. Can you imagine anything more dreary than weeks among people that can not understand one word that you say? Of life in Buitz and the little sunshine it gave us I have little time to tell you.

It was a happy morning when the captain came to tell us that our time of bondage had passed. We rested at Batavia several days while the captain attended to business. At the Hotel with us was an American circus company. We watched them with real interest because of their name, and their continual cries of 'Spider, Spider'—the American for the Malay 'Sparder,' meaning servant or boy, with the answering patter of the Spider's black feet, gave us the nearest approach to a laugh that we had attempted for many a day.

Out from Batavia in the little tug we went again to our ocean home with much cheer, for shortly we were to turn the *Besse's* nose towards country, home and friends. From the Dock Marten verandah we watched the vessel slowly move out from the arms that so long had held her, into the clearer water.

Sunday morning, August 26, 1883, we took our anchors, and with pilot on board proceeded down the Straits. The wind was light and what there was came contrary to law and order, for through Sunda Straits and Java Seas the wind blows six months to the Eastward and six to the Westward. The changes take place in April and October and are called Monsoons. From April to October the Easterly Monsoon prevails with clear sky and fine weather. From October to April the Westerly Monsoon blows, ofttimes with great force, especially during October and November, accompanied with strong squalls and dark, gloomy weather and torrents of rain. The current then runs with great velocity, making it very difficult for sailing vessels to proceed through the various Straits out of the Java Sea. The strength of the current is governed by the force of the wind. This unusual raging of the wind disturbed the pilot. We made little distance and finally came to anchor. As the chains rattled over the side there came answering echoes, above, around, beneath, until the vessel trembled so that it seemed as if the coral must again have clutched her. The thundering and cannonading continued louder and stronger until the pilot said, 'Krakatoa must be kicking up again.' His careless way of speaking gave us little cause for alarm, so we retired; but here he said that he did not like the look of things, so took a cot on deck and remained there through the night. All night volcanic thunder sounded like discharges of heavy artillery; fine lava dust fell all through the night.

As the morning broke the sky cleared, the atmosphere was less sulphurous, and all seemed favorable for a start. 'Man the windlass,' came the order, and soon we were under weigh. The pilot waited while we penciled a line to assure the watchers on the home shore that we were safe. Then came the God-speed, the little boat turned for the land, and we felt the voyage begun.

Sidney and I were on the main deck giving some order to the steward, when with a rush came the mate, saying 'Captain is at the wheel, he wants you at once.' Then he shouted 'All hands on deck!' Lowering sail and rattling anchor followed quickly. As I came to the companionway our captain said, 'Look at the barometer; tell me how it stands — I fear something dreadful is going to happen. I do not like the look of things. Tell me quickly how the barometer stands and every change it makes.' So violent were its movements that I could not give its record. It would rise and fall ten tenths at a time in quick succession. It seemed as though the thing was alive.

Our sails were all made fast when like a curtain fell a darkness so intense no human eye could penetrate it. Ashes were falling like snow. Lifelines were run for the safety of those who worked, for fingers and feet were eyes.

The air was so strong of sulphur that we were battened down in the cabin and every door closed. Lights were allowed only in the cabin, and this at mid-day. Do you wonder that we thought that the day of judgment had come? Soon the wind began to blow and howl about us; then the tide rose and rushed by us fearfully. Both anchors were down with 720 feet of chain on each, yet so strong and high came that tidal wave that those chains stood like bars of iron, dragging for miles anchors, chain and vessel, threatening to snap their links, and send us to the same coral from which we came six weeks before. Our captain flung the lead again and again, but though of thirty pounds weight it floated like a cork on the water. Every few moments the captain and mate would come to us that we might know they were safe. Their faces and clothes looked as though a mason had smoothed with careful hand his mortar over all. Hours passed slowly. At five o'clock our captain opened the cabin door and beckoning to us said, 'Come here.' We answered with trembling feet. Standing in the darkness he pointed to a little rim of light which seemed far, far on an unknown shore, and whispered 'Tis a promise of another day.' That night was quiet, save for a troubled sea which for hours had been smooth as glass, blown so by the force of the wind. The 28th of August was nearly all spent in heaving short our anchor.

The morning opened as fine and hot as usual at that season. Our chains were so foul and the sun so hot that we did not make sail until at six on the morning of the 29th, when it was thought best not to carry but little sail and to proceed cautiously, for with the exception of St. Nicholas Point neither land nor soundings were familiar or as they should be. Sight after sight was worked and every time the captain would say, 'I don't understand it; according to my sights we are sailing over the top of Angier.' And we have since learned that it was indeed so, for that night Angier with its 60,000 inhabitants, its wonderful Banyan tree and fort was wiped out of existence. I have been told that one hundred feet of water now covers much of the old city of Angier. Angier has been and is the halting place for vessels, many finding their orders to proceed to this or that port, which at the time of sailing could not be determined upon. Home letters there wait and cheer, and break many a long voyage. The new town is now nearly in the position of the old. Krakatoa has been a point of land much made by vessels entering Java Sea or Sunda Straits. It is now nearly all gone, and near to it another island appeared that day 700 feet high. It is stated on good authority that the missing mass of Krakatoa equals 200,000 million cubic feet, and that a fiftieth part of this mass suddenly dropped into the sea would create a displacement sufficient to make a circle wave nearly one hundred miles in circumference and twenty feet high. Dr. Verbeek estimated the dust to have been blown up nine miles into space.

On the 30th during the morning we were startled by our captain's cry of 'Hard up! Hard down! Easy! Hard up! Hard up! Hard down!', each order following quick after the other. A man was aloft, another on the lookout, and men stationed to pass the word along. Anxious voices were everywhere. We waited, knowing well that the master would tell us all as soon as he could. Shortly we were allowed to come on deck for a moment. 'Twas a sight I shall never forget. Our way seemed blocked by every conceivable thing: human beings bloated beyond recognition, boats, trees, fruit and animals. Should we ever be able to leave it all!

Like all other days that came to an end. We passed through the gates out into the Indian Ocean without other stain than the clinging ashes which never entirely left the vessel as long as she floated upon the water. At evening we passed Prineer[6] Island, which thus far was the first land that we had passed as it should be. The dock in which we repaired pulled from its moorings on the 26th and floated by us that day on an unknown and unreported voyage. Had we been overtaken while in its embrace it certainly would have been the last of us all.

For six hundred miles we sailed in the open sea ere we found blue water. Thus we knew Nature had sent her voice far and wide. Should we ever know or find our way—and where? Soon a dire stillness fell among us. One and another was taken; even the mate yielded, so that when we found the water blue about us and hope threw out a ray of sunlight we scarcely caught it.

[6] *Sic,* but no doubt 'Princes' in the original.

One evening just at nightfall we folded our flag over the box which held one of the crew. The captain read the burial service and into the ocean the box was lowered. Java fever or Beri beri as they called it lingered about us all the voyage, so that when off Hatteras we were ill prepared to battle with a hurricane.

However, when the three lights of Truro were sighted, and later Highland light, the home hawser was pulling so strong that courage came to every heart but mine. Even with pilot, tugs and assistance the home light was dim. Truly we were and had been Toilers of the Sea.

II

New England Grab Bag

The Dry Salvages and the Thacher Shipwreck   36
by Samuel Eliot Morison

The Disorderly Voyage of the Brig *Betsy*   51
from its log.

"Just Ease Her When She Pitches"   59
by William G. Saltonstall

The Battle of Priest's Cove   69
by Llewellyn Howland

The Merrimac River Gundalow and Gundalowmen   75
by Wallace B. Ordway

Until the industrial revolution New England's prosperity depended on the sea. Shipbuilding, fishing, and every marine industry thrived on the many-harbored coast. Trade flourished from the West Indies to Europe, China, the Spice Islands—any port that produced a viable product.

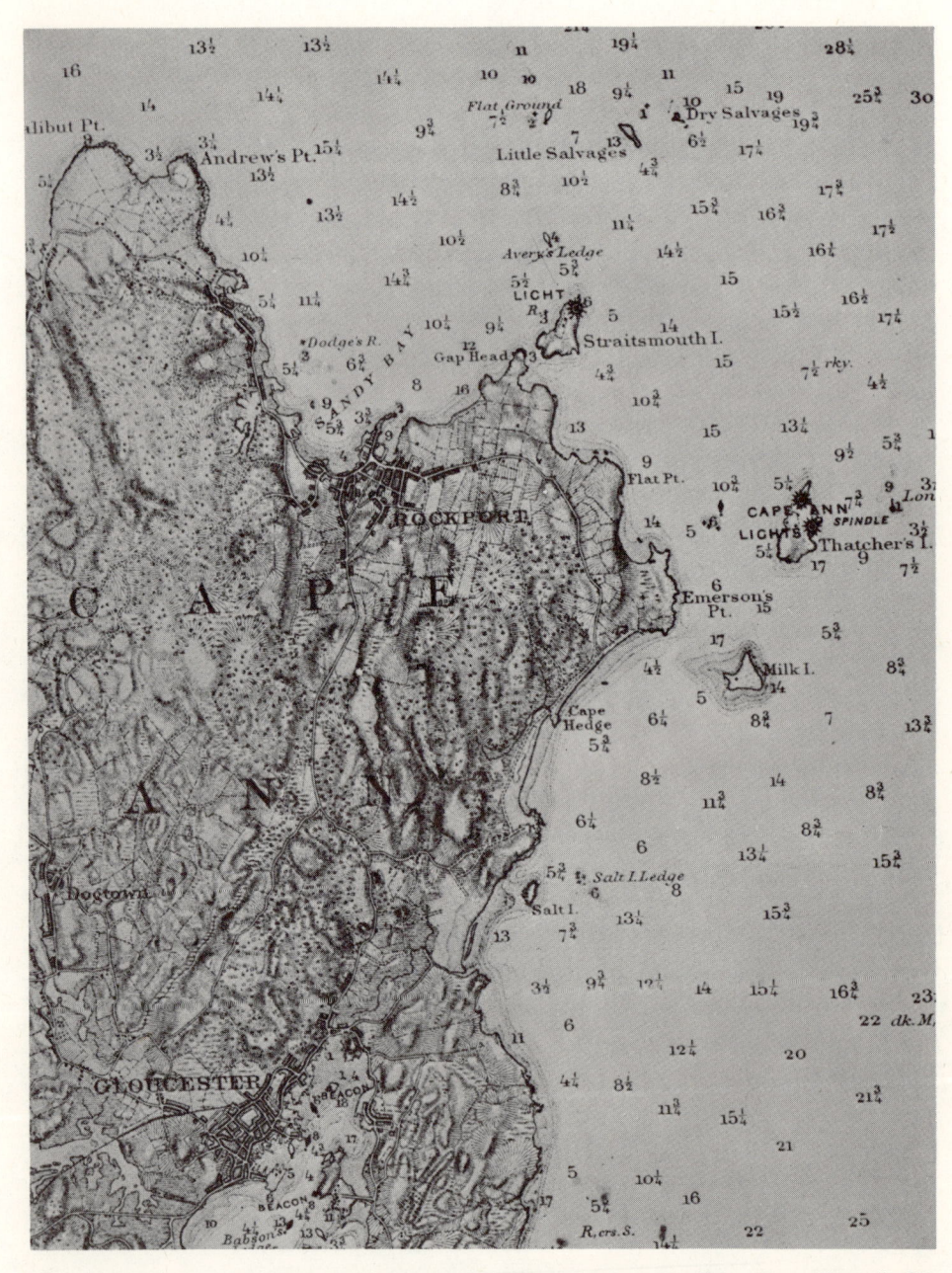

The Dry Salvages as shown on "Coast Chart No. 8 From Wells to Cape Ann," 1867
Courtesy of the Peabody Museum of Salem

The Dry Salvages and the Thacher Shipwreck

BY SAMUEL ELIOT MORISON

ONCE in a great while a rock or reef hitherto noticed only by seamen acquires fame through poetry. Such were Southey's *Inchcape Rock* and Longfellow's *Norman's Woe*. And now another reef off Cape Ann puts on immortality through T. S. Eliot's *The Dry Salvages*.

That is the title of one of his Four Quartets, first published in 1943. Many readers, including Eliot's latest biographer Herbert Howarth[1] and my humble self, believe it to be one of the greatest poems of the century. It has put this group of rocks off Cape Ann into literature for all time. Consequently one entertains a certain curiosity as to what the Dry Salvages are, how they got their name, and why they inspired Mr. Eliot.

As one may see on the attached reproduction of the 1867 chart, the Dry Salvages is a cluster of rocks lying about a mile east-northeasterly from Straitsmouth Island, off Cape Ann. The official *United States Coast Pilot, Atlantic Coast, Section A: St. Croix River to Cape Cod* (4th ed., 1941), page 260, describes the Dry Salvages as 'a bare ledge about 15 feet above high water near the middle of a reef about 500 yards long in a northerly direction.' Parallel to, and about 500 yards west of the Dry Salvages, is Little Salvages, a rocky reef bare at low water but covered at high tide, and half a mile to a mile northwesterly from Little Salvages is Flat Ground, a rocky ledge half a mile long with a least depth of two feet at mean low water. The *American Coast Pilot* of 1854 describes this as 'a large spot of flat ground which at low water will take up a small vessel.'[2] It 'took up' a Liberty ship during the last war, and a converted 110-foot subchaser in 1955. Tanker *Lucy* and minesweeper U.S.S. *Grouse* foundered there more recently. When an easterly gale is raging the entire group—Dry Salvages, Little Salvages and Flat Ground—becomes a seething mass of foam, as heavy swells from the Atlantic break and roar over it;

---

[1] *Notes on Some Figures Behind T. S. Eliot* (Houghton Mifflin, 1964), pp. 117-121.
[2] Edmund M. Blunt, *The American Coast Pilot* (17th ed., 1854), p. 211.

and at all times it is a menace to navigators attempting to round Cape Ann.

> ... The ragged rock in the restless waters,
> Waves wash over it, fogs conceal it;
> On a halcyon day it is merely a monument,
> In navigable weather it is always a seamark
> To lay a course by: but in the sombre season
> Or the sudden fury, is what it always was.[3]

At the time when T. S. Eliot knew it, Dry Salvages was marked by a wooden tripod; but, owing to the frequent need of replacing or repairing this beacon after a storm, it was removed in 1945, leaving the rock bare as 'it always was.' Since 1935 a big lighted bell buoy has been moored about half a mile to the northeast of the Dry Salvages.

Eliot's parents spent almost every summer from 1895 on, and during their son's years at Harvard, at Gloucester. He and his brother Henry, taught to sail by an ancient mariner of Gloucester, became familiar with these waters, and Henry continued to live on Cape Ann for many years after Tom went to England. The young men talked with James B. Conolly, author of *Out of Gloucester,* and with numerous fishermen and sailors. They read the story of Anthony Thacher's shipwreck in 1635, which further identified them with Cape Ann, because one of the passengers was 'Mr. William Eliot of New Sarum,' conjecturally a relative. T. S. Eliot eventually came to believe that his first American ancestor was in the shipwreck. 'Did you know,' he wrote to me on 28 July 1964, 'that the Reverend Andrew Eliot was in the company with the Reverend Mr. Thatcher when they went ashore on Thatcher's Island? What they were doing there I cannot imagine.' There is no evidence, however, of a relationship. Andrew Eliot of East Coker came over in about the year 1669, according to William Graeme Eliot's *Sketch of the Eliot Family* (1887). William Eliot of Salisbury, Wiltshire, preceded him in 1634 and had lived but a few months in Ipswich when he shipped on board the fatal pinnace. Nothing more is known about him.[4]

Tom was not only steeped in the lore of Cape Ann; he became familiar with the encompassing ocean. Cruising in college days with his friend Harold Peters, the Dry Salvages was the last seamark they passed outward bound, and the first they picked up homeward bound. Approaching or departing in a fog, they listened for the mournful moans of the 'groaner,' the whistling buoy east of Thacher Island, and the 'wailing warning' of

---

[3] T. S. Eliot, *Complete Poems and Plays* (Harcourt Brace & Co., 1952), p. 133.
[4] James Savage, *Genealogical Dictionary of New England,* II, 108-110.

Dry Salvages, 23 May 1965, looking southwest

the diaphone on Thacher's itself. They doubtless learned to allow an extra quarter point for set of current when sailing from the Maine coast to Cape Ann, as insurance against running on the Salvages.

These waters off Cape Ann are a real test of seamanship for sailors of small boats. There are numerous rocky passages that you can thread if you are 'acquainted,' and the *Coast Pilot* warns you to sheer off if you are not; big ships do well to keep outside the entire collection of reefs. The Dry Salvages, as Eliot writes, is 'always a seamark to lay a course by.' Leaving it well to starboard when approaching Cape Ann from the north, you shape a south-southwest course to pass between Thacher's and The Londoner. He did not have to consult the *Coast Pilot* to know that 'to avoid The Londoner, you must keep the lights close aboard the body of the island on which they stand.' The Eliot brothers learned that when sailing down East, after turning Thacher's, you must either steer north-northeast to clear the Dry Salvages, or due north to pass between Avery Ledge and Flat Ground.

Tom remembered the music of Cape Ann—'the sea howl and the sea yelp,'

> ... the whine in the rigging,
> The menace and caress of wave that breaks on water,
> The distant rote in the granite teeth,
> And the wailing warning from the approaching headland

And the 'tolling bell' off Flat Ground, which

> Measures time not our time, rung by the unhurried
> Ground swell, a time
> Older than the time of chronometers, ...[5]

These lines, and indeed all that follow, ring a bell in any sailor's heart. They are authentic, not synthetic like the great mass of so-called sea poetry. Take, for instance, 'the menace and caress of wave that breaks on water,' which Eliot could have observed at Flat Ground or Milk Island Bar. When a moderate wave from the ocean strikes a shoal, it suddenly lifts—a warning to an approaching mariner—and then breaks, with a susurration that may be rendered as a hissing menace or a wooing caress. Notice also 'the distant rote.' *Rote* or *Rut* is an old English word now seldom heard outside New England. It means a distant, continuous roar made by waves dashing on a long rocky coast.[6] Often have I heard a Maine

---

[5] *Complete Poems*, p. 131.

[6] In Robert Juet's account of Henry Hudson's voyage of 1609, 'We heard a great Rut, like the Rut of the shoare.' Levermore, op. cit., II, 396.

man say, 'Sea's making up. Hear that rote!' It may be ten miles distant, but you can distinguish it from traffic noises, jet planes or any other sound. T. S. Eliot doubtless listened to the rote from his parents' house, during the windless calm after a storm, or on a 'weather-breeder' day when swells from the eastward begin crashing on the 'granite teeth' of Cape Ann before a storm breaks.

These youthful impressions stayed with Eliot for almost twoscore years, producing at last the setting and background of his great poem.

* * *

Under the title to *The Dry Salvages,* the poet provided an explanation in parentheses: 'The Dry Salvages—presumably *les trois sauvages*—is a small group of rocks, with a beacon, off the N.E. coast of Cape Ann, Massachusetts. *Salvages* is pronounced to rhyme with *assuages....*'

This derivation as well as the pronunciation, both of which Mr. Eliot informed me he had from his brother Henry, surprised me. For I, too, have sailed in those waters, piloted by ancient mariners (as they then seemed to me), who pronounced the name of the rock, *savages;* and I reflected that *salvage* was a common spelling of *savage* in the seventeenth century.[7] As the rhyme accompanying the portrait of Captain John Smith on his Map of New England has it,

> Thy Faire-Discoueries and Fowle-Overthrowes
> Of Salvages, much civilliz'd by thee
> Best shew thy Spirit . . .

We may first dispose of T. S. Eliot's theory that the 'Dry' of 'Dry Salvages' is a translation of the French 'Trois.' This particular ledge has a dry part, out of water at high tide. 'Dry' is a not unusual designation along the Atlantic coast for ledges bare at high water, to distinguish them from others which, like the Little Salvages, are covered twice daily. Dry Bank and the Dry Tortugas off Florida are examples; and there are numerous 'Dry' ledges off the Maine coast. Moreover, 'Dry' appears on no map in connection with The Salvages until 1867, when any derivation from *trois* would be farfetched.

But how about *Salvages?* This is the older spelling of *Savage,* the *l* recording that it is derived from the late Latin *salvaticus,* meaning 'woodland' or 'wild.' One finds it in Shakespeare ('Doe you put trickes vpon's

---

[7] There is no possibility of the rock's name having been derived from the verb *to salvage;* for the Dry Salvages is the last place where one could salvage anything. On the contrary, it has been the scene of many wrecks.

with Saluages and Men of Inde?' *Tempest,* II.ii.60); in Thomas Fuller's *Holy and Profane State* of 1642 ('Let us not be naked Salvages'), and in George Withers' *Britain's Remembrancer* of 1628 ('When late the salvage bore'). This salvage spelling lasted later in New England than in Old England. The Laws of New Plymouth of 1677, page 187, mention 'Captive Salvages,' and James Franklin's newspaper *The New England Courant* of 7 June 1725 reports, 'We have through the favour of God, destroyed more of the Salvages.' But the spelling *savage,* as often found in Shakespeare as *salvage,* became increasingly popular after 1600, and there can be no reasonable doubt that it represents the common pronunciation of the word.

Local historians are unable to explain the name Dry Salvages. John J. Babson, writing in 1860, said, 'Tradition has preserved no account of the origin of the name.'[8] Lemuel Gott, writing in 1888, said, 'Nothing has been transmitted to us concerning the origin of the term Salvages.'[9]

Over thirty years ago I expressed the opinion that the name was a transfer from Cape Neddick Nubble which Gabriel Archer, in his account of Bartholomew Gosnold's voyage of 1602, called Savage Rock,[10] Transfers of geographical names are very common; the classic instance being that of the Portuguese *Lavrador* from Greenland to the modern Labrador.[11] One such transfer has taken place very close to the Salvages: the name Avery's Fall, as we shall shortly see.

Here is Archer's account of the southern Maine part of Gosnold's voyage:—'The fourteenth [of May, 1602] . . . we descried . . . another Rocke . . . that wee called *Sauage Rocke* because the Sauages first shewed themselues there; . . . From the said Rocke, came towards vs a *Biscay* shallop with saile and Oares, hauing eight persons in it, whom we supposed at first to bee Christians distressed. But approaching vs neare, wee perceiued them to bee Sauages. These comming within call, hayled us, and wee answered.'[12]

All historians who have studied Gosnold's voyage agree that this Savage Rock was The Nubble, a tiny round island off Cape Neddick in York, both being conspicuous landmarks on the southern Maine coast.

[8] *History of Gloucester,* p. 14 n.
[9] *History of the Town of Rockport,* p. 29.
[10] *Publications,* Col. Soc. of Mass., XXVII (1929), 300 n.
[11] Morison, *Portuguese Voyages to America in the Fifteenth Century* (1940), pp. 54-55. For the transfer from the Machias Seal Islands to Roque Island, see *Publications,* Col. Soc. of Mass., XLII (1964), 471.
[12] *Purchas His Pilgrims* (1625), IV, 1647, reprinted in Vol. XVIII of the MacLehose edition of 1905-1907, and in Charles H. Levermore, ed., *Forerunners and Competitors of the Pilgrims and Puritans* (published for the New England Society of Brooklyn, 1912), I, 44-45.

Archer continues: 'About sixteene leagues South-west from thence wee perceiued in that course two small Ilands, the one lying Eastward from *Sauage Rock,* the other to the Southwards of it.' The first must have been Boon Island; the second the Isles of Shoals, looking like a single island when seen from the northward. Gosnold's ship, *Concord,* passed Cape Ann in the night without sighting it, and next day reached Cape Cod, so named by Gosnold.

The following year, 1604, Martin Pring made a voyage along the same coast in ship *Speedwell,* and among her crew were two men who had been with Gosnold. After passing the mouth of the Kennebec, states Pring in his account of the voyage: 'We, . . . shaping our course for *Sauage Rocke,* discouered the yeere before by Captaine *Gosnold,* where going vpon the Mayne we found people, with whom we had no long conuersation, because here also we could find no Sassafras. Departing hence we bare into that great Gulfe which Captaine *Gosnold* ouer-shot the yeere before, coasting and finding people on the North side thereof.'[13] The *Speedwell* then anchored in the future Plymouth Harbor, which Pring named Whitson Bay.

Samuel de Champlain was the next explorer whose account of this coast has been preserved, and he was the first to attempt a chart of Cape Ann, which on his map of 1607[14] he called *Cap aux Isles,* and of Gloucester Harbor, which he called *Beauport.* On Champlain's map Cape Neddick is clearly depicted, and the Nubble is named *la ronde île,* suggesting that Champlain was not familiar with Archer's narrative of the 1602 voyage.

Champlain's exploration of 1605 with the Sieur de Monts, which his map illustrates, is described in *Les Voyages du Sieur de Champlain Saintongeois,* published at Paris in 1613. This was the voyage westward from St. Croix in a pinnace. After passing Mount Desert Island, exploring the lower Kennebec, entering the mouth of the Saco River, and anchoring in Cape Porpoise Harbor, they passed the Isles of Shoals and on 15 July arrived off Cape Ann.

'Next day,' states Champlain's account, 'we made our way to the above-mentioned cape [Ann] where, close to the mainland, are three islands which are covered with trees of different sorts.' These islands must have been the modern Straitsmouth, Thacher, and Milk. He continues: 'There is another low island upon which the sea breaks, which extends a

---

[13] *Purchas,* IV, 1655; Levermore, op. cit., I, 62.
[14] Plate LXXX in H. P. Biggar's Champlain Society edition (1922) of his *Works.* The original is in the Library of Congress. Plate LXXXI reproduces the less accurate and detailed *Carte Géographique de la Nouvelle France* from *Les Voyages* of 1613.

little farther out to sea than the others, and upon it are no trees.' This must have been the Dry Salvages. It is neither shown nor named on Champlain's 1607 map, possibly because the site is covered by an inscription. 'We named this place *le cap aux isles*,' continues Champlain. 'Near it we caught sight of a canoe in which were five or six Indians (*sauuages*) who came towards us, but after approaching our pinnace, went back to dance on the beach (*rivage*).' He then relates how he approached these friendly natives, gave them each a knife and a biscuit, and persuaded them to draw with charcoal an outline of Cape Ann and Massachusetts Bay. Sailing half a league further, the explorers 'perceived on a rocky point several *sauuages* who ran dancing along the shore toward their companions to inform them of our coming.'[15] The pinnace then anchored close to a small islet—probably Salt Island over against Bass Rocks—where the Frenchmen engaged in a friendly conference with the Indians. Champlain did not at that time enter Gloucester Harbor, but on his voyage the following year explored and charted it very accurately.

Thus Champlain is the first known explorer to mention the Salvages, though not by name. Yet is is possible that he did name it *Les Sauvages* after the friendly Indians whom he encountered on the cape shore, and that name was passed on to later mariners by word of mouth. The spelling *Salvages* is certainly not French; Champlain consistently calls the natives *les sauuages,* the second 'u,' in accordance with typographical canons of the seventeenth century, being meant for a 'v.'

Henry Hudson passed along the New England coast from east to west in 1609, before rediscovering the river named after him; but he sailed straight from the Kennebec River mouth to Cape Cod, and like Gosnold, overshot Cape Ann.

The next navigator to pass this way and leave an account of his voyage was Captain John Smith, in 1614. In his *Description of New England* (1616) he tells a good deal about 'the Salvages,' as he calls the natives, but not much about the land. Cape Ann he called 'the fair headland *Tragabigzanda*,' after the Turkish lady who had helped him to escape from captivity. It was 'fronted with three Iles called the three *Turks heads*,' so named after the gallant Captain's self-assumed coat of arms.[16] But his Map of New England, in his *Generall Historie of Virginia, New-England, and the Summer Isles* (1624), is more explicit. Off 'Cape Anna' (we owe it

[15] Translation in *Works*, I, 334-337. Local historians believe that he encountered these Indians in Whale Cove.
[16] E. Arber, ed., *Travels and Works of Captain John Smith* (1910), I, 204.

to Prince Charles, later King Charles I, that the name was changed from that of the unpronounceable Turkish lady to his mother's) are three islands, obviously Straitsmouth, Thacher and Milk; and, northeast of Straitsmouth, there are five dots representing the Dry and Little Salvages and the Flat Ground. But none are named.[17]

Governor John Winthrop, in his Journal of the voyage of *Arbella* in 1630, states: 'About the E: point of Cape Ann lye 3: or 4: ilandes which appeare aboue water & a ledge of rockes vnder water lyeth to the Eastward of the bigger E: Ilande, which ridge stretcheth about ½ mil to the E: . . . the most northeast of all the said Ilandes is a small Rocke, bare without wood or ought vpon it, the rest have shrubbes.'[18]

This "small Rocke" must be the Dry Salvages, still unnamed.

Charts or maps of the New England coast in the seventeenth century are few indeed. The earliest on which I have found the name that interests us is contained in *The English Pilot* (London, 1689). The chart included in this very rare book, John Thornton's *New Chart of the Sea Coast of Newfound land, new Scotland, new England . . . and part of Carolina*, has two dots off Cape Ann, labeled *Salvage* and *Thatcher*.[19] I have next found it in *The English Pilot,* the Fourth Book (London, 1706).[20] The chart at page 7, 'Part of New England, Sold by I. Thornton at the Platt in the Minories,' names the most prominent island off Cape Ann, *Salvages*. South of it are four crosses called *Sunken Rocks*. The sailing directions in this book, page 19, state, 'West from the high Hill of Cape *Ann* 2 Miles, lie the *Salvages Rocks,* a little to the Southwestward of Cape Ann lieth a small Island called Thatchers Island. . . .' West here is an obvious error for east; the Dry Salvages lie about two and three-quarters miles due east of Pigeon Hill, Cape Ann. Both map and text are repeated in the 1729 edition of *The English Pilot*.[21]

Captain Cyprian Southack's *New England Coasting Pilot* (London, 1724) is more accurate on Cape Ann than many later charts.[22] *Salvage Rock,* indicated as dry, is in approximately the right location. *Thatchers I.* is there, somewhat too far south, and off it is *Fishers Rock, seen at Low Water,* later named The Londoner.

The next chart in point of time that mentions the Salvages is Barnley's

[17] Id., II, 694.
[18] Mass. Hist. Soc. ed., *Winthrop Papers*, II, 281.
[19] Captain Cyprian Southack's copy, imperfect, in Massachusetts Historical Society.
[20] Copy in Harvard College Library.
[21] Map from this edition reproduced in *Publications,* Col. Soc. of Mass., XXVII, 298.
[22] Copy in Harvard College Library.

of 1757.[23] He has Thachers Island with approximately the correct shape and location, and, north of it, *Salvigis Rocks,* shown in such detail that Dry Salvages stands out distinct from the surrounding reefs, which are indicated by crosses to show that they were awash.

Within twenty years appeared the magnificent survey of the New England and Nova Scotia coasts by the British Admiralty, published as *The Atlantic Neptune* over the name of Joseph F. W. Des Barres. Here *The Salvayes (sic)* are inaccurately depicted as a long line of five separate reefs, none dry at high water.[24] The odd spelling need not trouble us; the *y* is obviously a copyist's or engraver's error for *g*.

Incidentally, the once famous twin lighthouses on Thacher's are shown on the 1781 edition of *The Atlantic Neptune*. First built by the Province of Massachusetts Bay in 1771, they were replaced by two taller towers in 1866. These twin lights, projecting their beams many miles out to sea, were among the most distinctive, reliable and comforting landmarks on the New England coast, enabling a vessel to shape a course to clear the Dry Salvages and all other obstacles. Great was the outcry when the Treasury Department, out of economy, extinguished the northern light on 1 February 1932 and substituted an occulting for a fixed light on the southern one. But the northern tower still stands, and makes a useful day mark.

The Atlantic Neptune and charts derived from it remained standard for more than half a century, since the United States Government did not attempt to chart the New England coast until after 1840.

Here are all charts that I have found in the Peabody Museum, Salem, which depict The Salvages or mention them by name:

1800: *A Chart of the Coast of New England from New York to Goldsborough Bay,* printed in London. *Salvages* appears as three crosses in line.

1812: *A New Chart of Massachusetts Bay,* by S. Lambert of Salem. *Salvages* shown as three dry rocks surrounded by reefs.

1813: Edmund Blunt, *New Chart of the Northeastern Coast of North America,* published in New York. *Salvages* indicated by five crosses—none dry. Halibut Point is called *Hallowbout Point*.

1828, with corrections to 1844: Edmund Blunt, *The North Eastern Coast of North America from New York to Sable Island. Salvages* indicated by three crosses in an oval frame.

[23] *A New and Correct Chart of the Sea Coast of New-England from Cape Codd to Casco Bay. Lately Surveyed by Capt. Henry Barnley.* Copy in Peabody Museum, Salem.
[24] Copies in Peabody Museum and Boston Athenaeum. But an early plate of this map, in Harvard College Library, depicts no fewer than five of these extended *Salvayes* as dry.

SALVAGES AND THACHER SHIPWRECK 47

1856: Captain George Eldridge, *A New Chart of the Coast of New England*. *Salvages* indicated by three dry rocks and three crosses, in circular frame.

We now begin to find results of the first official United States Coast Survey by its superintendent Alexander D. Bache, and Benjamin Peirce, the Harvard mathematician. It took the Survey about ten years to depict The Salvages correctly.

1856: An uncaptioned chart of the New England coast. *Salvages* indicated by two crosses in oval frame (Peabody Museum).

1857: *Sketch A—Shewing the Progress of Survey . . . from 1844 to 1857*. *Salvages* indicated as a single dry spot (Harvard College Library).

1867: *Coast Chart No. 8, Wells to Cape Ann* (Peabody). This we have chosen as illustration, since it is the earliest to differentiate between Dry Salvages, Little Salvages, and Flat Ground, all so named and depicted fairly accurately. The vignette or profile showing Cape Ann as approached from the north, we have also reproduced as it is the first attempt to depict the Salvages as seen by a seaman (Peabody).

1872, corrected to 1878: *Coast Chart No. 9, Boston Bay*. Similar to the above, with a different vignette, and *Little Salvages* as well as *Dry Salvages* shown as an island. *Oak Rock* off Thacher Island is first so named on this chart (Peabody).

1877: *Eldridge's New Chart from Lynn to Halibut Point*. Similar to the above, with a printed caution, 'From the Northeastward take care to . . . avoid the flat ground, and Salvages.' (Peabody.)

1877: *Coast Chart No. 108, Wells to Cape Ann* (Harvard). *Dry Salvages* is marked by a beacon; *Little Salvages* depicted as an island, not a reef. That is corrected in later editions of the same chart, which are substantially the same as those issued by the United States Hydrographic Office in the present century.

We may now consider the evidence both from spelling and pronunciation. Chart makers usually copy names from earlier charts; or, if they find no names to copy, ask fishermen or local mariners what an island or rock is called, and render it phonetically. This leads to some curious mistakes. For instance, Gott's Island south of Mount Desert, settled by the Gott family in the late seventeenth century, becomes 'Cross Island' in *The Atlantic Neptune*, and is not corrected back to *Gott's* for many years. Halibut Point, the northeast apex of Cape Ann, was originally Haul-about Point, old Gloucestermen tell me; and it is spelled *Hallowbout* on the Blunt chart of 1813. The spelling *Salvages*, first appearing in *The English Pilot* of 1689, is constantly repeated, with the one exception of the Barnley chart of 1757 where it is *Salvigis*. In England we have many instances of popular, traditional pronunciations of places which differ widely from the spelling. For instance: *Bicester,* pronounced *Bister; Cirencester,* pronounced *Cicester; Magdalen* Colleges at both Oxford and Cambridge, pronounced *Maudlin.* Eventually, with universal education, people begin pronouncing these names exactly as spelled; the two colleges in question being now pronounced *Magdalen* by the townspeople, who regard the pronunciation *Maudlin* as a donnish affectation.

In this case, it seems probable that the rocks spelled *Salvages* were originally pronounced *Savages,* as I heard them called by old salts early in the present century. But the repetition of the spelling *Salvages* led to a change, as more and more mariners began using charts. Modern yachtsmen pronounce it just as it is spelled, *Salvages,* with the accent on the antepenult. But the Reverend Thomas J. Carroll, who sailed in fishing schooners over thirty years ago, always heard the fishermen call it *Salvayges,* with the accent on the penult; and Captain John A. Muise, secretary of the Gloucester Master Mariners Association, assures me that this is the proper pronunciation. So Mr. Eliot's memory is vindicated. Other Gloucester fishermen call it *Salvigis,* with accent on the penult, as it is spelled on the Barnley chart of 1757.

I have no firm conclusion to offer. It still seems to me more likely that Archer and Gosnold's Savage Rocke (Cape Neddick Nubble) was transferred by later navigators or map makers to the present Salvages, using the then more common English spelling. This transfer is the more plausible because Archer's printed account, which any later navigator might have had on board, does not mention Cape Ann, which he never sighted. Consequently a later navigator might well have taken Archer's description of Cape Neddick as 'an out Point of woodie ground, the Trees thereof very high and straight,'[25] to have been Cape Ann, and his Savage Rocke —The Nubble—to have been the Salvages off Cape Ann.

It is possible, but hardly probable, that our unknown namer of the Salvages had Champlain's *Les Voyages* of 1613 on board, and, reading of his reception by friendly *sauvages,* decided to commemorate that event by calling this group of rocks after the natives.

No matter how it got its name, this 'ragged rock in the restless waters' has been a seamark ever since the first Indian *salvage* was bold enough to paddle a canoe around Cape Ann; and will continue to guide mariners into the unforeseeable future. For, again to quote Mr. Eliot's great poem:

[25] *Purchas His Pilgrims* (1625), **IV**, 1647; Levermore, op. cit., I, 44.

> There is no end, but addition: the trailing
> Consequence of further days and hours, . . .

*   *   *

Now for the Thacher shipwreck of 1635 in which T. S. Eliot supposed, erroneously, that his ancestor was involved. The story was first told in the words of Anthony Thacher's letter to his brother Peter, first printed in Increase Mather's *Remarkable Providences* of 1684. Thacher with his bosom friend the Reverend Joseph Avery and twenty-one other passengers, was sailing a pinnace from Ipswich to Marblehead, when they were overwhelmed by the sudden hurricane of 14-15 August 1635. In attempting to round Cape Ann the vessel struck on a rock a few hundred yards from an island. There 'Parson Avery' delivered his 'Swan-Song' (as paraphrased by John G. Whittier from Cotton Mather's *Magnalia*), and thence the poop of the vessel floated off, carrying Mrs. Thacher, grounding on the island ever since named Thacher's.[26] Anthony himself managed to swim ashore, where he found his wife alive. They took refuge for the night under a fallen cedar tree, 'I and my wife, almost naked, both of us, and wet and cold even unto death.' Next morning Anthony, scouring the shore, found his knapsack containing flint and steel and a horn of gunpowder, as well as some clothing, a drowned goat, a brass pot, two cheeses and some butter. Showing remarkable ingenuity for an English townsman, he dried his wife's neckcloth in the sun, kindled a fire on it with the flint and steel, skinned the goat and boiled it in the pot with water from a brackish spring. On that, and the cheese, they lived for 36 hours until a boat came by and rescued them from 'that desolate island, which I named after my name, Thacher's Woe, and the rock, Avery his Fall.' All four of their children, and the Averys and all their children, perished.

Now, what was 'Avery his Fall'? Avery's name, as *Avery Ledge,* has been attached to a rock off Straitsmouth Island, miles away. In mid-nineteenth century the local historians, studying Thacher's narrative and other contemporary accounts of the hurricane, put their heads together and decided that the rock could not possibly have been Avery's Ledge, or The Londoner, on the east side of Thacher's.[27] They decided that it must have

---

[26] *Remarkable Providences* (London ed., 1890), Chap. I. Also in Alex. Young, *Chronicles of Massachusetts Bay* (1846), pp. 485-495.

[27] The Londoner, a reef lying about half a mile easterly from Thacher's has been thought by some to have been the original Avery's Fall. The Londoner, formerly Fisher or Gannett Rock, was renamed from the ship *London* which struck there in the eighteenth century. Lemuel Gott, *History of Rockport*, p. 27. The name Londoner appears on the 1781 ed. of *The Atlantic Neptune*.

been a rock then called Crackwood's, but since the 1870's Oak Rock, between Thacher's and the mainland. Lemuel Gott, in his History of Rockport (1888) describes this rock as lying 'a gunshot from the western head of Thacher's, which looks like two rocks at half-tide but is really one rock with a passage admitting a small boat through.'[28]

The reasons for identifying 'Avery his Fall,' as Oak Rock rather than The Londoner, are that John Winthrop, in his contemporary account of the hurricane, says that the wind shifted from northeast to northwest about 8:00 A.M. at high water, and that in an hour's time the tide fell three feet. Winthrop gives several instances of ships being driven on a lee shore when the wind was northeast, and then blow off by the shift, drifting off to another lee shore with the northwest wind.[29] It therefore seemed reasonable that the pinnace struck on Crackwood's or Oak Rock (shown on our chart, halfway between Thacher's Island and the mainland), and that the poop with Mrs. Thacher aboard, and Anthony, swimming, would have fetched up on Thacher's Island with the northwest wind.

Winthrop records that 'The General Court gave Mr. Thacher £26 13s 4d towards his losses, and divers good people gave him besides.' He settled at Yarmouth on Cape Cod where he and Mrs. Thacher raised another family, and many of their descendants have been prominent as lawyers, judges and divines.

The elusive William Eliot was drowned, and no more is known of him than that he was a bachelor of Salisbury who had been in New England but a few months before the fatal voyage. But we may give him a word of long-posthumous praise, since his presence in the fatal pinnace helped to connect T. S. Eliot emotionally with Cape Ann, inspiring him to write his noble poem on the Dry Salvages. Eliot doubtless thought of him, when, in that same poem, he wrote:

> Also pray for those who were in ships, and
> Ended their voyage on the sand, in the sea's lips
> Or in the dark throat which will not reject them,
> Or wherever cannot reach them the sound of the sea bell's
> Perpetual angelus.[30]

[28] Lemuel Gott, *Rockport*, p. 27. This statement is confusing, since it describes The Londoner much better than Oak Rock. The latter consists of some five pinnacle rocks about 6 feet under mean low water, whilst The Londoner shows a distinct passage between two rocks at low water. If Winthrop erred about wind direction, and the pinnace struck when the wind was still northeast, The Londoner could be the fatal rock; but it is inconceivable that Thacher could have swum, or the poop floated, 700 yards to windward.

[29] John Winthrop, *History of New England* (Savage ed., 1853), I, 195-198. David Ludlum, *Early American Hurricanes* (Boston, American Meteorological Society, 1963), follows Winthrop, and apparently agrees that the rock was Oak Rock.

[30] T. S. Eliot, *Complete Poems and Plays*, p. 135.

The Disorderly Voyage of the Brig *Betsy*

THE Editors of THE AMERICAN NEPTUNE thank Count Pehr Sparre for lending them his manuscript of the log of the *Betsy*. It is written in neat clerkly fashion by the hand of, presumably, her much-tried mate. From his account it is difficult to determine whether the voyage suffered more from mismanagement or from bad luck. There was enough and to spare of both. Certain it is that disorderly behaviour and flat disobedience aboard the *Betsy* met with a forbearance which fortunately must at all times have been rare in what journalists will call the annals of the sea. Only one example need be mentioned. When after numberless misadventures the brig had at length reached Tarpaulin Cove and the pilot wished to up anchor for New London late Saturday afternoon, he could not do so for the crew, who had foolishly been given shore leave, had returned too drunk to work. As a result the vessel had to hang about till the following Wednesday before she finally got into New London harbor.

The mate's spelling puts one in mind of the kind of cook who, *because she has been taught how,* makes an exquisite Hollandaise but cannot boil an egg to specifications. Compensating for an utter lack of punctuation by his genteel use of capitals, the mate would make a pass at spelling names he had looked out on a chart, but the days of the week were forever beyond him. His innocent rendering of the spoken word, therefore, constitutes a perfect fossilization of our language. He writes *skuner* and *smoll* and *wotter* as they are still pronounced by many; he puts *lood* for load just as a New Englander today will say *loom* for loam. Such spellings as *marster, depater,* and *fartham* may strike us as strange for nowadays we say and write fathom. However there are people in Maine today who continue the process and pronounce the word father strictly as written — to rhyme with lather! But let the reader go on to make his own discoveries. It is not mainly because of the curiosities of their spelling that these extracts have been published, but because, after all, the brig *Betsy,* making her luckless rounds to Wilmington and Guadeloupe, is a humble little shuttle carrying the weft of history. Not the pattern of great events — Lord, no! — but a few of the threads of the unconsidered background fabric with which the pattern is interwoven.

Transactions on Bord the Brig Betsy *on her Passage from New London to Wilmilton North Carilina Capt John Clark Marster November 8th 1796*

Remarks on Tusday November 8th 1796   Saild From New London At 4 PM under All Sail Plesent Wether At 8 PM Montock Pint Bore West 2 Leagues Distance from Whitch I Take My Depater From   Latt in 40:18

Remarks on Wensday November 9th 1796   this 24 Hours Continurd Blowing hasey Wether At 4 PM under Single R & Top Sails Blowing Varry fresh And All the Passangers Varry Sik. Latter Part Continurard thik Fogy wether hevey Sea   Latt in 40:07

Transactions on Tusday November 16th 1796   this Day begins with Cler Plesent weather At 12 Clock Mrd. Com to Anker in 7 Fartham of Wotter 2 Leagues from the Land & Handed All Sail   At 11 Clock AM hove upt And Sot All Sail Lit winds from the Northard   And Run Donalong the Land   About SW Clear Wether Latter Part   4 Clock PM Com to Anker in 8 Fartham of wotter At 6 Clock AM hove oupt And Run Down Along the Land & At 10 Clock AM Com to Anker Little to the Northard of Cape Fare   And Sent the boat A Shore for A Pilot   And Clere wether

Wensday November 16th 1796   This Day Fine Clear Wether & All hans imployd in gitting the Brig in Order to Gow upt to the Toun & At 2 Clock PM the boat Com with A pilot & At 5 Clock PM got under way   And went Over the Bare   At 8 Clock PM Com to Anker And the River Pilot tuk Charg   At 9 Clock Com on A Varry hevy gail of wind About NE   And Last til 8 Clock the Nex Morning   And After that good wether & Sent the boat A Shore Awooding   And got A good Lood

thusday Wilmington November 24th 1796   This Day Fine Plesent wether & Cold Night & Mornings   All hans imployd Pon the Rigun & Sent Doun the Fore yard And over hold the Blocks & sentit upt Agin   And Landid 6 bbll Rum & 4 Sider & 8 bushel Potaters   And All Mr Lathrop Passangers went a way this Day in A Smoll Skuner for Charlston And glad wose wey to git Red of them.

Wilmington Tusday November 9th 1796   This Day Fine Cler wether All hans imployd Landing the Ballas Ston & Last Night A brig from New york wose Broken open And 600 Dollors taken out And Card of & Saild this Day 2 Brigs & 1 Slop Loodid with Lomber.

Wilmingto Satrday December 3th 1796   This Day Fine Plesent wether All hans im Ployd taking in Lomber & Shingles & Brought 2 boat Loods of Shingles from Mr. Gibbins 6000. Last Night the Cuck Run Away with All his Close And I went After him And Brought him Back in 2 Hours.

Wilmington Sunday December 4th 1796   This Day Fine Plesent wether & [*illegible*] All the Cheese And Maid Shelfs in State Rum And put them on & found 2 Broken ones And Sold them to the Peaple wt 16½.

Wilmington Sunday Night December 4th 1796   Isaac William Run Away from the Brig Betsey with All his Close. And wose found Missing Last Night At 12 Clock. Left Nothing but his old Chist & Bad.

Wilmington Munday December 5th 1796   This Day Fine Plesent wether All Hans imPloyd tekening [taking in?] Lomber & Corn & hiard A negro girl to cook & Negro Man to work in the hole & tuck Mr. Traceys Jack[?] from Capt Robinsons And sent him in to the Cuntry to keep   the girl 1/Day   the Man 3/Day

Wilmington Tusday December 6th 1796   This Day Fine Plesent wether All hans imploy Loding Lomber & Corn hiard A Negro Man for 3/ A Negro Girl to cook for 1/Day.   This night All hans has gon A Shore with out Aney Leve   Ant At 12 Clock Andrew Marting Coum Abourd Varry bad wondid & his wonds is Drest And has turnd in.

Wilmington Wensday December 7th 1796   Last Night All hans Left the Brig with out Aney Leve And went with Number More Ships Chru to A hore Hous Pon the hil   And at 10 Clock began to fit with sum Frenshman   And the Marakin Saillers had Nothing to fit with & the Frenshman had Sords & Pistols   And thay killd on Marakin & wondid 2 & the Marakins Most killd on Frenshman & wondid 3   And this Morning 6 frenshman Taken up And Put in to Jail. & this Day fine Plesens wether hiard 2 Negro Men to work in the hole to stoe Lomber @ 3/ 0.6.0 & A Negro Girl to Cook for 1/ Day And Sent Andrew Marting A Shore under the Docters Hands his board is 3½ Dolers A week.   And the Rest of the Peaple is to work pon the Lumber.

Friday Wlimington December 16th 1796 . . . At 12 Clock the Pilot Com Abord And horld of in the Streme — All hans drunk & fiting & shipt a boye to Cuck for 12 Dollars Month . . .

Saterday Wlimington December 17th 1796   This Day fine Plesent wether got under way from the Town And went over the flats About 18 Miles Down the River And thare Got Grond Laid All Night And A Black feller Com aboard to work his Passage — Andrew Marting Gits Sum better but Dus no Dutey.

Remarks on Friday 23th 1796   Saild from Wlimington Bar 12 Mrd under All Sail with the hole full of Lumber & Rice & Flour & Corn And 6170 feet of Lumber Pon Deck & 5 Hhd woatter & 1 of the Cables Pon the Quatter Deck   At 3 Clock PM Cape Far Light Hous Bore West 5 Legues Distance from whitch I take My Departer from. . . .

Remarks on on Wendnesaday 11th [January]   This 24 Hours Begins with Fresh Breeses And All Sail Sot At 8 Clock AM Sot Studssails At 11 AM Maid Martinico Baring SW & Dominico WbN   Bent Both Cables   At 12 Mrd Saw 2 Sail Rite had   Lattitude in 1517

Remarks on Thursday 12th 1796 [sic]   this 24 hours begins with Fine Plesent wether And fresh Breeses   Stering WbS   At 5 Clock PM A Smoll French Privetier Skuner Bodid us 5 Leagues from Martinico And Card Capt Clark Aboard in the Privetiers Boat And kept him board the Privetier And Sent A Prisemarster Abord to Carry us to Guddaloupe — the Privetier tuck 1 Doz of Capt Clarks fouls And then Steard NNW for Guadaloupe And the Privetier in Compeny with us At 8 AM Close under the Lee of Marigalant And thare stud of & on   And then the Privetiers Boat Com Abord And tuck All My Bucks & Papers & Card of   Lattd in 1604

Remarks on Friday 13th 1797   Now Remarks on this Day for thare wos Nothing Left Aboard to Right on

Saturday January 14th 1797   This Day Plesent wether And Fresh Breeses this Morning the Capt of the Privetier has Let Mea have Sum Paper to Right on   Last Night wey wose Chast in by A inglish Manerwore under the Lee Marigalant And thare Com to Anker in 12 feet of woutter At 6 Clock the Manerwore Run Close under the Land And Fiard Pon us Number of Times And oure Prisemarster had the Boat hove out And went A shore for fere that Shey wood Sink us   At 8 Clock Com back with the boat And thare Lay All Night & This Morning At 8 Clock hove upt And sot out for Pintpeter Got half Chrost And then Saw the Manerwore Agin And then wey hove About Run Close under the fort at Marrigalant And Com to Anker in 11 feet of woatter And thare Stade till Shee went of And then the Capt of the Privetier Brought Clark Aboar And Let him Shift his Close And then Carred him back Aboard of the Privetier the Capt of the Privetier Carred Aboard with him 6 fouls & 1 Chees   At 2 Clock this AfterNoon hove upt And Sot out for Pintpeter the Privetier in Compeny with us   At 7 Clock Com to Anker 4 Miles of the Toun handid All Sail

Pintpeter Sunday January 15th 1797   This Day Fine Plesent wether   At 8 Clock this Morning the Pilot Com Abord And hove up Run up to the Toun And thar Com to Anker of Pintpeter   At 1 Clock this After Noon

THE DISORDERLY VOYAGE

4 officers Com Abord And tuck An account of the Cargo Loock the hatches And Seald up the State Rum whare the Cheeses wose & Left the Prisemarster & 4 of the Privetiers Men And 2 Sogers to take Care of the Brig And then they Let Capt Clark Com Abord & No work Dun Aboard to Day This After Noon Capt Clark & My Self And Joshua Vallet went A Shore to the office to be Exsamend

Pintpeter Monday 16th 1797 This Day Continers Plesent wether the Prisemarster tuck the smoll Boat And went of with her Carred Away with him 7 fouls & 2 Larg Pices Beef, 1 Pot Butter & A Larg Bunch Candles Rold up in A pece of Canvice & Left Abord to take of us 7 Frenchman Living Pon the Brig Stores this day Capt Clark ordered Joshua Vallet to Com Ashore with the Boat at 11 Clock After him For hea wonttid to gow Abord & hea wod Not gow A Shore After Capt Clark But hea & John Glazier went of At 1 Clock this After Noon with Augusteen the Prisemarster with out Saying Enney thing About gowing

Pintpeter Tusday January 17th 1797 This Day fine wether Loust the Sails And Dried them handid them Agin No More work Dun to Day 6 Frenchmen Aboard Living Pon the Brig Pervisions And ant Contented with that But Carry Sumthing from the Brig Every time that one of them gows A Shore & At 10 Clock this Day Capt Clark sotout to gow to Bastar to the Brig Trial & No Nues from Joshua Vallet & John Glazier

Pintpeter Monday 23th 1797 This Day Continers Plesent wether All hans imploy'd About Ships Duty 2 Sogers Living pon the Brig Stores At 2 Clock this After Noon the Brig Betsey Capt J. Lord wose Brought in this this Place by A Smoll French Privetier And is to be keept till hea has his Trial At Bastar At 10 Clock this Eveing Capt Clark Got Back from Bastar And Brought the Condemnation of our Cargo And thay Are to Let us have the Brig And that is All

Pintpeter Saterday January 28th 1797 This Day fine Plesent wether All Hans imploy'd the Furst Part of the Day giting the fore & Main top Gallanmast up & the yards A thot & this After noon the officers Abord and Brok the Seels And Giv Lef to heave the Lumber of Deck And Make A Raft thay Left one old Sore Shind Soger to Take Care of the Cargo And to Live in the Cabing

Pintpeter Monday January 30th 1797 This Day Continers fine wether this Morning thare Com 28 Negroes (Sogers & 3 white Men) Abord and hove up our Anker And toad the Brig Close in A Shore And Com to Anker got a fast Shore And then went of Left 2 Frenchmen Abord to take An account of the Cargo Living pon the Brig Stors And Plunder All that thay Can

Pintpeter Wendsasday 8th [February] 1797 This Day fine Plesent wether All hans imployd About Ships Duty & this After Noon the Last Boat Lood went A Shore Loodid with Barrels And Sum went one way And Sum went Another No Anaccount taken of it And then the Sartchers Com Abourd And found Nothing But the Ships Stores And then All the Frenchmen went A Shore No More to Com Aboard And then All hans went to work Clearing out the hole & hove upt the Anker And Maid Fast A Sore Til to Morow Morning

Pintpeter Thursday February 9th This Day Continers Good wethe this Morning toade Down to the Refe to Ballas And thare Com to Anker And All hans imployd giting Ballas of the Refe & got 3 Boat Lood

Pintpeter Wendnasday February 15th 1797 This Day fine Plesent wether And fresh Breeses At 7 Clock this Moning the Pilot Com Aboard to Carrey us out & Capt Francis And Capt Dangefield to gow Doun to Bastar As Passengers with us And then wey hove up And Parted the Smoll Cable 2 Merican Boats to Toa us out At 2 Clock hove out the Boat And Cap Clark & the 2 Passangers went A Shore to Bastar And then wey Stud of & on waiting for the Boat At 5 Clock PM Capt Clark Com Aboard And Capt Buckley to gow as Passanger to New London

Remarks on Thursday February 16th 1797 Saild from Bastar the island of Guadaloupe At 5 Clock PM with Nothing Aboard But Ballas And Capt Buckley A Passanger to New London under All Sail Sot At 3 Clock AM wey wose Boardid By A inglish Manerwore of Mountserrat kep us 2 hours And the Let us gow ware wey Plese At 8 Clock AM saw 2 sail At A Distance Staning to the Northard

Remarks on Saterday February 18th This 24 hours Begins with Plesent wether And fresh Breeses under Refe Topsails And St Eustatia Rite had & Saba under the Lee Bow Saw A Larg Ship At A Distance Staning to the Northard At 8 Clock PM wey wose Boardid By A inglish Privetier And thay sartch oure hole & over horld the Papers And then Let us go whare wey Plese Latter Part thik wether And Blowing Varry fresh

Remarks on Tusday February 28th This 24 hours Begins with fine Plesent weth And Lite winds under All Sail & All hans imployd About Ships Duty At 12 Mrd wey wose Bordid by the Shipt thethis Capt Corkran And Card Capt Clark A board keept him 1 half houre And then sent him aboard And let us have Stores Help Carry us on the Coast Charg Nothing for them Lattd in 29.30

Remarks on Saterday March 11th 1797 this Day thik wether And fine Snow Now Laying in Tarpaulin Cove wating for a fare wind At 6 Clock this After Noon Mr. Harris Com Aboard to Pilot the Brig to New

London   All hans gon A Shore to Day Now work Dun Aboard   At 5 Clock this After Noon thay com Aboard All Drunk And got A Fiting with Clubs & A hammer And Bruse them selves varry Bad the Pilot wontid to heve up the Anker but wey cud Not git now work out of them

Tarpaulin Cove Wendnasday March 15th 1797   This Day Clear wether the wind At NNE   At 3 Clock this Morning hove up And Sot All Sail for New London   At 1 Clock this After Noon Com to Anker At New London harbour handid All Sail And hove out the boat And the Capt went A Shore & Capt Buckley & the Pilot

'Just Ease Her When She Pitches'

BY WILLIAM G. SALTONSTALL

THIS is an account of a strange trade between New England and India—a trade which exported New England weather by sailing vessel to Bombay, Calcutta and Madras. It is a story of the 696-ton ice ship *Arabella,* built in Portsmouth, New Hampshire, and commanded by thirty-year-old William H. Cobbs of Exeter, New Hampshire. Captain Cobbs's 262-page private journal, describing two voyages from Boston to India and back between July 1853 and November 1855, has recently been found in the course of a housecleaning at the Phillips Exeter Academy.

Exactly one hundred years ago *Arabella* lay at anchor in Bombay after a five-month voyage out by Cape of Good Hope. She had loaded some 160 tons of ice and sailed from India Wharf, Boston, on 27 July 1853. This cold and slippery cargo, packed with white pine sawdust, had to be sailed through the warm Gulf Stream, across the equator into the South Atlantic, around the Cape of Good Hope, and across the equator again up to India through the Indian Ocean where water temperatures ranged up to 82°. Though hatches were kept tight closed and the vessel was probably double-sheathed, the sawdust insulation preserved at best about one-half of the original cargo. Her most important piece of equipment was a reliable pump, to relieve the bilges of their cold water. The difficulties of such voyages were so many and so unpredictable, that it is not surprising that Captain Cobbs wrote the following verse opposite the first page of his journal:

'In navigating through this life,
In poverty or riches,
If fortune sends a head-beat sea
Just ease her when she pitches.'

The early efforts of Frederic Tudor, who pioneered the ice trade about fifty years before *Arabella*'s voyages, seemed pure folly to most Boston businessmen. Though Washington, Jefferson, and Monroe all harvested and stored ice, his friends thought Tudor mad. Crews were hard to get for they thought the ice would melt and swamp the ship. A Boston newspaper hoped that 'this won't be a slippery speculation.' But Tudor was able to make a profit selling ice from Wenham Lake in the West Indies. The market, of course, had to be created for there was no natural demand. Ice was a luxury enjoyed only by the rich in the tropics. Bar tenders were sent out to promote Tudor's idea. By offering cold drinks for sale at the same price as warm, by giving away substantial amounts of ice, by promoting the manufacture and sale of ice cream, by showing the use of ice in hospitals for yellow fever patients, and by teaching people how to preserve ice in their homes, Tudor quickly built up a brisk trade before the War of 1812. He at first froze out such competitors as challenged him by cutting his rates. He took savage glee over the failure of 'interferers.' His diary on 26 June 1818, says: 'This interferer will get about $5 in all for what must have cost him $100. This business is mine. I commenced it and have a right to rejoice in ill-success attending others who would profit by my discovery without allowing me the credit of teaching them.' Later on, however, Tudor had many successful competitors in the Yankee ice trade.

In the early 1830's the ship *Tuscany* took the first New England ice to Calcutta. The excited Indian reaction may be easily imagined. Alarmed natives ran away upon touching the ice. 'How this ice make grow in your country? Him grow on tree? Him grow on shrub? Mr. Mate, me buy one piece ice of you. Somebody make steal him. Me no find. Me want more piece ice.' Cold drinks were soon in great demand along the Anglo-Indian waterfront, and the arrival of a New England ice ship became the occasion for genial entertainment by skippers who mixed their drinks 'Yankee fashion.' These India voyages often lost at least half their cargo, but Boston ice delivered in Calcutta undersold native ice by 50 per cent.

The ice business flourished into the 1840's while the rest of our trade was declining. By this time Tudor had many competitors and the 'white stuff' was sold in distant parts for as little as one to three cents per pound. Boston's exports of ice more than doubled between 1847 and 1856, so *Arabella*'s voyages took place at the height of the trade. It was in the latter part of the nineteenth century that methods of manufacturing cheap artificial ice finally broke the 'bridge of ice' between New England and India. Many a pond near New England tidewater produced the ice which was harvested and stored in local wood and brick houses under the direction of Nathaniel J. Wyeth, harvesting expert, and then brought on demand by pung or train to the ice wharves—India Wharf in Boston and

Gray's Wharf in Charlestown. Hundreds of men were employed during the winters in cutting, transporting and storing the 'crystal blocks of Yankee coldness.' Early experiments with harvesting ice from North Atlantic icebergs proved unsuccessful. The trade required confidence, enterprise, and audacity. Only men who were sure of themselves would have taken such a long chance. Since there was no shortage of such men, the trade grew rapidly as the following United States export statistics show:

Year	Number of Ice Cargoes	Tonnage
1806	1	130
1816	6	1200
1826	15	4000
1836	45	12000
1846	175	65000
1856	363	146000

Arabella, a full-rigged ship, made the two round trips to India described in Cobbs's journal between the following dates: Boston to Bombay, Calcutta and return, 17 July 1853 to 4 October 1854; Boston to Madras, Calcutta and return, 29 November 1854 to 23 November *(ca.)*, 1855. These were slow passages. The ship was sailed hard. She frequently tore canvas and broke spars. Many a watch was spent repairing and replacing sails and fishing spars. But her daily runs rarely reached 200 miles and were frequently much less. She apparently steered poorly and lost a good deal of distance on this account.

Arabella was built in Portsmouth, New Hampshire, in 1841 by Messrs. Raynes and Fernald on Badger's Island. Her owners were Messrs. R. Rice, J. M. Tredick, and the estate of John Haven. One of the largest merchantmen built on the Piscataqua up to the time of her launching on Tuesday, 3 August, she was named for Arabella Rice, the daughter of one of her owners. Miss Rice later became a very wealthy spinster and at her death endowed the Rice Public Library in Kittery, Maine.

The following comments on and excerpts from her master's private journal suggest some of the situations and problems he faced in the Indian ice trade of one hundred years ago.

On the first of the above trips Captain Cobbs was accompanied by a Mr. Everett, supercargo, and Mr. and Mrs. Barker, missionaries. Casting off from India Wharf on 27 July 1853, they were towed out by steamer and were soon off Highland Light. They ran into large head swells, two men became sick and Mrs. Barker suffered from 'sea-uneasiness.' After a few days she managed to get on deck. 'She has only been married a month or two. Smily sweet looks, kisses, etc. are often visible.' An early subject of discussion at table concerned Mrs. Stowe and her recent book '"Uncle Tom's Cabin"—the minister and his wife for—Mr. Everett and myself against her Ladyship.'

The Reverend Mr. Barker held services regularly on Sundays. Other vessels were spoken almost daily—a Dutch brig, a French ship, an English ship and a topsail schooner. On 24 August 'at 4 P.M. received a visit from the boat of the English ship *Albatross*, 69 days from Melbourne bound to Liverpool with passengers. He wanted some small stores. Exchanged positions and found to agree with three or four miles of each other. Sent letters home by him—I wrote two, one to Mr. Tredick and the other to my mother. Requested him to report us.'

On 4 September 1853 'Twelve sail in sight at noon by the wind. Hard work getting South and no mistake! I am not the only one that has got jammed. Services by the parson.' And on the following day: 'Wind and weather the same. Hard luck. It beats the Dutch! Who is Jonah? It is said that you will have a long passage when you have missionaries on board.'

They crossed the equator on 8 September, about six weeks out of Boston. The SE trades were blowing fresh and 'a large flying fish flew aboard. He helped make a breakfast for Mrs. Barker.' Heavy rain and thunder squalls with rain in abundance throughout.' These gales continued for September, in the South Atlantic, 'fresh gale and thick weather. Pitching heavily. Hove to under a close-reefed main. Large sea running. Heavy squalls with rain in abundance throughout.' These gales continued for over a week, the ship 'scudding under close-reefed fore topsail, shipping considerable water and rolling heavily.'

On 9 October *Arabella* overtook the English ship *Tippoo Sahib*, 65 days out of Liverpool, and exchanged positions with her. Thanks to his willingness to carry sail, Captain Cobbs passed another English ship a few days later and left her hull down in six hours. There were fresh breezes all through late October and a few days' runs of over 200 miles were recorded. Sails were being torn very frequently, but *Arabella* carried an ample supply of spares ready to bend on when others blew out.

By late November *Arabella* was in the Arabian Sea and in early December she made her landfall off Bombay. There was a strong current setting down the coast, but on 14 December 1853, after ten days of light winds and head currents, she took on a pilot twelve miles from the lighthouse

'JUST EASE HER WHEN SHE PITCHES'

and dropped anchor in Bombay Harbor, 141 days out of Boston.

The following 'Remarks on Bombay' are found in the journal, immediately following arrival: 'The pilots have open boats, painted red, with their number on the bow of the boat. They are lateen rig—two masts and two sails. They do not cruise out, but as soon as a sail is distinguished from the Lt. House a gun is fired and then they go out. In the N E monsoons or clear weather a ship's masts can be seen from the Lt. House about 20 miles, and the pilot boat then meets you about 10 or 12 miles out. But in the S W monsoon it is generally thick stormy weather and you have to get close in before you can be seen. But it is well to keep firing as soon as you judge yourself near enough to be heard, for if possible they will come out as soon as they hear you. There are three lights—one a lighthouse and revolving—the other two floating lights and fixed. The pilots are not allowed to take a vessel in or out after sun-down. They are paid by government. The port charges in the S W monsoon for a vessel of 500 tons and over are pilotage in and out—110 Rupees. In the N E monsoon half that sum. Lighthouse dues @ 15 R's pr. 100 tons. Tonnage duty @ one anna per ton. Police fee 10 R's—2 an. In the S W monsoon the outer light ship is removed. The only port charges on Ice ships are tonnage dues and police fees, and *you get the best berth in the harbor.* Ships are moored with both anchors, 30 fathoms out on each chain. A custom house officer is kept on board during your stay in port. A list of ship's stores have to be put on the manifest—& be particular that they are correct.'

On 12 January 1854, a month after her arrival, *Arabella* took the pilot aboard and with the help of a few rupees he was persuaded to take the vessel to sea after sundown. Her skipper gives no account in his journal of unloading ice either here or in Calcutta, the next stop. The voyage to Calcutta was slow because of many calm days. Captain Cobbs exclaims on 29 January 1854—'Calm! Calm! Calm! If any poor mortal was ever troubled with light airs, I have been this voyage. It would make old Job swear I know. Dead calm and current against me! Not a breath of air till 9 P.M. Then took a light breeze from the N E.'

On 1 March 1854, *Arabella* hove to off Sangor Island and later moved up to anchor abreast of Garden Reach, Calcutta. She stayed in Calcutta almost eight weeks, but there are no entries in the journal during this period. On 26 April she sailed for Boston with a mixed cargo including saltpeter, cow hides, gunny bags, jute, cloth, goatskins, shellac, dye and linseed. The steamer *Powerful* towed her down the harbor. Robert S. Carter, pilot, found her drawing 20 feet 3 inches aft and 19 feet forward.

The next morning she grounded in three fathoms of water and laid over on her side for an hour until the flood tide floated her. Then she worked down channel and discharged the pilot on 1 May 1854 off Sand Heads.

Although his lady missionary had presumably been left in India, Captain Cobbs commented shortly after leaving for Boston: 'A woman abandons her opinion the moment her husband adopts it. Even in church the woman sings an octave higher than the man, in order not to agree with them on anything.'

As *Arabella* worked south and west toward the Cape of Good Hope she ran into a good deal of heavy weather. Pumping went on for long periods of time and many sails were torn or carried away. A typical entry during this period was that of 28 June 1854. 'Brings in strong breezes and passing clouds. 0-30 P.M. squally—took in light sails and Top Gall't sail. Parted rope to the Flying Jib and split the sail. 2 P.M. Breeze increasing with lightning and squally appearances in the N W—took in Top Gall't sails, crochic and outer Jib. 2:30 P.M. blowing fresh with a heavy squall with rain, thunder and lightning—double reefed main Topsail, close reefed Fore & Mizzen—weather threatening. Furled mainsail. 5 P.M. moderating—Set the mainsail—clear in the Westw'd, dark & threatening in the North'd—with continued lightning. 6:30 P.M. took in the mainsail & set it reefed as soon as the squall passed over. During the first watch blowing fresh from the N N E—clear overhead but a dark heavy bank in the north. A continued flash of lightning & distant thunder—and so continued till 1 A.M. when it suddenly rose and overspread the whole heavens—wind baffling from N E to N W—thunder heavy—& the whole heavens covered with one continued flash of chain lightning—raining in torrents—"Complaisance" at each masthead—Ship under close reefed Fore & Main, Topsails, Foresail & Jib. This continued without cessation till 3:30 A.M. when it lightened up in the N W & gradually settled. Morning & latter part fresh gales from N W & pleasant. Ship under double reefed Main & close reefed Fore & Miz Topsails, Jib & Courses. 58 days at sea.'

A week later, on 4 July 1854, 'the striking of the bell every half hour brings in this glorious day of the anniversary of our country's independence. Bessy [a cat?] who has been with us all the voyage departed this life at 3 P.M.—cause of death, coming in contact with the doctor's knife—her death was sudden and her blood flowed freely for the public good.'

On 16 July, *Arabella* shipped a heavy sea over the starboard bow, staved in the bulwarks, and filled the decks with water. The cook was washed off the Top Gall't forecastle aft 'bruising him considerable on his passage aft by water.' A week later 'caught a fine lot of Cape Salmon, about 200 in all. Quite a treat. Salted a barrel of them. Fed the crew on the rest of them for 2 or 3 days.'

On 29 July, having just rounded the Cape, *Arabella* was sailing north with pleasant breezes from the south and east. 'All stdg. sails set both sides. Struck a porpoise. At 5 P.M. a Bark passed across the bow standing to the Westward. Two Barks in sight off the stbd. quarter, standing same way and slowly gaining on us. If the "Old Maid" would only mind her helm & make a straight wake I could beat them. But she wiggles her stern like a girl of 17.'

The passage to Boston was apparently uneventful from here on and she arrived on 4 October 1854, 156 days out of Calcutta, and 14 months after her original departure from India Wharf. There is no account of what happened aboard during the next seven weeks, but on 29 November 1854, the 'sea account' of Captain Cobbs begins again, this time describing a voyage to Madras and Culcutta and back.

Again loaded full with ice, *Arabella* cast off from Devens Wharf, Charlestown, and proceeded to sea. It was to take her 141 days to reach Madras. This second voyage was much like the first except for some troubles Captain Cobbs had with his crew.

The following entry for 14 December 1854, explains why the crew was kept busy repairing sails and spars for the next two or three weeks. 'At 10 P.M. in a heavy squall carried away Fore Top Mast & Main Top Gall't Mast & sprung the Jib boom. Split Fore & Main Top Gall't Sails, Fore Topsail & Foresail. Lost both Fore Top Mast Stdg. sail booms, some running rigging blocks, etc. & did other damage. The mate had the watch on deck at the time, and to him I am indebted for the loss. He is not qualified for his berth. All hands clearing the wreck. Weather rainy throughout.' On the following day the captain dispensed with the services of Mr. Flagg as mate and took the second mate, Mr. Bridge, to act as mate and one of the men from before the mast to act as second mate. On 28 December, still less than a month out of Boston, he 'put Theodore, a Frenchman, in irons and close confinement on bread and water for refusal of duty.' Two days later Theodore was taken out of irons. 'He has come to his senses and promises to walk straight.'

On 11 January 1855, *Arabella* crossed the line, 44 days out of Boston. She passed close to a water spout but was not damaged. 'The mate's watch a little ugly today. Had to give them a talking to.' About this time the ship developed a list to starboard. All the chains were hauled aft and stowed on the larboard side along with spare anchors and everything of any weight to get the ship upright. From here on the passage to Madras was relatively uneventful. They caught an albatross and a shark on 5 February, were off the island of Amsterdam in the southern Indian Ocean 11 March, made Ceylon 13 April, and anchored Madras 18 April.

The next day Captain Cobbs 'went on shore & found that the Ice House lay about 3 miles to the Southward of us, & I found myself just so much dead to leeward from the neglect of not giving me instructions previous to my sailing from Boston. As the wind was blowing fresh & on shore did not get underway til April 21. In heaving up parted the chain about 6 or 8 fathoms from the anchor but kept on and worked ship down abreast of the Ice House & anchored in 6½ fathoms of water with 60 fathoms chain out. At 1 P.M. when Mr. Andrew Bancroft, the Ice Agent, came on board, opened the hatches and got all ready for discharging the ice. Got the spare anchor over the bow ready for use. April 22 discharged the ice only turning out 38 tons out of 160. Tuesday (23rd) discharged the boards & Wednesday morning in getting underway to proceed to Roads to take in cargo the ship cast in shore. Attempted to wear but finding she would not in time let go both anchors with 15 & 20 fathoms chain out. She dragged into 3 fathoms water under the stern when she brought up. Finding that it would be imprudent to attempt to get underway either by heaving up or slipping, made signals to the shore for immediate assistance & then for a steamer as there was one belonging to the E. I. Company at anchor in the Roads. She got up steam as soon as possible, passed me the end of her hawser, & towed me to the Roads & anchored in 10 fathoms at 10 A.M. Got ashore at noon and reported the ship ready for receiving cargo, but he said I must come into 9 fathoms before they would ship it. Took in cargo all day Monday, & Tuesday morning, May 1 at daylight hove up and got underway for Calcutta.'

On 25 April the local newspaper published a statement from the Master Attendant's Office describing *Arabella*'s close call. 'Her situation was most perilous. The steamer *Hugh Lindsay* proceeded to render every assistance, and brought her to the roadstead. The assistant Master Attendant had previously boarded the *Arabella,* and Boats with Lascars, a large kedge & hawser, had been despatched from the Master Attendant's office. The prompt & efficient assistance rendered to the *Arabella* has thus been attended with a happy result—but Commanders of Ships when riding near the shore should be very cautious in any attempt to get underway when the wind is not well off the land, because the groundswell has always a tendency to cast a ship inshore. At 1 P.M. the Commander of the *Arabella* called on the Master Attendant and expressed his most grateful acknowledgement to Government for the very able and effectual assistance he had received, which he declared had saved his ship from great peril, as he felt convinced that she must otherwise have drifted on shore.'

Arabella arrived at Calcutta on 6 May and sailed for Boston on 22 June 1855 with a cargo of saltpeter, linseed, indigo, gunny cloth, dye and shellac. The voyage home was difficult because of a strong list to port which developed in a storm on 1-3 July. She was rolling her lee rail under and the pumps were going constantly. She did not right from the list in calm weather, possibly because the water got into the saltpeter on the port side.

On Independence Day, Captain Cobbs reports, 'I have a sort of independent feeling, the only thing that reminds me of the day. It brings in fresh gales and rainy weather & ship leaky with a heavy list. Not very agreeable subjects to think about on the commencement of a long passage, but it can't be helped & the only way is to make the best of it.'

Early one morning Cobbs caught the second mate asleep during his watch on deck. This officer, Mr. Pasco, had been shipped in Calcutta and continued to give trouble until on 29 July he came to Captain Cobbs and 'requested to go forward. I willingly let him go as it saved me from sending him, for I certainly should as my patience was almost gone—a miserable specimen of a sailor & no officer or the capability of one. Now I have taken another man from forward, named Waters of Salem, & made a 2nd officer of him. Three first mates & four second mates I have had on this voyage. I hope the ones I have got now will last me home.'

During early August, near the equator, *Arabella* had tantalizingly slow going. 'Calm! Calm! Calm! & pleasant! pleasant! pleasant! throughout this day. Took a light westerly breeze, canting southerly towards evening.' Finally, on 15 August, the winds began to freshen. 'Huzza! for the Trades!' The ship leaked badly when it blew fresh and she was carrying sail. 'This keeping her off every four hours to pump her out is mighty disagreeable—especially in such a slow & wild steering tub as this one is. If she only steered well I could drive her when I did get a fair breeze. But there is no use talking. Can carry no after sail on account of bad steering.'

As she approached the Cape of Good Hope the usual albatross and cape pigeons made their appearance. She passed a dead whale 'stripped of his coat by man & getting finished off by the birds. On 9 September experienced a fresh blow with a large head sea—ship pitching bows under and filling the deck with water. Cabin not escaping the rush. The mate's stateroom & everything in it well soaked. "Piping" during the squalls & "whistling" darned loud between them.' During these storms she occasionally rolled her lee rail all under fore and aft. Finally, eighty-three days out of Calcutta, she reached the Cape—ahead of last voyage four days. 'Calm as a dock.'

As she headed north into the Atlantic control became steadily more difficult. 'Ship steering four points each way. I sometimes feel doubtful about her getting through between Africa & South Amercia without touching one side or the other in some of her yaws. She would be a good ship for an exploring expedition in search of unknown dangers!' In spite of it all she was 'wiggling off 8 & 9 knots by the log & making on a straight course about 2 knots less on account of bad steering.'

During early and middle November as they approached Boston the ship was painted inside and out. 'Caught a fish without a name, but made a good dinner off of him. Passed close by the hull of a vessel—keel up—probably a schooner about 80 feet long—copper bottom—and no barnacles on it. The prospect is not very promising,' wrote Cobbs on 18 November 1855; 'four of the crew already laid up with the scurvy, & several others have got it coming on fast. Their teeth begin to drop out, legs swelling etc. pretty sure signs. A scurvy crew, a winter's coast—fair winds now would be a comfort & a blessing too.'

The last entry in the private journal was for Monday, 26 November 1855. *Arabella* was then 152 days out of Calcutta. Captain Cobbs reported her position as lat. 37° 53' north, long. 70° 18' west, still a few days short of her destination. One can only guess at the reasons for the sudden termination of his regularly kept journal—a sick crew, winter storms in the North Atlantic, or further trouble with steering.

At any rate, he must have been home in time for Christmas with relatives and friends in Exeter, while New England ponds were freezing up with more ice destined for customers in India, 15,000 miles away.

The Battle of Priest's Cove

BY LLEWELLYN HOWLAND

EARLY in the 1890's that migratory shellfish—the 'Bay Scallop'—had earned for itself the distinction of a 'delicacy' in the metropolitan markets of our eastern seaboard. To supply a growing demand for these toothsome morsels, it followed that in the fall and early winter many of the fishermen of New Bedford and vicinity made a practice of 'scallopin'' as a substitute for the more arduous bottom fishing on the outlying 'grounds' such as Brown's Bank, Ribbon Reef, Noman's Land and Nantucket Shoals.

At this period I was a boarding school boy with the privilege of coming home for a stay of ten days during the Christmas-New Year holidays.

Across stone-walled fields and pastures a half mile from Father's house on Clark's Point—a long jut of land between Clark's Cove on the west and the entrance to New Bedford harbor on the east—sprawled a boat yard known as 'Beetle's', whence looking northeastward across the Ship Channel there was a commanding view of a broad expanse of sheltered water locally known as 'Priest's Cove,' the sandy shoals of which at that time were producing the plumpest, sweetest scallop 'eyes' available, in seemingly inexhaustible abundance. With a rowboat and light dredge of my own and the facilities of the boat yard at my disposal, what more delightful occupation could be contrived for the Christmas season than the dredging of a mess of scallops, when the weather served—or when it didn't, lending a hand on some simple job of work around the yard?

When in October 1892 the scallop market opened it was soon manifest that the supply was inadequate for the demand. As the season advanced so did the price mount until—almost to a man—the local professional fishermen, with due regard for the future supply of 'fish' and one another's rights, were engaged in restrained, yet profitable, dredging. But by 1 December this hitherto well-conducted business had been invaded by amateurs—virtually a mob of pirates—of whom a majority were 'vagrant foreigners'—that ancient and legally recognized term applying at that time to immigrants, particularly Portuguese, of foreign birth and speech. The inevitable result of this influx of newcomers was, when vacation time arrived, the glutting of the market, the dropping of the price to below cost, the depletion of the beds and all the portents of a factional row building up in the dredging fleet. From such gossip as I could pick up in Beetle's Yard during my first day of vacation, it appeared that the Yankee fishermen had already passed the word to 'the mob': 'Fish fair, or quit, or—take a licking'; and that the entire longshore community was waiting with held breath for the reaction to this ultimatum.

Another item of interest at the yard was a 42-foot boom, six inches in diameter at half length and tapering to four inches at either end, a formidable spar, had it been of spruce, but being worked out of a baulk of long leaf, southern pine, it was 'a hell of a stick'—and no mistake. All who hefted it agreed that Harry East—a young New Bedford fisherman, a high liner, who looked on scallop dredging as fit employment only for the aged and infirm—had fouled his hawse badly when he had ordered this boom, even though winter fishing called for rugged gear.

If this 'Cap'n Harry' of the thirty-two foot, catrigged *Bruiser* was aware of these strictures regarding his judgment and the new boom, he gave no sign of refuting them. A miser when it came to words, he was prodigal as to action; and it was an open secret that great pressure—even an appeal to his patriotism—had been exerted to induce 'Cap'n Harry' to assume command of the Yankee contingent in 'the scallopin' mess,' without to date eliciting from him a word of comment or deflecting him from his routine of silently and successfully minding his own business.

Such was the situation as far as I had been able to piece it together when, on the second day of my vacation, I hurried to the yard across the fields open to the sweep of an icy, boisterous nor'wester. Even in the shelter of the building-shed and bundled up, as I was, in warm clothes, the look of the weather was uninviting. Fat white clouds with dark edges and full of venom and the threat of snow squalls filled the sky. And even though I could see a numerous fleet of dredgers at work up river and in Priest's Cove—a majority of them mobsters by the brilliance and variety of color displayed—I was reluctant to try my luck with the scallops under the forbidding conditions.

In the hope that there might be signs of a coming lull I frequently gave over my self-imposed job of filling the trash bin in the boiler shed to peer out to windward through a dusty window. On one of these observations I caught sight of a sail coming down wind from New Bedford. On it came through the fleet of dredgers and headed for the yard. A moment later the hull came into view—unmistakably *Bruiser*. A few minutes more went by and there was 'Cap'n Harry' at the helm and his crew of two busy bending a warp to the anchor. I ran out to the beach in time to see the big catboat rounded-to in a shower of spray, the anchor let go and the close-reefed sail handed handsomely. An hour later that new hard pine boom had been rigged, replacing the lighter spruce stick, and *Bruiser* had swung on the way down river.

As I had lent a hand in this exchange of spars and the reeving of a new gang of running rigging, I had the opportunity to notice that, except for the stove—glowing a dull red in the dim of the cuddy—three long, stout-hafted boat hooks, two pairs of whale boat ash oars and a two-gallon stoneware jug, *Bruiser* was stripped of all her usual fishing gear and equipment—other than her heavy weight, winter sail.

As I made a move to join Will Lucas and Sam Slade—two of the yard crew—in the skiff that bobbed alongside preparatory to towing the spruce spar ashore, 'Cap'n Harry' said:

'Stay where yer be—Bub—and we'll land yer at the wharf to Bedford by noontime—y've earned the trip and you c'n tell 'em all how the new boom works when y're ashore.'

Delivered as it was, this invitation gave no choice other than acceptance, which I indicated by a nod, and while the crew were tucking in the close reef again and hoisting sail I struggled into a crackling suit of oilskins which the Captain tossed up to me from down below.

At 10:30 by the cabin clock, after short tacking the anchor off the bottom, the sheet was flattened down and *Bruiser* laid sharp on the wind for the beat up-river. As she gathered speed and began knocking into the feather-white chop the spray commenced coming aboard pretty lively. Presently she shipped a good heavy dollop that searched out the chinks of our waterproofs to start cold trickles running down inside on backs and bellies. Jamming his hard felt 'bean pot' hat—moss green from long exposure to salt water and sun—down hard on his head, 'Cap'n Harry' ordered: 'Pass the jug.' Due no doubt to my tender age I was excluded from this rite—a ceremony, I noticed with growing concern, that was repeated after every heavy dusting of spray, until by the time we had worked well to windward of the fleet of dredgers, though the skipper gave no evidence of unusual animation, the crew showed signs of having *their* jibs bowsed up pretty taut.

Abreast of Palmer's Island *Bruiser* was brought round onto the starboard tack, the helm put up, the sheet let go on a run to the knot and a moment later we were flying down wind straight for the weather-most scalloper—a sloop with red bottom, blue top sides, green rails and lemon spars, proof she was 'foreign' owned. Scissors and thumbscrews—how *Bruiser* rolled and yawed as she bore down on that head-reaching dredger! And how those dark-skinned Iberians yelled as 'Cap'n Harry,' without so much as a twitch of a cheek muscle, held his course until, at the moment when collision appeared inevitable, *Bruiser* was sailed by-the-lee, the new boom lifted ominously, and then—with the swing of a giant scythe—it gybed and with a crash and crackle sheered off the mast and rigging of the *Jacintho Jesus* as we cleared her stern by inches and plunged on without a check!

Before this explosive maneuver I'd been shivering cold; but now I was feverish—hot and cold in turns—my teeth chattering and mouth too dry to spit. Again the jug was passed and this time offered to me. A swig and a swallow, and the sensation of turpentine on fire pouring down my gullet and followed by the kick of a mule in the midriff best describes this, my first introduction to that raw, red Miquelon rum. But I 'kep it down' in spite of involuntary spasms to be rid of it, and found it stood by me like a friend while we performed two more effective gybes on boats, as in the case of the *Jesus,* that were towing more than the prescribed limit of dredges. We then ran down through the rest of the fleet in order that the character and menace of that boom might be impressed on all the scallopers present, and when we were clear to leeward hauled aft again for the beat to New Bedford.

Shortly after noon *Bruiser* was neatly luffed into her berth at the head of a slip occupied by several old whale ships long since out of commission. After furling sail a careful examination of the new boom discovered no more serious injuries than a gaudy bruise here and there. Later as all hands sat round the stove drying out the Skipper said:

'That boom don't owe me nothin' now—and as a mob soother I never see its beat—give 'em the good news to Beetle's—when yer get there—Bub!'; another of 'Cap'n Harry's' left-handed invitations that sent me promptly ashore to start the four-mile journey home on shanks' mare and an empty stomach, as I'd found from past experience a pocket full of change was both an encumbrance and a liability around a boat yard. But in spite of wet, heavy clothes, a cold wind and eyes full of the dust it raised, I enjoyed that walk as few that I've taken since. To have played a part in such a straight-forward action to right a wrong was elating beyond words to express it. And though I did not mention my trip on *Bruiser* in the family circle, the thought of it lent savor to my supper and a sense of blissful well-being when I got to bed.

Next morning—one as cold and windy as the day before—I was early at the boat yard to find a big Saturday morning crowd of old men, boys and loafers all agog for news of yesterday's action in Priest's Cove and also crammed with rumors as to 'Cap'n Harry's' reception should he dare to come down river with *Bruiser* and attempt to repeat his tactics of Friday. To be hanged at his own masthead was one of the more conservative predictions. The entire waterfront was evidently at full boil and the yard considered as a ringside seat in the event of an encounter which it was expected would be a fight to a dramatic finish; for there across the ship channel, for all to see, was a fleet of scallopers more numerous than that of the day before and of a complexion indicating that 'them foreigners' had brought up all their reserves.

Cold as it was standing round in that press of eager watchers, there were few deserters. And when a yell went up—'Here she comes!'—all hands stampeded from the lee side of the buildings, where there was some shelter, to scramble for points of vantage—the tops of boulders, piles of timber, two or three derelict boats—on the weather side of the long building-shed whence a sight was to be had of that unmistakable sail with an American flag at the peak bearing down on the dredgers.

Yet, though the stage seemed set for a 'ripsnorter' such as I had not before nor have since witnessed, there was a hair in the soup; for that wind was sharp as a skimming knife that cut ever deeper and deeper until I, for one, prayed that if 'Cap'n Harry' was to be hanged he'd get it over with soon to release me from this rôle of suffering spectator.

And, as if in answer to this prayer, *Bruiser* held her foaming, rolling course straight for the centre division of the scalloping fleet. But before she came within range, and as if she had been an approaching flag-ship with an admiral on board signalling for maneuvers, every boat in the fleet up with her dredges and joined herself to one or other of two squadrons which promptly took form, one standing close hauled on the starboard tack, the second on the port tack. This latter division, numerically less than the first, rapidly closed with *Bruiser* and when abreast of her came about in her wake, started sheets and followed the flag-ship on a broad reach to intercept the other division standing inshore towards Beetle's Yard. Hurrah—what price Priest's Cove now as against Trafalgar! And as *Bruiser* and her consorts closed with the Iberians and their consorts there was action aplenty as boat hooks were flourished and yells of defiance heralded the imminent collision.

'But Hell!'—as one of the old hands at the yard exclaimed—'You ain't goin' to ketch Harry East smashin' up gear when he can scoop the school 'ithout so much as partin' a rope yarn'; for with the suddenness and precision of a flight of peeps that Yankee division, with 'Cap'n Harry' leading four of the eight boats, divided to threaten both van and rear of the pirate squadron which tack, wear, run, reach or beat, together or in unit, was unable to shake off the menace of an assault that ever threatened but was never driven home, until after two hours that gaily painted fleet was herded to an anchorage to the westward of Palmer's Island known, even then, as 'the Portugee Navy Yard'—and I went home feeling somewhat like a pricked balloon.

Sunday came—a beautiful, clear day with a gentle breeze from the south. Again I was early at the yard to be rewarded, as I looked across to Priest's Cove, by the sight of *Bruiser* anchored peacefully and no other boat in sight. There she lay 'til toward sundown, her ensign at masthead, flapping gently in the faintly stirring air, while 'Cap'n Harry' and his crew lazed in the cockpit, no doubt refreshing themselves at intervals from that two-gallon jug and with the regulation Sunday cigar—Connecticut wrapper and God knows what filler—of that era.

Monday morning—another pleasant day—and there working the 'beds' under orderly, peaceful conditions were twelve Yankee dredgers—and no pirate boat in sight. Except for the regular crew, the yard was deserted and the work going on quietly. At ten o'clock on the making up of a nice, whole-sail southwest breeze, *Bruiser* came-to off the beach once again, unshipped the new hard pine boom and took on board and rerigged her spruce spar—in silence as far as conversation went—except that when the war-scarred stick splashed overboard alongside, 'Cap'n Harry' paused for a moment to look down on it contemplatively and remark:

'That's the *father* and *mother* of a boom when it comes to gybin' in a breeze o'wind.'

Thus befell the Battle of Priest's Cove—a battle hitherto unsung, yet one of international flavor and far-reaching effect in that it was responsible for the inauguration of enlightened laws for the protection of that lowly bivalve—the 'Bay Scallop'—in whose succulence many take delight and for whose preservation—and that of my own neck—I, the last known survivor of that action, offer a special prayer of thanksgiving on the anniversary of the engagement.

The Merrimac River Gundalow and Gundalowmen

BY WALLACE B. ORDWAY

WHEN John Greenleaf Whittier in his poem 'The Countess' described the little settlement of Rocks Village on the Merrimac River, he wrote:

> The river's steel-blue crescent curves
>   To meet, in ebb and flow,
> The single broken wharf that serves
>   For sloop and gundelow.
>
> With salt sea-scents along its shores
>   The heavy hay-boats crawl,
> The long antennæ of their oars
>   In lazy rise and fall.[1]

During the nineteenth century gundalows were a familiar sight on the beautiful stretch of the Merrimac between Haverhill and Newburyport[2] and in the salt marshes of Newbury and Rowley that were reached from the Merrimac by the Plum Island River, but they have now entirely disappeared. The Piscataqua River gundalow has been well described by D. Foster Taylor,[3] but little has been printed about the similar type used on the Merrimac River.

The model which is reproduced on page 74 was made for the construction of his own gundalow by Joseph Lowe of West Newbury, Massachusetts, and is therefore a contemporary and authentic record. As so little has been written about the type, it seems worth while not only to describe the model but also to include whatever can be drawn from old account books and from the recollections of older people in the vicinity of West

---

[1] John Greenleaf Whittier, *Complete Writings* [Amesbury edition] (Boston: Houghton Mifflin Company, no date), I, 255.

[2] The region is well described in Samuel T. Pickard, *Whittier-Land, A Handbook of North Essex* (Boston, 1904), which contains a good map. The end-paper maps of John A. Pollard, *John Greenleaf Whittier, Friend of Man* (Boston: Houghton Mifflin Company, 1949), are good though not detailed.

[3] 'The Piscataqua River Gundalow,' THE AMERICAN NEPTUNE, II (1942), 127-139; 'The Gundalow *Fanny M.*,' ibid., 209-222.

Model of Merrimac River Gundalow built by Joseph Lowe,
West Newbury, Massachusetts, in 1862

Merrimac River Gundalow near Parker River Bridge,
Newbury, Massachusetts, about 1895

Newbury who were familiar with the many and varied uses of gundalows.

According to his daughter, Jennie Lowe Foss, Mr. Lowe whittled this model to scale with his pocket knife in 1862. Scaling one inch to three feet, we find the length of the vessel to have been 41 feet, and beam 10 feet 4 inches from the turn of her bilge; at the turn of her bilge forward to the cutwater, 10 feet 3 inches, which was 9 inches thick. She measured 12 feet 4 inches beam aft on deck, and 13 feet 6 inches forward. Starting 10 feet aft of the bow, the bottom sloped upward to the lower edge of the bow timber, and aft the bottom sloped up for a distance of 9 feet. The model shows that there was a 4-inch deadrise at the bilge. From the sheer bilge down it was 1 foot vertical. The fourteen frames measured 6 inches, moulded about 5 inches, and were 2 feet 6 inches between centers. The mast was 8 inches in diameter at the step, was 22 feet 6 inches long, and was placed 9 feet aft. The yard measured 16 feet 6 inches, and was raised by a halyard reeving over a shieve at the masthead and belaying within reach of the steersman. Saillocks on the sheets and tacks were peculiar to gundalows. They were referred to during the eighties as reeflocks.

Gundalows were essential for the farmers of the lower Merrimac valley, as well as for the building of roads, wharves and bridges. Extracts from diaries and account books will give some idea of their varied uses. 'Went to Amesbury and engaged John Huntington and David Goodwin's gondola[4] and wharving to go after mud,' wrote Newell Ordway, the Quaker preacher and friend of Whittier in his diary for 13 May 1844. '14th Jacob Morrill, Moses Stevens, William and Lewis Farrington went with me after mud. 16th Joshua Stevens drew two loads of mud. P.M. Finished unloading the boat of mud.' From the eighteenth to the twenty-seventh there were more trips after 'mussel mud' from the shore of the lower Merrimac River. While men were employed at 83 cents a day in hauling mud ashore from the gundalow at Emery's Landing, and in spreading it on the land, there were other activities on the farm. 'Joshua Stevens here with four oxen ploughing. Jacob Morrill here planting corn. 20th repairing fence round William Wheeler's meadow. P.M. My cow inclining to push down fence I put a preventitive on her horns. 22nd 3 oclock we had a daughter born, I then went to Newburyport and got mother to take care of my wife. I then went to Seabrook to meeting, Jared

---

[4] There are many spellings of the word. Newell Ordway used the original Venetian form of 'gondola'; Whittier followed the spelling 'gundelow.' John Huntington of Amesbury billed Thomas G. Ordway on 24 September 1850 'to a gundalo in the meadows 2 days at $2.00,' and Thomas H. Balch of Bradford on 10 August 1852 billed the same Mr. Ordway 'To gondola 2 days $2.50.' The men most intimate with the vessels, who shared the hard pulls against cross-winds and tides as the great sweeps (measuring sometimes as much as 28 feet in length) swung on their 'sniple pins,' or sculled at the stern with twenty or more tons of hay aboard, often contracted the pronunciation of the name to 'gunlo.'

Patterson of Indiana, Charles Taber of Farnham, Lower Canada, and Daniel Clapp of Pomfret, Connecticutt, was there. 27th took John Huntington and David Goodwin's gondola home, then went fishing where we caught four shad, two salmon, one sturgeon and one bass.'

A perusal of the account books of John Huntington, his son John Dean Huntington, Philip Jones and Joel Davis, gundalow owners of Pleasant

Poling the Gundalow against Tide

Valley, Amesbury, from 1826 to 1884, disclosed some interesting items. There were both 'Old boat engagements' and 'New boat engagements.' The accounts began 7 August 1826 with a new gundalow *Ruth Jones,* so named for the wife of Philip Jones. Through 1826 and 1827 the prevailing price for leasing *Ruth Jones* appears to have been two dollars per day. In 1828 a Mr. Carten paid 75 cents for 'a boat to Newburyport,' Robert Colby one dollar for 'a boat to bring 1 load of mud,' and on 13 June of that year Captain Tigue settled $6.00 for 'two boats to move a building at 50 cents per day each.' In 1832 fifty cents was charged 'to a boat to bring a load of wood from Pattens break.' On 30 June 1832 John Huntington and Joel Davis leased a new gundalow to John Sawyer to go to Haverhill for five days for a total of $5.00, but some mishap must have occurred as a charge was made to Sawyer of '33 cts for one plank.' The name of Captain Valentine Bagley, the hero of Whittier's poem 'The Captain's Well,'[5] appears with a charge of two dollars on 17 and 18 August 1831, and the account books show that men came long distances to engage gundalows. The longest trip mentioned was made by 'Amos Little to Ipswich after Rockweed.' One of the most amusing entries concerns E. Moody Boynton, the picturesque inventor of the Bicycle Railroad System and the Lightning Saw.[6] On 14 July 1878, while he was attempting to deepen the channel of the Merrimac River at Mitchell's Falls above Haverhill, there appears a record of a rented gundalow to 'E. M. Boynton to go up to the Rappids to take lumber,' but instead of the usual entry of cash paid there simply appears the comment 'a disappointment'!

During the active period of Newburyport shipping, gundalows were often used to load and unload vessels in the harbor. When there were one hundred and three West Indiamen, more than seventy vessels in the Labrador fleet, and more than one hundred sail of mackerel vessels there was plenty for gundalows to do in Newburyport harbor.[7] They also were used by the shipyards, and in the construction of wharves and bridges, including the Eastern Railroad bridge built across the Merrimac in 1840.[8]

[5] Shipwrecked on the coast of Arabia, Captain Bagley resolved if saved to pay his debt to the Lord by digging a well by the roadside in Amesbury on his return home. John Greenleaf Whittier, *Complete Writings*, IV, 289-294; Pickard, op. cit., pp. 83-84.

[6] The story of E. Moody Boynton's life is picturesque and amazing in its contrasts. As a young man teaching in the little district school at Pleasant Valley he sometimes crossed the river on thin ice by using two boards, pushing one at a time forward and walking on it, while veteran river men, who dared not venture out, watched from the shore. In 1877 he represented the City of New York Board of Trade at a meeting of the Association of Chambers of Commerce of Great Britain in London and was presented to Queen Victoria and the Royal Family at Buckingham Palace. As a young man he navigated the Merrimac in a boat with a contrivance of his own operated by treadles connected with paddles, but later in life he owned the fastest steamboat of its time on the river, the *Startled Fawn*. Although this was a pleasure boat, it was sometimes used in towing gundalows. Some of the trees that hold the banks at Pipestave Hill in West Newbury were planted under his supervision, and he is credited with the plan of tree planting used to hold the banks of the Panama Canal. A letter which Mr. Boynton wrote to the Honorable George W. McCrary, Secretary of War, on 18 November 1879, is claimed to have influenced him to approve of his plan to construct the jetties at the mouth of the Merrimac River. Mr. Boynton evidently had great confidence in his Bicycle Railroad System—according to which a train would run with one wheel below and one above the cars—or in those who were expected to buy stock in it when he proclaimed: 'We will scale the Rockies like a moonbeam.' Whittier heard Boynton speak at the dedication of the statue of Josiah Bartlett and then wrote:

"I hear the wild waves rushing
From Boynton's limber jaws,
Swift as his railroad bicycle,
And buzzing like his saws."

[7] In December 1804 Captain Samuel Rolfe paid David Coffin $1.50 for the use of a gondola for two days for unloading. In 1803 the gondola was used by the brig *Active* for two and a half days.

[8] George L. Whitmore at the age of 92 said: 'There used to be a lot of them come down river. All the shipyards used them to pick up wedges. There would be hundreds of them in the river when they launched the ships. A sturgeon one time landed in one.'

Gundalows contributed much to the social life of the region, for many a one was converted into a house boat where friends were entertained. Occasionally the excursion of a neighborhood group or a Sunday School would provide an event long to be remembered. Warren Plummer, now ninety years of age, recalls the details of one of the annual Oldtown Parish picnics, which took place about 1868. The picnickers had enjoyed a trip

Noonin' Gundalow Days

with two gundalows through Plum Island River to the farm of 'Marm' Small, otherwise known as Halfway House, and during the picnic the boats were left 'sitting' with one end on shore. By mutual understanding one was reserved for the younger folks. Eventually, after a day of pleasure, the farmers were anxious to get back for their evening chores, and besides there was need to return on the rising tide at an appointed hour. Evidently at least one of the young people had a special desire to remain after the time agreed upon, for as the picnickers returned to the gundalows they found that someone had removed the drain plug from the bottom of the one reserved for the young people so that it had filled with water. It requires considerable time either to bail that amount of water from a gundalow or to wait for the tide to run low enough to drain out.

The second alternative was decided upon and the young people remained for the night. During the 1880's and 1890's the farmers and their families of Newbury and other towns would meet at Parker Hall as the Oldtown Farmers' Club. Long seats and chairs would be placed in gundalows and a trip made through Plum Island River to Ipswich Bluffs for a picnic. 'Gundalows were part of the fun,' said Howard Noyes in retrospection. The *Weekly Messenger* of 16 July 1892 described an up-to-date gundalow outing in the following romantic and high-flown language:

> As in the olden time, years gone by when the busy tillers of the soil among the hills and valleys of Groveland took their autumnal outing, so the Methodist lads and lasses floated out on the tide Monday evening and voyaged down the Merrimack in the moonlight. In the place of the primitive scow used in those days for the conveyance of hay from the meadows, a gondola was pressed into service. No Venetian arm and muscle propelled the silent craft. With her living freight she quietly stole over the mirrored waters. The little steamer at her side patiently turned her propeller measuring off miles of beautiful shore and shadowy valley. Frank Sargent with one finger directed the prow of the ongoing vessel.

Perhaps the most characteristic use of the gundalow was bringing salt hay from the marshes near the mouth of the Merrimac to the farms along the river. This traffic had an inland extension, for farmers from towns in southern New Hampshire would come with horses and oxen to the river below Haverhill for the hay brought up by gundalow. In 1865, 4195 acres of salt grass were cut from the marshes contiguous to the lower Merrimac River.[9] Gundalows were essential to this harvest, for they could penetrate the streams winding through the marshes, and could sit happily on the mud when the tide went out. The cutting of the salt grass was originally done entirely with hand scythes, but toward the end of the nineteenth century horse-drawn mowing machines were introduced. The Sargents of Bear Hill, Merrimac, were responsible for the first horse-drawn mowing machine at Black Rocks, Salisbury, in 1878, but the farmers who cut the larger marshes extending for miles along both sides of Plum Island River were not to be outdone for long. These men—descendants of those who first settled along the upland nearby—knew their marsh was too soft for their horses' hoofs, but they were accustomed to overcoming obstacles. Soon someone fashioned large flat wooden shoes and found an old

---

[9] There is a good account of the salt marshes of Rowley, with illustrations of salt haystacks and the staddles which raised them above the marshes in Amos Everett Jewett, *The Tidal Marshes of Rowley and Vicinity with an Account of the Old-Time Methods of "Marshing"* (Rowley, 1949), which was reprinted (with additions) from *Essex Institute Historical Collections*, LXXXV (1949). Mr. Jewett's personal knowledge of the Rowley marshes goes back to the late 1870's. A somewhat later picture of the same region was given by Dr. Charles Wendell Townsend in *Sand Dunes and Salt Marshes* (Boston, 1913). The pen and ink sketches by F. J. McGregor, made to illustrate this article, record details of the use of gundalows in the salt marshes.

dobbin patient enough to allow them to be fastened on his feet.[10] Once the problem of shoeing had been straightened out, gundalows carrying horses and mowing machines to the marshes were seen on the Merrimac. Philip Corbin of Rings Island remembers seeing Arthur Smith propelling through Black Water Creek a gundalow loaded with hay, and topped by a pair of horses.

Loading the Gundalow

Preliminary to trips down the river to the marshes, farmers studied for weeks the *Old Farmer's Almanac* for a period of low tides, better known as 'salt hay season.' As the time drew near, there were busy days for the farmers' wives, as each employer was expected to provide an ample supply of food for his crew. This included beans, sometimes baked in a large

[10] These shoes were made from a piece of oak plank 9¾ x 10¼ inches and weighed 4¼ pounds each when dry. Cutouts were made for the hoofs, and a flat piece of iron was bolted across the bottom for them to rest on. Large leather straps held them to the hoofs. Sometimes a hamestrap was used. These were drawn through four loops of the same material on opposite sides of each shoe. Shortly after, there began in Rowley the manufacture of the Dodge shoe. These were fastened on with iron clamps that were tightened by a nut which drew them tight against the hoofs about 3 inches above the conventional iron shoe. Before long these became an important accessory to the cranberry growers' equipment on Cape Cod. Other makers in limited numbers were George Randall of Newbury and Fred Brown of Salisbury.

two-handled earthen pot, loaves of bread comparable in size to a hassock in the old meetinghouse, a variety of pies baked in large brown glazed redware plates and white ones with various borders of blue Staffordshire. Pork apple pie was considered one of the favorites. There were 'Tap Ann' tarts, and the traditional apple pan dowdy, often sweetened with molasses.[11] A plentiful supply of clams in nearby flats was often dug for a chowder, and cooked with a fire in the brazier, usually called the fire-pot. Always a cask was filled with water for washing and drinking, and, as John Mullen recalled, 'some demanded something strong to drink,' and so a second cask was provided for them. 'Never heard no angry words among them,' Mullen added. Others were content with a swigler.[12] Scythes, rakes, forks and haypoles were necessary. Sometimes a grindstone was included and a boy to operate it, eager and happy with the privilege of comradeship with the men.

With a gundalow all prepared, and the 'top of the ebb' coming at early evening, there was nothing more to be desired. While the tide was still rising, men came from back roads to join the crew. Seven were needed for the larger 26 to 36 ton boats.[13] While final preparations were going on, there would be discussions about the probable time of return. John Mullen, when recently asked how much time was needed to make the trip of 18 miles from Whetstone Landing in West Newbury[14] to the marsh for a load and return, replied, 'By gorrys, that's according to the crews. Big load in four days. Sometimes three tides to load.' He believes that four hours down with the tide was fair time for the distance of about six miles from Pleasant Valley to the marsh.

When the tide had risen until only one end of the gundalow rested on shore, someone would exclaim, 'She is sitting.' Soon all would be aboard, the pikes would be pushed into the ground, and as the boat started moving, someone would remark, 'She's fleeting.' Soon all would

[11] At the Emery farm in West Newbury chests brought from Romsey, England, in 1635, by John Emery were again and again brought from the attic of the old farmhouse to be packed with food and utensils.

[12] I have one of these little wooden containers in the form of a cask used on a gundalow during the Civil War. It has the capacity of less than a quart, or a considerable number of swigs.

[13] Occasionally the boy who came to join in this rugged work was paid 35 cents per day. John Mullen said, 'Never wanted any pay. Had a good outing for a few days.' When a boy would be seen coming over the hill to the landing for a trip, Elbridge Merrill would exclaim, 'By gosh and blazes, there's a youngen.' When Gene Drake and Ellie Macintosh were sighted, he would say, 'Here come them two apostles.' His son Willie was called 'Skipper,' and was depended upon as 'he knew the river,' said Fred Poore. For years Willie and his six-seated 'mountain wagon' were famed from Newburyport through the White Mountains. His tally-ho is now at the Wolfe Tavern, Newburyport.

[14] At Whetstone Landing is a stone with a hole drilled a few inches deep which served a unique purpose for some of the farmers who used this landing for unloading their hay. They would watch the rising tide until it ran into this hole. Then they would know that the water was beginning to flow over the salt marshes and their men would be quitting work there.

be in position. With the largest sweeps,[15] two men were needed for each. Sitting on cross planks, one faced forward and the other aft. Two men sculled, with an oar each, at the stern, with the skipper between them at the tiller. Once well into the stream the slow, even motion of the sweeps began. Discussion would turn to the question of who else had gone. Two and a half miles above is 'Duck Hole,' and someone has dimly seen a gun-

Fair Tide and Wind Homeward Bound

dalow making the upper turn, not to be seen again by them before Hughes Creek. Below, another comes in sight around a point, and trained eyes soon see that no sweeps are dipping into the water and no sail is on the mast, yet the gundalow is making good time. Any Merrimac River gundalowman would know that this boat could belong to but one man—Otis Dwinnels—who, with back much bent, was alone in the stern, sculling as no one else on the river could. They knew that he would scull the nine miles to Pork Island in Plum Island River, cut his load alone with scythe,

[15] A gundalow was built by Prescott Spofford for Joel Davis in 1877 for $325. I have in my collection a pair of the sweeps made for this gundalow, and they measure 28 feet 2½ inches in length. This gundalow was sold to the Wonnesquam Boat Club in 1892 for $25 to spend its last years as a float.

and, by fastening a cleat across his two haypoles, drag tons of hay to make his load.[16]

As the journey down river continued, the gundalow would move faster as the sweeps came into a more even tempo. Often a man standing on the shore would cup his hands around his mouth and call out: 'Got any pan dowdy aboard?' Gundalowmen expected this good-natured banter to be heard from the shore, from the bridges, and from other boats as they progressed along the way. At 'The Narrows,' where a rocky point projects into the river, the current becomes quite swift. Of this spot John Mullen recalled, 'Didn't have so much work. Float along easier.' The Old Ferry Road Landing would soon be passed. Someone would start a discussion about the amount of grass cutting he was going to do. Another would tell a big story of some of his own past accomplishments. If Sam Ordway had any doubt about this boasting, he might be expected to comment, 'That's all poppycock.'

Rocks and ledges add to the rugged beauty of the shores.[17] Immediately upon coming within sight of the famous Chain Bridge,[18] boatmen

[16] There is no record of the weights of Otis Dwinnels' loads of salt hay, but he had, without help, made trips with not less than 25 tons of coal from Newburyport to Whetstone Landing to distribute to his customers. Men on the gundalows used to blow their horns and call to the drawtenders, 'Hoist the draw,' until it became the custom to give the call as a friendly greeting when passing on the river. Otis Dwinnels brought the phrase ashore and when meeting an acquaintance would substitute 'Hoist the draw' for a greeting of common usage. To this day this form of greeting is occasionally heard from men who never knew Mr. Dwinnels. I have been told that Otis Dwinnels once stood in a bushel basket and grasped a handle in each of his hands. Then in an attempt to raise himself with the basket from the ground, he pulled with his mighty arms until both handles were ripped from the basket. This tale, although never written down, has been current in West Newbury for seventy-five years. In 1914 Mr. Dwinnels was walking along River Road in West Newbury. It had been a long time since he had last propelled his gundalow, and he was so bent that he appeared able to see by his bushy beard only the ground at his feet. His left arm lay across his back, and his right arm was in position to suggest the grasping of an oar, just as if he were sculling a gundalow. He was offered a ride—his first—in an automobile in which I was also a passenger. Soon the motor stalled on a sharp incline and started to move backwards. Mr. Dwinnels in all seriousness gave his opinion that the machine should carry an anchor for such emergencies. He was, even in old age, still a gundalowman in mind and body.

[17] In 1839 Thoreau, who had just passed his twenty-second birthday, journeyed here from Haverhill in a steamboat, and was much impressed by the beauty of this particular portion of the river. His journey was made eleven years after the first steamboat had passed down river from Haverhill. He wrote in part: 'Between Amesbury and Newbury it is a broad commercial river, no longer skirted with yellow and crumbling banks, but backed by green pastures, with frequent white beaches on which fishermen draw up their nets. It was a pleasant sight to watch the fishermen dragging seines on the distant shore as in pictures of a foreign strand.'

[18] During the latter part of 1791 the question of a bridge across the Merrimac River from the Newbury side to Salisbury by way of Deer Island was agitated and petitioned for by Nathaniel Carter and eight others, and the bridge was built in 1792. Although the portion of the bridge extending from Deer Island to the Salisbury shore remained in use until 1882, the long wooden arch from the Newbury side of the island was removed in 1810 and replaced by a chain suspension bridge. It is a matter of tradition that this portion of the bridge was very unpopular with the upriver navigators, especially the gundalowmen carrying salt hay, whose highly piled freights often scraped the shore side of the great arch. Evidently the bridge was annoying to the many boatmen of the time. Emphatic threatenings were made in regard to this 'damnified obstruction' to navigation, and it is said that the stockholders placed watchmen nightly on this portion of the bridge for its defence and

needed to be especially alert for hidden rocks. One can hardly look upon Deer Island, which supports one end of the bridge, without being struck with wonder at the men who brought their gundalows through these waters without mishap. Immediately below are cross currents by some rocks, which prompted the crew with John Mullen to call the locality 'Pull and Be Damned Point.' Then Eagle, Ram and Carr's Islands have

Whetstone Landing, West Newbury, Mass.

to be passed before reaching the shipyards, from which would come banter from the ship carpenters and calls from young men on wharves inquiring for plum duff and lob scouse. If the tide was up enough, the route inside of Woodbridge Island would be chosen and Plum Island River soon reached.[19]

protection during the hay season. See John J. Currier, *Ould Newbury: Historical and Biographical Sketches* (Boston, 1896), pp. 593-604.

[19] Deacon Plummer, who lived in the First Parish of West Newbury, on one occasion employed an Irishman fresh from the old country, to help him bring hay from the salt marshes by gundalow. On

On 1 October 1949 I cruised into Plum Island River with a few members of the Massachusetts Archaeological Society, travelling in two boats with plans to dig at Grape Island for Indian kitchen middens. While the skippers of both boats were struggling with their motors, I refreshed my meager knowledge of the vicissitudes of the river, and had an opportunity to meditate on the skill of the gundalowmen of the past. In 1949, instead of thousands of stacks of hay extending for miles southward on the marsh, and ending in a mirage of them above the distant sound, only a few small clusters could be seen. The only life visible in the tall grass, sweetening the air as it waved in the wind, was an occasional Great Blue Heron. Water fowl crisscrossed from one feeding place to another. The only cloud in the sky was a thin distant one, and it spelled 'Cola'! Of the many creeks, I saw Hackers, Hole In The Wall, and Labor In Vain, with no directional signs to warn the novice. There are landmarks known as Jericho, Pork Island and Tony's Rocks, which are hidden except at low tide. In surveying the deserted marshes, I was glad that in my younger days I had volunteered for a short season among the haymakers, and so could make myself believe that I was entitled to a measure of common interest in this occupation.

In my imagination, I saw a few of the scenes of former times. Men were busy on the 'sweepage lots' again. Some were mowing, raking and stacking. Others were poling the hay to gundalows 'laid off' against the mud banks. Voices could be heard above the whirring of the horse-drawn mowing machines. As our two disabled boats, now roped together, drifted against Pork Island, it reminded me that there Alfred Moore[20] of West Newbury used to 'lay off' his gundalow, and cut the twelve to fifteen acres. I saw Cyrus Ordway measuring in the goose grass with his haypole as a suggestion for the length of the stroke he expected of his men as they mowed. I could see some of the different grasses. Fox grass was said to be the hardest to cut and goose grass the easiest. There is black grass and fire

coming through Plum Island River, the deacon and the newcomer were sculling at the stern, while two men toward the bow were using the long oars. The incoming tide rushing up the river made the steering more difficult, and, as they rounded a turn, the force of the water caused the Irishman to lose his grip on the oar. Struggling to regain it, he lurched into the deacon, sending him overboard. Immediately the oarsmen, sensing something was wrong, looked and saw only the Irishman. They cried, 'Where is the deacon?' and he replied 'He just stipped off now.' An extended oar was soon grasped and the wrathful deacon pulled aboard.

20 I thought of the times when Alfred Moore used to come to the West Newbury Co-operative Creamery. One day when a patron drew from the tank more skimmed milk than was his due, Mr. Moore remarked, 'The Creamery not only tests the milk, but it also tests the patrons.' He sometimes wore for a necktie an old black cloth, formerly used as a cover to pull over a closed umbrella, and it served him quite well! He used to leave his bootjack on the kitchen floor where his wife would trip over it, and then she would throw it out through the doorway. One day he nailed it solidly to the floor, and said, 'There now, Hannah Moody, let's see you kick that around.'

grass, so called because it is so red. When this was cut it was usually 'lopped on.'[21] I remembered being told of my great-great-grandfather Joshua Ordway with his eight sons mowing together, the father leading and the sons following according to their age.[22] I saw some young men mowing with their scythes, and I seemed to hear their slow chant, which was supposed to be a reflection on the slowness of older men. It went like this

> Milk and whey,
> And that all day.

Suddenly at a faster tempo, to imply their own superior ability, they would recite

> Bacon and eggs
> Look out for your legs.

I thought of the drainage ditches, so necessary for each lot, but often hidden by the tall grass from the casual observer, so that horse and men might suddenly find themselves in one.[23]

With the help of oars we rounded the far end of Pork Island and could see where 'Marm' Small's isolated boarding house—also in the old days called Halfway House—used to be. When this point was reached, the gundalowmen would always begin a chant established by long custom, which went like this: 'Old Marm Small is dead, and the last words she said, were Johnnie take care of my cranberry bed.'

Returning on the incoming tide, we were glad of a borrowed motor to bring our boats along without effort from us,[24] and I thought of the long pull the gundalowmen used to have. I remembered how John Mullen had told me of his crew of long ago, 'When they started to come home they gave Indian war whoops and threw each other into the water, and nobody got mad.'

[21] An exception was Herb Keith of Peddycodiac, N. B., who refused, and so used the English grass clip.

[22] This must have been before 1814, as William, one of the sons, died in that year. It was said that Thomas Ordway, the seventh son, born in 1776, could light his pipe using flint and steel while on a galloping horse. Believe it or not!

[23] In poling hay, the man in front was expected to warn the one following. Parker Nason told of an incident in this way: 'I remember we were poling hay. The man in back was John Salkins and he couldn't see the ditch. I said "Ditch" too late. "I know, I'm in it," said Salkins.'

[24] In the twilight where the black grass grew, I tried to visualize the Indians and their wigwams, for once an Indian village stood there. There is now an airport and planes were coming in for the night. Our expedition had been a failure so far as reaching the Indian kitchen middens on Grape Island was concerned. There were apologies expressed, especially to the oldest man in the party, who had that October day, by no fault of his, been required to wait for hours in a marooned boat, and then to wade deeply in mud and water and walk across the marsh over ditches. But Robert Forsythe said, from his heart, 'I have enjoyed every minute of it.' After all, he was an old gundalowman.

The last load of hay brought up the river by gundalow from the salt marshes was cut near Ipswich Bluffs in 1899 for the Training Field Farm of William E. Merrill in West Newbury, 15 miles away. Of the crew of ten, three men are now living: John Kirkpatrick, William and Murray Coffin. The remainder were Eugene Bradley, George Brown, Dan Donahue, Warren Coffin, Sam Fowler, Jarvis Gambrell who was engaged as cook, and Mr. Merrill. 'That was the biggest freight brought up the river. My father said so. We were down there more than a week,' declared Murray Coffin. 'We went down to Pleasant Valley and got the gundalow. I think it was Colby's,' added William Coffin. 'We had fun on that one. We poled it all off the marsh by hand. We sculled and rowed all the way to Plum Island bridge. We had to swim the creeks.'[25] Those who swam ahead would hold the rope taut for those who could not swim to work their way across over the water. The traditional practice of easing the rope and giving ducking was indulged in on this occasion. 'Jack Kirk' was the victim this time. 'Didn't he holler,' said William Coffin. 'We hit the piling on Plum Island bridge an awful crack. They had hard work to close the draw after that. We laid down Joppa all night and I never saw the midges so thick,' said Murray. In reference to the steamer engaged to tow them, William Coffin said, 'They didn't show up. Merrill had to go and get another. It was the *Bronx*. They charged fifty dollars for the towing. They were mad. They tried to soak us. We were not supposed to carry more than 25 tons and we had 50. I heard a man on the boat say it was the largest load he ever saw. We got out in midstream before they would hitch onto us. That was a green freight. It was spread all over Training Field,' said Murray. 'All around in the hotel field,' added William.

Recently I walked with Philip Marquand along a path near Emery's Landing, overlooking the river, on the ancestral estate made famous by his son John, the novelist, as Wickford Point. 'It makes me tired not to see any gundalows on the river. There used to be two of the Goodwins' over there,' he said, as he pointed across to Pleasant Valley. 'They were a nuisance. I used to sail boats, and they were a nuisance when going under bridges.' John Mullen, drawtender at Newburyport railroad bridge for nearly thirty years, whose viewpoint came from experiences with gundalows from 1880 to 1885, recently said, 'Sailboats bothered gundalows. They had the right of way. They wouldn't give in. They done it more for deviltry than anything else.'

One of the best photographs of a Merrimac River gundalow is of the ves-

---

[25] It was often necessary to swim across the creeks with a rope and pull the gundalow after.

sel that was bought of Nat Dole by Tom Thornton, W. Burke Little and Moses Noyes, taken about the year 1895 near the Parker River bridge. It is only by photographs and models that the type can be studied today, for the last true gundalow built with wooden trunnels afloat on the Merrimac River has disappeared. This, which belonged to Captain Hunt, spent its last days at Rings Island where, filled with water, it served as a swimming pool, and was frequently referred to as the 'community bath tub.'[26] About 1933 it broke away from Rings Island in a storm and has never been seen again.

Many of the riverside farms below Haverhill are also gone. In 1875 there were upwards of two hundred cows on River Road farms of West Newbury receiving their evening ration of salt hay, which was mostly brought by gundalow. The assessors in 1949 found not a single cow on this road. Many of the old landing places are clogged with driftwood and covered with lush growths of rushes, loosestrife and trees. The ruts from ox and horse carts disappeared. Miss Georgianna Emery in her ninetieth year recently viewed the scene at Emery's Landing. Close by was an old grist mill on the site of one built by her ancestor, John Emery, more than three centuries ago. She looked toward the mill at a rise of land between the landing and the mouth of the Artichoke River, and saw trees with trunks measuring more than four feet in circumference. 'They kept this place for drying the hay,' she said, 'but these trees have grown up.'

The vigorous gundalowmen[27] too have gone from the river. We no longer hear their horns echoing from the river banks, nor their voices calling, 'Hoist the draw! Got any apple pan dowdy aboard? By gorry dormans, I'm purty nigh ruinated. By June, I'm tuckered, stiff, used up and wore out!' I, for one, regret it.

[26] Mrs. Philip Corbin, who must have been quite young at the time she knew the 'community bath tub,' recently said, 'Gee, it was swell. You pull the plug out and let it fill. It would drain out when the tide went down.' Josie Worthen of Pleasant Valley has memories of her childhood when the Davis gundalow on land served as a skating rink.

[27] They did not have an easy life, and there were accidents now and then. Oliver Knight was injured at Curzon's Mill bridge when a young man in the early eighteen sixties. A gundalow loaded with 'mussel mud' was brought in at high tide and the mud wheeled in wheelbarrows on planks over the gates to small rowboats and rowed up the Artichoke River to be spread on the farm by the bridge at the main highway. A plank gave way, dropping him and the wheelbarrow. Although he lived until 1913, he never fully recovered from the injury. Samuel Ordway, in nervous haste to lift the end of a gundalow while aground, injured his shoulder, so that his right shoulder was obviously lower than his left. Although these men were not afraid of work, they wasted few words in conversation, and even fewer in written accounts of their activities. A three-day gundalow trip in 1872 by John Dean Huntington was recorded in this laconic manner: 'Aug. 31 Grate storm. Sept. 1 Left boat and come holm. Sept. 2 Put on hay.'

III

Some Distinctive Coastal Craft

The Boston Packets *by Henry C. Kittredge*	93
Enchanted Voyage *by Alexander Crosby Brown*	104
The New England Double Enders *by David Cabot*	117
Johnny Woodboat *by George MacBeath*	137

Until recently, various ports and regions of the Atlantic seaboard had their own peculiar types of fishing craft, work boats, or coasters. The best way to see them—and one of the most delightful ways to travel—was provided by the numerous steamboat lines that ran between principal ports.

The Boston Packets

BY HENRY C. KITTREDGE

IT has long been the fashion when we look back at earlier decades, to sigh faintly and call them the good old days. There is no harm in the habit, certainly. Every generation has done it. Go back to the good old days of fifty years ago, and you will find men of that day looking enviously at the simplicity of life and the abundance with which their grandfathers had been blessed. In the same way you may chase Time back to its very beginnings and find men singing the same sad song: O! for the good old days!

Well, in the following pages we shall take a brief backward look at some of the old days on Cape Cod and at one phase of seafaring that flourished a hundred years ago—the story of the Boston Packets. The business was at its best from about 1800 to 1875 or thereabouts, old days, certainly, but if we look at them with the naked eye of the historian instead of through the rose-tinted glasses of the sentimentalist, neither better nor worse than our own.

It is useful to keep some such reflections as these in mind when we contemplate the era of the local packets—those stout little sloops and schooners which for two generations or so furnished the principal means of transportation between the Cape villages and Boston. That era, like every era, had its pleasant features and its unpleasant ones, and it is my purpose to depict it briefly and without bias. Then each can decide for himself whether on the whole, those times were better than our own, or worse; whether, if it lay within our power to do so, we should bid Time turn backward in its flight to the days when our roads, ankle deep in sand, were bare of automobiles and our harbors were white with the sails of fishermen, coasters, and Boston Packets.

The first fact that strikes one in examining this period is that, like the era of the clipper ships, it was brief. Two generations, as we have said, just about covered it. This does not mean, of course, that nobody ever went to Boston by water before 1800, but that if he did so, he embarked as the lone passenger on a chance fisherman or coasting schooner. There were stagecoaches, to be sure, but one trip by stagecoach was usually enough. Men of God, like Timothy Dwight, or philosophers like Henry Thoreau, might rise above the hardships of such an experience; but then, as now, there was more salt than dust in the blood of Cape men and women, and they preferred a boat to a carriage. They knew more about the wind than they did about horses, and after one trip overland on rough, sandy roads in a coach that rocked and jolted and in air thick with dust, they either went by water or stayed at home.

Nor was it a very difficult matter to find a vessel of some sort that would take them, for communication by water between the Cape and Boston began early. Stubby little sloops and schooners made occasional trips as far back as 1660. One of them was owned by Thomas Huckins who, at least as early as this, was the landlord of the Barnstable tavern and found that the surest way to keep his taproom supplied with rum was to bring it himself from Boston in his own vessel. And no doubt he took a passenger along with him once in a while. Rum, in fact, seems to have formed a not inconsiderable item in the merchandise of these early and sporadic coasting skippers. Captain Jeremy Bickford, about 1670, brought a cargo of rum and molasses—and one lady passenger—from Boston to Truro.

Some of these men were real sailors, but a good many were Jacks-of-all-trades, versatile mechanics and farmers who would never have left dry land if they had not had something to sell in Boston. Their seamanship, though adequate, was often rudimentary, and according to the trend of their genius, they regarded their trips as pleasant interruptions to the monotony of farm work, or as disagreeable necessities. Many of them were sharp traders, a Yankee trait which, if I am not mistaken, their descendants have not yet lost. If, therefore, their business methods sometimes lay open to criticism, let him who is without sin among us cast the first stone.

Take, for example, the trick that Isaac Bacon played on his neighbor, Samuel Huckins. Both were Barnstable farmers who specialized in onions and were in the habit of carrying their crop to Boston in their own vessels. Huckins had agreed with parties in Salem to deliver a cargo of onions there. Bacon learned of the arrangement, got to Salem ahead of Huckins, sold his own onions as Huckins' and was half way across Cape Cod Bay, headed home, before Huckins reached Salem and learned how he had been tricked.

It would be interesting to know what kind of looking vessel Bacon's was, for local wags nicknamed her *Somerset* after the celebrated British frigate that was wrecked at North Truro during the Revolution. Obviously she was not a queen in her class. That Bacon's seamanship was as rough and ready as his business ethics appeared during one of his trips to Boston. He rounded the point of Sandy Neck with a strong S.W. breeze, when suddenly the vessel developed an alarming leak. Bacon brought her about on the other tack, no doubt with a view to beaching her, but found to his surprise that on this tack she was as tight as ever. He had himself lowered over the windward side to investigate, and found (so the story goes) a neat round hole, about three inches in diameter, in her planking. He whittled out a soft pine plug to fit it, pounded it well in with a caulking mallet, came about once more, and continued his voyage to Boston. One may well ask how a neat round hole could suddenly appear in a vessel's planking. An underwater woodpecker? A salt-water rodent of a new species? Something very strange about that story!

But these sporadic sailors bore small resemblance to the real packet captains of later years. The term *packet* implies some degree of regularity in making trips, something at least approaching a schedule; and since none of the men who have been mentioned had any reason for following schedules they cannot be called packet captains in the proper sense of the word, nor can their vessels be called packets. After the Revolution, however, conditions on the Cape improved greatly. By 1800, salt was being made in every town, and though much of it was used by local fishermen, a surplus often remained for the Boston market. Farmers kept on raising onions, and sometimes they had a cargo of flax. The forests of Sandwich yielded more wood than the citizens could burn in even the coldest winter. All this merchandise called for transportation. So, about 1800, with freight as their mainstay, and with passengers as a side issue, packets to Boston began to appear and eventually to flourish.

By 1830 boom times for the packets had begun because business of all sorts was booming. More salt was being made every year, and what was just as significant, the number of deepwater shipmasters in every village had grown enormously, and those lordly mariners, most of whom sailed out of Boston, demanded something pleasanter than stagecoaches and stuffy sloops to carry them to and from their commands. With such men on board, speed was essential and regular meals and comfortable accommodations.

There is no keener rivalry than the rivalry between the towns of Cape Cod, and there is no more exciting sport than boat racing. When these two factors are combined, and when the question of money is also involved, the cords of competition are stretched extremely taut. This was precisely the situation that existed between the owners and the captains of packets in one Cape town and the next. No sooner did a new schooner appear in the business in Provincetown, let us say, than the citizens of Truro would see what they could do to go her one better. If Orleans came out with a new flier, Brewster, within a month, was looking around for something bigger and faster.

A fine instance of this kind of rivalry existed between the neighboring towns of Barnstable and Yarmouth. During these flush times these two towns strove mightily to surpass each other in the packet business, and Yarmouth, in spite of a woefully inadequate harbor, no more than a creek in the marsh, was first to carry off the laurels. About 1830 its citizens came out with a new schooner, *Commodore Hull* which, under the able command of Captain Paddock Thacher, could pass anything on the Bay without putting her lee rail under. Barnstable, as the shire town, swallowed its chagrin for a time, but after a few years of defeat two of the leading citizens, Matthias Hinckley and Thomas Percival, took a trip to Boston and called on Captain Daniel Bacon, a retired shipmaster in the China trade and a leading Boston merchant and shipowner. More important, he was a loyal son of Barnstable, and had built the Bacon farm there for a summer place. He told Hinckley and Percival to go ahead and get a packet that would beat *Commodore Hull* and he would pay the bill. They came back with a new sloop called *Mail*, built to order somewhere on the Hudson River, and the fun began.

At the end of the first race, *Mail*, under the joint command of Hinckley and Percival, slid into her dock at Central Wharf a bare length ahead of her Yarmouth rival, which was now commanded by Captain Thomas Matthews. Whether or not the tables were turned in subsequent races does not appear, but the two towns long remained rivals, with races between one or another of their vessels becoming almost weekly occurrences. Barnstable had another vessel at this time, a sloop called *Emerald*, and Yarmouth's second string packet was *Eagle Flight*. If we may believe the vainglorious strains of a nameless Barnstable bard, *Emerald* could beat not only *Eagle Flight* but the redoubtable *Commodore Hull* as well. Here is the ditty which makes up in sprightliness what it may lack in truth:

> The *Commodore Hull* she sails so dull
> It makes her crew look sour;
> The *Eagle Flight* she is out of sight
> Less than half an hour.
> But the bold old *Emerald* takes delight
> To beat the *Commodore* and the *Flight*.

One point the commendable bias of the poet forbade him to mention. *Emerald,* so loudly lauded, had originally belonged in Yarmouth, and having grown old in the service, had been sold to Barnstable. Nor need we suppose that many five-dollar bills found their way from Yarmouth to Barnstable pockets to pay wagers won by the 'bold old Emerald.'

Dennis was an active town, too, in packeting, with Captain Orren Sears, of East Dennis, and his schooner *David Porter* well up in the front rank. The calmness and skill of Captain Sears were well demonstrated in a famous gale that struck the Cape from the southeast in the fall of 1869. Beginning as a hard blow, it steadily increased until it approached the strength of a hurricane. Trees were blown down; roads were turned into rivers. It caught Captain Sears and *David Porter* off Plymouth, but so far north that there was no hope of his being able to beat into harbor there. The jib halliards parted; the fore gaff and the main boom broke, one after the other, leaving the schooner under bare poles. Nothing daunted, Captain Sears scudded before it, edging in bit by bit as he got a chance, and finally, working her up under a lee, he beached her on a strip of sand not far from Scituate. When the tide ebbed, he discharged his passengers dry shod. *David Porter* floated off on the next tide, her hull as sound as ever—none the worse for the terrific beating she had taken.

But Dennis, always a seagoing town until some years ago, when it became the theatrical center of the Cape (second only to Provincetown), had plenty of other packets and packet captains besides Orren Sears and *David Porter.* From the days of Captain Nathaniel Hall, who was prospering just after the Revolution, up to 1874 when *David Porter* lowered her flag for good, the town carried on a brisk packet trade with Boston. There were Judah and Jacob Sears of East Dennis, who in 1820 were joint commanders of the schooner *Polly and Betsy,* named for their respective wives. And there were two other particularly celebrated men in the business, Captains Dean Sears and Joseph H. Sears, also of East Dennis. Both of them gave up the command of their packets, *David Porter* and *Combine,* to become masters of ships on deepwater.

And herein lay one of the less immediate but very important results of packeting: it opened the eyes of young Cape men to the roadsteads of the world. The humble, necessary packets served as a primary school for seafaring, and like all good schools, they furnished their pupils with the incentive to fare farther and reach higher, until many a youngster who began his career coiling halliards on a Dennis packet, finished on the quarter-deck of a full-rigged ship, bringing tea and silk from Penang or linseed and jute from Calcutta. The late Mr. Edgar Jones, of West Barnstable, who was in his day mate of such fine ships as *Radiant, Comet,* and *Royal Arch,* told me that his first desire to go to sea came to him when, as a boy, he watched the sloop *Mail* leaving her dock at the foot of Scudder's Lane and heading for Boston. And how, in truth, could it have been otherwise? What boy could sail into Boston Harbor on *Combine,* or *Emerald,* or *Commodore Hull* and there see the spars of tall ships cutting the sky with the intricate tracery of their rigging, without longing to join the ranks of the conquerors and command such ships on voyages that would take him across four oceans and into half the harbors of the world?

No town could have been less favorably endowed by Nature for the packet business than the proud town of Brewster. There was nothing anywhere along its shore line that could even remotely suggest a harbor —not even a creek in the marsh big enough for a schooner to lie in. But the citizens, undismayed, went ahead with the business, harbor or no harbor. For the ten years between 1820 and 1830 Captain Joseph Crosby and his successors used to bring their schooner *Republic* to anchor off a wide sandy cove near Point of Rocks and let her ground gently on the flats with the ebb tide. Then the passengers and cargo went over the side into wagons and were driven ashore as comfortably as on the highway— more comfortably, in fact. In writing reminiscently of her early years, Augusta Mayo, daughter of one of the principal Brewster packet owners, says,

> We had great enjoyment in riding down to the packet [Lafayette] with Father at low water, where he had to go frequently for goods in the summer. We would drive up to the vessel's side, climb a ladder, and go on board. While the wagon was being loaded with goods from the hold, we children would go down into the cabin where Captain [John] Myrick would treat us to pilot bread from the table drawer.

In spite of this unorthodox method of making port, the packet business grew so fast (owing partly to Brewster's being the port for Chatham and Harwich passengers as well as her own) that about 1830, when business of all kinds was booming on the Cape, owners felt justified in building a breakwater which gave the town a makeshift harbor and a dock to tie up to. Thenceforth it was plain sailing. In 1833, thanks to these improved facilities, the schooner *Patriot* made forty-two round trips—not bad when we realize that about 1 December all the vessels were pulled up for the winter. Her profit was about $400 a season over and above all expenses.

But even before the breakwater was built Captain Crosby and *Republic* had rivals in the business. The old sloop *Fame,* which by 1824 was well along in years, was brightened up during the winter by her Captain, Solomon Foster, preparatory to resuming business in the spring. Her owners, following a custom that was common in the business, suggested that Captain Nathaniel Lincoln should take joint command of her, but he refused, and Foster had to go it alone. He did so well with her that the next season she was fitted out with more bunks and mattresses and everything was done to put her, in the language of her owners 'in prime order for the accommodation and convenience of passengers.'

But not every packet could make the same claim by any means. Young Albert Smith, who in 1847 made the trip from Boston to Orleans in the leaky old schooner *President Washington*, has left a lively account of the voyage, the more interesting as he was only fifteen years old at the time. She cast off from her dock in Boston in a flat calm at 9:00 o'clock of a July morning, drifted a few miles with the tide, and anchored. In an hour or so a breeze sprang up which, though dead ahead, was better than swinging idly at anchor. She set sail again, beat down Harbor as far as George's Island, and anchored once more. Apparently, windward work was not *President Washington*'s strong point. While waiting for the wind to shift, the captain obligingly had a boat lowered so the passengers might while away the time by rowing over to the Island and having a look at the castle. By suppertime they were back on board, and toward sunset the anchor was weighed and the voyage resumed. Only ten bunks were available for the twenty-five passengers, but they obligingly slept in shifts, one group turning in early and sleeping until midnight, then rolling out and finishing the night on deck while the second shift crawled into their beds. They woke in the morning (those who had been asleep) to find that they were off Cohasset, seventeen miles (and twenty-four hours) from Boston. But the tedium of this day was enlivened by a chowder made of five fish which one of the passengers caught between Cohasset and Plymouth. After another night of turn and turn about in the bunks, they arrived off Orleans, but the tide being low, they had to anchor off the flats and row into Rock Harbor in the tender. So ended a seventy-mile voyage that had taken forty-eight hours!

The monotony of such a trip as this was bad for the business. Even ministerial patiences were tried at such times. There is the story of Captain Edward Gorham, of Yarmouth, who was taking his schooner in light airs, dead ahead, through the narrow, twisting channel that connects Yarmouth with the Bay. His emotions may be imagined; tack followed tack with scarcely perceptible progress, but all hands had to be polite because Mr. Simpkins, the minister, was on board and though no sailor, he was, like all ministers, a figure to be revered. He watched at first in bewilderment, and finally in exasperation, the painfully slow progress of the vessel, until, man of God though he was, his patience was gone. He approached the captain and said in a pompous voice: 'Captain Gorham, why do you zig-zag back and forth in this aimless fashion? There lies the channel; why do you not sail right along it?'

'Go below, you damn fool!' snapped the captain.

Later, after he had calmed down, Captain Gorham may have been sorry for his brusqueness, justifiable though it was, for part of the business of a packet captain was to keep his passengers happy in all weathers. A past master at this art was Zoeth Rich, of Truro, captain of *Postboy*. *Postboy* is said to have been the finest packet in the Bay, her cabin finished in bird's-eye maple and adorned with silk draperies. However this may be, it was the captain's geniality quite as much as *Postboy*'s luxurious fittings that kept the passengers happy. The same urbane qualities that made Captain Rich an immensely popular figure on shore robbed long stretches of calm in the Bay of much of their tedium.

Another royal entertainer among the genial company of packet captains was Simeon Higgins, of Orleans, master of the sloop *De Wolfe*. It was no accident that led him to become a well-known hotel proprietor after he retired from the sea. He was merely continuing to give his genius the true bent, and to exercise among his guests on shore the same genial qualities that had charmed his passengers on *De Wolfe*.

But captains had plenty of assistance in keeping life pleasant. If *David Porter* was becalmed off Duxbury, a veteran of foreign voyages was pretty sure to be on board with tales of outwitting a Britisher in Canton or giving the slip to Malay pirates in the China Sea. The squire would pompously admit that it took a smart man to get ahead of a Yankee, and there would follow jingoistic reminiscences of Commodore Raggett and the War of 1812; for few Cape sailors who had tried to leave port during that dreary period had failed to encounter that celebrated officer of His Majesty's Navy. Perhaps a retired shipmaster would be on board who was now serving as Representative to the General Court. He would enlighten the company in affairs of State and the ways of governments until the schooner docked at Central Wharf and each man went his way, the squire having practiced democracy and the humbler citizen having broken bread with the great. The fare was $1.50 for the round trip; meals were twenty-five cents. But after one or two experiments most passengers wisely took their own provisions with them!

Another way in which the captains made themselves and their commands popular was by turning themselves into errand boys for their neighbors. Edmund Jarvis, of Orleans, the most casual of a necessarily casual group, was particularly accommodating in this regard—partly, it may be, because his little sloop *Nancy* was a good deal more of a tramp than most, putting in at Plymouth, Sandwich, Barnstable or any other town along the Bay shore where there was a chance to sell some cargo. His staples from Boston were rum, molasses, potash, lime, indigo, tobacco, sea coal, and now and then a passenger. Much of this merchandise was on order, no doubt, but Captain Jarvis was a trader at heart and never hesitated to take on a part of his cargo as a speculation. He it was who on one occasion bought an umbrella in Boston for an Orleans lady, and again put in at Plymouth to pick up two chairs for another neighbor. A Barnstable citizen (his name, fortunately perhaps, is not recorded) asked Captain Matthias Hinckley to get a jug of rum for him in Boston. He was the first man on the wharf as the captain's famous sloop, *Mail,* appeared off the Sandy Neck lighthouse on the return trip; and no sooner was she made fast than he jumped on board and confronted the captain.

'Did you do that, —er, —er, —little errand for me, Captain?' he asked.

'If you mean rum, say rum,' roared Hinckley: 'There's your jug.'

When it came to actual performance, though, the laurels went to Captain Whitman Freeman, of Provincetown, and his lovely schooner *Northern Light.* Her graceful lines and lofty spars were a match for even the famous Georges Bankers; and under Captain Freeman she held to a schedule of three round trips a week between Provincetown and Boston, a performance unrivaled in the annals of Cape Cod sailing packets. After a brilliant career on the Bay she was sold to parties in San Francisco and was lost in the Straits of Magellan on the long voyage out.

It was steam, of course, in one form or another that tolled the knell of the sailing packets. The beginning of the end came as early as 1848 when the first locomotive puffed into Sandwich. Sandwich had had a lively packet business for years with close races between Captain George Atkins of West Sandwich, who commanded *Henry Clay,* and Captain Calvin Fish, of the village, in the sloop *Sarah.* Another man who was active in the business was Captain Roland Gibbs of the schooner *Cabinet,* and the sloop *Osceola.* These men hung on after the arrival of the railroad, but fewer and fewer passengers graced their decks and they had to content themselves with cargoes of cordwood for the Boston market.

A few enthusiasts tried to answer the challenge of the railroad by starting steam packets—one of them, with Sandwich as her home port, was hopefully named *Acorn,* and two others, both of Provincetown, were *George Shattuck* and *Longfellow.* These, and perhaps one or two more, splashed back and forth between the Cape and Boston in a vain but valiant attempt to keep the business alive. The towns between Sandwich and Provincetown had a few more good years because the march of the rails was slow; it was 1873 before they reached Provincetown; but other changes, too, contributed to the ruin of the business. As early as 1840 the salt from the Turks Islands mines was crowding out that made locally by evaporating sea water; farming had long since given way to seafaring, so no more Cape onions or flax were unloaded on Boston docks. The packets, that had been kept so trim and shipshape during the busy years of their prosperity, grew dingy and neglected. They sailed halfheartedly if they sailed at all. The business was stone dead in Yarmouth in 1871, yet had outlasted its old rival, Barnstable, by ten years. The lower Cape, as has been said, hung on a little longer, but even there the end was in sight long before owners would admit it. Seafaring men are a strange mixture of conservative and pioneer. Blind to the inevitable, Wellfleet and Provincetown captains sailed their packets stubbornly until even they had to realize that the end had come.

The old vessels themselves, their usefulness as packets ended, fared variously. Some spent their last years as fishermen; one was sold as a pilot boat in New Orleans; the tragic end of *Northern Light* has already been mentioned. Another, on her way south, went down in a collision off Hatteras. One by one, they faded from sight, and a lively and often prosperous epoch in the annals of the Cape was at an end.

It may have been observed that nothing has been said about any of the South Side packets, which had their home ports in Falmouth, Cotuit, Hyannis, South Yarmouth, Harwich, and Chatham, and from the east side of Orleans and Eastham as well. The reason for this omission is that, barring accidents, these vessels were freighters pure and simple. If a citizen of Chatham or Harwich or Hyannis had business in Boston, he watched for a flag to fly or a barrel to be raised on the nearest of a scattering line of poles set along the high wooded ridge that forms the backbone of the Cape. This was a signal for South Siders that a packet would sail before long, and the traveler packed his bag, drove across the Cape to the appropriate Bay village, and embarked in comfort on a passenger carrier. This is how it came about that the vessels of his own village had nothing but freight to carry. Furthermore, Boston, not New York, was the metropolis for the Cape. A hundred Cape Codders headed for Boston for one that had business in New York.

Our song of the packets, then, has been sung; not a grand opera number, it is true, but a cheerful lay of a busy and prosperous time, a ballad, too, of a day that some of us find it pleasant to contemplate.

At the wharf, Pasque Island

Leaving the wharf at Pasque Island about 1916

Hauled out on the marine railway at Fairhaven, Massachusetts
From a photograph owned by William H. Tripp, New Bedford

Wooden hull screw steam tug *J. T. Sherman*

Enchanted Voyage

BY ALEXANDER CROSBY BROWN

THE writing of memoirs is a privilege, usually reserved for those of advanced age and wide experience. It is a moot point, however, just when enough of both has been acquired to justify the recording of past events. A back-log of years is certainly a help, for it automatically reduces the number of contemporary critics to challenge the recital, but meanwhile, memories wane.

Possibly I have no business invading a field for which neither time nor performance have qualified me. But, since the following brief travelogue is neither world-shaking nor profound, I may perhaps be excused for the portentousness of taking pen in hand to jot down some events of my youth, the details of which are dim enough as it is.

From the time I was very small, it was the custom of our family to leave Philadelphia and its environs to stew in their own juices while we embarked on an annual hegira that brought us to the more salubrious climate of a small island southwest of Cape Cod. Since this happened at the beginning of every summer, I naturally cannot now remember details as having taken place on any one particular trip. But I will attempt to record an 'odyssey' of the Brown family between the Main Line and Pasque Island, Massachusetts, as it might have taken place, say, in the year 1913, at which time I was eight years old and probably fresh. The way travelled seemed natural enough at the time, but today, many of the means of conveyance then involved are as thoroughly dead and gone as the dodo. This was just prior to the general use of the automobile and, looking back, one is appalled at the inconvenience and expense by which countless families such as ours transplanted themselves annually in order to be more uncomfortable in a maritime or mountain environment.

Our Mecca, Pasque Island, known to countless cruising yachtsmen as a God-forsaken blot of land, is, on the contrary, the most beautiful island in the world. I say this advisedly, having since compared at first hand

Tahiti, Samoa, Bali, Maderia, Capri, and (lest Sam Morison point out a sin of omission) Mount Desert. It is true that Pasque's mile-long boulder-strewn terrain is shaded at one point only by a cluster of half a dozen moth-eaten pines, that Robinson's Hole is branded by Eldridge's *Coast Pilot* as one of the meanest little harbors on the coast, and that the freak set of the currents sweeping to a ledge known as the Graveyard has caused the destruction of many worthy vessels. The critics of Mother Nature's handiwork have not, however, at the age of eight experienced the thrill of 'treasure' hunting on restless Cobbley Beach, caught cunners from the bridge across the tidal creek, sighted wild deer in a West End swamp, or nightly sneaked out of bed to look for the friendly gleam of Gay Head Light's slow cycle of three white flashes followed by a red.

Pasque is one in the chain of Elizabeth Islands which point westward from Woods Hole at the elbow of Cape Cod to divide Vineyard Sound from Buzzards Bay. In 1602 Bartholomew Gosnold, Gent., of Falmouth, England, first set foot ashore in the Western Hemisphere on the Elizabeth Islands, as he called them, and their names were as familiar to me as a Mother Goose rhyme, for one of the first jingles learned by heart in our family was:

> Cuttyhunk, Penikese,
> Nashawena, Pasquenese,
> Naushon, Weepecket,
> Uncatena and Nonamesset.

The names look appalling in print, but actually sound very musical. Pasque Island, originally called Pasachanest by the Indians and termed Pasquenese for the purpose of the rhyme, lies in the center of the group, about ten miles from Woods Hole, fourteen from New Bedford and seven from Martha's Vineyard. In the late 1860's some sportsmen bought the island and incorporated the Pasque Island Fishing Club whose avowed purpose was the catching of striped bass, then plentiful in those waters. I still shudder when I think of the club's engraved stationery: a fat bass serenely swimming over a ribbon bearing the legend, 'To see me, drop a line.'

My grandfather was one of the early members of this club and was followed by my father and all his brothers and sisters and their husbands. My generation was bolstered by countless cousins as well as by the cousins, uncles, aunts, mothers and fathers of other members. Each family owned rooms in one of three barracks-like weather-worn buildings at the east end of the island. By day, the older generation fished for bass from stands built out over the surf, played tennis, or sailed their boats in the Hole. A

Pasque Island Club Houses looking across the creek

Pasque Island Club members in the Smoking Room about 1895
From a photograph by John Stettinius

wagon made the circuit of the island to deposit the fishermen in the morning and to pick them up again in the evening. And there was much ceremony at the fish house in the weighing-in and recording of the day's catch. If Father had been lucky, he might give us a taste of his daily 'tipple' of port before supper. This formal meal concluded, the male members of the club drew lots for the choice fishing stands to be used the next day, then withdrew to the smoking room to the stimulating pastime of dominoes, chess, or cards which they played with their hats on until bedtime. Sunday nights we all sang hymns.

Children were restricted from most of these activities, but there were plenty of other things to occupy us and I know of no more exciting place for the young. The pleasures of anticipating the trip to Pasque were in my case sometimes sufficiently keen to produce nervous indigestion and the resultant parental warning that I might have to be left behind.

Well, finally June thirtieth would roll around, the trunks would have been dispatched the day before, and the big moment would be about to begin.

There was undoubtedly a 'Clarence Day-esque' quality to the arrival of our family and faithful retainers at the railroad station. Already Father would have discovered that something vitally needed had presumably been left behind. It would, of course, turn up in my brother's trunk ('where that stupid new maid had put it') when we finally reached the island and unpacked. But meanwhile, Maurice Hayes, the coachman, would receive explicit instructions for sending on the article as soon as the horses got him back home.

Although it was fully an hour before the New York express was due (the family were believers in being on what was invariably called 'the safe side'), there would be innumerable details about the tickets; the baggage had to be counted, checked and then recounted and, of course, magazines and candy had to be obtained for consumption on the trip. I remember the magazines as being for grown-ups and thus uniformly dull; and during the entire two-hour train ride to Jersey City I would be permitted only two of those round Peters chocolates wrapped like silver dollars, with the warning that more would make me sick on the boat.

Finally, after an eternity of squirming in the green plush seat and being permitted to play with only one or two of the most accessible toys in the top of my straw suitcase, the train would come panting into the Jersey City depot. At this point, the excitement really began. As we were lowered off the train, our hands were secured in vice-like parental grips so that we would not get lost in the crowd bent on getting down the platform and across to the ferry in nothing flat. Railroad station and ferry house were in the same enormous building and I remember that provocative smell of soft coal smoke, wet wood, salt air and horse manure as we crossed the apron and entered the glass doors on the ferry. I would have liked to remain on the fantail to see what happened when the boat started up, but by the time we had been shepherded to the upper deck, she was under way.

This thrilling prelude to the larger navigation to follow would be over quickly. Other ferries seemed to miss us narrowly as they passed at breakneck speed, and there was much hooting of whistles on the river. I remember being intrigued with our fellow-passengers and pitying the poor dray horses confined to the semi-darkness of the deck below. A dear old lady who wished to speak with me on a trifling matter involving the donation of a few cents for coffee, would find that Father had something to say and move on. My life was too sheltered then for me to appreciate a very drunken sister when I saw one.

Suddenly the damp cavern that was the slip on the Manhattan side gaped before us. Not appreciating the effect of currents in the North River, I was surprised in the docking maneuver at the rashness or incompetence of the ferry captain. He seemed to derive a perverted pleasure from bumping into the sides of the slip several times before the boat was secured. I claim today that my frequently expressed concern for the pilot's ability to locate the right slip was natural curiosity, Freudian interpretations to the contrary.

There was the same mad rush to get off the boat as there had been to board it. Father anchored us to a pile of luggage while he located transportation. Motor taxies were common then, but I do not believe that my family considered them quite dependable or even safe and, being allergic to such new-fangled gadgets, Father usually rounded up hansom cabs. Here our party would perforce be divided since one cab could not take all, and I would experience a twinge of anxiety lest in as losable a place as New York I might never see my mother or my brother again. The jolting ride over cobblestones on the lower West Side seemed particularly hazardous in such an eccentric contraption, since a driver was nowhere to be seen and apparently the horse could do as he pleased. Once under way, the only means of communication with the driver (I was assured there was one) was to stick one's head out of the window and call back to him on his lofty and unsheltered perch.

Finally we would pull up before Pier Forty, North River, and in an instant the cab would be surrounded by an avalanche of shouting Negro porters with gleaming silver buttons on their uniforms. Their caps, I recall, were suggestive of those of Civil War snipers. Two or more porters, as required, took immediate possession of our luggage as it was checked off the cab and whisked it away inside the head of the pier. Meanwhile, our other hansom cab had arrived and, reunited, our family started to board what I thought was the epitome of the naval architect's genius, the then twenty-one-year-old steamboat *New Hampshire* which, with her 300-foot sister-ship, the *Maine*, maintained over-night service between New York and New Bedford for the New England Steamship Company. Alas, both are gone today: one to the scrap heap and the other, a victim of a winter storm on Execution Rocks.

To my mind, these noble vessels with their furnishings of Victorian opulence put our poor house and all within it to shame—a view not likely entertained either by my family or even the owners of the boats, for the New Bedford Line was a step-child using old vessels not wanted on the Fall River or their other more fashionable services. But travellers today who board the stuffy (though air-conditioned) so-called sleepers for their journey to the Cape, will never know the comfortable luxuries of a trip on one of those night-boats. The privilege of viewing Long Island Sound by night is now reserved for yachts which get becalmed on the way home and a few freighters kept up late by waning commercial necessity.

Having crossed the gangway, inevitably tripping over the high, well-polished, brass doorsill on entering the main deck saloon, the final goal was attained and we were on board and ready to go.

Not only in point of splendor, but in size, was the New Bedford boat as noteworthy a creation as I had then encountered. Even the enormous brass keys which Father obtained from the purser were significant—keys which must inevitably open one of the stateroom doors which stretched along corridors of infinity before us. Meanwhile, flight after flight of richly carpeted stairs had to be mounted and more corridors traversed until at last the porter stood before that very special door which he opened with a rattley flourish, at the same time cupping his hand discreetly to receive the tip.

There was then no time to survey the snug apartment properly; that could come later; now we had to get right out on the foredeck below the wheel-house to see what was going on. Once on board, we were accorded more liberty than had been permitted on the train and ferry and proceeded forthwith to a point of vantage. It was, of course, a three-ring circus. It was patently impossible to see at the same time the trunks and cargo rolling up the fore gangway, the lighter unloading across the slip onto the neighboring pier, and the shipping in the river beyond. All this, and keeping an eye out for acquaintances among the new arrivals, kept my brother and me on the jump. I remember being disturbed by the fact that the harbor water was so dirty and full of broken crates and garbage. And I really was alarmed when a wise guy pretended to throw me overboard, an inferior joke of irresistible appeal to some so-called adults.

Meanwhile, the tempo of activity on the *New Hampshire* would be mounting. New arrivals hit the foredeck every minute and spaces at the rail filled up. Since transportation between the mainland and Pasque Island was effected only once or twice a week by chartered tug, there were bound to be other club members and their families on the *New Hampshire* for this particular trip. With whoops of joy we soon recognized some cousins approaching and, a minute later, Uncle Artie.

My bachelor uncle, passionately adored by his countless small nieces and nephews, was, thought I, the wisest person in the world. At least he must have had a preternatural patience to withstand the battery of questions we all put to him, ranging in scope from, '*Now* when is the boat going to go?' to 'What's that man trying to do?'

I recall that invariably Uncle Artie provided a plausible answer, although more than once I was admonished not to ask so many *foolish* questions and was reminded of the predicament of Kipling's Elephant's Child. I remember being at a loss to discriminate between approved and foolish questions and must have shut up for as long as half a minute as a result of it while I mentally compared my own relatives with those of the hero of the great grey-green greasy Limpopo River. In all, I considered myself fortunate not to have within my family circle a hairy baboon uncle or a broad hippopotamus aunt to spank me for 'satiable curiosity.

Pretty soon a steward would start his rounds of the decks ringing a bell and calling, 'All ashore that's going ashore!' And at five P.M. sharp the deep-throated steam whistle would cut loose with three long blasts. I disliked this noise very much and remembered vividly a previous year when I had been obliged to cry as a result of it. I also remembered asking Father to speak to the captain to request the ceremony be omitted as a special favor to me, but to no avail.

The noise over, the *New Hampshire* would gather way imperceptibly, the pier would slide slowly backwards along her hull, and the voyage began.

New York City as seen from the Hudson River in the late afternoon of a clear summer's day is an inspiring sight. Once out in the stream and headed south, the *New Hampshire* skirted the shore at about three hundred yards off the pier ends. Here Uncle Artie really shone. He would point out and identify the towers of Manhattan: the Singer Building, the Equitable, and of course the brand-new spire of the 60-story Woolworth Building. But we were more interested in the ships a-loading for the globe's proverbial four corners. I cannot remember any of them today, but undoubtedly on this trip or another we saw a giant, four-stack Cunarder like the *Lusitania*, banana boats of the Great White Fleet, four and five-masted coasting schooners, and even an occasional square-rigger, not to mention lesser craft—countless puffing tugs neatly managing unwieldy carfloats, the many-windowed ferries, and glistening white steamboats such as our own. Side-wheel propulsion was no rarity then, and many ferries and steamboats were surmounted by walking beams, their paddles giving them a waddling pomposity. I can recall the distant hum of the city sounding across the water and the fragrant smell of coffee as we passed the Munson Line piers.

Soon we were abreast of the tip of Manhattan and changing course to round the Battery and come into the East River. A fresh breeze from the southwest meeting the falling tide raised a slight chop. Here, naturally, we had to cross over to the starboard rail to see Governors Island and the Statue of Liberty and then mount to the top deck to be ready to go under the Brooklyn Bridge. My grandmother's house was on Brooklyn Heights and undoubtedly Uncle Artie pointed out nearby Grace Church spire, but I cannot remember ever seeing it.

The navigation under the East River bridges was thrilling. It seemed a certainty that the *New Hampshire's* masts would be snapped off, but, miraculously, there was always room to spare, and nothing impeded our steady progress. Uncle Artie obliged with the names of all the bridges and I could not realize that the gossamer-like threads that supported them were cables a foot and more in diameter.

By the time that we had reached Blackwell's Island with the Brooklyn Navy Yard well astern, it would be supper time, but we would resist all parental suggestions to go inside until we had passed Hell Gate. As we approached this blatantly profane landmark, mysterious doings went on in the roped-off portion of the foredeck about the brass-topped capstan. The *New Hampshire* had old-fashioned stock anchors and one of them was invariably catted and swung out ready to let go at a moment's notice in case the swirling tide race put the steamer out of control, or the engine failed at a crucial moment. Once the danger was past, we would reluctantly admit that there was now nothing much more to see outdoors and let ourselves be led off to wash for supper.

In those days, the boats carried a small string orchestra to compete with the rattling of the crockery, and the dining saloon was a cheerful place. All I can presently remember about the meal was the quantity of small, thick dishes necessary to complete it and that supper concluded with macaroons and a sort of super Neapolitan ice cream in which the black specks showed in the vanilla.

The captain and his officers ate at the head table and, since the captain was obviously the most important individual on board, I felt that my family would do well to cultivate his acquaintance, elevate its social caste, and afford me the opportunity of enjoying a personally conducted tour of the engine room. Every year I passionately wanted to see what made the boat go, but somehow never made it until I was too old to have it matter much. I remember hearing that even then, timorous people desired their cabins to be located at some distance from the machinery casings lest the boiler 'blow up.' Perennially we were spared this excitement.

A very brief tour of the deck was permitted after supper, but it was now cold and windy and there were only distant, and to us unidentifiable, lights on the horizon. By this time I would be worn out, even though rebellious at the thought of bed. One intriguing feature of the New Bedford boats, always good for a few extra minutes at the end of the day, was the news stand featuring a variety of desirable objects which I was erroneously advised I did not want. Being permitted one small purchase, it would be a toss-up between a cheap replica of the Statue of Liberty, or a cheaper unhollowed sailboat model, until finally I discovered a fascinating gadget which I must own. This consisted of a round box with a celluloid top through which a magnetized spindle projected. Small snakes cut out of bright metal would be attracted to the spindle and wriggle briskly around it when one gave the shaft a spin. I believe I obtained one of these snake outfits on every trip, but they must have soon become lost or broken, for today I can only associate them with the New Bedford boat.

Finally led off to bed, I found compensatory excitement in undressing in the tiny cabin. I regretted that my brother, being older, was awarded the upper berth. When the lights went out, all the mysterious shipboard noises, of which I had previously been unaware, asserted themselves. The cabin walls creaked, the door rattled a rhythmical tattoo and, outside the peculiar wooden-slatted shutter, the waves splashed and danced. There was a slight motion to the ship and my brother and I prayed that it would not be rough off the Point Judith we had heard the family discussing, the nemesis of even cast-iron stomachs. For then, alas, the china container under the bed would be broken out to play a tragic rôle.

When I woke up, the early morning sun was streaming in the window. There had been some anxious moments during the night, I recalled with pain, but on this trip catastrophe was averted by lying flat on my back and holding on to the side of the bed. We were soon dressed and out on deck, but by this time the *New Hampshire* had passed Butler's Flats and was well on her way up New Bedford harbor.

We had to hurry through breakfast, for there was much to be done ashore in New Bedford before leaving for Pasque. Across from the *New Hampshire's* berth, the Nantucket boat, the side-wheeler *Gay Head*, was already impetuously blowing her whistle as signal of imminent departure.

Our suitcases repacked, we would make our way as quickly as possible along corridors already festooned with piles of used bed linen and descend to the door leading out to the gangway. Here it would be my privilege to deposit the brass stateroom key in a carpet covered box so labeled for the purpose. A brief glance backwards, a stumble over the same brass door sill, and we would say farewell to the New Bedford boat, now metamorphosed into the New York boat, until the sad retracing of the journey in the late summer.

New Bedford was full of attractions. Next to the whaling museum below Johnnycake Hill, where the family would take us if there was time, I enjoyed going with Father on his rounds of the hardware and fishing tackle shops on William and Purchase Streets. The discussion of size of hook and weight of sinker made me feel very grown up, and Father promised that soon I would be big enough to have a proper rod and reel of my own. There were many other things to do and look at, and the bustle of Union Street with merchandise piled up on the sidewalks was different from anything I had ever seen in the John Wannamaker section of Philadelphia. Finally, after obtaining still another pair of sneakers (on Pasque at least one pair was always out drying), we would make our way down from the center of town, past Briggs and Beckman's sail loft, to Merrill's Wharf.

New Bedford was still a whaling port in 1913. On both the New Bedford and Fairhaven sides of the Acushnet River whaling barks like the veterans *Andrew Hicks, Morning Star*, or *Charles W. Morgan* were moored to the many wharves that projected into the harbor. The smell of whale oil and the ring of the cooper's mallet were in the air, and Uncle Artie explained to us about 'greasy luck' and 'blo-o-ws.'

The steam tug *J. T. Sherman* was already along the south side of Merrill's Wharf opposite the coal loading pier, and the trickle of steam that came out of her escape pipe abaft the funnel showed she was all set to go. I was a little disappointed that the *S. C. Hart* was not the one to take us on the last fourteen-mile lap of our journey. Not that there was much difference between the little vessels; both were wooden-hulled harbor tugs with gilded eagles poised on their pilot house roofs and both would roll their hearts out in the usual Buzzards Bay seaway. Either one of them might be chartered for the weekly trip out to the island. The 73-foot *Hart* was three feet shorter than the *Sherman* and, having been built in 1896, was seven years older, but was only a slightly less palatial craft. Both hulls were painted black, with red superstructure on the *Hart* and green on the *Sherman*. But my preference for the *Hart* was not based on outside appearance. I naturally would not have understood then and I know of no one to ask now, but apparently the engine of the *Hart* was a compound, steeple job with a lot of crossheads, pistons, tail rods, and connecting rods flying around in plain view of the engine room door. It is true that for an eight-year-old boy, the *Sherman's* reciprocating engine was pretty exciting to watch, but it was harder to see below the varnished wooden-slatted cylinders, and apparently not as much was going on in the engine room. I pity the present generation of boys who must grow up with only memories of dull and uninspiring turbines or diesels, whose neat and efficient casings conceal all moving parts.

By eleven o'clock the trunks and provisions would have been stowed in a neat pile on the towboat's fantail and covered with a tarpaulin, the last of the Pasque Island clan arrived, and the *J. T. Sherman* slipped her lines from the well-worn bollards and headed down the harbor. The *Sherman* was not famous for her passenger accommodation, but canvas camp stools already liberally sprinkled with grit were provided on the upper deck between the lifeboats, and sometimes the captain let us sit on the leather-covered settee in the pilot house and watch him spin the wheel. Fire buckets stowed in a rack around the funnel were available for other purposes in case it got too rough. The power of suggestion being what it is, I avoided looking directly at them as much as possible.

A complete tour of the tug was not a lengthy process and, after two or three of them, I began to get impatient to have the voyage over. In the middle of Buzzards Bay a spar buoy with an old broom tied to it indicated the half way mark and, once that was passed, we began to be able to pick out familiar landmarks on the island. First the cliffs on the north shore showed up and then the lone cluster of pine trees on the east end detached itself from the surrounding highland.

Pretty soon Robinson's Hole opened up, and we could see clean through to the Vineyard beyond and note the small flotilla of island cat boats and sailing dories (called 'peanuts') bobbing at their moorings. The tide was low and, as we approached the Hole, the jagged point of Peaked Rock was visible by the eel grass on the west side of the channel. A minute later we were abreast of the club houses and could see the white plume of smoke followed by the sharp crack of the signal cannon. This little brass gun had been salvaged from the wreck of a palatial schooner yacht, the *Tidalwave*, claimed by the Graveyard in 1891, and custom dictated it should salute the approach of visiting craft.

By this time a knot of people had gathered at the long pier and the wagon was clattering down the road leading to it. With slackened speed the *Sherman* nosed her way in, lines were passed, and in another minute were were alongside and scrambling up the gangplank. Utopia was gained.

The New England Double Enders

BY DAVID CABOT

ONE rainy afternoon in mid-November I wandered into the boat yard and was agreeably surprised to find a group of local yachtsmen sitting around the pot-bellied stove, their feet up on coils of line and nail kegs, filling the air with pipe smoke and strong talk. I sat down and applied myself to the task of sorting out the cross-threads of salty conversation. It soon became evident that the subject was sea-going craft, and one man was trying to argue that his superbly constructed light racing craft was as good as the best of them in anything short of a hurricane, provided you knew when to shorten sail, but he was generally outvoted by the others, who wanted a heavy sea boat so that they would never have to worry about carrying away 'light racing gear' in a blow. Many types were proposed and discussed: the Colin Archer boats, copied from the Norwegian ketches and cutters, the British and French pilot cutters, the Brixham trawlers, the Arab dhows, and various others, but after a while I was struck by the fact that here was a group, most of whom had hardly ever left New England, whose discussion totally excluded the multitude of types developed through years of experience for the very waters in which they spent all their time afloat. This preoccupation with foreign craft was probably due mainly to the extensive publicity that they have received, while our own, being just 'common local boats,' have been sadly neglected.

A great part of what has been written about New England boats has concerned the Gloucester schooners, the fishermen's races, driving home with water seven feet over the lee rail, topmasts snapping like popcorn, and all the rest, which parallels the clippers for sheer romance. But what of the boats in the days before the 'Golden Age'? The subject as a whole would require an immense amount of research, and a reasonable way to divide it is to draw the line between the double enders and the square sterned boats.

A double ender is any boat whose stern is pointed like the bow, the best known example being the canoe. Before 1800 there were two distinct types of boat growing up parallel to one another on the New England Coast: the double ender and the square sterned craft. These latter, of which the dogbodies and heeltappers are examples, gradually overtook and then overshadowed the double enders as the clamor for speed became more and more overbearing. This in turn was caused by a mounting demand for fresh fish and the consequent decline in the percentage of salt fish, by the great profits that fell to those who could get the first fish to a starved market, and by the sheer stubborn pride of the Yankee skippers, who hated to be beaten even by a better boat. Thus the wholesome square sterned fisherman of an earlier day grew into the slim, heavily sparred, light capacity racing fishermen of Gloucester and Boston fame around the end of the nineteenth century.

A century earlier, however, it was a different story. There was a large number of double enders, probably well over half of the fleet, for their seaworthiness and comfort was something not to be belied. One advantage of the double ender is that when running in a following sea, the seas unless very large do not lift the stern and send the bow rooting they way they will do with a counter or transom sterned boat which has her bulk down closer to the water. Rather the seas will be split and will rush on harmlessly past. Another result of this quality of relatively small reserve buoyancy in the stern, is that when the bow is lifted by a wave, it is not impeded in its rise by any pressure of the stern on the water aft, and hence there is less danger of solid water rolling aboard over the bow.

The surface of the subject has been scratched by two books from which I draw a good part of my information,[1] but the rest has had to come from personal interviews, old copies of *Yachting* and *Rudder* magazines, rare old books and small pamphlets. The list of types (complete to my knowledge) including only boats primarily propelled by sail, is as follows: the Quoddy boats, the carry-away boats, the Hampton Whalers, the Crotch Island boats, the Isles of Shoals boats, the Chebacco boats, the pinkies, the Martha's Vineyard-Noman's Land boats, the Block Island boats, and, including Nova Scotia as the logical extension of the New England coast, the Tancook Whalers as well. I will not try to duplicate material which has already been published in books on these craft except where it is the only material available, and in this case my discussion will be kept at a minimum.

The Tancook Whalers of Nova Scotia were not what their names im-

---

[1] C. G. Davis, *Ships of the Past* (Salem, Mass., 1929); H. I. Chapelle, *American Sailing Craft* (New York, 1936). Since this article was set H. I. Chapelle's comprehensive book *American Small Sailing Craft* (W. W. Norton: New York, 1951), has been published.

ply at all, since they were in no way connected with whaling, but were descended from the Hampton Whaler, through the Labrador boat. The only information available on these slim, beautifully lined schooners is from an article in *Yachting* magazine.[2] E. A. Bell mentions that the lines have been attributed to the Viking boats which visited the Northeast Coast. This I believe to be very doubtful. The Tancook Whaler, shown by Mr. Bell, was 41 feet overall, 34 feet 3 inches on the waterline, 9 feet beam, 4 feet 3 inches draft without centerboard. The earlier boats had no centerboard. Bell states that they were developed from the 'Labrador Whaler,' a 30-foot ketch-rigged type, by the boatbuilders of Tancook Island, but Chapelle says that this was the 'Labrador boat' which was the same as the 'Hampton Whaler.' Planking was either smooth or lapstreak (which is the same as clench or clinker-built) and they were ballasted with rock. The Tancook boats were undoubtedly rather tender, because of their relatively small beam and draft in proportion to waterline length. Therefore the low schooner rig with big, club-headed topmast staysail for light airs was well suited to the hull form. As with most fast, fine-lined boats, the men who sailed them must have needed a nice feel for the point when they were overpowered and sail reduction was necessary, for they could not be driven like the Gloucester schooners because of lack of bearings aft, among other things. The overlapping foresail, common on many of the double ended types, shows that the modern yachtsmen have discovered nothing new with their overlapping genoa jibs. These boats started from a length of about 30 feet overall and evolved into craft as long as 50 feet. They were designed to be able to run home quickly before a rising gale, but they probably seldom had to do any heavy weather beating to windward. Hence they could be slimmer and sharper than their sisters further to the southward. Their high stern, sweeping sheer, and long-reaching bow topped by a short bowsprit made them, in my opinion, the most beautiful of all the double enders.

In a letter of 11 February 1948 to Paule Loring of Wickford, Rhode Island, from Howard I. Chapelle of Cambridge, Maryland, marine architect and historian, which was one of a number that Mr. Loring kindly lent me, Chapelle says:

First about the Tancook Whaler—Bell's article in Yachting, for which I made the plan as you noted, does refer to a white whaler and I have a record of a gray one as well, but I was informed by both former owners and sons of builders that the boats were commonly black, a number were dark bottle green, and most of these had black sheer strakes. The boats had red bottoms and gray decks.

[2] E. A. Bell, 'The Passing of the Tancook Whaler,' *Yachting* (Feb. 1933), p. 55.

120 THE NEW ENGLAND DOUBLE ENDERS

As is the case with some of the other types, the Tancook Whalers have been copied and 'improved' for use as yachts, by Ralph Wiley of Oxford, Maryland, but he has spoiled the original by making her too high-sided, giving her a tall, jib-headed rig, and omitting the centerboard. He has, however, retained the strong sheer and beautiful ends.

Fig. 1. Quoddy Boat

Going a little further westward we meet the Quoddy or Lubec carry-away boats used around Quoddy Head and Passamaquoddy Bay. I can find only three published sources on this type.[3] Davis, whom Chapelle claims to be incorrect, gives meager information stating that they were

---

[3] Davis, op. cit., pp. 14-16; H. I. Chapelle, 'The Lubec Carry-Away Boats,' *Yachting* (July, 1940). p. 54; G. B. Goode, *The Fisheries and Fishing Industries of the United States* (Washington, 1887), Sec. V.

cat-rigged, 35 feet overall, 12 feet wide, and 4½ feet deep (in the hold, I presume) and shows a picture of a model in the U. S. National Museum which has the mast 3 or 4 feet abaft the stem, well raked, with no standing rigging. The gaff was quite short though not as diminutive as those of the Block Island boats. The model has a companion slide forward leading to a small cuddy, with a large cockpit aft.

Chapelle's article is much more complete and gives valuable insight into their origin. He says that they probably were developed either from the Eastport pinkies, with a change in rig from the schooner to the sloop, and in a few cases, the cat, or from the carry-away boats of the menhaden fisheries, used to carry the fish from the seines to the factories. These carry-away boats were developed to the west of Cape Cod in conjunction with the invention of the purse-seine in Portsmouth, Rhode Island, around 1845 according to Goode.[4] They resembled the Block Island boats very closely, according to Captain Reynolds of Wickford who observed them in his youth, but were beamier if anything and of course had a cat rig. They were also, I believe, used on Long Island Sound. These carry-aways, along with the similar mate and purse boats, used to manipulate the seine, were 'soon replaced by steamers,' according to Chapelle. Whether 'soon' was before 1864, when two companies from Rhode Island erected factories at Bristol and Blue Hill, Maine, is hard to say, but it is reasonable to suppose that the Rhode Islanders would have brought their own boats, or at least their model, with them. It is easy to see how the type could have spread eastward from here.

However, there seems to be a slight difference in model between the Maine and the Rhode Island carry-aways, which would seem to substantiate the theory of development of the Lubec boats from the pinkies. The lines given by Chapelle show two models, similar in rig and profile, but different in section. The first is sharp, with hard bilges and fairly light displacement, while the second is fuller and rounder in section, altogether a more burdensome boat. The sheer of both the boats is sweeping, but not excessive, giving them low topsides amidships to make net tending easier, and both exhibit strong rake to the stern post, and moderate drag to the keel, with a deep forefoot. Both are short-gaff sloops of moderate sail area to my eye, but Chapelle considers the rig large. The dimensions of the sharper model are 38 feet 4 inches overall, 11 feet 4 inches beam, and 6 feet draft, while the smaller, heavier boat is 34 feet 2 inches overall, 30 feet 7¼ inches on the water, 11 feet 2½ inches wide, and draws 5 feet 9 inches.

[4] Goode, op. cit., Sec. V, Vol. I, p. 368.

Goode shows several plates which substantiate Chapelle's article, but he gives a minimum amount of text.[5] The first set of plates that I have noted show the Lubec or Quoddy boats engaged in several aspects of the herring (sardine) trade. Some, the smaller, cat-rigged boats resembling the picture of the model in Davis, are gill-netting, while others, larger boats, one a cat and the other a sloop, are being used as carry-aways.

Fig. 2. Carry-Away Boat (Lubec)

The second set of plates that I have noted shows the Rhode Island carry-aways and points up a few important differences from the Lubec boats. Although their rigs are very similar, the hulls differ in several respects. First, the sheer of the Rhode Island boats, if we are to trust Goode's plates, was somewhat like a Dutch shoe with two toes, that is, it kicked up suddenly at both ends. Secondly, their stern post was nearly perpendicular, while that of the Lubec boats was strongly raked. Thirdly, the Rhode Island carry-aways seem to have resembled the Block Island boats in section, having very slack bilges, bearing little resemblance to the harder-bilged Lubec carry-aways in this respect. Finally, the Maine boats are smooth planked, while the Rhode Island boats are lapstreaked.

There is an immense amount of misunderstanding surrounding the subject of the Hampton or Hampden boat and its relatives which Chapelle has attempted to clear up in a number of letters in this magazine. At the risk of further confusing the issue I shall attempt to draw some order from the welter of information.

[5] Goode, op. cit., Sec. V, Vol. I, pp. 430, 509; Atlas, Plates 123, 132, 135; 99, 100, 101, 102, 108.

THE NEW ENGLAND DOUBLE ENDERS

First let us consider the Hampton Beach boat, sometimes termed the Hampton Whaler. I have examined a set of lines taken from a wreck at York Beach, Maine, by Chapelle in 1936 which shows a small schooner, 24 feet 3 inches overall, 7 feet 6 inches beam, 3 feet 1½ inches draft at the stern, with gently raking stem and sternposts, and the deep forefoot and strong sheer characteristic of most of the local double enders. She has hollow waterlines fore and aft, nicely balanced ends, and a fairly full mid-

Fig. 3. Hampton Whaler

section. There is a pronounced S curve in the sections aft, which permits sharpness near the water while allowing enough bulk higher up so that she will lift to a following sea. Her schooner rig as shown by Chapelle is low with a single jib set on a short bowsprit. There is a note on the plan that the sail plan seems too large for the hull. I believe she is lapstreaked, although there is no indication.

These were the boats which, according to Goode, were taken on deck by the vessels of the Labrador fleet before the dory came into use.[6] He gives the same approximate overall length, placing their waterline at 19 feet, and says they were clinker built and carried two sails, either leg-of-mutton or sprit. This does not agree with Chapelle's schooner rig, but it

[6] Goode, op. cit., Sec. V, Vol. I, pp. 137-138.

is my belief that his boat was kept in the water and had no need for a demountable rig.

Paule Loring says he believes that the Hampton Whalers were actually used for whaling in what was known as the 'shore fishery.' This is quite possible, since the waters north of Cape Ann are much frequented by whales. Also Chapelle's lines show oarlocks on the gunwales, which would be used when pursuing the whale in a calm.

Not to be confused with the Hampton Whaler is the Hampden or Hampton boat. These boats were square sterned, very sharp forward, with the midsection well aft, and were descended from the ship's yawl boat, according to Chapelle.[7]

The New England or pinky boat was, as nearly as I can discover, just the Hampton Whaler with a few modifications. They had more drag to the keel and were a bit longer. From these, Chapelle claims, came the Crotch Island pinky of Casco Bay, which has been claimed elsewhere to be just a sharp sterned version of the Hampton boat. At any rate they were sharp sterned with a strongly raking sternpost, vertical stem, slightly curved, strong sheer with a 'kicked-up' stern like the true pinky, and had hollow floors in the midsection. The rig was always that of a spritsail cat ketch, with a jib on a temporary bowsprit for light airs. This then is the totality of the relatives and descendants of the Hampton Whaler except for the Isles of Shoals boat, which I shall discuss soon. The Hampton Whaler was perhaps one of the most widely used of all the New England double enders, but they failed to gain the recognition accorded the pinkies, largely because they lacked any sharply distinguishing feature like the pink-stern.

The Isles of Shoals are a cluster of small islands situated about sixteen miles north of Cape Ann, Massachusetts. They are surrounded by comparatively shoal water, and make an ideal base for fishing.[8] Inhabited by fishermen for two centuries after being sighted in 1605 by Champlain and explored by Smith in 1614, they declined in importance after the Revolution, and I believe that it was during this later period that the Isles of Shoals boat was developed. In the earlier period it was one of the largest settlements in New England, although women were prohibited for some time because with their arrival the annual production of fish became sadly depleted. There is no record of any particular type of boat

---

[7] Chapelle, AMERICAN NEPTUNE (July 1941), p. 311. Other references: AMERICAN NEPTUNE, Vol. I, 66, 90, 173; Vol. II, 249-250; Vol. III, 141-147.

[8] E. V. Bigelow, *Brief History of the Isles of Shoals* (Congregational Summer Conference, Star Island, 1923), p. 62.

developed there at that time, the boats apparently coming from other places. At any rate it is known that in the latter half of the nineteenth century there was a fleet of small boats native to the islands (although probably built on the mainland) which would go out handlining in the

Fig. 4. Isles of Shoals Shay

shoal waters around the islands. An old picture in the possession of L. Francis Herreshoff of Marblehead, Massachusetts, shows this fleet fishing near the islands and forms part of the pictorial basis for my discussion of this type. There were a good number of these boats, as there are over a dozen in the picture, with others intruding on the edges, so it may be assumed that the entire fleet is not included. From the picture it is evident that they ranged from about eighteen to twenty-four feet overall, were clinker built, had a nearly plumb stem, a raking sternpost, with the bow somewhat higher than the stern. The sheer was straighter than was common in the other double enders. They resembled some of the Quoddy Boats in their cat rig with the mast set well aft, but they had a headstay and the sail was smaller and higher in proportion, the end of the boom being well inboard.

There is another source of information on these boats, besides the histories which are very informative on the early fisheries but contribute little after the Revolution. This book, by the one-time owner of the hotel on Appledore Island, while it is maddeningly inexact, does give us a few revealing hints.[9] To begin with, there is a picture showing two boats in a calm, one of these being apparently one of the boats we are seeking although it is rather hard to tell because of the small scale. Further on we discover a reference to a 'sailboat' eighteen feet long, 'very wide and seaworthy' which was hauled out on a 'slip' by means of a windlass. More important, she had a single mast which could be unstepped. Later, however, he mentions that two 'whaleboats' were bought by his father, and that the type was used by the men of Star Island for fishing. They were apparently rigged as cat schooners, that is, with no jib. We may safely assume that these boats were not the whaleboats carried by the whaling ships, as these would have been unsuited for such a service, but rather boats of the 'whaler' type, the origin of whose name I have already explained. It is reasonable to expect that these boats were either Hampton Whalers or closely related to them, since the picture shows a close similarity between the two hull forms, perhaps the greatest difference being in the rake of the sternpost.

The third source on this type is a book by Morris.[10] He has a photograph which shows a lapstreaked cat schooner about twenty-seven to thirty feet long. The hull closely resembles those of the Herreshoff photograph, but we get a better view, which shows sharp, hollow ends swelling quickly to a fairly full midsection. Her beam is the same over a good portion of her length. Her masts are evidently unstayed so as to facilitate unstepping when hauling, while her foresail is loose-footed. She is decked over forward for about one-third of her length and has a short after deck. I consider this to be the most authentic source on the type. I have a the-

---

[9] O. Laighton, *Ninety Years at the Isles of Shoals* (Beacon Press, Boston, 1930), pp. 2, 19, 41, 56.
[10] E. P. Morris, *The Fore and Aft Rig in America* (New Haven: Yale University Press, 1927), p. 127.

THE NEW ENGLAND DOUBLE ENDERS

ory about the rig shown in the Herreshoff photograph, which may or may not be correct. Since these boats were hauled out they had no bowsprit, but were cat schooners. For fishing close to the islands a single masted rig would have been the handiest and it is likely that they simply unstepped the mainmast and hoisted the boomed mainsail on the foremast in place of the loose-footed foresail. I have already noted that the end of the boom was well inboard, which helps substantiate this theory.

There is one other source of information, which I am hesitant to trust, however.[11] It gives dimensions (29½ feet overall, 26 feet waterline, beam 9½ feet, draft 4 feet) of a replica of *Alice*, last of the Isles of Shoals double enders, and says that *Alice* was lapstreaked. The rest of the article contains several obvious fallacies, and I dare not draw any conclusions from the pictures and sail plan of his replica. The method of fishing known as 'jigging' described by Laighton is rather astounding, and, to my knowledge, unparalleled elsewhere on the coast. When the mackerel were schooling off the Isles, the fishermen would sail out armed with 'jigs,' light poles with a barbless hook lashed to the lower end. Then they would begin a process known as 'tolling' north of Cape Cod, and 'chumming' on the south side. Old bits of stinking fish, clams and other offal were ground up and scattered around on the surface of the water. This would attract the mackerel in such numbers that the men would only have to jab their jigs down into the mass of shimmering, squirming bodies and on the upstroke they would have at least one fish impaled on the hook. A far cry from the fishermen of today with their radio telephones and underwater detection units.

In Jenness there is a passage which seems worth citing:[12] 'During the entire sixteenth century fishing vessels came hither from our eastern waters. Doggers and Pinkies of the English, clumsy Busses of Holland, light Fly-boats of Flanders, the Biskeiner and Portingal and many other odd high peaked vessels were attracted thither summer after summer.'

This shows that double enders were not novel to our coasts even in earliest times and it is therefore not surprising that in the late eighteenth century, when there was a need for small, inshore fishing boats, there was a type of double ender built near Essex, Massachusetts, known as the Chebacco boat.[13] These boats were developed from the early shallops according to Chapelle. They were cat schooners not often over forty feet overall and had what was known as a 'pink-stern,' in which the bul-

[11] 'Palm, a Modern Pinky,' *Yachting* (May 1931).
[12] J. S. Jenness, *Isles of Shoals* (New York, 1873).
[13] Chapelle, *American Sailing Craft*, Ch. 9; Davis, op. cit., pp. 14-16.

warks were carried out beyond the stern and ended in a 'tombstone' similar in shape to the stern of a fishing dory. As time went on they grew larger and by 1800 were used in the offshore fisheries. After the War of 1812 they gained the full schooner rig, with jib and bowsprit and became known as 'pinkies.' There were four distinct types of pinky according to Chapelle. The Essex pinky resembled the ships of her day, carrying her beam on deck for a great part of her length, having a bluff bow and a fine stern with a barrel-shaped midsection. These were wonderful sea boats,

Fig. 5. Chebacco Boat

riding the seas duck-fashion, but must have been very slow to windward. They had a pronounced sheer and the bowsprit was steeved up to carry out the sheer. The Maine pinkies had less sheer, lower bulwarks, more deadrise and more beam in proportion to their length. The Canadian, or Yarmouth pinkies were much like the Essex boats, except that they had more deadrise and were very beamy. The Eastport pinkies were built for speed, and were easy to distinguish from the other types. They were much sharper, and had more deadrise; the stem, and even more so, the stern, were well raked, and there was a strong drag to the keel. The peculiar pink stern served several purposes, not least of which was that of a seat of ease. This would seem to have been a bit disagreeable in sloppy weather, but Chapelle says, 'Indeed no.' Otherwise it was used as a support for the mainsheet horse, a protection for the rudder and windbreak for the helmsman, a frame to hang nets on, and the 'tombstone' had a notch to serve as a boom crotch. The distinctive pinkies are perhaps the most famous of all the New England double enders due mainly to their novel construction. There have been several developments of the pinkies in recent times for use as yachts and commercial craft, perhaps the most authentic being Chapelle's *Glad Tidings*, and Jim Anderegg's *Surprise*, built and now located at Bucks' Harbor, Maine.[14] Because of the comparative wealth of information on this type I have purposely limited my discussion to the barest essentials.

Moving south of Cape Cod we find that there they faced an entirely different problem. On the two islands where double enders were used, Martha's Vineyard and Block Island, they needed a boat which could be hauled up on the beach between trips. The men were farmer-fishermen, and since they did not spend all their time afloat, on Martha's Vineyard their homes were not near the harbors on the east end of the island but were spread all along its perimeter. The Block Islanders had no natural harbor at all.

The Martha's Vineyard or Chilmark boats, cat schooner rigged, evolved into a type ranging from about 15 to 22 feet overall.[15] For a boat 18 feet overall the other dimensions were $15\frac{1}{2}$ feet waterline, $6\frac{1}{2}$ feet beam, and 3 feet of draft with the centerboard. This was an improvement added by George Butler in the 1880's, the previous boats drawing about $1\frac{1}{2}$ feet with no board. While the early boats were quite full and chunky, eventually they became sharper. They were lightly constructed of cedar planking over oak frames, fastened with copper nails, some of which may well have been made by Paul Revere. Three or four thwarts were well kneed in place by natural crooks, and in general they were of the best construction, for their owners' lives were dependent upon these staunch little craft. The shores of Martha's Vineyard were at one time liberally dotted with them. As time went on and fish grew scarce around the Vineyard it was found advantageous for the fishermen to have camps on the island of Noman's Land to the southwest, and soon there was a permanent settlement there. The Vineyard boats, which had differed widely in size and detail, became more or less standardized into the Noman's Land boat which was of the dimensions of the typical Vineyard boat previously mentioned.[16] Some of them were smooth planked while others were lapstreaked, and all were rigged as cat ketches with spritsails.

As there was no harbor on the island the boats were hauled ashore after every trip, in the same manner as those on the Vineyard. They would be sailed in, the sails lowered, the masts dropped overside, and the bow allowed to ride up onto the hollowed rungs of an oak ladder laid flat in

---

[14] Chapelle, 'Return of the Pinkie,' *Yachting* (Feb. 1938), p. 35; *Rudder Magazine* (Feb. 1937), p. 57; (June 1943), p. 36.

[15] J. C. Allen, *Martha's Vineyard Boats* (Reynolds Printing Co., New Bedford, Mass.), copy in Widener Library, Harvard University.

[16] W. H. Taylor, 'A Noman's Land Sailboat,' *Yachting* (March 1932), p. 74.

the sand, a bolt slipped through a hole in the stem, a strop clapped on, and they would trundle up the ladder in tow of a team of stunted oxen kept specially for this purpose.[17] In later days the oxen were owned by Israel Luce, and he would charge each boat five dollars a season, no matter how many times she was hauled.[18] The boats fished fairly close to the

Fig. 6. The Noman's Land 'Double-Ender' of the '70's
With double-reefed foresail and full mainsail these little boats would work to windward in a gale, providing there was 'one man to sail and one to bail'

island, the seasons lasting from April first to the end of May, and from October to December fifteenth. A few of the hardier souls would fish all winter. The method of fishing was mainly line trawling; hauling 3600 fathoms of heavy trawl over the roller was very heavy work.[19] The loose footed sails were easy to roll up on the sprits if one knew how, but were superseded by more efficient gaff sails in some of the boats. One of the reasons why the boats were so small was to enable them to be rowed, and

[17] Goode, op. cit., Sec. V, Atlas, Plate 250.
[18] A. M. Wood, *Noman's Land, Isle of Romance* (Reynolds Printing Co., New Bedford, 1931).
[19] L. Howland, *Sou'West and By West of Cape Cod* (Harvard University Press, 1947).

THE NEW ENGLAND DOUBLE ENDERS

often the men would row great distances when the breeze failed. The foresail (as they persisted in calling it, although it had grown to mainsail proportions) was overlapping and the sheets were led to wooden pegs in the underside of the gunwale, the main (or mizzen) sheet working through a block on an iron traveller around the tiller, and a wooden bullseye on the sail. All their gear was correspondingly simple, yet handy. While not fast, they were weatherly, and with a double or triple reefed mainsail and full mizzen, 'one man to sail and one to bail,' they would be taken out in the most ferocious weather. A more perfect small boat for launching stern first through the surf could hardly be imagined, for they were modeled with the S shaped sections aft which kept them sharp at the waterline while being full enough higher up to rise to the seas. That they were extremely able craft sailed by skillful seamen can be seen from their record of only two boats lost in their history of trips to the mainland and neighboring islands as well as fishing about Noman's Land in all weathers.

The Block Island boats are probably the oldest and one of the most unusual types on the New England coast, having been in use for over two hundred years. Their closest relative is probably the neighboring Noman's Land boat, but there are several marked differences which set them in a class by themselves. Contrary to popular opinion (if the opinion of the few people who even know they existed may be called popular) there are two types of Block Island boat between which it is necessary to distinguish, although they are very similar in type.

Block Island lies ten miles off the shore of Rhode Island, and after its exploration by the Dutchman, Adrian Block in 1614[20] during which he built a fort and a few houses, it remained in Indian hands until they massacred the crew of a ship which landed there, whereupon an expedition landed, wiped out the Indians and made it the property of the Massachusetts Bay Colony. Shortly thereafter, in 1661,[21] the first settlement was made by a group from the Colony who wished to establish a 'free State and Church which never sought to impose restrictions on others.' Naturally these settlers were dependent upon the sea for at least part of their livelihood as well as for their transport to the mainland. The Island, like Noman's Land, has no natural harbors, and its history is one of a long struggle against the elements to make and maintain artificial harbors.

[20] R. Dodge, *Tristram Dodge and Descendants* (J. J. Little Co., New York, 1886), pp. 198-201.
[21] Rev. S. T. Livermore, A.M., *A History of Block Island* (Case, Lockwood & Brainard Co., Hartford, 1877).

On the west side of the island lies Great Salt Pond, separated from the ocean by a narrow strip of beach and 'large and deep enough to hold the entire British Navy.' It was here that the first attempt at a harbor was made in 1680 by the cutting of a breachway across the narrowest part of the sandspit. This quickly filled in, despite all their efforts, and the project was abandoned in 1705. The next solution was the building of a breakwater known as 'The Pier' in the bight on the east side of the island. The boats could only lie here in calm weather, however. The Pier was finally broken down by a storm after twelve years' service. In 1773 another attempt was made at the Salt Pond, only to be abandoned in 1735 in favor of building an addition to the old pier or a new one near it. In 1736 both of these were done, but the result was not too successful. During subsequent years there was much agitation for a harbor of some sort. The Revolution put off the execution of another cut into the Salt Pond. In 1816 some unknown soul started the 'Pole Harbor' on the east by sinking a few oak spiles into the sand at right angles to the breakwater, to tie his boat to. Others soon followed suit and eventually there were over 1000 spiles, with short stone piers built out between the rows. The blackened remnants of some of these stakes are still visible at low water. This was still only a calm weather measure, however. In 1870 the government began construction of two breakwaters which now form the 'Old Harbor.' At the beginning of the present century the breach was again opened into the Salt Pond and protected by a stone groin on its south side so that there are now two harbors on the Island.

The result of all this vacillation was that until 1870 the Islanders had no place where their boats could be secure in foul weather, and they had to resort to the same tactics as the Noman's Landers, hauling their boats up on the beach, and although they used greased planks instead of ladders, the motive power was a similar team of stunted oxen. Also the boats had to be weatherly and able because the greatest traffic was with Newport, and the stretch of water including Point Judith, and the channel into Newport can become the nastiest on the Atlantic coast. The 'cowhorns,' as the boats developed for this usage were called, were not over 22 feet overall, 19 feet waterline, 9 feet beam, 4 feet 2 inches draft. They were lapstreaked, with straight raking stem and stern posts, and their sections showed the pronounced V with only a little rounding off above the water which is one of their most unusual features. As a result, despite their immense beam of a little under half their length, they were actually rather fine at the waterline and this effect was retained even when they heeled. Some of the better boats had the S sections aft whose advantages have already been noted. They could carry a prodigious load of fish or other cargo for their size at the water because they increased their buoyancy so fast when loaded. Their rig, which has been thought by the best authorities to be that of a cat schooner with tall masts of equal height (twenty-seven feet) set perpendicular to the keel, has recently been thrown in doubt. There is a model in the National Museum which shows them to be cat ketches with the mizzenmast about three-quarters as high as the main. This model has been largely discounted by the experts, since it is grossly inaccurate in hull form. However, Goode gives evidence to substantiate the ketch rig and Paule S. Loring, whose *Glory Anna II* was built to a set of lines as closely approximating an old cowhorn as he could get by taking the lines from an old wreck on Block Island, says that he very often sails with a reef in the mizzen (or main, if you wish) because she balances better.[22] With this evidence then, it seems more probable that the cat ketch is the true rig of the cowhorn. The sails were loose footed, the foresail overlapping, and were suspended from extremely short gaffs hoisted with a single halliard, reminiscent of Dutch practice, except for being straight instead of curved. There has been a good deal of talk about this 'Dutch influence' and mention of 'early Dutch settlers' is accompanied by wise nodding of heads, but the fact is that the Dutch did not have a great deal to do with the Island after the initial discovery, and the idea of short gaffs must have come through the English who used this rig from 1600-1700. The boats were fully as well built as their counterparts on Noman's Land, the same construction of copper-fastened cedar over oak being used. While little or nothing is known about the builders of the Noman's Land boats, on Block Island an early builder in Revolutionary times was John Rose and he was succeeded by Lemuel Rose. In later times Deacon Sylvester D. Mitchell was the builder and it is recorded that he would cut his timber on the mainland and bring it back (in a cowhorn) to build with. The cowhorns were ballasted with cobble stones from the beach which were tossed overboard as the boats were loaded or when they were to be hauled out. They were completely open, being crossed by three or four thwarts securely kneed in place. Their method of fishing was unique as far as I know. Having reached the grounds they would drop the foresail, let the mainsheet run, and let her drift off to leeward as pretty as you please, while they fished over the weather side.

With the building of the government harbor in 1870 came the end of the necessity of hauling the boats for every storm, and thus the limita-

[22] Goode, op. cit., Atlas, Plate 46.

Glory Anna II, the only existing Block Island cowhorn, owned and built by Paule Loring

tion on size was removed. They probably had been needing bigger boats for some time, as everything that came to the Island had been brought in the cowhorns, and so the size of the boats after this time increased to a maximum of around forty feet, and this is the Block Island boat about which the greater part of the existing literature has been written. They represented only a minor part of the total number, however, for while there were about a dozen of the later type, there were five times as many of the cowhorns. The later boats, of which *Lena M.* and *Island Belle* were examples, resembled the cowhorns in general appearance, but were narrower in proportion.[23] Also, since they were not hauled out, at least part of their ballast was permanent, and it is reported that they would cover over the rocks with sand and then sow beach grass to tie the sand together and keep the ballast from shifting. Construction was, on the whole, heavier than that of the cowhorns, and with the event of the gasoline engine some of the boats had a large cuddy forward, separated from a galley amidships by a space of deck.

There have been two replicas of the Block Island boats built thus far: *Roaring Bessie,* a carvel planked boat to the lines of *Lena M.* by Martin C. Erismann, and *Glory Anna II,* the replica of a cowhorn. I am much indebted to Mr. Loring for his assistance in gathering material on these boats. Several of his stories are quite informative as well as amusing. It seems that there was a rumor going around that two brothers who owned one of the last Block Island boats could not agree as to who was the rightful owner and so they sawed her in two, each taking half. Mr. Loring dispelled this rumor when he discovered that there was truly one of the boats which had been sawed in two, but that it was only because she leaked too badly to be any good, so her owner cut her in two, set her bow on a stone wall and built a foundation under it to make a chicken house, while the stern was set off in a field to be used as an icehouse. He also relates of the time he was overboard while at anchor cutting away a line which had fouled in *Glory's* propeller and, after doubtfully eyeing her lofty topsides was wondering 'just how the hell the old boy like me was going to get back aboard.' He was swimming round the boat a bit hopelessly when he noticed that the notch in the afterside of the rudder, which he had previously considered only an ornamentation, was ideally placed for a step, the mainsheet horse forming a convenient handhold, wherewith he clambered back aboard, rejoicing not only at being saved the in-

---

[23] W. M. Thompson. 'Roaring Bessie,' *Yachting* (April 1912), p. 261; P. S. Loring & K. Littlefield, 'Old Glamor Girls of the Bay,' *Providence Journal,* Feb. 1948.

conveniece of drowning, but also at having discovered one more useful 'kink' devised by the resourceful Islanders.

There are several similarities which mark the New England double enders as a group. As a rule they all have a sweeping sheer with high ends and a low midsection. Many have raking stem and sternpost, and practically all have the S section aft which, though harder to build, makes a great difference in the sailing qualities. The schooner rig takes preference, with cat rigs of all kinds being popular. There is a noticeable simplicity in rig, saving needless labor and expense, and lapstreak construction is used more than carvel, mainly for the boats where lightness is an important factor. There tends to be a good deal of similarity between the various types to the east of Cape Cod, and the jumble of names and slight modifications make the subject a hard one to unravel. In the light of past experience I have no doubt but that I will find other types that I have overlooked. A topic such as this is subject to constant revision.

Finally, it seems to me that a yachtsman desirous of a rough, inexpensive boat which will take him to sea in all weathers can find something among the multiplicity of craft developed on this coast that will suit him far better than a type imported from abroad. The proof of the question lies in the satisfaction of those who have already tried it.

Acknowledgments

Besides my sincere thanks to Mr. Paule S. Loring for giving so freely of a wealth of information on Block Island boats and for lending me the lines of several types, as well as for his fine illustrations which say more than pages of my prose, I wish to thank Mr. Llewellyn Howland of South Dartmouth, Mass., and Mr. L. Francis Herreshoff of Marblehead, Mass., for their invaluable aid in tracking down little-know boats. Mr. Alfred Brownell of Providence, R. I., who is making a series of excellent models for the Providence Public Library depicting New England fishing boats, was kind enough to lend me two photographs of his work. I also thank Mr. Chapelle for the information obtained from his letters to Mr. Loring and refer the reader to his new book, soon to be published, on New England fishing craft.

Johnny Woodboat

BY GEORGE MacBEATH

ONE hundred years ago the St. John River was teeming with a peculiar type of craft called the woodboat. Today not a single woodboat plies the river nor indeed can the remains of one be found along its shores. They have completely disappeared. They were part of the scene for so long and died so peacefully that New Brunswickers seldom think of them in terms of historical data. I was no exception; it took an outsider—Colonel Howard Chapelle—to make me realize the importance of this distinctly local craft. Intrigued with the subject, I spent many pleasant hours searching the records, talking with the people who remember these boats and poring over pictures and plans. As the pieces of the puzzle were put together, the picture of a lovable old workhorse that was very much a part of a life that is no more began to emerge. Here was an unusual craft that was of great economic importance during the last century, and a craft that has a connection with the early schooner types.

Of the theories advanced as to the woodboat's origin, the one most often heard is that it originated on the St. John, the place where it was most used. This claim can be accepted for the boat's final development, but both the rig and the hull of the late eighteenth-century models were based closely on the pre-Revolutionary 'Two Mast Boat' to be found farther south. These craft themselves were special adaptations of English craft of the seventeenth century to the new conditions found along the Atlantic.

One of these colonial types was the Chebacco dogbody, a small, two-masted, gaff-rigged open boat without headsails which became popular in Massachusetts after 1750. Such a craft would be familiar to the trading company of Simonds, Hazen and White who had established themselves at the mouth of the St. John in 1764 and carried on trade with New England. It is quite possible that it was this vessel that they had in mind when in November 1783 they determined to build two boats to bring wood to market. Each boat was to be undecked, carry a crew of two, and have a capacity of about eight cords.[1] But from present records it is impossible to describe the hull and form of these first woodboats, which must have averaged about fifteen tons. However, one thing points clearly to the fact that they were modeled after the Chebacco dogbody: the sailboats which brought wood and country produce to Saint John during the early nineteenth century were known as Chebacco boats.[2]

With the rapid settlement of the St. John River valley by the Loyalists after 1783 there was a great need for boats. Almost every farmer within reach of the water required the use of a versatile craft that would carry cordwood and country produce to the ready market at Saint John and bring back lime, ashes, and manufactured goods for his use. It is highly probable that those among the Loyalists who had been boatbuilders responded to this need and began constructing improved models of the Simonds, Hazen and White boat. The result was indeed a successful one, since the boats that they built were among the chief factors in the development of this part of New Brunswick in its early years.[3] Serving primarily as a river cargo carrier, the woodboats, as they came to be known, proved so superior that no other conveyance was able to compete with them until nearly the middle of the nineteenth century.

With the experience gained in constructing these early woodboats, the builders began to make changes and there gradually emerged a craft better adapted to local needs and quite different from the early boat. It is for this reason that some consideration can be given to the claim that the woodboat is a distinct local type. That she is worthy of greater interest than she has received is unquestionable, especially in view of the fact that the woodboat was one of the last survivors of the shallop rig which ceased to be common early in the nineteenth century. The craft survived here because it was admirably suited to its peculiar situation.

Exactly when the true woodboat form was established is impossible to determine.[4] Between 1783 and 1815 there were a number of developments of which we are certain. There was an increase in size, the 1815 tonnage being twice that of the wood carrier of 1783. A lithograph of Saint John Harbour in 1815 shows the woodboat of the period to be a longish craft, rather similar in appearance to the Hudson River boats and much less chunky than the Chebacco boat. Between 1815 and 1825,

---

[1] Hazen Papers, The New Brunswick Museum.

[2] *Acadiensis*, III, No. 4 (Saint John, 1903), 275.

[3] Until less than 150 years ago there was an almost complete absence of roads in the Province and it was apparent to settlers of those days that water must primarily be depended upon for communications.

[4] The earliest reference I have to them by the name 'woodboat' is in a pamphlet printed in 1812, but the term was almost certainly used earlier.

Common woodboat carrying a moderate load.
Courtesy of the Peabody Museum of Salem

Typical woodboat off the New England coast. The number of coastal woodboats without headgear was probably small.
Courtesy of the Peabody Museum of Salem

the size of the woodboat doubled, breadth had increased in relation to depth, and it would appear that by 1830 a distinct type of craft called the St. John River woodboat had been established.

What did the woodboat look like? It some ways this is a difficult question to answer. Each builder seems to have had his own ideas, the result being great variety in form and quality of workmanship. Another difficulty is the range in size of these boats. Records show that they ran between eleven and ninety-seven tons.[5] In the matter of dimensions, length varied from 36 to 84 feet, depth from 4 feet to 7.9 feet, and breadth from 13.8 feet to 27 feet. The average, however, was somewhere around seventy tons. The dimensions of *Lida Gretta* are more or less typical. She measured 68 tons, had a length of 71 feet, a breadth of 25 feet, and a depth of hold of 6.5 feet.

The hull of these picturesque craft was constructed with carvel planking. The bow was full, with a stout, curved stem often shaped with much tumble home above the water line. The bulldog bow gave maximum cargo space at a sacrifice to speed; but this was not an important consideration since they were not designed to carry perishable cargoes. It was also found that this type of bow prevented deep plunging and caused the boat to lift quickly in a heavy sea. This buoyancy was due to the fact that the resistance was all in the bow; almost all the boats had a pretty midsection and aft end.

The heavily sheared hull was usually a somewhat shallow keel model with very little dead rise. They varied greatly in the matter of run; some had a very fine, rather long run; more seem to have had a short, full run. Apparently, there was no standard.

There was no overhang aft, although in a few of the later models the counter stern was to be found. The stern was cut off, usually with a raking transom like the stern of a modern dinghy. The exposed sternpost had a utilitarian 'outdoor' rudder attached. George Wasson in his excellent *Sailing Days on the Penobscot* states that this type of stern and the general 'chunky' look of the boat brought about this imaginary conversation between two skippers:

'Where's the other one?'

'What other one?'

'Why, the one they turned to and sawed that one off'n.'

The common type of steering gear, especially for those used exclusively on the river, was a tiller attached directly to the sternpost. The tiller often

[5] Tonnage figures are the registered tonnages unless otherwise specified.

ran to seven feet in length.[6] A local resident told me about being in a woodboat at Evandale one night and hearing music coming over the water. He called one of the crew who agreed that it was indeed music. In a few minutes another woodboat sailed past. Seated sideways on the tiller was the captain, a fiddle tucked under his chin and giving forth with some ditty like 'Turkey in the Straw.' He was able to change course by simply walking backward or forward, and didn't need to miss a note!

A word should be said on the anchor. For many years, the common type was wooden, being simply two huge pieces of curved wood set at right angles to one another and securely pinned. A large rock held in place by 'withes,' or twisted saplings, was placed in the center of the curved timbers. A hemp hawser served as anchor chain.

These boats were all rigged with two masts. The foremast was three feet or less from the stem and the taller mainmast amidships or slightly abaft amidships. Being stepped as far forward as possible, the foremast took the place of a headsail. This helped the boat head off the wind, and would steady it and prevent yawing when the wind was from the quarter. The tongue-in-cheek reason given by George Wasson for the absence of headsail is that 'they often loaded wood in such remote sylvan spots that bowsprits were too likely to get mixed up with trees on the steep banks!'[7] The truth of the matter is that with the towering deckloads they often carried it would have been awkward to work the jib.

The rigging was simple. The fore and mainsails were hooped to the masts, the foresail being almost as large as the main. The foremast boom was on the average only a foot longer than the gaff. It was not unusual to find a main boom that ran up to sixty-four feet in length, or to have a main gaff made from a large tree. A woodboat of forty tons carried about 1,700 square feet of canvas, usually managed by a two-man crew. Neither the main nor the foremast had stays so that the crew had to use the hoops or shinny up the mast if it were necessary to go aloft. There was the odd boat, however, that used the boatswain's chair. The gaffs, especially that of the foremast, had little peak when hoisted. The shape of the foresail was 'barn door,' or square. In the early days the sails were treated with ocher, giving them a dull red or brick color. It was felt that this treatment would protect them, but there was no proof that it actually did and for the most part the practice died out.

This rig proved to be handy in crowded waters and could be worked

---

[6] Boats built toward the end of the century were almost all equipped with a wheel. It was mounted on a wooden tiller and the whole worked like a windlass from steering lines leading from the drum to the rail.

[7] George S. Wasson, *Sailing Days on the Penobscot* (New York, 1949), p. 221.

by a small crew. Moreover, it enabled woodboats to navigate the long and sometimes treacherous tributaries under sail power alone. The rig also contributed to make the woodboats better than average sailers. With a stiff wind and reasonably calm water, and winged out,[8] they were able to make between nine and ten knots on the river. An even better speed was sometimes achieved by these workhorses in the Bay of Fundy. Speaking of their speed, it is related that *Comrade* once beat a Boston pilot boat in a race up the harbor of that port. The pilots were so impressed that they tried to persuade the woodboat captain to put his boat in dry dock at their expense to give them a chance to study her underwater lines.[9]

Most of the owners saw no sense in spending money for looks alone and no figurehead, no bow badges, no decoration of any kind was to be found. For years, tar and pitch served as paint which was considered to be a needless luxury. When paint finally did come into use, the hull was nearly always painted black and the railing or bulwarks another or a combination of contrasting colors. To my knowledge, however, the woodboatmen never developed the passion for paint and gaudy colors for which their deep-sea brethren were noted.

The usual plan of the flush deck was simple. Right abaft the foremast was the old handspike wooden windlass, although it was sometimes to be found in the space between the foremast and the stem. It was a primitive arrangement, a drum with a hand-operated lever at both ends which was worked with a see-saw motion. At least two strokes, two up and two down, were required to bring in a link in the anchor chain.

Just aft of the windlass on the center line was a small hatch for storage in the forepeak room. Amidships there was a large rectangular hatch, and one or two pumps with wooden barrels abaft the mainmast. A large, rather high cabin trunk, with a cabin slide to port of center line, was placed at the stern. This lead to the cabin which was aft under the deck and had space for three men. There was no regular plan for this dingy and stuffy cuddy, made all the more uninhabitable by the smoke from the brick fireplace used for cooking and heating. The wheel or tiller was close abaft the trunk. A yawl or jolly boat was hung on clumsy wood davits, although many of the woodboats used exclusively on the river were not equipped with davits and simply towed their tenders. On the early vessels the rail was open and stopped at the after end of the main hatch. Solid bulwarks were uncommon if not unknown, being consid-

[8] 'Wung out,' to use the expression of the crews of the woodboats, meant having one sail swung out to starboard, the other to port.

[9] Recounted by William Holder, an octogenarian and a well-known sailmaker of Saint John.

ered dangerous in a small craft. Of course, solid bulwarks were to be seen on the majority of the later boats. These were about two and one-half feet in height. There was usually a large break in the rail amidships at the main hatch.

Their low sides made it comparatively easy to pass wood by hand over the railings. Due to the moderate dead rise and bilge keels the craft were able when grounded on the shore to sit upright, a necessary position for convenient loading and unloading. This was an important consideration since the boats had to cope with Saint John's thirty-foot tides which leave many of the slips dry at low water. Other features in their favor were that they could carry large loads in very shallow water and were usually smart sailers. The story is related of how a captain sailed his boat into the crowded waters of Market Slip, Saint John, and left instructions with the mate to 'Just jolly her around until I get back.'

Some of the woodboats were skilfully built of the best materials. It is quite evident from the records, however, that more were rough and primitive in construction, being most often built of odds and ends. As a class, they won the dubious distinction from some authorities of being the least expensive vessel, ton for ton, ever built on this side of the Atlantic.[10] Yet there is no question about their popularity and their importance in the economic life of the Province during the last century.

The St. John River woodboats received their name apparently from the fact that they were built almost exclusively on the lower St. John River and its tributaries. There are records of a few being built elsewhere but these are rare indeed when the total number of woodboats built in the last century is considered. Yards were located at Moss Glen, Long Reach, Holderville, Victoria Wharf, Whelpley's Point, Greenwich, Oak Point, the Belleisle, the Washademoak, Jemseg, and Grand Lake, to name but the more important. Although Grand Lake was the one considerable boatbuilding center in the lower St. John River valley, it is Harvey Whelpley of Whelpley's Point who is credited with having constructed more woodboats in his yard than any other builder.[11]

Many of the boats were built by farmers in winter to keep themselves and their hired hands busy. It was not unusual to find a boat built, sailed and owned by the same man. The vast majority were owned either by farmers or lumber merchants.

The first step in constructing a woodboat was to cut the lumber. Very

---

[10] George S. Wasson, op. cit.

[11] It was felt to be of no vital importance in this study to list the name and particulars of every such craft known to have been launched. It might be well to point out however that much of this information is now on file at the New Brunswick Museum.

often this was to be found on the land of the builder, within a half mile or so of the shore where the vessel was to be built. The timber for planking was mill sawn or more often, at least until 1875, whip sawn or hand hewn on the spot. Many preferred hand-hewn timber, believing it closed the pores of the wood. Two or three farmers living near the Devil's Back on the St. John built a woodboat some distance inland. Then they tore it apart and carried it to the river where it was reconstructed. This ingenious plan was followed to save cartage!

The regular 'yard' was simply a cleared, leveled space on the shore where a platform of planks had been laid. The keel, stem, sternpost and ribs would then be raised on the platform. The pattern of construction was that employed in building seagoing vessels.

A master builder or experienced foreman was usually engaged to oversee construction, at least in its early stage. But there was more than one case of complete novices building such a boat. I was told recently of one such person who decided to build. He fashioned the model without difficulty, but was at a loss as to how to take off the lines. He solved the problem by imprinting the model in the deep snow and got his lines by placing shingles in the impression.

As the manner of building varied, so did the kinds of lumber used. These included birch, beech, maple, oak, pine, spruce, hackmatack, and elm. They seem only to have drawn the line with poplar, which was termed 'good for nothing.' The better constructed woodboats were planked below the water line with birch or some other hardwood, and with spruce above, as well as for the deck. The deck planking was usually cut first and put on last so that it would be well seasoned. Hackmatack was used for knees, keel, keelson, stem, stern, and stanchions, and white pine for the masts. The poorer boats were built almost wholly of spruce.

In the early days, no model of any kind was used. The builder relied on 'rule of thumb' or trial and error in building. They were later almost wholly built from a model or half model designed by the master builder. There is no record of paper plans ever having been used in building a woodboat.

The planking was held in place by wooden pins or trunnels made of birch or hackmatack. Oakum, of course, was the common caulking used, but it is related that the early builder found cow dung just as good. I am told that on more than one occasion a builder found such large gaps between the planks that he had to insert gads or wedges before caulking.

Some of these woodboats were so rough and primitive in construction as to be veritable curiosities of shipbuilding. 'Some enterprising soul once put an extreme specimen on exhibition at a Boston wharf. For ten cents were to be seen crude and even startling make-shifts of every description. It was easy to believe that the unique craft grew far inland, as a distinctly bucolic touch was given by an anchor which had flukes consisting of plough-shares, fastened on by wire lashings, while the stock was simply a limb of yellow birch to which bark still adhered. In this strange outfit the skipper who built it, together with his wife, were no small part of the show and the wonder grew that Boston was ever reached.' [12]

Since the majority were crudely constructed and since they received much rough handling in the many uses to which they were put they did not prove to be very durable. What with the devastating effect of being afloat in fresh water, plus the fact that they were not always tight and usually had cuts in the planking and poor spots in the seams, many of them were unfit to put to sea. Indeed, afloat at any time the pumps had to be kept going constantly. There are records to show that some were kept afloat simply by the buoyancy of the cargo they carried. The skipper of one woodboat once admitted that in ten years it was time to junk the best of them.

Yet there are dozens of boats whose long careers disprove this generalization. The thirty-one-ton *Favorite* was built in 1816 and operated on the river for over nineteen years. Another of the early boats, *Salmon River*, was built in 1814 and operated for about thirty-four years. David Coombes built the sixty-four-ton *Guitar* at Greenwich in 1853, and she wasn't broken up until 1883. *Marysville*, seventy-eight tons, was built at Westfield in 1869 and not pronounced 'unseaworthy' until 1907. But the record for long life must go to the sixty-nine-ton *Sea Bird*. She enjoyed a career of forty-four years, from 1868 to 1912. On the other hand, the forty-seven-ton *Dolphin* was built in 1838 and condemned and broken up in 1844, a period of only six years.

Only eleven woodboats were built during the 1820's, but eighty-one were launched in the 30's. The total then began to decline: seventy-one in the 40's, seventy-three in the 50's, sixty-nine in the 60's, fifty-nine in the 70's, twenty-four in the 80's, fourteen in the 90's, and only six between 1900 and 1917.[13]

J. A. H. was the last woodboat to be built. Constructed during the winter of 1917, she registered fifty-six tons. She was rebuilt the following year and equipped with a gasoline motor. This is the only instance re-

---
[12] Wasson, p. 222.
[13] Official records prior to 1820 were not available.

corded of a woodboat being equipped with motor. Happily, they died out in time to escape this fate. The last woodboat on the river was condemned and broken up at Indiantown, Saint John, in December 1930. She was the fifty-one-ton *Maggie Alice*, built in 1897.

The St. John River woodboat in its final form was designed to carry wood on the river. Indeed, the majority were operated as lighters in the lumber business on the St. John River. However, they were put to other uses.

They conveyed deals from the hundreds of water-powered sawmills to the port of Saint John where they were reloaded on deep-sea vessels for the overseas market. The cargoes of ten or twelve woodboats were required to fill one of the square-riggers. The woodboat would be tied up at the bow of the ship and the deals loaded directly through the timber ports.

There was also a constant demand for their services in carrying timbers, planks, knees, and so forth, to the many shipyards at the mouth of the river. It was customary for many of the farmers on the lower part of the river to use their spare time during the winter months to cut these materials for shipbuilding on their property. As spring approached teams of oxen would haul the lumber to the shore of the lake or the river where it would be loaded on the woodboat for transportation to Saint John.

Still others brought cordwood down river to be used to heat the homes of the residents of Saint John. Most of the woodboats carrying this type of cargo were beached in Market Slip and the stove wood piled in two-wheeled carts. Market Slip was the popular congregating place for the odd-job men who were looking for work. Some of these men waited around with bucksaws and when a cart loaded with wood pulled away from the Slip they would follow it to its destination in the hope of getting the job of cutting the wood into stove lengths for the purchaser.

Woodboats were also extensively used to carry coal from the Minto and Newcastle fields to Saint John and Fredericton, some of it to be reloaded into ships at Saint John. The coal for many years was loaded aboard the woodboats by means of wheelbarrows. Those woodboats carrying coal destined for Saint John were usually beached at York Slip where the McCormack and Zatzman fish establishment is now located. Two-wheeled dumpcarts would be drawn up alongside the woodboat and a plank run from the cart to the break in the rail, then wheelbarrows were used to do the unloading. Most of the coal used in Saint John was sold to the blacksmiths.

Mention must be made, too, of the staggering deckloads of hay which these boats carried on the river. These loads of hay were often so high that the man at the helm could not see over them and on occasion was directed by shouted orders from forward.

The woodboat became widely known through the coastal trade. In this use it served principally to carry kiln wood to the limekilns at Rockland, Camden, Rockport, and Thomaston. The wood, cut in four-foot lengths, was purchased by the captains at various places along the river at $1.50 a cord and sold at a limekiln for $5.00 a cord. These limekilns which dotted the Maine coast during the last century used approximately thirty cords of wood at each burning with the result that there was a constant demand for wood. Due to the comparatively short run, the woodboats were able to carry towering deckloads. As with hay, these loads were sometimes so high that the helmsman had to be directed by another member of the crew stationed on the top of the load. The favorite practice was to load the vessel until she was deck to. In fact, very often, they were so deeply loaded that water stood several inches deep across the deck amidships. Although there was always a constant risk of losing the deckload in a rough sea, there was little danger of the craft sinking even should a serious leak develop since the buoyancy of the cargo would keep her afloat. Some of these farmers in the Rockland trade had only a hand compass and an almanac, which gave course from buoy to buoy, as navigational aids.

This seems a good point to note that back in 1812, when we were squaring off with our American cousins, serious consideration was even given to converting woodboats into gunboats! In an order entitled 'Primary arrangements to be observed in assembling the Militia in case of emergency,' dated 9 December 1812, were these instructions: 'and should the alarm [of an American attack] take place whilst the Water communication is open, the Officers commanding Corps should press all the Wood Boats in their respective Districts, to convey them to the places of Assembly and, afterwards, to assist in concentrating the force. The Boats to be provided with plenty of Sweeps, for the use of them. The Crews are to do their Militia Duty on board of them, instead of in the field; and, if time will permit the forecastle in the boats may be extended, with sufficient Supports, twelve feet in the rear of the fore-mast, to carry a gun....'[14]

With the signing of the Canadian Reciprocity Treaty in 1854, there was a great increase in trade with New England, and the ever adaptable woodboat proved that it was equally useful for carrying firewood, coal,

---

[14] This information is contained in a letter written by Ward Chipman in 1812 and forms part of the Hazen collection of papers in the New Brunswick Museum.

fish, flour, provisions, grain, ice, and dairy products to the New England ports. Woodboats were such a familiar sight on the St. John that they were mostly ignored, but once they ventured forth along the Maine coast their crews came in for many a jibe. Some of the Americans swore that the woodboats were built on the ice and in the spring were simply sawed off at the desired length. Crews signaling vessels which passed them would shout: 'Hey, cap! Better take your rudder in, it's outdoors.'[15]

Badly built and unseaworthy as many of them were, most of the captains preferred to hug the coast figuring that the danger of going aground was to be preferred to being caught in a sudden storm some distance from shore. If a gale did come up, most of the woodboats sought shelter in the first convenient harbor, bay, or cove, sometimes remaining there two or three weeks until the weather improved sufficiently to permit them to continue their voyage.

On their return trip up the coast the woodboats would carry products from the West Indies, manufactured goods, whaling products, hides, and especially lime and wood ash for the farms. Many, however, had no freight to bring back and returned light. Ballast, apparently, was never used.

There are records to show that woodboats were used as lighters on the east coast of New Brunswick and that they were occasionally pressed into service to refloat sunken steamers and sailing vessels. I am told, too, that the St. John woodboats went fishing, probably in the inshore fisheries. But only a handful of the boats in operation were used for such diversified purposes. One further, rather interesting use should be mentioned, however. About the middle of the last century it was quite common for the female members of the country household to make a trip to the city in a woodboat, usually owned and sailed by members of the family. The ladies generally enjoyed this experience as it meant a welcome break in their otherwise lonely lives. Apparently the woodboat crew was glad to see them too as it meant that the cabin would be straightened up and dishwashing would no longer be a problem, to say nothing of the home cooking which the ladies brought in their baskets and prepared over the brick fireplace.

Although after their advent the steamers handled most of the passenger traffic, some of the woodboats managed to capture a share of this trade. In 1855 a line of three woodboats was advertised to sail twice a week for Fredericton. Just what degree of success this project had we do not know,

[15] They were known the length of the New England coast as 'Johnny Woodboat,' but this name was not used in New Brunswick.

but a few of the best-equipped boats continued for thirty years to carry passengers. As late as 1879 *Duke of Newcastle* under command of Captain J. W. Anderson was still carrying way freight and passengers; she was one of the best-equipped vessels for this purpose. Another, *Teneriff,* sailed by Captain Heran Humphrey a few years later, carried freight and passengers between Washademoak and Indiantown.

Although, as we have seen, the last woodboat was condemned at Saint John in 1930, it was long before this that they had begun to wane in popularity. The schooner had proved to be much more suitable in the New England trade. The two-sail scow had replaced it in popularity on the river because of its shallow draft and its ability to sail in waters inaccessible to the woodboat. The cargoes of country produce and general freight were taken over by the steamers. The 'coup de grace' was administered when scows towed by small tugs captured the wood-carrying business.

IV

Perils at Sea

Murder at Sea　　　　　　　　　　　153
by R. C. Holmes

Mutiny on *Junior*　　　　　　　　163
by Sheldon H. Harris

A Tidal Wave at Huanillos, Chile, in 1877　　183
by Lincoln Colcord

The bountiful sea, a worldwide highway for commerce, is also a perilous sea. In the days of sail and long voyages, fire, storms, mutiny, and a lee shore were but a few of the hazards encountered by the sailor as part of his day's work.

Murder at Sea

BY R. C. HOLMES

IN 1884 Dudley and Stephens (master and mate of the yacht *Mignonette*) were indicted at Exeter Assizes for the murder of the cabin boy Parker. What the indictment did not mention though the law report (Regina *v.* Dudley and Stephens, L. R. 14, Q. B. D. 273) does, was that they ate him, too, an effective if unusual way of getting rid of the incriminating evidence, though one which may cause a deprecating eyebrow or two to be raised among more conventional landlubberly murderers.

The two prisoners, together with a seaman named Brooks and the *pièce de résistance,* took to a boat when the yacht sank in the South Atlantic over one thousand miles from Cape Town. The only food in the boat was two one-pound tins of turnips, which in itself is curious. There was apparently no time to provision the boat properly, yet tins of turnips are hardly the things one finds on the decks of yachts in much profusion. However, that was all they had; not a very appetizing, and even less a sustaining, stock of food with which to be adrift in a small boat on the high seas.

Apart from this, they had nothing to eat for three days, but on the fourth they caught a small turtle, which lasted them until the twelfth day. Thereafter they went hungry until the twentieth day, when the act for which they were indicted took place. The only drink they had was a little rain water collected in an outspread oilskin.

On the eighteenth day Dudley suggested to Stephens and Brooks that one of the boat's occupants should be sacrificed to feed the rest, but Brooks demurred, and it appears that the boy was not asked for his opinion. On the nineteenth day Dudley renewed his proposal, and again Brooks dissented, nor was the boy consulted. So Dudley proposed that if no vessel were sighted by the next day, the boy should be killed, but still Brooks would not assent. The following day Dudley told Brooks that the latter had better try to get some sleep, and made signs to him and Stephens that the boy should be butchered, but though Stephens agreed, licking his lips, Brooks still objected. The boy, according to the evidence offered to the jury 'was lying in the bottom of the boat, quite helpless and extremely weakened by famine and drinking sea water, and unable to make any resistance, nor did he ever assent to being killed. Dudley went to the boy, telling him his time had come, put a knife to his throat and killed him.'

According to the evidence, the boy provided the remaining three with food for four days. They seem to have consumed him with improvident speed, considering the privations they had just experienced, and the prospect that those privations would be resumed and possibly prolonged after their gruesome *plat du jour* was eaten. After all, even the small turtle had lasted the four of them for eight days, but possibly they thought it advisable to swallow their last helpings hastily, or even throw the remainder overboard uneaten, for on the fourth day after the murder a passing vessel sighted them, and they would naturally not wish their rescuers to notice any embarrassing leftovers on the sides of their plates.

So much for the story, and the evidence offered in court. The legal position, however, was complicated by the jury, whose decision was that 'if the men had not fed upon the boy they would probably not have survived to be rescued but would within four days have died of famine; that the boy, being in a much weaker condition, was likely to have died before them; that at the time of the act there was no sail in sight nor any reasonable prospect of relief; that in these circumstances there appeared to the prisoners every probability that unless they then or very soon fed upon the boy or one of themselves they would die of starvation; that there was no appreciable chance of saving life except by killing some one for the others to eat; that, assuming the necessity to kill any one, there was no greater necessity for killing the boy than any of the other three men; but whether, upon the whole matter, the prisoners were and are guilty of murder the jury are ignorant, and refer to the Court.'

In other words, after giving a summary of what might have, should have, and couldn't have happened, the twelve good men and true confessed that they could not decide if what actually did happen was right or wrong. So the five senior judges of the Queen's Bench sat to consider this unusual verdict, the moot point being 'does necessity excuse murder?', and Lord Coleridge, in announcing the findings of the five, made it abundantly clear that though it was comparatively easy to give a legal definition of 'murder,' it was extraordinarily difficult to lay down any ruling as to what constituted 'necessity,' especially in view of the fact that future murderers might benefit from the definition, or even create conditions of necessity as an excuse for killing. The judges did appreciate the appalling choice which confronted the prisoners, but felt legally bound to find them guilty of murder, for which they were sentenced to death, a penalty which was almost immediately commuted by the Crown to one of six months imprisonment without hard labor.

Except for the turnips, the affair is strangely reminiscent of the gruesome though purely fictitious event supposed to have occurred on board *Nancy Brig* in the Indian Ocean. It is interesting to note that W. S. Gilbert, the author of 'The Yarn of the Nancy Bell' (written and published several years before the case of cannibalism just cited) tells us that the poem was originally offered to *Punch,* but was, however, declined by the then editor on the ground that it was 'too cannibalistic for his readers' taste.'

Nearly a century before Parker went the way of most flesh, a somewhat similar incident had occurred in very nearly the same locality, the greatest difference being that cannibalism followed suicide instead of murder. In 1799 six deserters from the garrison at St. Helena stole a boat and tried to row to an American ship which was in the offing. Failing to make her, they decided to carry on to Ascension Island, over 600 miles away, a foolhardy plan, considering that they had but two pairs of oars, no sails, and only one of them had any seafaring experience. They were better off than the crew of *Mignonette,* however, for though they had no tinned turnips for hors d'oeuvres, they did have 25 lbs. of biscuits and a small breaker of water in addition to a chart and a compass.

They started to row on 10 June, and on the 26th they were still at it, in-out, in-out, having sighted no land and their food all gone. On 1 July they caught a small dolphin, which lasted them five days, after which they agreed to draw lots to decide who should be eaten by whom, and one McKennon lost. He calmly opened a vein and bled to death, whereupon the others fell to with hearty appetites. Two days after they had pulled the wishbone and swallowed the last toothsome morsel, they sighted land (the Bahamas, of all places; about five times as far from St. Helena as was Ascension), but in beaching their boat, two more lost their lives. Some time afterwards the ringleader, John Brown, whose conscience or digestion was troubling him, gave himself up to the authorities, and so the story became known.

That, however, was a suicide, and should really not be included in this article, considering its title, but to make up for it, the next is a threefold murder, which will more than bring up the average.

The barkentine *Herbert Fuller,* loaded with lumber, sailed from Boston in the summer of 1896, bound for Rosario. The master of her was Captain Charles I. Nash, and his wife accompanied him on the voyage. The mate was Thomas Bram, a naturalized American citizen, though born at St. Kitts, and there was also one passenger, Leslie H. Monks, a Harvard undergraduate.

Soon after sailing the master had a bitter quarrel with both the mate and the second mate, and also did not seem to approve of most of the crew. A few nights later, when the barkentine was about 800 miles from Boston, the passenger was awakened by violent screams from the chartroom where the master was sleeping. Monks called out to him several times, but receiving no reply, he went to investigate, and was horrified to find that both Captain Nash and his wife had been brutally murdered, apparently with an axe, for a very bloody one lay on the deck near them.

Monks immediately told the mate, who, after viewing the bodies, decided that a mutiny had broken out. So the two men armed themselves and remained on guard all night, the mate keeping his eye, doubtless his weather one, on the helmsman, another Brown, though Charlie this time, while Monks watched the forecastle. The fact that they made no attempt to call the second mate, whom they could have presumed to have been on their side in the case of a mutiny, was, as was pointed out at the subsequent trial, very curious.

The conduct of the crew when it turned out at dawn proved that the men had no thoughts of mutiny, nor were they aware of the tragedy. At the same time the steward discovered that the second mate would not have answered even if he had been called, for the simple reason that he had been murdered, too, and in a similar fashion.

Everybody knew that the murderer was still on board, and most seem to have suspected Charlie Brown, who, as he was steering the ship, apparently under the supervision of the mate who was on watch (or, at least, presumed to be), would appear to have had the least opportunity of any of leaping from cabin to cabin applying the axe to the inmates.

The vessel was headed back for Boston, and when land was sighted, the crew put both Brown and Bram in irons. The passenger Monks, who had the best opportunity of committing the crime, and no means of proving that he had remained in his cabin until he himself discovered the corpses, seems to have escaped any suspicion at all.

Bram was indicted for murder before a Federal Court at Boston, where he was found guilty and sentenced to death. His lawyers appealed against the sentence, but at the retrial he was again found guilty, but this time was not sentenced to be hanged but to life imprisonment. In each trial the defense accused Brown of the murder, the critical question being whether he could have left the wheel long enough to commit the murders without the vessel falling off her course, which the mate would have noticed. As usual, the expert witnesses who testified for each side proved conclusively to their own satisfaction (never a difficult task for expert witnesses) that this could and could not be done, nine ancient mariners stating at the first trial that he could have lashed the wheel and left it for twenty minutes, but at the second trial Captain Nash's brother, who had taken command of *Herbert Fuller,* testified that she would be off her course with the sails lifting in two minutes under such circumstances. Nobody seems to have suggested that it would (or should) have dawned on the mate that something was amiss if the ship was careering round the ocean with nobody at the wheel. Bram served fifteen years of his sentence in Atlanta Jail, being paroled in 1913, and granted a free pardon by President Wilson in 1919.

Thoughts about murders at sea had been brought to my mind by a novel I was reading, in which a sailor on board a sailing ship attempted to kill the master of her by dropping a marlin spike on him from aloft.

Death-dealing showers of tools, which the author appears to assume were part of the everyday life on board a sailing ship, seldom occurred at all in real life. In fact, during the seven years I was in sail, I cannot recall it happening once. The sailors in such ships were craftsmen in both senses of the word: they not only took great pride in their work—sailorizing, as they called it—but they were also proud of not doing certain things, and foremost among these was dropping things from aloft, whether by accident or negligence.

It is true that the sailor in the novel in question was supposed to be mad, but are not all sailors, not because they go to sea, but because they continue in that calling? The Romans spoke of the sea as 'the pasture of fools,' and Emerson, in *English Traits,* says 'the wonder is always new, that any man can be a sailor.' If we distrust the opinions of foreigners, as we generally do, our own Dr. Johnson 'opined' that no man would go to sea who had wit enough to get into jail, for being in a ship was being in jail with the added chance of getting drowned.

The only time I can remember anything falling from aloft through human agency was in a steamer, a troop-cum-hospital ship, on 12 Nov. 1918, when we were bound from Durban to Fremantle. A religious service was being held to give thanks for the Armistice; the ship's chaplain, surrounded by the officers, conducting it from the after part of the saloon deck, while the troops, who formed the main, and probably the most thankful part of the congregation, were grouped round the foot of the mainmast. Two sailors were working aloft on that mast: what they were doing I cannot remember, but it necessitated the use of a top maul, the nautical equivalent of a sledge hammer. The chaplain, in his address, gave little indication, I thought, of the Christian virtue of humility; he was grateful to God, but gave us the impression that He had no choice but to be on the side of the British. At this stage of his discourse there was a cry from aloft of 'stand from under,' and the top maul, like one of Jupiter's bolts, came whizzing down, striking the deck with a mighty crash at the chaplain's feet, and fortunately hurting nobody. After this tactful hint from one above, it was gratifying to observe that he finished his talk on a more humble and contrite note.

I myself was the innocent victim of a dastardly and cold-blooded attempted murder when I was an apprentice in the full-rigged ship *William Mitchell* when my indentures had nearly run their course. I was about twenty years old, and I considered I was as good a sailor as any on board the ship, an opinion which was apparently not shared by one of the best AB's in the forecastle, Joe, sometimes called Dago Joe, a hot-tempered man whose native tongue was Spanish, though Spain was not his homeland.

We were bending a main lower topsail in the tropics, and the watch was spreading along the footropes, preparatory to stretching the head of the sail. Joe had been one of the first aloft and was making for the post of honor, the weather yardarm, to take the responsible job of reeving and hauling the head earring. I resented him doing so, and, disdaining the footropes, ran along the top of the yard, reaching the coveted position just ahead of him. He was considerably peeved, but I think he would have accepted the situation as calmly as his temperament permitted, had I not, in my arrogance, made a disparaging remark. However, there I was, sitting astride the yardarm, hauling on the head earring with both hands; he was next to me, inboard, standing on the footrope and hauling on the head of the sail with one hand, while with the other, which Nature had supplied to ensure his own safety (one hand for yourself, one for the ship, we used to say), he gave me a hearty shove, making a rude remark in Spanish as he did so, from which I gathered that I had done something to annoy him. I slid gracefully off the yardarm, but in falling managed to clutch the lower-topsail sheet, which had been hauled up on the clewline, in readiness for shackling on to the clew of the sail. Thus was I able to climb down safely to the main yard below.

Unfortunately for Joe he did not have the opportunity of admiring my agility. He had leaned well outboard when he gave me that totally unmerited push, and as I let go the head earring, the head of the sail automatically slackened. The combination of these two circumstances caused him to lose his balance and his feet slid inboard along the footrope. He fell, too, whizzing past me when I was about halfway through what the second mate afterwards referred to (rather callously, I thought) as my Indian rope trick. But Joe was luckier than I think he deserved, for the mainsail was bellying out with sufficient rigidity to take his weight and he slid comfortably down. Evidently the shorn lamb is not the only one for whom the force of the wind is adjusted. He landed on the eiderdown-like lower topsail which we had previously unbent, and heaped, as if to catch him, on the main hatch; and he suffered only a severe shaking, proving to his satisfaction that a benign Providence looks after the just.

I should like to be able to add that after this we shook hands and became firm friends, but the very reverse was the case. We hated each other the more, but I soon sensed that he feared me as well; or rather, he feared the waiting in expectation of the revenge he was sure I would seek, and wondering how it would befall. In my charitable mood, I took advantage of his anxiety and suspense, and added to it whenever I could. I would steal up behind him at night, like the dusty curates of Grantchester, with lissom, though nautical rather than clerical, printless toe, holding a belaying pin, or other lethal but legal weapon, and then purposely stumble or make a noise just before I reached him. I hoped to make him feel like one that on a lonesome road doth walk in fear and dread, and having once turned round, walks on and turns no more his head, because he knows a frightful fiend doth close behind him tread; the confessed sensations of another, though more ancient, mariner with a killing on his conscience. I was solicitous in my offers to accompany him aloft after dark, especially when he was bound for a lonely, little-frequented part of the rigging. I was in the van when any heavy weight had to be lowered if he was at the receiving end, underneath. We were both glad when the voyage ended, for I found the strain of inventing menacing situations almost as unbearable as he did the anticipation of them.

That last example was not a successful murder at sea, nor even a premeditated one, but merely a case of a grown man feeling justifiably annoyed with a precocious youth. So to make up for the anticlimax we will finish with a coup which produced three dead master mariners in the same ship, and of which I am reminded by the name of Dr. Adolph Meyer, a New York physician, who, in the 1870's, augmented the profits derived from his practice by insuring the lives of his patients, and then prescribing a sea voyage, i.e., a trip in his rowing boat on a hot afternoon. When they became thirsty he hospitably pressed on them iced beer, laced (unknown to them, of course) with nitroglycerin, a refreshing beverage which, apparently, not only assuages the thirst, but causes those who drink it to die with all the superficial symptoms of sunstroke.

Dr. Meyer is not mentioned here because he prescribed his lethal nostrums afloat, but because his trial recalls that he was defended by the then well-known lawyer William F. Howe, who had previously appeared (in 1863) for the killer of the three dead master mariners.

William Griffin was the accused, and he was mate of a merchant ship which had been commandeered by the Union in the American Civil War. He was in sympathy with the Confederates, and he tried to persuade the master of his ship to sail south, run the blockade, and join them. This the master refused to do, and soon after he was found dead in his cabin. A new captain was appointed, and when he, too, would not fall in with Griffin's suggestions, he died in similar circumstances.

When a third master was found dead, the suspicions of the owners and the government authorities were aroused, and the body was sent to Boston, where an autopsy was performed. As the stomach was found to contain more copper sulphide than a sailor's stomach should, Griffin was arrested.

His guilt was unquestionable, for he pleaded guilty to manslaughter, but the Federal government, which was prosecuting, refused to accept this plea because of the taint of treason in his actions. The principal witness was the steward, who testified that he had seen Griffin rubbing the master's claret glass with some substance, the prosecuting counsel contending that, if good wine needs no bush, even less does it require the addition of copper sulphide. The defending lawyer, Howe, suggested that the steward himself was the guilty party, and as the jury disagreed in their verdict, a new trial was ordered.

This took a similar course to the previous one, no new evidence or witnesses being called, but the prosecuting counsel visibly swayed the jury by producing, during his final speech, the very obviously bereaved widows of the three captains, who filed silently into the court, weeping copiously, and dressed completely in black. Things would have looked even blacker for Griffin had he not been defended by a quick thinking and not too finicky advocate. Seated in court, listening with scarcely concealed admiration to his forensic skill were Howe's wife and young daughter. Without a moment's hesitation he pointed at them. 'Will you,' he asked the jury, 'on the unsupported testimony of this disreputable scullion make that woman a widow, and an orphan of that innocent child?' Mrs. Howe gazed pleadingly at the jury: in filial duty Miss Howe looked as innocent as possible at such short notice. Of course they wouldn't! Tears welled into twenty-four eyes as, without leaving the box, the jury decided that enough blood had already been shed, and William Griffin left the court without a stain of copper sulphide on his character.

Mutiny on Junior[*]

BY SHELDON H. HARRIS

I

NINETEENTH-century American whaling has always fascinated writers of the sea. Romance and adventure have abounded in the plethora of whaling literature. The image of a few men in an open boat, armed solely with a toggle harpoon, conquering a sixty-to-one-hundred-ton monster has fired the imagination of many; the whaleman's slogan, 'a dead whale or a stove boat,' reinforces the impression that only the strong and the pure of heart engaged in whaling. Even the more unpleasant aspects of whaling life have been clothed in the protective coloring of the picturesque by present-day spinners of whaling yarns.[1]

A detached examination of the facts, however, reveals much which was unpleasant about life aboard a whaling ship. Working conditions in the American merchant marine in the nineteenth century were generally appalling, and whaling was no exception. Ships' officers were often petty and cruel taskmasters. Sleeping quarters for the men were cramped and overcrowded. Ventilation was almost nonexistent. Food was of the cheapest quality, and because of poor packing, the rations served to the seamen were so decayed that often they were inedible.[2] The boredom and monotony of the long voyages[3] tended to break the morale of even the most adjusted 'green' hands.

As a result of these disgraceful conditions, sailors deserted in large numbers whenever a ship put into port. Fights between officers and crew broke out frequently.[4] Mutiny attempts occurred with remarkable fre-

---

[*] The *Junior* logbook is in the New Bedford Free Public Library, and I am indebted to Mr. Laurence G. Hill, Chief Librarian, for permission to quote from the manuscript.

[1] See for example, Edouard A. Stackpole, *The Sea-Hunters* (Philadelphia and New York, 1954), *passim*; Robert B. Robertson, *Of Whales And Men* (New York, 1954), *passim*; Chester S. Howland, *Thar She Blows!* (New York, 1951), *passim*; A. B. C. Whipple, *Yankee Whalers In The South Seas* (New York, 1954), *passim*.

[2] A brief, brilliant account of the actual conditions aboard a whaler may be found in Samuel Eliot Morison's classic, *The Maritime History of Massachusetts 1783-1860* (Second ed., Boston, 1941), pp. 314-326.

[3] Most whaling voyages took three to four years to complete.

[4] A federal grand jury in Boston on 18 September 1858 returned twenty-five separate indictments for assault at sea. New York *Times*, 24 September 1858.

quency. Stories of suppressed mutinies appeared with such regularity in the New Bedford and Nantucket newspapers in the 1840's and 1850's that citizens were no longer shocked when they read headlines as: 'More American Atrocities on Shipboard.'[5] Reporters became so accustomed to writing mutiny stories that they handled them in routine fashion. 'A mutiny occurred on board the whaleship *Warren*,' a typical account began, 'and we hear nine of the seamen are confined in irons. It is not a serious affair, however. . . .'[6] But on the evening of 25 December 1857, a mutiny erupted on board the New Bedford whaler *Junior* which was so horrible that the most hardened reporters regarded it as a 'serious affair.'[7]

II

In July 1857, there was considerable hustle and bustle along the burgeoning New Bedford wharves. The whaling capital of the world was enjoying its golden age of prosperity and, in this glorious year of rising whale-oil and whalebone prices, it was sending more than three hundred and thirty vessels to the whaling grounds throughout the world.[8] Nowhere was there more excitement and activity than in the offices of David R. Greene & Co., for the owners of *Junior* were outfitting her for another journey. Built at East Haddam, Connecticut, in 1836, *Junior* was a typical whaling ship of the era. One hundred fifteen feet in length, twenty-seven feet in width and thirteen and one half feet in depth, the vessel displaced about 378 tons. A two-decker, she was square sterned. Carrying three masts and a billethead, but no galleries, *Junior* had seen much service in the northern Pacific whaling grounds in a twenty-year career.[9]

Junior returned in May from a successful four-year expedition and her owners, typical Yankee ship's agents, were hopeful that their present investment in supplies and equipment for the long voyage to the Sea of Okhotsk, north of Japan, would bring back the usual huge profits. Careful not to waste one extra penny, they ordered stowed below decks some

[5] New Bedford *Evening Standard*, 3 May 1858.

[6] Ibid., 14 May 1858; also see the New Bedford weekly *Whalemen's Shipping List*, 16 January 1844, 23 January 1845, 29 February 1848, 1 July 1851, 10 May 1853, 19 January 1858, for representative reports of whaling mutinies.

[7] There are many popular accounts of the *Junior* mutiny. They all suffer from similar failings of insufficient research and an over-abundance of imagination. This has led to the citing of conversations and incidents which never took place. See New Bedford *Evening Standard*, 27 November 1896, 21 December 1919; New Bedford *Standard-Times*, 22 April 1934; Howland, op. cit., pp. 88-223; Whipple, op. cit., pp. 228-258; Foster Rhea Dulles, *Lowered Boats: A Chronicle of American Whaling* (New York, 1933), pp. 174-177.

[8] Morison, op. cit., p. 316.

[9] Alexander Starbuck, *History of the American Whale Fishery From Its Earliest Inception To The Year 1876* (Waltham, Massachusetts, 1878), pp. 374, 410, 444, 468, 502; Federal Archives Project, *Ship Registers of New Bedford, Mass.* (Boston, 1940), II (1851-1865), 135.

casks of meat and bread purchased in the Sandwich Islands on *Junior*'s previous voyage. This food, not in good condition when originally acquired, was now considered unfit for hog's food, but apparently good enough for the seamen aboard *Junior*.[10]

The ship's official papers listed four officers and twenty-nine crewmen. *Junior*'s former captain was unavailable for this trip. Consequently, the owners employed Archibald Mellen, Jr., of Nantucket, as his replacement. Mellen was only twenty-seven years old in 1857; *Junior* was his first ship. A dull, unimaginative person, lacking experience, and understandably awed by the great responsibility imposed upon him, the captain was to rely inordinately upon the advice of his first mate, Nelson Provost, of New Bedford. Provost was a man with a checkered past. Poorly educated, and with a quarrelsome disposition, he considered himself superior to most of the riff-raff with whom he was forced to associate. Nelson T. Lord, also from New Bedford, was second mate; John Smith, of Boston, was third officer. Lord and Smith were both good officers and had a knack for obtaining the best from a crew.

Since able seamen were difficult to find for the whaling fleet, *Junior*'s crew reflected the decline in the quality of men who went to sea. There was a good sprinkling of foreign-born, non-English-speaking hands on board. Of the Americans, most were young men who were unable to obtain employment in other fields and were going to sea for the first time. Some were running away from an unhappy home life; others were ex-jailbirds. The majority were of low intelligence and semiliterate. Because one or two had been to sea before, these were assigned to the responsible position of boatsteerers (harpooners).

Preparations were completed on 20 July, and on the twenty-first *Junior* set out to sea. All went well at first, but the crew began to grumble after a few weeks. Provost started to mistreat the men. His contempt for the crew, bordering almost on hysterical hatred, soon became apparent as he vented his fury. He had a habit of cuffing and kicking them whenever they displeased him—which was almost all of the time. Almost every crew member suffered from his cruelty. He appeared to take special pleasure in sadistically beating the green hands. One of these, Richard Cartha, Provost knocked senseless with a club. Provost rarely called a man by his name. Instead, he would address him, a seaman recalled, as 'd-d Irishman' or 'd-d Mickeys.'[11] Another later testified that he had

---

[10] Three casks of bread and twenty of meat were repacked and sent out with the ship. Boston *Evening Journal*, 16 November 1858.

[11] Ibid., 23 November 1858.

seen Captain Mellen interfere to prevent one of the crew from receiving a beating, and that 'Provost threatened to shoot half the men before he got home.'[12]

At first, the men were served adequate food, but they were soon introduced to the repacked Sandwich Island meat and bread. These staples were now moldy and wormy. The cook tried to disguise the quality of the bread by mixing it with grease and frying the mixture for the crew's breakfast pudding, 'scouse.' But this did not appease the men. 'We could eat wormy bread,' a seaman declared, but he could not eat the 'scouse' because 'sometimes there would be half a dozen worms in a cake, and sometimes more. . . .'[13] The meat was equally bad. It was 'not fit for anybody to eat,' Hugh Duff, *Junior*'s steward, testified. The meat was 'short . . . it was so soft that it would not hold together to boil . . . it smelt dreadfully,' he remembered. To make matters worse, a cask of the stinking meat would last a long time because the crew would not eat much of it at dinner. The few vegetables furnished to the men were of equally poor quality. Duff declared the beans served were 'old and moldy, and after being boiled was hard as stone.'[14]

Their patience wearing thin, the crew protested to the captain about Provost's brutal treatment and of the bad food. Mellen, spurred by Provost, told them conditions would not improve. Provost, however, warned the men he would have his revenge because they dared complain. He became so infuriated, he threatened to 'learn them to go aft and complain.'[15]

The crew was patently on edge, and nothing happened to divert their unhappiness. Day after weary day, month after monotonous month, *Junior* sailed over the vast expanse of ocean. Her ports of call were few; the men were refused shore leave at the infrequent stops. The ship rarely met another vessel; whales were nowhere to be found. Captain Mellen had nailed a $10 gold piece to the main mast as a prize to be given to the first man sighting a whale, but after six months at sea, no one could claim the reward. Tension and frustration among the men continued to mount. Gradually the crew began to come together in little groups at the end of the day's labor to commiserate with each other over their unhappy plight. One group gathered about the boatsteerer, Cyrus Plumer.

Plumer was a strange, moody, unstable person. He was perhaps no

[12] New Bedford *Evening Standard,* 16 November 1858.
[13] Ibid., 17 November 1858.
[14] Ibid., 23 November 1858.
[15] Ibid., 17 November 1858.

more than twenty-three or twenty-four years old in 1857. A tall, thin, gangling fellow, he was not at all impressive looking. His features were sharp, but the lower portion of his face was masked by a large blond mustache and a heavy beard; his most prominent feature was a long, thin hooked nose which obscured his tiny, half-shrunken, brown eyes and gave him a bird-like appearance.[16] Sly, scheming, with the craftiness which the not overly bright sometimes possess, and with so poor an education that he could barely scribble his name, Plumer, nevertheless, had a quiet air about him that inspired the crew's confidence in his ability.

His past was mysterious. It had been bandied about on the New Bedford docks and on board *Junior* that he was a black-sheep member of Massachusetts Senator Charles Sumner's family.[17] Whether he encouraged this rumor is unknown. Although he gave his home address on *Junior*'s crew list as Providence, Rhode Island, Plumer actually came from a prominent up-state New York family.[18] He had been to sea before and some said that, while he was a capable seaman, he could be a troublemaker when aroused. He sailed from New Bedford on *Daniel Wood*, in 1852, but left the ship in Honolulu because of some difficulty with the captain.[19] In 1855, he shipped out on *Golconda* of New Bedford. Somewhere off the South American coast he stole one of *Golconda*'s boats and, with two companions, deserted ship.[20] It is amazing that with this background, with which many in New Bedford were aware, Plumer, using his own name, was able to secure a berth on *Junior*.[21]

Plumer's closest companions aboard *Junior* were Richard Cartha and William Herbert. Cartha, a heavy-set youth of eighteen or nineteen, was hot-tempered and quick to nurse a hatred for anyone insulting him. He had not forgotten the beating Provost administered to him, and he longed to even the score. Herbert was only sixteen when he signed aboard *Junior*. The runaway son of a New Jersey clergyman, he had received a fair education and often was called upon by both officers and men to write letters

[16] New York *Times*, 26 August 1858; Boston *Daily Courier*, 26 August 1858.

[17] John W. Seymour to James Buchanan, Utica, New York, 4 July 1859, Department of Justice Records: 'Office of the Pardon Attorney, Case File Record Group 204, Pardon Case A-187,' National Archives.

[18] New Bedford *Daily Mercury*, 1 December 1858.

[19] New Bedford *Evening Standard*, 1 July 1859; 'Ms. Port Society Crew List, 1852,' p. 104, Old Dartmouth Historical Society Library, New Bedford, Mass. Plumer gives here his home address as Portland, Maine.

[20] Ibid. (1855), p. 33.

[21] Plumer later allegedly boasted (*Junior* ms. logbook, 4 January 1858) that he had 'taken two or three vessels' in the past, but he was obviously exaggerating the events described above. Ships' agents, although willing to sign on practically any petty criminal or troublemaker, would have refused from selfish motives to enlist former pirates.

for them. Young and impressionable, with a wild adventurous streak, he was willing to embark on any venture which would prove exciting. From time to time, other younger members of the crew would join the three in gripe sessions.

Some five or six weeks out of New Bedford, Plumer and his friends began planning to jump ship at the first opportunity. *Junior* was scheduled to make port at Fayal in the Azores, and the dissenters hoped to effect their escape at that landing. Their plans were frustrated, however, because the ship's officers were stationed on deck to prevent the men from leaving.

The men now made plans to seize *Junior*'s officers and force them to sail her to another port where they could flee to safety. They deliberately cut the whip of the flying jib and lured the second mate, Nelson Lord, forward to fix it. Lord climbed the boom to check the damage. Charles Fifield, one of Plumer's confederates, was to give the signal for the uprising by knocking the mate down. Fifield could accomplish his assignment only by causing Lord to fall into the sea to be drowned. He was willing to knock him down and tie him up, Fifield later testified, but he 'shrunk from the idea of murder.'[22] So, this attempt also failed.

On Friday, 25 December 1857, *Junior* cast anchor to celebrate Christmas at latitude 37° 58′ S, longitude 166° 57′ E. The vessel was some six days sail off the southeast coast of Australia. *Junior* had been to sea six months, and in all that time had not sighted a whale. Discipline on board was as rigid as ever, and the food served the men did not improve. Bored, frustrated and disgusted, the crew continued to grumble about their treatment.

At about six o'clock that evening, Captain Mellen distributed a small glass of brandy to all the men in honor of Christmas. The second mate, feeling sorry for the crew, gave Plumer a bottle of gin to pass among them.[23] Then, making certain all positions were fast and that all was safe and secure, the officers and most of the men retired for the night.

Plumer, Fifield, Cartha, Herbert, Cornelius Burns, John Hall and one or two others, however, sat around for hours brooding about how cruelly fate had handled them. Towards midnight, Plumer, exclaimed: 'By G-d this thing must be done tonight!' Someone asked what thing and Plumer replied, 'take the ship.' Then, apparently to fortify his own determination and that of his audience, he produced a coconut shell containing the

[22] Boston *Daily Courier*, 10 November 1858.
[23] Boston *Evening Journal*, 14 November 1858.

gin Lord had given him earlier. Everyone took a drink and plans were made.[24]

Quickly and silently the men gathered all the whaling guns, hatchets and harpoons available. Their plans set, each conspirator took his appointed station.[25] Two men were assigned to guard the entrance to the crew's quarters. Another two were placed outside the officers' cabin. About one o'clock on the morning of 26 December, Plumer, Cartha, Burns, Herbert and Hall crept quietly into the officers' quarters. Guns extra-loaded and cocked, the conspirators silently took aim at each of the sleeping men in their berths.[26] The muzzles of the guns nearly touching the victims, all was ready, and Plumer gave the order to fire. Instantly three large balls from a whaling gun wielded by Plumer entered Captain Mellen's left side. The balls penetrated with such force that they passed under his ribs and came out at his right side and lodged in the cabin wall. Mellen jumped up and exclaimed: 'Oh My God, what is this?' Plumer replied, 'God damn you, it is me.' He then caught Mellen by his hair and started whacking at him with a hatchet. Three or four strokes finished him and Mellen fell to the floor dead.

While Plumer was performing his bloody task, John Hall killed the third mate, also with a whaling gun. Burns, to make doubly certain Smith was dead, ran a boarding knife through him several times. Lord was shot and then Cartha insanely tried to carve him up. Using another boarding knife, Cartha struck at him repeatedly, but Lord finally managed to catch the blade in his hand and bent the point over the berth board. Cartha then wildly fired a pocket pistol into Lord's breast. But by some miracle, Lord managed to survive the attacks. Provost was shot six times, but all he suffered were flesh wounds in his shoulder. The gun had been held so close to his left cheek that its discharge took some of the skin off his cheek and set his clothes and the bedding on fire. Stunned by the shots, and suffering from loss of blood, the first mate fainted.

The rest of the crew was awakened by the shooting, and the gang temporarily abandoned their grisly work to inform the hands of the latest events. Although one of them later testified, 'We were then *made* come on deck and were *made* [to] arm ourselves with . . . Harpoons, spades, Axs

[24] Ibid., 10 November 1858.

[25] Although Fifield appears to have been in on the conspiracy from the first, he apparently hung back at the last moment and was not implicated to any large degree in the subsequent events.

[26] The following account is drawn principally from *Junior*'s manuscript log entry of 4 January 1858. This narrative was dictated by Provost and entered by one of the hands. Since the first mate was directly involved in the affair, his version must be used with care. I have accepted his statements in only those instances where they have been confirmed by other more objective reports.

[sic] & other things & were *made* stand at the Fore Main & Mizzen Hatchways,'[27] they were not unduly disturbed by the turn of affairs. The men did not really need much urging to undertake their new duties. Few had an abiding sense of loyalty to the officers, and those who did felt it prudent to conceal their feelings for the time being. After gorging themselves on decent food for the first time in months, they went below and broke into the officers' possessions and appropriated liquors, tobacco and everything else they could lay their hands on. All whaling equipment was thrown overboard; the officers' clothing and 'the Articles on board to recruit ship were destroyed.'

Provost recovered consciousness during the excitement and confusion on deck. He armed himself with a pistol and crept stealthily below to hide. Lord was not so fortunate as he was seized as he emerged from the cabin. Despite his wounds, he was put in irons and stowed in the forecastle for safekeeping.

The ship was taken and Plumer assumed complete charge of its direction. The officers' quarters were on fire. Therefore, Plumer's first task was to direct the hands in quelling the flames. Plumer, once the cabin was safe to enter, then assigned some men to dispose of the bodies. A rope was fastened to one of Mellen's ankles and he was hauled on deck. His body was weighted down with a heavy chain and cast overboard. The same procedure was used with John Smith's body, except that he was weighted down with a grindstone.[28]

The mutineers were under the impression that Provost, too, was dead, and assigned Anton Ludwig, a not-too-sober seaman, to search for his body in the cabin. The cabin was so filled with stifling smoke that Ludwig had a difficult time getting his bearings. His foot touched something while he was stumbling about, and he shouted, 'Another body, hard fast to a rope.' Plumer asked, 'Large or small whiskers?' Ludwig replied, 'Small whiskers.' A rope was thrown to him and he fastened it to the body. He soon discovered his error, however, for he found that he was hauling up the ship's dog. It had stumbled into the cabin during the shooting and suffocated to death when the cabin was set on fire. The incident, it was later noted, 'excited the merriest laughter,' and the men 'poked fun at the Dutchman.'[29]

With the bodies disposed, the men turned their attention to repairing the damaged ship. Then, an intensive but fruitless search for Provost

[27] 'The Proceedings On Deck As I Was Told,' *Junior* ms. logbook, 4 January 1858. Italics are in the original.
[28] Boston *Daily Courier*, 24 August 1858.
[29] Ibid., 26 August 1858.

was begun. Plumer now prayed that the first mate would be located alive because he discovered, to his horror, that no one except the hated Provost could navigate the ship. *Junior* was no good to him and his fellow mutineers if it could not be sailed to a safe berth. He wanted to escape to Australia, but as far as he knew, Australia could be in any direction; it might be six, ten, twenty, or forty days sail away.

Provost managed to elude his hunters for five awful days. During that period he suffered unspeakable pain. Locating some casks of bread and water, he managed to subsist on this fare, but it is remarkable that he stayed alive. Finally, on 30 December 1857, his hiding place was discovered, and he was brought on deck. His suffering was so apparent, and his appearance so pathetic, that even his captors were moved to pity him. The foremast hands told him, 'that if there had been any other person with me they could not have told who it was. I was so much altered. My hair stood upright from fear of being shot.'[30]

His captors handled him tenderly and dressed his wounds, but Cartha now attempted to have his revenge. Coming up to Provost with a 'pistol cocked and a hatchet raised,' he struck 'me on the lame shoulder with the Hatchet, & said I am going to shoot you,' the first mate later recalled. He made wild motions with the hatchet and roared, 'I will cut your nose off and kept striking near my face. Plumer told him to keep still and not shoot me. But had hard work to hold him back.'[31]

Plumer then took Provost aside and struck a bargain with him. He promised him his life and assured him that he would not be harmed further. He also promised that the ship would be turned over to him again once the mutineers were in sight of land. The first mate, in return, was to navigate *Junior* to Cape Howe, Australia. Provost frankly expected to be killed once *Junior* reached its destination but, having little to lose and everything to gain, he agreed to the proposition.

On Monday, 4 January 1858, *Junior* hove within twenty miles of land. Two whaleboats were loaded with food and equipment and all the ship's arms. Surprisingly, now that the time for separation had arrived, Plumer kept his promise, and Provost was not murdered. He was forced instead to swear on a Bible that he would head the ship for New Zealand. Plumer apparently expected that he would then have plenty of time to vanish into the Australian interior without trace.

Provost now asked Plumer for a favor. He was fearful of facing the authorities without some evidence that the remaining officers and crew

[30] *Junior* ms. logbook, 4 January 1858.
[31] Ibid.

had not participated in the mutiny. Plumer magnanimously replied that he would be delighted to leave a testimonial absolving the innocent of blame. The log was brought on deck, and he had William Herbert enter in it the following:

This is to testify that we Cyrus Plumer, John Hall, Richard Cartha, J. Cornelius Burns and William Herbert did on the night of the 25th of December last take Ship *Junior* and that all others in the Ship are quite innocent of the deed.

The Captain and third mate were killed and the second mate was wounded and taken prisoner at the time. The mate was wounded within the shoulder with the balls from a whaling gun and he was obliged for fear of suffocation to take himself to the lower hole [sic] where he remained until Wednesday afternoon. We could not find him before that but undertook a strict search and found him then. We promised his life and the ship if he would come out and surrender without any trouble and so he came out. Since he has been in the Ship he has been a good Officer and has kept his place. We agreed to leave him the greater part of the crew and we have put him under oath not to attempt to follow us; but to go straight away and not molest us. We shall watch around here fore [sic] some time and if he attempts to follow us or stay around here we shall come aboard and sink the ship. If we had not found Mr. Nelson[32] the ship would have been lost. We are taking two boats and ten men and everything that we want. We did not put Mr. Nelson in irons on account of his being wounded but we kept a strict guard over him all the time. We particularly wish to say that all others in the Ship but we five aforesaid men are quite innocent of any part in the affair.

	Signed	
Witnesses	Hugh Duff	Cyrus Plumer
	Henry T. Lord	John Hall
	Herman Graf	Richard Cartha
		Cornelius Burns
		William Herbert

Herbert signed the mutineers' names because the men could not write well. As he affixed their names to the document, each man touched the pen to give it a sense of legality.[33] As for the extraordinary document itself, comment would be superfluous.

Their business aboard *Junior* completed, the mutineers, and five crewmen who decided to throw in their lot with them, bade the men good-by and rowed happily to the near-by land. Provost waited until the two whaleboats were out of sight and then headed the ship in the direction of the nearest port, Horbart Town. This was a violation of the solemn oath given to Plumer, but he salved his conscience with the knowledge that the oath had been forcibly imposed upon him. The following day

[32] The first mate's name was Nelson Provost but he signed the ship's papers as 'Mr. Nelson,' and he was addressed by the crew as 'Mr. Nelson.'
[33] Boston *Daily Courier*, 12 November 1858.

MUTINY ON JUNIOR   173

Junior met the brig *Martha Ellen,* and her captain advised Provost to head directly for Sydney. There he could have his wounds attended to properly, and he could report the affair to the authorities and to the American consul. Provost accepted this advice and on Sunday, 10 January 1858, *Junior* set anchor in the port of Sydney, New South Wales. The long, horrible nightmare was over.[34]

III

News of the *Junior* mutiny spread quickly through the streets of Sydney and set off a wave of alarm. The Australian port was an important provisioning station for the whaling fleet, and the Australian authorities there were aware of the effect the recent events would have on the industry if the men were not apprehended quickly. *Junior*'s crew was interrogated; then, the steamer *Illawana* was hastily dispatched to the vicinity where the mutineers made their gallant farewell. It did not take the police long to catch up with them.

Plumer and his followers had split up after leaving *Junior*. Five men were assigned to each whaleboat and the two boats sailed in different directions. The former boatsteerer, with Charles Stanley, Richard Cartha, Jacob Rike and John Hall, landed along a deserted stretch of sandy beach near the tiny town of Merembula. Hall immediately took off for parts unknown and was never seen again. The remaining four were given a pleasant reception by the few settlers in the desolate area. Plumer assumed the name 'Captain Wilson' and had a gay time. He tantalized the residents with stories about his 'interesting' and romantic past. Plumer made such an impression on the local beauties that he was soon affianced to one of the loveliest neighborhood belles. But his dream of peaceful paradise was shattered as word reached the police of the presence of strangers in the area. Plumer and his companions were arrested in early February and hauled back to Sydney for a hearing.[35]

The remaining five, William Herbert, Adam Canell, Joseph Brooks, William Sampson and Cornelius Burns, fared no better. They headed for Port Albert but never made it. Their boat had to be abandoned on Gabo Island. Burns took off for the interior and was never found. He was believed to have been murdered by headhunters who inhabited the region. The other four were eking out a miserable existence when the police, again tipped off by settlers of the presence of strangers, swooped down

[34] *Junior* ms. Logbook, 4, 5, 6, 7, 8, 9, 10 January 1858.
[35] Boston *Daily Courier,* 24 August 1858; Robert D. Merrill to Lewis Cass, Sydney, 10 February 1858, Department of State Archives: 'Despatches from United States Consuls in Sydney, New South Wales,' National Archives.

and arrested them in late February. They, too, were sent back to Sydney.[36]

A lengthy court hearing was held in February and March. Depositions were taken from Provost, Lord and the crew. Plumer and the other prisoners were carefully interrogated. As a result of this hearing, the authorities recognized United States jurisdiction in the case. The men were turned over to the United States consul to arrange their transportation home for trial. The celebrated mutineers were lodged in the local jail until proper accommodations could be prepared.

This was a busy time for Robert D. Merrill, the able and conscientious American consul. Under his direction, the remaining damage to *Junior* was repaired and the vessel made seaworthy again. Eight sturdy cells were constructed in the steerage compartment of the ship for, ironically, the prisoners were to be returned to the United States in *Junior*. A new captain was hired because the crew, still burning with hatred for Provost, absolutely refused to sail under his command. Five men jumped ship in Sydney rather than chance the possibility of having to sail with him. So great was the personal danger to Provost that Merrill put him aboard another ship heading for America. He feared Provost might not reach New Bedford alive if he embarked on *Junior*.[37]

Toward the end of April 1858, preparations were completed, and the prisoners were placed on board *Junior* for the long voyage home. Each man was heavily manacled and was assigned to one of the newly built cells. They remained shackled for the duration of the trip and were not allowed to communicate with their fellow inmates. Six soldiers and two officers were sent along to prevent trouble.[38]

IV

News of the mutiny reached New Bedford on 5 April 1858. The whaling capital was horrified. Mutinies were an accepted risk in the whaling trade to most New Bedfordites, but the enormity of the *Junior* affair appalled even the most sophisticated citizen. The newspapers were full of the crime for New Bedford had not had such excitement since the British, during the American Revolution, had unsuccessfully attempted to burn the town.[39]

Junior arrived in New Bedford on 20 August 1858, after an uneventful

[36] Ibid., 10 March 1858; New Bedford weekly *Whalemen's Shipping List,* 20 April 1858.

[37] Robert D. Merrill to Lewis Cass, Sydney, 9 April 1858, Department of State Archives: "Despatches from United States Consuls in Sydney, New South Wales,' National Archives.

[38] New Bedford *Daily Mercury,* 21 August 1858.

[39] New Bedford weekly *Whalemen's Shipping List,* 6 April 1858. News of the crime was reported over a wide area, and the New York *Times,* 17 April 1858, published a detailed account.

voyage, and was given a tumultuous welcome. 'When the *Junior* was signalized there was considerable excitement in the streets,' a newspaper reported, 'the arrival of a vessel with such a freight being somewhat new in our local history.'[40] Almost the entire population was waiting at the docks to greet the vessel. It is no wonder that some of the prisoners suspected they were being given a hero's welcome, rather than being viewed as alleged murderers and pirates.

The prisoners were posed for daguerreotypes, and were then introduced to the crowd. The pictures were later placed in the window of a store in the center of town, and the shrine attracted tremendous crowds for more than a week. They were then sent on a tour of Cape Cod and the Islands. Nantucket staged almost as elaborate an exhibition of the daguerreotypes as New Bedford.[41] *Junior* became a tourist attraction and thousands of curious citizens visited the ship. 'No whaler that ever belonged to this port,' a newspaper observed, 'has been an object of so much interest....'[42]

The prisoners were sent to Boston on 21 August for arraignment before a United States Commissioner. A hearing was held in a tiny courtroom where, because of the public interest in the case, every seat in the room was filled; many of the curious were forced to stand throughout the proceedings. The windows were ordered shut to prevent the possibility of escape, and the hearing room became so overbearingly hot that some of the spectators fainted. 'The room was dark,' a reporter noted, 'and the rattling of the chains by which the prisoners were held together, created something of a sensation as they were marched in.'[43] Preliminary testimony taken, the Commissioner held the men without bail on two charges: murder and piracy.

V

The arraignment and all subsequent hearings were held in an atmosphere inimical to the interest of Plumer and his confederates. Most Boston and New Bedford newspapers were convinced that the men were guilty, and they did not conceal their views. 'In the annals of crime upon the high seas,' one typical editorial declared, 'we do not know where to look for [*Junior's*] . . . parallel since the days of the buccaneers on the Spanish Main.'[44] A surprised reporter noted at the preliminary hearing

[40] New Bedford *Evening Standard,* 21 August 1858.
[41] Ibid., 14 September 1858.
[42] New Bedford *Daily Mercury,* 5 October 1858.
[43] Boston *Daily Courier,* 23 August 1858.
[44] Ibid., 24 August 1858.

that the prisoners 'appear anything but the hardened villians [sic] their crime shows them to be, and this morning appeared to be in the most genial and contented humor.'[45] Another correspondent observed that, 'so plain is the case against them that they are as good as dead men.' They were, he continued, 'a fine-looking set of men as ever scuttled ships or cut a throat.... We have not had a multitudinous hanging for years, and the United States laws admit of open execution.'[46]

Hangings, however, could not take place until the men were tried and convicted and, much to the dismay of many, the mutineers were given all the privileges accorded defendants under the law. Further proceedings were postponed until suitable defense counsel could be obtained. This took some time to accomplish. Since they lacked funds to hire lawyers, the defendants were allowed to choose from a pool of court-appointed attorneys. The best legal talent in Boston thus became available to them, and they selected their defenders with care.[47]

Plumer obtained Benjamin F. Butler and Charles R. Chandler as his attorneys. Butler, who was soon to win notoriety for his conduct in the Civil War and in the Reconstruction era, was perhaps the best criminal lawyer in New England at the time. Now at the peak of his powers, he was noted for his unorthodox trial techniques and for his ability to sway juries with his masterfully emotional pleadings. Chandler, an extremely able criminal lawyer, possessed a fine reputation at the bar. The remaining defendants secured equally competent counsel.[48]

In September, Plumer, Cartha, Herbert and Charles Stanley were indicted by a federal grand jury on two counts of first-degree murder—that of Mellen and Smith—and one count of piracy. Trial was set for 6 November 1858. Rike, Canell, Brooks and Samson were considered passive bystanders during the mutiny and were, therefore, not indicted at this time and did not become involved in the subsequent proceedings.

All Boston and New Bedford were talking about the case for weeks preceding the trial. So much interest was generated that on the trial's opening day, the Boston federal courthouse was jammed to capacity. The

[45] Boston *Evening Journal,* 23 August 1858.

[46] 'Tyme' in the New York *Times,* 26 August 1858; see also New York *Herald,* 23 August 1858.

[47] The persistent rumor that Plumer was related to Charles Sumner would not be stilled. The New Bedford *Daily Mercury,* 1 December 1858, learned from an 'authentic source' that Plumer's real name was William Y. Sumner and that the sum of 'one thousand dollars was raised by the Sumner family, in the vicinity of Boston, to defray the expenses of employing counsel for his defense,' Professor David Donald, of Princeton University, is preparing a definitive life of Sumner, and in a conversation with the author in October 1958, doubted the authenticity of the *Mercury*'s source. Professor Donald has found no evidence in his researches that the Sumner family contributed to Plumer's defense.

[48] Ms. Records of the *Junior* Trial: 'Original Trial Record,' United States District Courthouse, Boston, Massachusetts.

corridors outside the courtroom were clogged with a struggling mass of humanity eager to obtain admittance; guards were hard-pressed to maintain order. The crowd made so much noise that the presiding justices, Peleg Sprague and Nathaniel Clifford, struggled to maintain judicial calm.

Despite the obvious public excitement and interest, the trial was a dull affair. Plumer and the others were tried solely for Captain Mellen's murder, the prosecution holding in reserve the other indictments in the event something went wrong at this trial. Day after day, the United States District Attorney, Charles Levi Woodbury, and his assistants, ploddingly laid before the court overwhelming evidence of the defendants' guilt. Provost, Lord, Fifield and other members of the crew reviewed the bloody events aboard the ship.[49] *Junior's* logbook was entered into the record, and the mutineers' extraordinary confession made a devastating impression. The evidence was so overwhelming that Charles Chandler noted in his diary after the fifth day of the trial: 'Mr. Plumer you will get hung I think if this is all the truth. I am sorry for you Poor Boy. You must look to your God for help for we can not do much hear [sic].'[50]

There was little that the defense could do for the men. Butler and the other defense counsel realized from the start that they would not win their case. If they could not have the case thrown out on technical grounds (Butler tried just that tack by denying United States jurisdiction in the affair, attacking the wording of the indictment, etc.),[51] the best they could hope for was a lenient sentence. By emphasizing the cruel conditions that prevailed aboard *Junior*, the defense hoped to arouse the sympathy of the jury and the judges. State witnesses in cross-examination testified freely to Provost's inhuman conduct and to the unbelievably bad food served the men. The few defense witnesses called confined their testimony exclusively to the first mate's behavior and the quality of the food.

The prosecution took fourteen days to present its case. The defense needed but one afternoon. On the sixteenth day of the trial, 26 November 1858, the defense and the prosecution summed up. Woodbury reviewed the evidence ably, but it was in Butler's speech that the true significance of the case was revealed. The points he made were to be repeated by others over the years.

He did not deny the men's guilt. He freely admitted the charge. How-

---

[49] The stenographic record of the trial has disappeared, but the Boston *Daily Courier* printed a detailed daily report of the trial. I have used also the accounts in the Boston *Evening Journal*, New Bedford *Daily Mercury* and the New Bedford *Evening Standard*.

[50] Department of Justice Records: '*Junior* Case Scrapbook,' p. 19, Office of the Pardon Attorney, Case File Record Group 204, Pardon Case A-187, National Archives.

[51] The court overruled every defense objection. Boston *Evening Journal*, 6 November 1858.

ever, Plumer and the others were not guilty of premeditated murder, he declared, but of the lesser crime of manslaughter, which was provoked by the brutal conditions aboard *Junior*. Their crime was sordid, but the practices of the ships' owners and the officers serving them were equally sordid. He called for laws to protect seamen from the abuse to which they were constantly being subjected. 'There is no Mrs. Stowe or *Uncle Tom's Cabin*, to depict before the world the horrors of shipboard,' he noted, but 'he thought it would be well for Congress instead of legislating so incessantly for black men, should make an effort for the protection of white, who without such protection, are obliged to answer for an act freeing themselves from tyranny.' Heatedly, he urged the jury not to believe that 'the merchant commerce of the United States cannot go on if Plumer is not hanged.'[52]

Butler spoke for over five hours. His was an emotional address, and he pulled out all stops. The appeal was so effective that a hostile reporter was moved to note the 'feeling and beauty of [his] language.' At the close of his address, 'he was applauded for a moment by many of the spectators whom the eloquence of the advocate had caused for a moment to forget the proprieties of the place.'[53]

The jury, too, was impressed with his speech. They brought in a verdict of manslaughter for Herbert, Cartha and Stanley. Butler's persuasive eloquence could not, however, save Plumer who was convicted of first-degree murder.[54] Sentencing was delayed until the other charges against the men were resolved.

Reaction to the trial's verdict was mixed. Commercial interests and their newspaper supporters raged that three of the men had cheated the gallows. They feared the effect the relative leniency of the verdict would have on discipline in the merchant fleet. They refused to recognize the need for reform; their only concern was with the possible breakdown of the officers' control over the seamen.[55] It was charged that the decision was 'unjustifiable compromise; that one juror refused to agree to a verdict of murder in regard to Plumer, unless his fellows would let off the other three' with a manslaughter conviction.[56] But, they consoled themselves, perhaps the next trial would bring a better result, since the third mate's murder indictment was still pending.

[52] Boston *Daily Courier*, 27 November 1858.
[53] Boston *Evening Journal*, 26 November 1858.
[54] Ms. Records of the *Junior* Trial: 'Memorandum of Verdict, Boston, November 30, 1858,' United States District Courthouse, Boston, Massachusetts.
[55] See Boston *Daily Courier*, 1 December 1858; New Bedford *Daily Mercury*, 1 December 1858.
[56] Boston *Daily Courier*, 21 April 1859.

The second *Junior* trial opened on 9 April 1859. The District Attorney, satisfied that Plumer would be hanged on the basis of his previous conviction, spared him the ordeal of this trial. Only Cartha, Herbert and Stanley were tried for killing John Smith, the third mate. After short and uneventful proceedings, the trio was convicted of manslaughter.[57]

VI

The four mutineers were sentenced for their crimes on 21 April 1859. Plumer was given an opportunity to make a statement before sentence was pronounced, and his appeal took a leaf from his brilliant counsel's argument. Picturing himself as the victim of the brutality of the maritime service, he begged for mercy because 'it would not be for the interest of commerce to put him to death.' He reminded the court that he had spared Provost's and Lord's lives, and if he was executed, 'the effect of his death would be, in any future similar case, to induce mutineers to act upon the maxim, that dead men tell no tales.'[58]

His plea did not move the judges, and he was sentenced to be hanged sometime between the hours of eleven in the morning and one o'clock in the afternoon on 24 June 1859. Cartha, Herbert and Stanley were sentenced to two years and ten months hard labor for their rôles in Captain Mellen's murder. In addition, they were fined one thousand dollars each.[59] The penalty for Smith's murder was a little higher, and the men were given three-year sentences and again fined one thousand dollars. The sentences were to run consecutively.[60]

The lines were now drawn between those who hoped to use the *Junior* trial verdicts as a vehicle to promote reform in the merchant marine, and those who feared the decline in discipline on board ship because all the mutineers were not to be executed. Reformers agitated for commutation of Plumer's sentence. Leniency shown to Plumer, they argued, would act as a spur to the shipowners to clean up conditions in the service. The commercial interests and their allies, on the other hand, were disturbed by the sentences. Reflecting their reaction, the Boston *Daily Courier*[61] warned that 'it is not possible to estimate the injurious effect...

---

[57] Ms. Records of the *Junior* Trial: 'Circuit Court Records, October 1858, Term,' pp. 643-647, United States District Courthouse, Boston, Massachusetts.

[58] Boston *Daily Courier*, 22 April 1859.

[59] Ms. Records of the *Junior* Trial: 'Original Trial Records,' United States District Courthouse, Boston, Massachusetts.

[60] Ms. Records of the *Junior* Trial: 'Circuit Court Records, October 1858, Term,' pp. 645-647, United States District Courthouse, Boston, Massachusetts.

[61] 21 April 1859; see also New Bedford *Daily Mercury*, 23 April 1859; New Bedford *Evening Standard*, 22 April, 7 July 1859.

[of the prison sentences] upon the discipline of our merchant marine.' They shuddered to think what would happen aboard whalers if Plumer were not hanged.

Reformers adopted Plumer's courtroom plea as their central argument. They urged clemency because his execution 'will not arrest mutinies in whaleships while the owners select the meanest men for masters & officers because they can get them cheap & while the same owners put food on board not fit for men to eat merely because they can buy that cheap.' Plumer's commutation would be 'an instructive lesson to such shipowners & outfitters, which would redound to the mercy & comfort of the thousands of seamen who toil so patiently . . . to increase the wealth of New England.'[62]

Working alone, the reformers might have failed in their efforts, but they were aided by some strong allies. Plumer's family had connections in the New York Democracy, and political figures began to pressure President Buchanan.[63] The country had been swept in the 1840's and 1850's with a strong anti-capital-punishment movement, and leaders of this movement joined in the cry to spare Plumer's life.[64] Petitions calling for commutation of his sentence were circulated by these diverse elements throughout New England and the Middle States. Incredible results were achieved in a short period of time. Over twenty thousand people signed the petitions in the two months following Plumer's sentencing.

The prospect of possibly displeasing twenty thousand voters made James Buchanan hesitate, and on 23 June, he postponed the execution for two weeks.[65] Pressure continued to mount on the President. After consulting with the Cabinet, he decided on 5 July to commute Plumer's sentence to life imprisonment.[66]

---

[62] C. F. Winslow to James Buchanan, Washington, 15 June 1859, Department of Justice Records: 'Record Group 204, Records of the Office of the Pardon Attorney, Pardon Case Files, Letterbook B,' National Archives.

[63] John W. Seymour to James Buchanan, Utica, New York, 4 July 1859, Department of Justice Records: 'Office of the Pardon Attorney, Case File Record Group 204, Pardon Case A-187,' National Archives.

[64] Sheldon H. Harris, 'The Public Career of John Louis O'Sullivan' (ms. doctoral dissertation, Columbia University, 1958), pp. 105-114, 122-123, 156-157; David B. Davis, 'The Movement to Abolish Capital Punishment in America 1787-1861,' *The American Historical Review*, LXIII (October 1957), 23-46; New Bedford *Evening Standard,* 7 July 1859.

[65] Horace Greeley's New York *Tribune* could not help getting in a dig at Buchanan, even in this gesture of mercy, and declared the President would not commute Plumer's sentence, since he was 'neither an Irishman nor been engaged in the slave-trade piracy.' Quoted in the Boston *Daily Journal,* 24 June 1859.

[66] Ms. Records of the *Junior* Trial: 'Proclamation of James Buchanan, Washington, July 5, 1859,' United States District Courthouse, Boston, Massachusetts.

VII

Plumer received the news philosophically. His previous appeals had been turned down, and he had 'given up all hopes of a commutation and had made up his mind to die like a man.' He had even taken the precaution of becoming baptized a few days before the execution date.[67]

If the principal in the case received the news stoically, the shipowners did not. Panic bordering on hysteria swept through their ranks. Many predicted the end of the whaling fleet now that mutineers could 'get away' with murder. In the future, they predicted, there would be no holding the men in line; discipline on ships would now vanish. The New Bedford *Whalemen's Shipping List* raved[68] that 'the influence that has been brought to bear on this case is without a parallel . . . the most strenuous measures have been resorted to with the view to prejudice the public mind against . . . [whaleship] owners and those in command.' If the Executive extends clemency, it continued, to 'those who aim to take life and burn our property, the prosecution of the whalefishery will be materially lessened, if not wholly abandoned.' Whaling captains 'in these days must go well-armed, and expecting no favors at home, must exercise their own judgment for the maintenance of order, the preservation of peace, and protection of life.'

The Boston *Daily Courier* seconded the *Shipping List*'s lament.[69] Plumer's commutation, it declared, was a 'hard blow at the commercial welfare of the country.' If he, 'who has been guilty of cold-blooded piracy and murder, can be rescued from the just fate usually awarded such crimes, we might as well haul our ships up and dismantle them at once.' Chaos will prevail, it predicted, because seamen, knowing they could appeal to popular prejudice, would not hesitate to rebel against their officers, and the officers, 'in case of any difficulty or suspicion of insubordination, may be led to feel that their safety requires harsher and prompter measure than they were otherwise likely to resort to.'

VIII

The dire predictions of the pessimists did not come true. The bloody mutiny on board *Junior* was symptomatic of the cancer in the American merchant marine, but the outcome of the affair brought no immediate modification of the existing evils. The trials of the mutineers momentari-

---

[67] Boston *Daily Herald,* 7 July 1859.
[68] 12 July 1859.
[69] 8 July 1859.

ly focused attention on the plight of seamen, but the public's gaze was soon to be distracted by the drama of the Civil War.

Plumer's commutation did not serve as a landmark in the struggle to ameliorate brutality at sea.[70] Discipline on board ship remained as harsh as before. The hands were treated by their officers with a savagery that is incomprehensible today. Venal ships' agents remained unremitting in their efforts to devise new ways for cheating sailors of most of their hard-earned pay. The ships' owners continued their economizing at the expense of the crews' health and morale. And, as a result, mutinous outbreaks plagued the industry for years.[71] Working conditions for seamen did not improve until almost the end of the nineteenth century. In fact, it was not until the passage of the LaFollette Seaman's Act of 1915 that a serious effort was made to protect the rights of the men who went to sea.

The American whaling industry did enter into permanent decline shortly after the *Junior* trials.[72] Its demise was not due to the light prison sentences accorded mutineers, but to Edwin Drake's momentous discovery in Pennsylvania, in 1859—a cheaper illuminant than sperm oil: petroleum.

[70] Half insane after serving fifteen years, Plumer was pardoned by President Ulysses S. Grant in 1874. He, thereafter, faded into obscurity. W. F. Peddrick to the Warden of the Massachusetts State Prison (Boston), Washington, 18 July 1874, Department of Justice Records: 'Record Group 204, Records of the Office of the Pardon Attorney, Letterbook B,' National Archives.

[71] The New Bedford weekly *Whalemen's Shipping List* reports a mutiny at late as 5 April 1887.

[72] *Junior* made one more whaling voyage, and her owners then sold her to a New York firm in 1862. In 1865, she passed into foreign hands. Federal Archives Project, op. cit., II, 135.

A Tidal Wave at Huanillos, Chile, in 1877

BY LINCOLN COLCORD
Penobscot Marine Museum, Searsport, Maine

THE following letter was written by Captain E. D. P. Nickels, master of the American ship *Resolute,* to his brother in Searsport, Maine, Captain J. C. Nickels, who was managing owner of the vessel. It tells in vivid and seamanlike terms the story of a famous earthquake and tidal wave that devastated the coast of Chile on 9 May 1877.

The port of Huanillos, from which this letter was written, is situated on the straight north-and-south coast of Chile about a hundred miles south of the important nitrate port of Iquique. It is an open roadstead in the extreme sense of the term, fronting the Pacific on a bold shore without shelter and overshadowed by the mighty range of the Andes. It constituted, together with Lobos Point twelve miles to the northward and Pabello de Pica twenty-five miles to the northward, a group of three localities known in the days of the west coast guano trade as the 'southern guano ports.' They were not ports at all, but merely loading points, which had grown up because of important local deposits of guano. Nowhere in the world could shipping be so completely at the mercy of seismic disturbances as in these exposed anchorages which literally hung on the edge of a volcanic mountain range.

The fleet at Huanillos evidently consisted of twenty-six vessels; this is the number listed by Captain Nickels. Of these two were sunk outright with loss of life, two were completely wrecked on shore, eighteen were seriously damaged, and only four escaped without injury. The fleet at Pabello de Pica, Captain Nickels states, consisted of twenty-seven vessels, of which ten were sunk and only two escaped without damage. Assuming that a similar fleet of twenty-five odd vessels lay at Lobos Point, the catastrophe affected some seventy-five square rigged ships in this immediate locality.

I have never seen a first-hand account of the 1877 tidal wave from Pabello de Pica or Lobos Point, with lists of vessels in these ports and the damages sustained by them, although such accounts undoubtedly exist in letters from ship masters who went through the experience there. It would be interesting if we could receive some of these for publication in THE AMERICAN NEPTUNE.

The ship *Resolute,* Captain Nickels' command, was built by William H. Webb at New York in 1857, to be operated in the Black Star line of Liverpool packets under the management of Williams & Guion. A vessel of 1645 tons, 190 feet in length, 40.3 feet in breadth, and 28 feet in depth, she had three decks and was diagonally iron strapped for strength. Built just as the depression of 1857 was coming on, she was soon diverted to the general carrying trade.

In 1871 the *Resolute* was purchased from Williams & Guion by Captain J. C. Nickels, who recently had lost the clipper ship *Wild Rover* on Long Island. Thereafter for fourteen years she was owned and managed in Searsport, Maine, though hailing from New York, commanded by various Searsport ship masters. One of these, Captain Wilson C. Nichols, disappeared from her deck on a voyage from Cardiff to Rio de Janeiro under circumstances which have never been explained. The *Resolute* finally was sold to Dutch account, going under the flag of Holland without change of name. Re-rigged as a bark, she was abandoned in a sinking condition in March 1886, on a passage from Philadelphia to Europe.[1]

CAPT. J. C. NICKELS,   Huanillos, Chile, May 13, 1877.
   Searsport, Maine, U. S. A.
Dear Sir:—

Since I last wrote you a most terrible calamity has visited the shipping and towns at these southern guano deposits. On the 9th inst., at 8.30 P. M., occurred one of the severest earthquakes ever experienced by anyone here, followed by a tidal wave. I will try to describe it, but the terrors must be imagined.

On the morning of the 9th I found on heaving in the starboard chain, (having re-moored the ship the day before,) that it had unshackled at 30 fathoms and that the anchor was lost. We got the spare anchor over as soon as possible, and then took in the guano lying alongside, which was finished at 7 P. M. When I came on board at 6 P. M. and found that the mate had not time before supper to overhaul a range [of cable], I told him as it was so late he might let the men get supper and overhaul the range afterwards. But he, thinking it better to finish at once, did so before supper. The men had just finished their supper and hoisted the boat when the ship began to tremble.

[1] Frederick C. Matthews, *American Merchant Ships: 1850-1900* (Salem: Marine Research Society, 1930-31), I, 260-263.

The Earthquake

At first we experienced a trembling which increased for one-half minute or more; it kept growing stronger, lulling at times. It shook the ship like a leaf and you could hardly stand on the deck. The shock lasted in full strength perhaps two or three minutes; then it passed away. Then came a most terrifying noise from the shore, rocks rolling from the mountains into the water, making a deafening roar, which in the intense darkness was appalling.

After this had subsided, (perhaps ten minutes after the earthquake,) Capt. Adams of the ship *Theobald* shouted to me to slip stern moorings, as his ship was coming down on us. Before we could slip they parted, and we swung half around. We immediately let go the starboard anchor and paid out all the chain on deck. All this was caused by the first receding wave.

Scene 2nd.

Then the tidal wave came in like a boiling cauldron, ships taking anchors and chains with them as though they were feathers, and in the rush vessels shot round and round and collided with each other, going at the rate of eight to ten miles per hour. All we could do with the ship was to steer her. All around us we could hear crashing vessels. One vessel crossing our bow carried away the jibboom and fittings attached.

Scene 3rd.

After a lull of perhaps fifteen to twenty minutes, again the ships began to revolve and twist about and again vessels crashed and groaned in collision. Several were sunk at about this time. Howbeit, Almighty God kept us clear of all vessels doing us serious damage until 11.30 to 12 midnight, when the British bark *Samuel* backed stern first into the stern of this ship, striking us about the upper part of the stern moulding, breaking two planks only. Soon after, (at this time the rush of tide was greatly diminished,) the British ship *Wm. Leavitt* struck this ship, carrying away the bumkin on the port side, crashing the main rail for ten feet, etc. Again we swept clear, and soon after the ships circled completely around each other, and being entangled, we lashed the ships together to prevent further damage, or rather to prevent very serious damage. From midnight until daylight the tide became gradually diminished, and at last subsided with frequent shocks of earthquake.

When daylight broke all in sight was wreckage. Two ships were sunk, the *Geneva* and the *Avonmore*. The crew of the former were saved. But the fate of the *Avonmore* was shocking. Capt. Corfield (the master) was an old acquaintance of ours, having been with us in Callao and Lobos the last time, and having been well acquainted with him when mate of the ship *Live Oak* with Capt. Coombs at the Chincha Islands. He had on board Mrs. C., a most amiable lady, and three of the loveliest children I ever saw, Harold, the eldest, four years old, Mabel, two years old, and an infant five months old, together with the nurse. Capt. Trick of the British ship *Arctic* was visiting them. They all went down together, and only Capt. Corfield, with Harold, who died in his father's arms an hour after, were saved. On the next two days one by one his family were found, and services and prayers read over them. The poor father, who was so proud of them all, is nearly heart-broken, but he has been our guest and we have done all in our power to alleviate his sorrows. Besides these about eight seamen were drowned from the ships that sunk and went ashore.

At 4 A. M., and as soon as I dared, I sent Emma [Mrs. Nickels] in charge of Mr. Curtis [mate of the *Resolute,* afterwards Captain Henry G. Curtis] on board the ship *C. F. Sargent* of Yarmouth, which vessel was lying clear and apparently uninjured. I have just taken her [back] on board tonight. She behaved splendidly and I am proud of her bravery. I had her forward three times to avoid falling spars while in collision.

We have since had frequent moderate shocks, but of course nature will not find its equilibrium at once after such convulsions. The Governor's house, safe, Consul's building, Captain of the Port's house and office containing every ship's register, have been swept away. Only a few hovels remain at the upper part of the town. Strange to say we have saved the [guano] launches, which hung on alongside throughout the whole disaster.

Out of the fleet at P. de Pica[2] of twenty-seven vessels, only two escaped without damage; the rest are all seriously damaged, ten of which have been sunk. At the town of P. de Pica only one house remained; about 100 lives were lost on shore but only one life lost in the fleet. About half of the ships at Lobos Point were lost or seriously damaged.

At daylight we commenced, aided by half of the crew of the *Geneva,* to clear the ship from the ship *Wm. Leavitt.* The chains of both ships were around each other one or two turns, and the ships could not be swung without getting afoul of other ships. The *Resolute* and *Wm. Leavitt* were grinding heavily and chewing up fenders nearly as fast as we could put them in. The Capt. [of the *Leavitt*] went on shore in the morning to get a steamer. It was impossible for us to slip, as we had no spare anchor, and when we got his spare anchor over, the Capt. was away ashore drinking. The consequence was that after our ship had been pounding with the

---

[2] Pabello or Pabellon de Pica, twenty-five miles north of Huanillos.

W. L. for 30 hours, the *W. L.* slipped and was towed outside. She went to sea to-day badly cut up, bound to Callao.

After all our hard knocks, only three vessels lying in our part of the fleet have escaped with as little damage as we. Our anchors are so entangled together with those of the other ships that I doubt if we ever get them. Damages received, as far as can be seen at present: mizzen topgallant-mast carried away; 2 stern planks and sheathing broken; main rail and bulwarks, 10 feet in length, crushed aft on the port side; bumkin and fashion piece, port side, carried away; lower mizzen guard boards crushed; rail on after house broken, ten feet; main sheet bolt carried away; main lower guard boards badly crushed, and chain plates badly bent; several planks about the fore rigging considerably bruised; forward side, port, badly bruised; head rails, jibboom, fiddle head, etc., carried away, besides jibboom guys and jumpers; several lanyards and ropes in fore, main, and mizzen rigging chafed; several treenails started in the bends; three lodging and two hanging knees in upper and lower between decks started.

I have been sounding the ship on the port side with caulking irons, which [side] has been caulked since our arrival here, and have found the seams good thus far, although she has been severely shaken. Nearly all the ships which have received much damage have gone to Callao, and I know not what to do. I know not how the ship is insured, but if I hear nothing shall act for the good of all concerned.

One of the most serious parts of this dilemma is that no ships can get their anchors, and as all ours are on the bottom God only knows when we will be able to save them. About 12 of the original fleet will remain here to finish loading, and many more are bound here. The north shoots [chutes] with stages, etc., were washed down by the terrible surf this morning. Here more than two-thirds of the guano was shipped, and it will take at least six months to repair the damage, as the whole structure is demolished. I cannot predict when they will begin to ship guano from the other shoots. I don't think our lay-days by the charter party are counting. I wish I knew what to do with the ship, but I shall wait a while and learn more before I act.

Since sitting here writing we have had quite a shock of earthquake.

You have now the particulars as nearly as I can write. Trusting that however I act in this matter you will be satisfied,

I remain

Yours Truly

Emma joins me in love to you and Nettie. E. D. P. Nickels.

Ship *Benjamin Sewall*, built at Brunswick, Maine, 1874

Reproduced from a photograph by Thomas A. E. Luke in the Peabody Museum of Salem

A TIDAL WAVE AT HUANILLOS

LIST OF SHIPS AND DAMAGES RECEIVED BY THE TIDAL WAVE OF WEDNESDAY

Huanillos, May 12, 1877

American ship *Geneva*. Total wreck.

[Built by Houghton Bros. at Bath, Maine, in 1874. 1535 tons, 216.4 x 39.9 x 24.6. Hailed from Bath. ED.]

American ship *Benjamin Sewall*. Fore royalmast gone. Starboard side badly bruised. Slipped port anchor, gone to Callao.

[Last vessel built by C. S. Pennell & Co. at Brunswick, Maine, in 1874. 1362 tons, 202 x 38.9 x 24.1. Hailed from Boston. Wrecked on the Pescadores in the China Sea in 1903. ED.]

American ship *Theobald*. Fore topgallant-mast gone. Windlass carried away, besides other slight damage.

[Built at Richmond, Maine, in 1861. 981 tons, 172 x 34 x 23.6. Hailed from Richmond. ED.]

American ship *C. F. Sargent*. Rudder head carried away.

[Built by C. F. Sargent & Co. at Yarmouth, Maine, in 1874. 1704 tons, 220.3 x 41.2 x 26. Hailed from Yarmouth. ED.]

American ship *Jeremiah Thompson*. Jibboom and head gear all gone. Starboard bulwarks all smashed in fore and aft. Whole of starboard side badly cut and bruised. After house smashed in. Copper badly cut and torn. Slipped both anchors and gone to Callao.

[Built at Greenpoint, Long Island, N. Y., in 1854. 1904 tons, 216 x 43 x 28. Hailed from New York. Probably built for a packet ship in the Black Ball line. ED.]

American ship *Resolute*. Jibboom and head gear all gone. Billet head and head boards all smashed in. Whole of port side badly cut and bruised. Port channels all gone. Bulwarks from mizzen rigging aft all gone. After house smashed in. Copper on both sides badly cut and torn. Mizzen topgallant-mast carried away, besides other damage.

English ship *King Cholric*. Jibboom gone, besides other slight damage.

[Wooden ship, built by J. K. Dunlop at Portland, New Brunswick, in 1875. 1582 tons, 222.2 x 40 x 24. Hailed from St. John. ED.]

English bark *Sir John Lawrence*. Fore topgallant-mast gone. Topgallant forecastle badly smashed.

[Wooden bark, built at Aberdeen, Scotland, in 1864. 879 tons, 186 x 32.1 x 20.4. Hailed from Aberdeen. ED.]

English ship *Gov. Tilley*. Fore topgallant-mast carried away. Jibboom and head gear all gone. Both sides from water to rail badly cut and bruised. Channels all gone. Copper badly scratched and torn.

[Wooden ship, built by Cruickshank at St. John, New Brunswick, in 1875. 1420 tons, 201.6 x 38.5 x 24.2. Hailed from St. John. Ed.]

English ship *Canute*. No damage.

[Wooden ship, built at Quebec, Canada, in 1869. 1215 tons, 197.5 x 38.4 x 23.4. Hailed from Liverpool. Ed.]

English bark *Arctic*. No damage.

[Iron bark, built at Glasgow, Scotland, in 1875. 616 tons, 176 x 30.1 x 17.4. Hailed from Swansea. Ed.]

English bark *Conqueror*. Foremast gone to the deck. Jibboom and head gear all gone. Main topgallant-mast gone. Bulwarks badly smashed fore and aft.

[Wooden bark, built at Middleboro, England, in 1866. 599 tons, 165 x 29 x 18. Hailed from Liverpool. Ed.]

English ship *Wm. Leavitt*. Jibboom gone. Fore topgallant-mast gone. Both sides badly smashed fore and aft. Channels all gone. Slipped both anchors and sailed for Callao.

[Wooden ship, built at St. John, New Brunswick, in 1863. 1183 tons, 179.9 x 37.6 x 23.8. Hailed from Liverpool. Ed.]

English bark *Samuel*. Jibboom and bowsprit all gone. Fore and mizzen topgallant-masts gone. Stern badly smashed.

[Wooden bark, built at Quebec, Canada, in 1866. 360 tons, 130 x 28 x 14. Hailed from Bangor, Wales. Ed.]

English bark *Eliza Campbell*. Completely dismasted. Bulwarks all smashed in.

[Wooden bark, built at Maitland, Nova Scotia, in 1873. 597 tons, 148.9 x 28.9 x 17.8. Hailed from Glasgow. Ed.]

English ship *Avonmore*. Sunk. Complete wreck.

[Formerly American ship *Longwood*, built at Newburyport in 1863. 1260 tons, 193.7 x 38 x 24.2. Hailed from Bristol. Ed.]

English ship *Conference*. Complete wreck. Gone to pieces on the rocks.

[Wooden ship, built at Richibucto, New Brunswick, in 1858. 967 tons, 177.2 x 36.3 x 21.8. Hailed from Bristol. Ed.]

English ship *Conway Castle*. Complete wreck.

[Wooden ship, built at St. John, New Brunswick, in 1866. 1299 tons, 188.6 x 38.3 x 24. Hailed from Liverpool. Ed.]

Norwegian ship *Cleveland*. Damage slight.

> [Wooden ship, built at Quebec, Canada, in 1873. 1221 tons, 207.6 x 37.8 x 23. Hailed from Skien. ED.]

Swedish ship *Gauthiod*. Foremast gone to the deck. Main topgallant-mast and jibboom gone, besides other damage.

> [Wooden ship, built at Gefle, Sweden, in 1869. 803 tons, 146.9 x 32.8 x 19.7. Hailed from Gefle. ED.]

Swedish ship *Atlantic*. Lower main topsail yard broken. Port side badly cut and bruised.

> [Formerly American packet ship *Atlantic*, built at Williamsburg, Long Island, N. Y. in 1846. 736 tons, 141.7 x 30.8 x 19.7. Hailed from Härnosand. ED.]

Swedish ship *Ugglan*. [?] No damage.

German ship, name unknown, iron. Jibboom and bowsprit gone. Fore topgallant-mast carried away. Bulwarks and stern badly smashed.

Italian bark, name unknown. Completely dismasted.

Italian bark, name unknown. No damage.

German bark, name unknown. Jibboom carried away.

V

The Nineteenth-Century Navy

Men, Monotony, and Mouldy Beans—Life on   195
   Board Civil War Blockaders
     by James M. Merrill

     The Battle of the Rams   207
  by Lee Nathaniel Newcomer

     The Iron Sea Elephants   219
      by Walter Millis

A period of transition in naval warfare, the nineteenth century saw the development of the ironclad warships, the introduction of steam, and such experimental transition ships as rams and monitors.

Men, Monotony, and Mouldy Beans—Life on Board Civil War Blockaders

BY JAMES M. MERRILL

TO American volunteer seamen, life on board any ship carrying out routine assignments can be irksome and dull. Whether on board a Yankee gunboat off the African slave coast in 1844 or on board a cargo ship anchored in the back waters of the South Pacific a hundred years later, the average sailor fidgets, complains, and longs for a layover at a liberty port. Much Civil War duty was monotonous. Some bluejackets, who served on board Union blockaders off the Southern coasts, described ship routine as 'Pretty stupid,' and one declared it 'a perfect hell.'[1]

To the Union Navy in the Civil War went the task of blockading more than 3,000 miles of coastline from Virginia to Texas. This meant stationing gunboats off Confederate ports and in lonely rivers and sounds, whose shores were held frequently by enemy guerillas.[2] Although the work in the navy involved neither the degree of peril nor the amount of privation that attended the Civil War military campaigns, the awful monotony was broken only by exposure to the elements, and, occasionally, by Confederate blockade runners dashing out for the open sea. At night aboard the Yankee gunboats, no lights or noises were permitted, hatches were covered and lanterns were dimmed with casings. Expecting any minute to sight enemy craft, crews were ready to slip anchor cables and man the guns; steam was kept up; officers slept half dressed with their side arms within easy reach. One naval lieutenant declared in a letter home that he was 'being used up so fast by the anxieties and climate together' that if he

---

[1] See anonymous, 'Life on a Blockader,' *The Continental Monthly*, VI (1864), 50; Charles A. Post, 'A Diary on the Blockade in 1863,' *United States Naval Institute Proceedings*, XLIV (1918), 2346; and Smith to his family, on board *Bienville*, off Florida, 26 December 1861, Franklin E. Smith Papers, Duke University.

[2] James M. Merrill, 'The Hatteras Expedition, August, 1861,' *The North Carolina Historical Review*, XXIX (1952), 204-219.

should spend more time on blockade duty he would not be 'worth much.' Another summer of blockade duty, he stated,

will finish the breaking down. . . . The publick give credit for feats of arms, but the courage which is required for them, cannot compare with that which is needed to bear patiently, not only the thousand annoyances but the total absence of everything that makes life pleasant and even worth living.[3]

Characteristic of any navy at any time, complaints from Union bluejackets in 1861 increased as the Civil War lengthened from months into years. The men grumbled about everything from the daily routine, hard work, and heat, to food, homesickness, and the absence of girls. Journals, letters, and newspaper accounts all attest that the commonest grievance of the sailor in the Federal Navy concerned monotony. 'During the last week,' a seaman wrote home, 'I have seen enoughf [sic] of the sea. I am not sea sick but I am sick of the Sea.'[4] On board *Florida*, off Wilmington, North Carolina, a sailor penned in his diary:

I told her [his mother] she could get a fair idea of our 'adventures' if she would go on the roof of the house, on a hot summer day, and talk to half a dozen hotel hallboys, who are generally far more intelligent and agreeable than the average 'acting officer.' Then descend to the attic and drink some tepid water, full of iron-rust. Then go on to the roof again and repeat this 'adventurous process' at intervals, until she has tired out, and go to bed, with every thing shut down tight, so as not to show a light. Adventure! Bah! The blockade is the wrong place for it.[5]

For those 'raging lions' who believed that wars were won by firing cannon, the quiet and usually uneventful work of the blockade seemed to accomplish nothing.

Many sailors, especially those in more southerly waters, complained of the excessive heat. When the ships lay at anchor, ready to get under way at a moment's notice, the men were oppressed by the heat generated in the engine rooms. Off Charleston, South Carolina, one officer grumbled that he was in 'one constant drench of perspiration.'[6] Heat prostration was not uncommon.

But if life on board the wooden ships was hard, it was worse on board those vessels with 'steel corsets,' the monitors, which, as a class, were barely seaworthy. As waves dashed over one ironclad, which was headed for Charleston, one sailor yelled to his friend: 'I'd rather go to sea in a diving-

---

[3] Drayton to Hamilton, on board *Passaic*, Port Royal, 16 March 1863, Percival Drayton Papers, New York Public Library.

[4] Osborn to his girl friend, on board *Vanderbilt*, at sea, 2 October 1864, Joseph Bloomfield Osborn Papers, Library of Congress.

[5] Charles A. Post, op. cit., p. 2346.

[6] Smith to his wife, on board *Bienville*, off Charleston, 22 July 1862, Smith Papers.

bell.' Another cried out: 'Give me an oyster-scow! anything!—only let it be of wood, and something that will float over, instead of under the water.'[7] There was a general dislike for the ironclad service. Quarters on board were 'damp, dark, and dingy.' In hot climates, the monitors were 'almost impossible to live in.' The condensed moisture ran 'in streams from their bulkheads.' 'In fact,' an ironclad skipper observed, 'you can write your name with your finger on the walls of the cabins.' When the hatches were shut, temperatures below decks became 'intolerable' in the course of a few hours. In the colder climates, 'it was very much like living in a well.'[8] So arduous was the monitor service that crews' wages were increased one fourth, and the wooden steamer *Home* was sent South so that monitor men could have an opportunity to recuperate after becoming exhausted by the continued hard service.

Sailors of the entire fleet complained about seasickness. It was not unusual for recruits to write home, as one did: 'I am not used to bob[b]ing up and down on the Sea. . . . I tell you it made me disy [*sic*] the first day.'[9] Complaints were also leveled at the food which, in one instance, consisted of 'Moldy and Musty Beans' for twenty-five days.[10] One officer on board *Brazileira* recorded in his diary that he was awakened at night by the rats playing on him, nibbling at his fingers and pulling his hair.[11] Another sailor wrote to the Secretary of the Navy: 'Give me my discharge and let me go home. I am a poor, weak, miserable, nervous half-crazy boy . . . everything jar[s] . . . upon my delicate nerves. . . .'[12]

Routine on board the blockaders started at 5:30 A.M., when crews were rousted out of their hammocks, and the decks swept fore and aft, clothes scrubbed and the 'bright work' polished. Breakfast was served at 8:00 A.M.; dinner, at noon; supper, at 4:30 P.M. During the day's work at sea, the sailors were employed in the usual shipboard duties of cleaning guns, painting, polishing and standing watch.[13]

Drills were frequent. An article in *The Continental Monthly* described a typical exercise. Gun practice started with the rapid roll of the drum.

[7] Grenville M. Weeks, 'The Last Cruise of the Monitor,' *The Atlantic Monthly*, XI (1863), 368.
[8] See Gillett to [Lowry], on board *Sangamon*, Port Royal, 10 January 1865, Miscellaneous Papers of the Naval History Foundation, Library of Congress; Post, op. cit., p. 2339; and Drayton to Hamilton, on board *Passaic*, Washington Navy Yard, 5 December 1862, Drayton Papers.
[9] Osborn to his brother, on board *Vanderbilt*, at sea, 18 September 1864, Osborn Papers.
[10] Richards & Cambel to Livingston, Norfolk, 10 January 1863, Letters from Officers Commanding Squadrons, North Atlantic Blockading Squadron, National Archives.
[11] Manuscript log of U. S. bark *Brazileira*, Library of Congress, p. 10.
[12] Phillipson to Welles, Rip Raps, 11 February 1862, Letters from Rear Admirals, Commodores, and Captains, January-March 1862, National Archives.
[13] See Watch, Quarter, and Station Bill, U. S. frigate *Wabash*, National Archives.

'Here, there, everywhere,' men jumped to their feet and rushed to their battle stations fully equipped with cutlass and gun. 'Pass nine inch shell and load!' roared the captain. 'Now run out! train her two points off port quarter; elevate for five hundred yards! Fire! Run her in! Run out starboard gun! Run her home! Train her three points off starboard quarter! Fire!'

On the bridge of the hurricane deck, the first lieutenant supervised the men as they worked the guns, trained, loaded, and 'mimic[ked] fire.' He shouted through his speaking trumpet: 'Boarders and pikemen at port quarter! First boarders advance! Second boarders advance! Repel boarders! Retreat boarders! Pikemen cover cutlass division! Fire! Repel boarders!' In fifteen seconds, the writer recalled, men had crowded around the port bulwarks, and were 'slashing the air with the most Quixotic fury.' Crouched on bended knees, marines and pikemen aimed their rifles, snapped the triggers and poured into 'an imaginary foe a vast volley of imaginary balls.' Retreat was ordered, and the men returned to their respective watches, work, or recreation.[14]

The roll of the drums occasionally signaled a false alarm or a real attack. One humorous incident, which occurred at midnight on board *Flag*, was described by an officer in a letter to his parents. The slumbering men were awakened by the boatswain bellowing: 'Slip the cable! Slip the cable!' Rushing out on the spar deck, sailors saw a floating object bearing down on the ship, and heard the boatswain yell: 'Back her, back her, for God's sake back her; she is right under our bows.' One tar jumped for the deck, expecting to take his 'next breath among the stars.' As *Flag* backed her engines, the imagined torpedo boat glided harmlessly past in the swift current. A shot from one of *Flag*'s guns cut it in two, and the 'torpedo' proved to be merely a mass of floating seaweed.[15]

Although the work on the blockade was hard and monotonous, Yankee seamen improvised simple recreation. On board the blockaders, from sunset to 8:00 P.M., all hands assembled in groups on the forecastle to sing, or to listen to the violin or to old salts, who were 'proud to give . . . a song or a yarn.' One sailor's diary contains the notation that he heard two 'acting wardroom officers swap lies' until he nearly 'exploded with laughter.' Other groups sat on bitts making their own shoes, blouses and grass hats. Runaway 'Plantation darkeys,' who had managed to escape to

---

[14] Anonymous, 'Life on a Blockader,' op. cit., p. 50.

[15] Butts to his parents, on board *Flag*, off Charleston, n.d., in Frank B. Butts, 'A Cruise along the Blockade,' Rhode Island Soldiers and Sailors Historical Society, *Personal Narratives of Events in the War of the Rebellion, No. 12*, II (1881), 14.

the Union Navy, sang and danced and, on board *Minnesota,* their comical efforts brought 'roars of laughter' which could be heard in the captain's cabin.[16]

Music, the traditional entertainment at sea, was the staple morale raiser. On board *Vanderbilt,* officers bought a full set of musical instruments and formed a band of 'minstrels.'[17] Music was so popular in one squadron that the commander wrote the Secretary of the Navy:

> I have refrained all I could from troubling the Department with secondary matters, but will now ask of it the favor to order a Band of Music, to be enlisted for this ship.... My opinion, founded on long experience and observation, is that the moral and indeed physical effect, upon a large crew by music at stated hours is most satisfactory.[18]

Sailors who could not play, danced to the tunes of their more talented shipmates. In one wardroom, officers threw off their 'quarterdeck dignity,' and engaged in an Indian war dance. At the sound of a gong, a 'most ludicrous band of Amazons' appeared from the different staterooms wearing short dresses made of coffee bags, tarpaulin hats and heavy sea boots. Starting their dance, the fun was 'fast and furious' until one officer tried 'to cut a pigeon wing,' and fell flat on the deck, 'jarring the ship.'[19] After weeks of struggle, *Brazileira's* theatrical company held its first performance, which included a skit entitled 'Stage Struck,' a dance, several songs and the comic operetta 'Ethiopiana.' This proved so popular with the 'captive' audience that other shows were staged. A platform was rigged on the port side of the quarter-deck, running from the house to just aft the mainmast. Sails were swung around overhead so that the audience was entirely covered, and the stage was decorated with flags and greens. The printed programs announced:

> The manager has the honor to inform the officers and crew of the U. S. Bark *Brazileira* that he has fitted up at enormous expense this Truly Magnificent place of resort New Scenery, Costumes, Etc. No pains will be spared to make this Theatre the Best in the Country. Special Police will be in attendance to preserve order.

That evening, the show included 'The Laughable, Burlesque Operetta of Bombashes Furioso,' the 'Grand Trial Dance,' a song and a recitation. A diarist recorded that the whole thing was 'really very funny' and that

---

[16] See Gratten's journal, John W. Gratten Papers, Library of Congress; and Amos Burton, *A Journal of the Cruise of the U. S. Ship Susquehanna* ... (New York: Edward O. Jenkins, 1863), p. 76.

[17] Osborn to his girl friend, on board *Vanderbilt,* Boston, 22 October 1864, Osborn Papers.

[18] DuPont to Welles, on board *Wabash,* Port Royal, 12 December 1861, Letters from Officers Commanding Squadrons, South Atlantic Bloackading Squadron, National Archives.

[19] Gratten's journal.

one officer, although 'too heavy in figure,' looked 'the handsome woman to perfection.'[20]

The more salty on board the blockading ships spent hours in the tatooers' quarters. The most popular designs included hearts, bridal wreaths, 'true love-knots,' anchors and the 'mysteries of Religion' with the 'All seeing eye.' Seamen, who had a 'taste for the fine arts,' could select portraits of shepherds with their 'pipes—not tobacco,' crooks, lambs and cottages. A victim of 'the tender passion' from his girl friend, one sailor had himself embroidered with two hearts and two sets of initials, 'the whole surrounded by a nuptial wreath.' Another in the same predicament ordered crossed daggers and a bleeding heart pierced by a flaming dart.[21]

The more serious bluejacket, who was lucky enough to be on board a ship with a library, passed the hours by reading. Newspapers were one officer's greatest enjoyment, although he admitted that he often read Thackeray. For use with the forces afloat, the Navy Department, in 1864, purchased seventy-five Bibles, eighty Webster's English dictionaries, twenty-five atlases, and twenty copies of George Bancroft's *History of the United States*.[22] But the Bible, 'with few exceptions,' as an officer recalled in his memoirs, was 'thrown aside.'[23] The monitor *Dictator* possessed 'quite a nice library' of 200 volumes. 'Some of the books,' the captain wrote home, 'are valuable and some pretty editions. For instance Motley's rise of the Dutch republic $12 ... Halls Arctic Voyage—Harper made a deduction of 40 per cent on all the prices and much more on some of them ... and he threw in some books.'[24] The library on board *Penobscot* included, besides technical books on gunnery and steam, the Bible, the Constitution of the United States, an English dictionary, Cooper's *Naval History of the United States,* and Washington Irving's biographies of Columbus and George Washington.[25]

The emotional and psychological reaction of the Civil War sailor was no different from his counterpart in World War II. Like the fictional Mr. Roberts on board his AK in the South Pacific, seaman Osborn on board

[20] Log of *Brazileira*, pp. 3, 5, 7, 13, 17.

[21] *Colburn's United Service Magazine*, n.d., quoted in *The United States Army and Navy Journal*, 1 October 1864, II, 251.

[22] Contract for books for the United States Navy, 30 June 1864, 'Report of the Secretary of the Navy, 7 December 1863,' *House Exec. Doc., No. 1*, 38 Cong., 1 Sess. (Washington, 1863).

[23] Amos Burton, op. cit., p. 76.

[24] Rodgers to his wife, on board *Dictator*, New York, 11 December 1864, John Rodgers Papers, Library of Congress, box 124.

[25] 'List of books belonging to the Library of this vessel [gunboat *Penobscot*], Cape Fear, N. C., 1862,' Correspondence of Commander John M. B. Clitz, National Archives.

his gunboat off Charleston in 1864 complained that music, dancing, theatricals, and books could not replace the companionship of women. 'I like it well enough,' Osborn wrote his girl friend, 'only I miss Ladies society *yours* especial[l]y. Was it not for that I would be contented here.'[26] Whenever a blockader was anchored in a friendly port after months at sea, those on board watched for the 'petticoats.'[27] When women were reported passing on steamboats, tugs, or ferries, sailors rushed to the side, and all the spyglasses on the ship were immediately put into use. There was excitement when wives or nurses from nearby military camps visited the blockaders. 'A captain's lady was on board this morning,' noted an officer in his journal, 'the only white woman we have seen during the last five months.'[28] When it was reported that 'real-alive young ladies,' who were headed for a military camp down the coast, had arrived in Ossabaw Sound on board the transport *Neptune* and were coming on board *Brazileira,* the crew was thrown into 'a state of mild phrenzy,' although one diarist pointed out, 'few of us believed it really possible until we saw them distinctly undeniably before us.' As the women neared the ship, all hands were drummed to their battle stations. The diarist described the youngest as having 'great big black eyes of the most destructive character, exquisite feet and ankles . . . dazzling white stockings. Mem.' Ushering them into the wardroom, he recorded that the executive officer boasted that he was 'a sailor from the top of his head to the end of his big toe nail,' which made one woman's eyes open 'like saucers.' Everything in the wardroom was delightful except 'for that damn liquor.' One officer was a 'very little gone'; another, a 'little lively'; a third, 'pretty bad.' The ladies 'noticed it.' When they were about to leave, a crew member appeared on the starboard side leading a blanket horse on which was mounted another sailor in woman's clothes, who was introduced as 'Mrs. Jeff Davis.' Returning the ladies to *Neptune, Brazileira*'s boat crew circled the transport singing 'Good Night.'[29]

If the subject of women was foremost in the minds of the seamen, food and drink were a close second. Life was so dull on the blockaders that one man reported: 'When breakfast's done, the next thing I look forward to is dinner, and when that's done, I look for supper time.'[30] This seems hardly credible when, on board *Augusta,* a sailor's daily ration consisted

[26] Osborn to his girl friend, on board *Vanderbilt,* at sea, 30 October 1863, Osborn Papers.
[27] Log of *Brazileira,* p. 83.
[28] Amos Burton, op. cit., p. 102.
[29] Log of *Brazileira,* pp. 46-48.
[30] Anonymous, 'Life on a Blockader,' op. cit., p. 50.

of navy bread, salt beef or pork, flour, dried apples, desiccated potatoes and vegetables, sugar, tea, vinegar, molasses, rice and butter.[31] For those on board ships anchored in the calm waters of the sounds, peas, new potatoes, beets, blackberries and other 'garden produce' could be obtained from abandoned patches on shore. Oysters and crabs were found without difficulty.[32]

On special occasions the fare was improved. For Thanksgiving on board *Vanderbilt,* the ship's company ate 'hot bread and canned roast beef'; while on another vessel, the officers 'handsomely demolished' champagne and turkeys.[33] Although on Christmas the sailors ate pork and bean soup for dinner, packages from home, consisting of 'All sorts of good things, Sugar plums, [and] fruit cake,' filled the void.[34] Not satisfied even with Christmas boxes, one man promised in a letter:

If we come to N. Y. I want to lay in a large box of provisions consisting of Boiled ham, canned tomatoes and fruits, cake, bolonies [*sic*], sardines, herrings, onions, Lima beans and butter, cheese. . . . Our living here consists of hard crackers, pork, corned beef, tea, coffee, boiled flour, called duff, can[n]ed meat pickles and butter.[35]

'If you want a Sailor to work give him his whiskey and he is true to the letter,' one bluejacket commented in his journal.[36] Drunkenness among their crews drove most commanders to despair. In 1862, Congress passed a law stopping the sailors' grog ration[37] and, when the statute was read to enlisted men, it was met with 'disgust.'[38] They immediately started signing petitions to have the law repealed. Some called it 'an act of tyranny.'[39]

The law did not curb drunkenness. 'Strong drink,' a captain reminisced, was absolutely forbidden, but 'bottles labeled "Navy Sherry" were good substitutes.'[40] On board one ship, an officer went aft into the steerage, where he found a mess kettle full of ale and an officer 'pretty

---

[31] Manuscript journal of U. S. S. *Augusta,* October 1861-September 1862, National Archives.

[32] Rodgers to his wife, on board *Weehawken,* Port Royal, 15 May 1863, Rodgers Papers, box 124.

[33] Osborn to his girl friend, on board *Vanderbilt,* at sea, 27 November 1864, Osborn Papers; and Gratten's journal.

[34] Log of *Brazileira,* p. 8.

[35] Osborn to his brother, on board *Vanderbilt,* at sea, 4 October 1864, Osborn Papers.

[36] Kent Packard, ed., 'Jottings by the Way: A Sailors Log—1862-1864,' *The Pennsylvania Magazine of History and Biography,* LXXI (1947), 136.

[37] Welles' general order, Navy Department, 17 July 1862, *Official Records of the Union and Confederate Navies in the War of the Rebellion* (Washington, 1910), VII, 584. (Hereafter cited as *ONR*. All notations are to series 1 unless otherwise indicated.)

[38] Smith to his daughter, on board *Bienville,* off Charleston, 28 August 1862, Smith Papers.

[39] DuPont to Nickles, on board *Wabash,* Port Royal, 23 August 1863, *ONR,* XIII, 275.

[40] William G. Saltonstall, 'Personal Reminiscences of the War, 1861-1865,' Military Historical Society of Massachusetts, *Papers,* XII (1902), 280.

MEN, MONOTONY, AND MOULDY BEANS

well set up.'[41] 'I have never been so much impressed with the dreadful reality of sin,' a volunteer wrote home, 'as I have been here.'[42] Traffic in spirituous liquor was secretly pushed by private traders. When ashore in Port Royal, tars could buy liquor for $10 a bottle from men on the wharf. Some of this was described as 'the most wretched stuff, worth perhaps 10 cents.' Ten gallons of whiskey were stolen from the medical supplies on board *Powhatan* and, when petty officers confessed, they were promptly clamped in irons to await court-martial.[43] One seaman begged the commander of *Sabine* to disregard the charge of drunkenness against him because he was 'not a drinking man.' 'I have a wife,' he begged in a written statement, 'who will become crazy when she learns that [the] one . . . to whom she had always looked up with respect, has in an unguarded moment . . . blighted his future prospects . . . .'[44]

Commanding the ironclads in Charleston harbor, Admiral John Dahlgren ordered six barrels of whiskey from the army to be used 'under medical direction' for his men while in action.[45] This act was denounced by Secretary Welles, who sent the monitors a shipload of ice, and suggested the use of 'strong iced coffee' or 'Oatmeal mixed with water' as a substitute.[46]

The officers and enlisted men of the navy looked forward to liberty at towns occupied by Federal troops along the seaboard. When news arrived that the ship would go to a liberty port for provisions and possibly overhaul, the crew was 'perfectly electrified' and in 'a swirl of excitement.'[47] 'The Southern Federal capital,' Port Royal, chief naval base for the South Atlantic Blockading Squadron, was regarded as the most desirable liberty port along the rebel coast. Here were the headquarters of the military forces operating in the area and, consequently, there were many attractions which could not be found at the smaller stations. Port Royal had a 'good deal of society,' for many army wives had accompanied their husbands to the camp. All supplies for the squadron were received and distributed, and transports arrived daily, bringing fresh provisions and mail. For the officers and men, who had been stationed for months on some

---

[41] Log of *Brazileira*, p. 84.

[42] Osborn to his girl friend, on board *Vanderbilt*, at sea, 3 October 1864, Osborn Papers.

[43] See Lloyd Phoenix manuscript journal, United States Naval Academy, pp. 71-72; Drayton to DuPont, on board *Pawnee*, Fernandina, 11 May 1862, *ONR*, XIII, 3-4; and Packard, op. cit., p. 124.

[44] Wade to Ringgold, on board *Sabine*, 10 November 1861, Letters from Rear Admirals, Commodores, and Captains, January-March 1862, National Archives.

[45] Dahlgren to Bradford, on board *Dinsmore*, off Morris Island, 26 July 1863, *ONR*, XIV, 398.

[46] Welles to Dahlgren & enclosures, Navy Department, 5 August 1863, ibid., XIV, 418-419.

[47] Log of *Brazileira*, p. 78.

lonely river or at sea, steaming for Port Royal was 'like going to a city from some barren desert.'

Port Royal gave the appearance of a bustling town, and its little shops offered a variety of 'staple as well as fancy goods' to the sailor on liberty. Once ashore, the bluejackets usually went first to the Port Royal House, where they downed glasses of ale, and then walked to Beard and Co., a sutler's place, to buy needed articles or to have their pictures taken to send home. If, at the butcher shop, the 'jolly red faced' proprietor took a fancy to a sailor, he would ask him into the back room for some 'very fair whiskey.'

On Sunday liberty, sailors could attend church services at a theater which had been constructed by soldiers who had been 'weary of doing nothing.' Here, an Episcopalian minister in a 'rusty black gown' stood on the stage, while an army private played a melodeon and conducted the singing. Nearby, at the African Baptist Church, 'a tall copper-hued negro' pastor preached from behind a pine pulpit.

The leading liberty port for the North Atlantic Blockading Squadron was the 'queer old place' of Beaufort, North Carolina, which was 'neither London, Vienna, St. Petersburg, nor New York.' One man described the town 'as a string of houses, a number of churches, and lots of sand'; another, 'a sleepy Rip-Van-Winkle, dead-alive, gone-to-seed, fishing-smack town.' For recreation, the tar had a choice of either the bowling alley, 'where poor beer' was sold, or the billiard saloon.[48]

The happiest day of the sailor's life came when his ship was assigned to Philadelphia, New York, or Boston, for extensive repairs. When a captain gave the order to up-anchor for home, the men sprang to the windlass. 'I venture to say,' one man observed, 'that no anchor of equal weight and dimensions ... ever came up ... within the same space of time as ours did on that occasion.'[49] About to go home, one sailor counted his 150 greenbacks and wrote to a friend that he was 'going on a regular tare [sic]' when the ship docked.[50] Not fortunate enough to be homeward bound, another seaman commented: 'What luck some people do have! If one of the shells

[48] See Charles Nordoff, 'Two Weeks at Port Royal,' *Harper's New Monthly Magazine*, XXVII (1863), 112; Robert S. Davis, 'Three Months around Charleston Bar; or the Great Siege as We Saw It,' *The United States Service Magazine*, 1 (1864), 169; Charles C. Coffin, *Four Years of Fighting* ... (Boston: Ticknor & Fields, 1866), pp. 224-225; log of *Brazileira*, pp. 85-86, 90; and I. E. Vail, *Three Years* ... (New York: Abbey Press, 1902), pp. 79-80; Post, 'A Diary on the Blockade in 1863,' op. cit., p. 2572; and [John W. Adams], 'The Failure at Fort Fisher,' *The Overland Monthly*, IV (1870), 493.

[49] Vail, op. cit., pp. 68-69.

[50] Arthur M. Schlesinger, ed., 'A Bluejacket's Letters Home, 1863-1864,' *The New England Quarterly*, I (1928), 566.

had only hit us the other day *we* should be going home to glory, cool drinks and our best girls.'[51]

Although heroic in the face of enemy fire, this remark sums up the typical attitude of the seamen who felt themselves to be in the backwash of the Civil War or, for that matter, in any war.

[51] Charles A. Post, op. cit., pp. 2569-2570.

The Battle of the Rams

BY LEE NATHANIEL NEWCOMER

FRIDAY, 6 June 1862, dawned mild and clear and beautifully still on the Mississippi River with a bright sun and every indication of fair weather. Ardently Confederate Memphis, the 'Charleston of the West,' was astir unusually early that morning. Just after five o'clock, while ever-larger groups of spectators gathered on the bluffs and on the broad levee between the city and the river, a Confederate River Defense Fleet of eight steamers converted into gunboat rams left the landing, backed out into the stream, and with paddle wheels gouging holes in the muddy water, turned to form a double line of battle across the river. Upstream past a Federal fleet of ironclads in Hopefield Bend, United States Army rams were assembling. The stage was set for a unique incident in the history of American warfare, a battle between steamboat rams.

Of the three fleets the ironclads had been first on the river. Early in October 1861 *St. Louis* slid down the ways near her namesake city in the West, the first of a fleet of seven river ironclads meant to spearhead the Federal advance on the western waters.[1] On top of each wide, flat-bottomed hull was an oblong casement with sloping sides and a flat roof. Heavily armored on the front and more lightly on the sides, there were ports for thirteen guns, the three of heaviest caliber in the bow, four on each side, and two at the unarmored stern. The paddle wheel was placed just forward of the stern and sheltered on all sides. This center-wheel method of propulsion made the boats miserably slow, capable of only two or three miles an hour against a moderate current.[2]

Under Flag Officer Andrew H. Foote, an old salt who at first disliked his assignment to duty on 'the catfish front,' the ironclads fought at Forts

---

[1] Stevens and Westcott, *A History of Sea Power* (New York: Doubleday, Doran & Company, 1941), p. 248; Fletcher Pratt, *Civil War on the Western Waters* (New York: Henry Holt and Company, 1956), pp. 15-19.

[2] Ibid., p. 20; H. Allen Gosnell, *Guns on the Western Waters, the Story of River Gunboats in the Civil War* (Baton Rouge: Louisiana State University Press, 1949), pp. 16-17; W. D. Porter to Secretary Welles, 6 May 1861, *War of the Rebellion . . . Official Records of the Union and Confederate Navies* (30 vols., Washington, 1894-1914), series I, 23: p. 83.

Henry and Donelson. Then, joined by a number of small mortar boats, they went down the Mississippi where in April *Carondelet* skippered by Henry Walke ran the batteries at Island No. 10. This Confederate bastion surrendered, but the ironclads were soon stopped by formidable Fort Pillow, situated on the second Chickasaw bluff forty miles above Memphis. While Foote was held at bay, the Confederates assembled a fleet of gunboat rams to attack the ironclads.[3]

Composed of eight river steamboats purchased and converted at New Orleans, the River Defense Fleet was under the command of J. E. Montgomery, a well-known riverman who before the war had operated a line of steamboats between Louisville and Cincinnati. The machinery on the Confederate boats was protected with cotton bales and iron rails and guns were mounted on their decks, usually one forward and one aft with no shields for their gun crews. Designed to get behind the unwieldy Federal ironclads and ram their unarmored sterns, their bows were packed solid with timber; one-inch iron strips were bent around the bows and extended back to make them as effective as possible.[4]

Above Fort Pillow, Flag Officer Foote, his energy sapped by a foot wound received at Donelson—'aggravated by the miserable treatment of a horse doctor from Cincinnati'—and his digestion deranged 'by the disease of the climate,' was cautious. The guns he faced were on a steep red clay bluff opposite the lower end of a long horseshoe bend; their plunging fire could be very rough on the Federals. Foote pointed to the disadvantages of fighting his ironclads down river against either the fort or the Confederate gunboats, for if one of Foote's boats were disabled, it would drift down into the hands of the enemy, and if an enemy boat were captured the slow ironclads would lack the power to tow it upstream.[5]

So for day after day, as the redbud trees and the dogwood bloomed and faded on the Tennessee shore, Foote lay idle sending only a mortar boat down to lob thirteen-inch bombs into the fort to annoy the Confederates. The weather was hot—'Confound the mosquitoes with secession sympathies!'—there was no sea breeze on the river, and the interior of an ironclad was like an oven. For this reason some of his captains neglected Foote's order to keep up steam.

---

[3] Pratt, *Civil War on the Western Waters*, p. 55; James B. Eads, 'Recollections of Foote and the Gun-Boats,' *Battles and Leaders of the Civil War* (New York, 1884-1888), I, 343.

[4] *Confederate Veteran*, X: pp. 416-417 (Sept. 1902); Gosnell, *Guns on the Western Waters*, pp. 19-20; Ben La Bree, Ed., *The Confederate Soldier in the Civil War* (Louisville, 1897), pp. 388-389.

[5] Foote to M. C. Meigs, 23 April 1862, ibid., p. 71; [Henry Walke], *Naval Scenes on the Western Waters: The Gunboats Tyler, Carondelet and Lafayette* (n.p., n.d.), p. 247; [William G. Stevenson], *Thirteen Months in the Rebel Army* (New York, 1863), pp. 59-60.

Eventually the flag officer, on crutches, requested sick leave although 'my heart is still with the flotilla.' Captain Charles H. Davis, another career navy man and scholarly Boston Brahmin with gray rim whiskers and a flowing brown mustache, arrived on 9 May to take command. Foote turned his fleet over intact to his successor, also leaving him his mosquito net and straw hat as the new commander had not brought these necessities along. Davis wrote home that he enjoyed the venison, ortolans, and wild turkey shot nearby for his mess, as well as the mackinaw trout brought from afar, but that he had no wine, 'nothing but water, and Mississippi water at that—more dirty than that which runs down the gutter of Beacon Street in a summer shower.'[6]

Captain Davis soon had other things to worry about. Dashing General Jeff Thompson, former mayor of St. Joseph, Missouri, now 'the swamp fox of the Confederacy' and fresh from guerilla exploits, had just joined Montgomery's fleet, placing his men as sharpshooters aboard the various boats. It was decided to attack. Pressed by his men to open up his liquor supply, Thompson refused, saying, 'We'll go into this one dry.'[7]

Early on 10 May, a beautiful Sunday morning, the River Defense Fleet steamed up past Flower Island and around Craig's Head Point. In the lead was the fast *General Bragg*, a former Gulf steamer, 'cutting the wind with her tall spars like the swoop of an eagle.' The Federals were fairly caught at Plum Point Bend, tied up to the bank and most of them with steam down. Mortar boat No. 16 and its guard boat, *Cincinnati*, lay near Bulletin Bar, the crew of *Cincinnati* holystoning her deck. Seeing *Bragg* coming around the point with her walking beam churning up and down at a furious rate, *Cincinnati* tried desperately to get up enough steam to be maneuverable, her engineers throwing oil and anything that would burn on the fires. But in quick succession *Bragg* and two other attacking rams struck her, and one of Jeff Thompson's marksmen shot Captain Stembel through the neck. The last two rams found *Cincinnati*'s unarmored stern; the force of their blow sent her bow under, and water poured in from three sides. She just managed to make shallow water on the Tennessee side before she sank. Her crew scrambled for the wheelhouse which remained above water and soon were all perched there, as one of them said, 'like so many turkeys on a corn crib.'[8]

[6] Davis to his wife, 9, 28 May, Foote to Davis, 15 May 1862, Charles H. Davis, Jr., *Life of Charles Henry Davis, Rear Admiral, 1807-1877* (Boston, 1889), pp. 222-223, 229, and see p. 244.

[7] Jay Monaghan, *Swamp Fox of the Confederacy: The Life and Military Services of M. Jeff Thompson* (Tuscaloosa: Confederate Publishing Company, 1956), pp. 51-53.

[8] Jeff Thompson to General Beauregard, 10 May 1862, S. L. Phelps to Foote, 11 May 1862, *Official Records*, 23: pp. 54-55, 18-19; Walke, *Naval Scenes on the Western Waters*, p. 256; Eliot Callender, 'What a Boy Saw on the Mississippi,' in *Military Essays and Recollections: Papers Read before the*

In the melee which followed, Captain Kilty's ironclad, *Mound City*, was holed by the rams, run on a towhead, and put out of action. In another few minutes with *Carondelet* and other ironclad reinforcements appearing, Commodore Montgomery hoisted the recall signal.[9] He had done well enough and with only minor casualties. The Federals had been caught by surprise; however superior their firepower and armor, it had availed them nothing for they were defeated in detail. With Captain Davis licking his wounds—the two sunken ironclads were raised and towed up to Cairo for repairs—Fort Pillow was safe from the Federal ironclads.

Meanwhile a second Union fleet, the Army rams, had been taking shape under the direction of a fifty-two-year-old, slightly built civil engineer, Charles Ellet, Jr. Ever since the war began, Ellet had made almost incredible efforts to be of service to the Washington government: interviewing officials, publishing pamphlets denouncing what he called the military incapacity of General McClellan, writing and talking to anyone who would listen. At his home in Georgetown, Maryland, all other topics were ignored; the war formed the ordinary chitchat around the dining room table because none of the Ellets felt any interest in anything else. Ram warfare was on Ellet's mind: 'convert the steamer into a battering ram, to enable her to fight, not with her guns, but with her momentum.' Heavy armor was not wanted, he said, since it would slow the ram down, nor was it needed, for naval guns were too unwieldy and inaccurate 'to shoot flying, to hit a steamer on the wing.'[10]

On 8 March 1862 *Merrimac*, by easily ramming and destroying a blockading Union warship, showed what a steam-powered ram could do. Within a week Ellet was in Secretary of War Edwin M. Stanton's office talking rams. Stanton wanted control of the Mississippi River, and he was concerned over reports of Confederate ironclad construction at Memphis. Ellet might be a useful man: 'He has ingenuity and courage. He can beat anybody at figures, and he has more enterprise than anybody else I have ever seen.' So at noon on 26 March, with the rank of colonel, Ellet took the train for Pittsburgh to build rams to meet the Confederate threat on the river. Two days later at the Monongahela House he sat

---

Commandery of the State of Illinois, Military Order of the Loyal Legion of the United States (Chicago, 1891), I, 60-61; *Memphis Avalanche*, 13, 20 May 1862.

[9] Ibid., *New York Times*, 23 May 1862; Montgomery to General Beauregard, 12 May 1862, *Official Records*, 23: pp. 55-57.

[10] C. Ellet, Jr., *Coast and Harbour Defenses: The Substitution of Steam Battering Rams for Ships of War* (Philadelphia, 1855), pp. 8-9; 'Memoirs of Mary Israel Ellet,' H. P. Gambrell, ed., in *The Bucks County Historical Society Papers*, VIII (1940), 319; C. Abbott, 'Charles Ellet and His Naval Steam Rams,' *Harper's New Monthly Magazine*, CLXXXIV (1866), 298-300.

down to write his wife, Ellie, not to neglect the asparagus and to plant some little poplar trees.[11]

Clad with ample authority from Stanton, the new colonel bought the fastest coal-burning boats he could find on the Ohio River and with the aid of local businessmen at Pittsburgh, Cincinnati, New Albany, and smaller ports he pushed work on their conversion. 'I have been crawling to-day in the hulls of boats only fitted for a cat to slip through.' Eight of the boats were made into rams, others into tenders and dispatch boats. In all, Ellet soon had the Ohio River ports busy on nineteen vessels.[12]

Most of the work was carpentry. There was no iron prow but, as on a Confederate ram, the bows were packed solid with timber. In addition, three heavy solid timber bulkheads of hemlock, poplar, or pine, sixteen inches thick, were run fore and aft and strongly trussed to one another and to the sides. Iron tie bars were installed from gunwale to gunwale to prevent the sides from spreading on impact. The result was one rigid unit capable of delivering the impact of the whole mass at the point of collision. As the boilers could not be dropped into the holds for their protection, oaken shields were placed around them. Ellet, polishing and perfecting his weapon, decided to sacrifice armor, guns, boiler protection, everything, to advance the one purpose of his ram, to deliver a crushing blow to the enemy without wrecking itself.[13]

Floods on the Ohio River caused delays in construction. Ellet, with no take-it-easy temperament, raced to beat the Confederate ironclad construction at Memphis. He was everywhere, hiring rivermen for his pilots and crews, prodding contractors and discouraging their jobbery, their demands for extravagant contracts, and their speculating on the government. Too many did not seem 'to care a fig whether the boats are got ready or not—provided they can make money out of it.' Yet he did temporarily forget about McClellan: 'I am myself surprised to find how much incessant occupation with pressing business relieves one's anxieties about public affairs.' It was May before Ellet found time to buy his colonel's uniform, but then he found that 'the eagle on the shoulder, and a military hat, are better passports than brains or character.'[14]

[11] General Halleck to Stanton and Stanton to Halleck, 25 March 1862, *Official Records*, 22: p. 672; C. Gorham, *The Life and Public Services of Edwin M. Stanton* (Boston, 1899), I, 290-292; Ellet to Ellie, 28 March, Charles Ellet, Jr., Papers, Transportation Library, University of Michigan, Ann Arbor.

[12] Ellet to Ellie, 29 March, 3 April 1862, ibid.; Ellet to W. McGunnegle, 10 April 1862, *Official Records*, 23: pp. 78-79; [W. D. Crandall and I. D. Newell], *History of the Ram Fleet and Mississippi Marine Brigade* (St. Louis, 1907), pp. 16-19.

[13] Ibid., pp. 28-29; Ellet to John Jeffrey, 19 April 1862, Ellet Papers. See also Gosnell, *Guns on the Western Waters*, pp. 21-23.

[14] Stanton to Ellet, 28 March, 12 May 1862, *Official Records*, 22: pp. 681, 23; Ellet to Stanton, 6 May, to Ellie, 5, 8 April, 3, 7 May, Ellet Papers. See also 'Memoirs of Mary Israel Ellet,' p. 59.

His brother, Captain Alfred W. Ellet, was sent by Stanton from Missouri to be second-in-command of the ram fleet. As sharpshooters he brought his son, Eddie, and other volunteers from his own regiment. Colonel Ellet's nineteen-year-old son from the East, Charles Rivers Ellet, joined the fleet as a medical cadet.[15]

After Plum Point Bend telegrams came from Stanton urging haste, and Ellet began to dispatch his boats to Cairo, the wharves at their departure points crowded with relatives and friends. Carpenters continued working on the way down the river, and to make them look more formidable, the rams were painted black. At Cairo, where Ellet spent a wretched night unable to sleep from the heat and mosquitoes, final supplies were taken aboard. By 19 May most of the fleet, each ram with a crew of about thirty rivermen—officers, two pilots, carpenters, engineers, firemen, and deck hands—were on their way to the front. A few days later they joined the ironclads above Fort Pillow. Although Stanton gave Ellet orders to operate 'with the concurrence of the naval commander,' he was not placed distinctly under Captain Davis.[16]

Ellet wanted to push right on down, run the batteries, ram the Confederate gunboats below, and sweep the river. Impossible, rash, and foolhardy, said Davis, remembering Plum Point Bend; his first duty was to protect Cairo and St. Louis. Ellet could not persuade him to commit even one ironclad to the effort. Angered by the independent Ellet, Davis spoke of the unarmored rams—'brown paper Rams'—as nothing more than light skirmishers to assail stragglers and assist any disabled ironclad. To expose such frail craft 'to the first brunt and shock of battle would be to misapply their peculiar usefulness and mode of warfare.' To which the colonel replied that 'the only efficient service these rams can render is that for which they were especially built, viz, to run into the enemy with good speed head on and sink him.'[17]

In daily letters to his wife in Boston, Captain Davis rarely mentioned his brushes with Ellet. On 31 May he was 'highly gratified, greatly pleased' with the good opinion of his Cambridge neighbors and vowed that if he ever got near the rebel fleet again, 'I shall destroy it.' Meanwhile there was little news, although on 2 June, 'A man was killed in the mortar fleet this morning in a curious way. He had a cylinder of loose

---

[15] Ellet to Ellie, 6 May, Ellie to Ellet, 10 May 1862, Edward Ellet to Ellet, 22 April 1861, Ellet to A. W. Ellet, 2 May 1862, Ellet Papers; Crandall, *History of the Ram Fleet*, pp. 37-39.

[16] Ellet to Captain Joseph Ford, 10 May, to Captain David Millard, 10 May 1862, Ellet Papers; Ellet to P. H. Watson, 15 May, A. W. Ellet to Ellet, 26 May, Stanton to Ellet, 25, 26 April 1862, *Official Records*, 23: pp. 95, 107, 74.

[17] Ellet to A. W. Ellet, 2 May 1862, Ellet Papers; Ellet to Davis, 28 May, 1 June, Davis to Ellet, 2 June 1862, *Official Records*, 23: pp. 34, 37-39.

powder over his shoulder and lighted cigar in his mouth. His head was blown off. These mortar-men are said to be very careless.'[18]

Ellet raged. Davis, like McClellan, had the slows: 'His purpose seems to be to idle here, and put me off.' To Stanton, Ellet wired for permission to proceed alone: 'I want to make the rebel fleet our own game.' To Ellie he wrote, 'this confounded Commodore won't move.' As the river was falling, his rams would soon lose some of their down-river speed, and at any hour two Confederate ironclads building at Memphis might join the rebel fleet.[19]

Actually, by June, Fort Pillow was already in the process of being evacuated. With Corinth, Mississippi, captured by the Federal army, both Fort Pillow and Memphis were effectively outflanked, their doom sealed. Early on the morning of 5 June, Ellet discovered what was going on and immediately sent a boat to raise the American flag over the deserted and demolished fort. When the ironclads got underway, Captain Davis was 'not a little surprised at seeing the Stars and Stripes already waving over the rebel works.'[20]

In fact the two fleets were now acting independently, each steaming down river on the watch for the retiring Confederate gunboats. Knowing his pilots would have no difficulty keeping the channel on a falling river Ellet pushed the chase. At 11:30 A.M., chewing camphor and taking a little blackberry wine for his diarrhea, he sat down to write his wife: 'I am now well in the advance, and hope to maintain this position.' Later, a postscript found Ellet delayed, awaiting his coal barges while the ironclads pushed on ahead, as 'they don't wish the rams to do all the work.'[21]

A newspaper correspondent on board Davis' flagship pictured for his readers back home the huge, squat, black ironclads, *Benton, St. Louis, Carondelet, Cairo,* and *Louisville*, with flags flying and black clouds of smoke pouring from their funnels, steaming down the river with the pea-soup color past Hatchie Landing and then the little village of Fulton. Behind them came tugs, tenders, and white-painted, troop-filled transports, carrying two regiments that had been camped on the Arkansas shore fighting only mosquitoes for the past two months. Along the banks smoke above the treetops confirmed that the Confederates were

---

[18] Davis to his wife, 31 May, 2 June 1862, Davis, *Life of Charles Henry Davis*, pp. 235, 236.

[19] Ellet to Stanton, 3 June, to 'Ma,' 2 June, to Ellie, 3 June 1862, Ellet Papers.

[20] Ellet to Stanton, 5 June 1862, Ellet Papers; *Cincinnati Gazette*, quoted in Frank Moore, Ed., *The Rebellion Record: A Diary of American Events with Documents* (New York, 1861-1868), V, 167. J. D. Milligan, focusing entirely on the river war, implies that Memphis' doom was not sealed, 'The Federal Fresh-Water Navy and the Opening of the Mississippi River,' Ph.D. thesis, University of Michigan, 1961, p. 247.

[21] Ellet to Ellie, 5 June 1862, Ellet Papers.

burning cotton to prevent its capture. Some had been dumped into the river. Opposite the widow Craighead's place and again at Pecan Point the water was spotted with the white cotton in bunches and bales. The Confederate transport *Sovereign* burning cotton below the mouth of the Hatchie River was surprised by *Benton* but would have escaped if it had not been for the Union tug *Spitfire*. Taking a short cut across the bar at the head of the chute of Island 37, the tug got within range of *Sovereign*, forcing her ashore with three rounds from her 12-pounder howitzer. It was fortunate for *Spitfire* that she did not have to fire a fourth, for the next round of fixed ammunition had been rammed home shell first, and for some time the gun crew was busily engaged trying to unload.[22]

The ironclads passed deserted Fort Randolph, and late afternoon found them steaming through the group of islands known as Paddy's Hens and Chickens; it was nearly dark when they anchored in the stream four miles above Memphis. While the men slept, those on watch could see the lights of Memphis appear as twinkling stars in their glasses.

Now that New Orleans had fallen to the Federals, Memphis, a city of 22,000 and boasting of its skyline of four and even five-story buildings, was the industrial heart of the western Confederacy with machine shops, foundries, and ordnance workshops. One nearly completed ironclad ram, *Arkansas*, had been towed southward from the city; but a second one was not far enough along to move and was still there. For several weeks while Federal mortar boats at Fort Pillow boomed like distant thunder, a quiet sense of doom had taken hold of the city as rumors of a retreat from Pillow came down the river. Business slowed to a standstill, real estate advertisements filled the papers, and people were leaving for the interior by the hundreds.[23]

Then Pillow did fall, and excitement pervaded the city; Montgomery's River Defense Fleet attracted much attention. Along Cotton Row the question was, 'When do you think the Federals will be here?' or 'Will there be a battle?' Most citizens seemed to think that the fleet should fight to save the city, although some hoped the battle would be far enough away so that stray cannon balls would not fall in Memphis streets.[24] Commodore Montgomery, short of coal, decided to stay and fight for the city even though the five ironclads had him outgunned and outarmored. It

[22] *Cincinnati Commercial*, quoted in Moore, *Rebellion Record*, V, 177-178; W. Knox, *Camp-Fire and Cotton Field: Southern Adventures in Time of War* (New York, 1865), pp. 171, 173-174; *Memphis Avalanche*, 16 May 1862; *Official Records*, 23: pp. 138-139.

[23] J. Trezevant to General Beauregard, 21 March, letter of 28 February 1862, *Official Records*, 22: pp. 741, 830; S. McIlwaine, *Memphis Down in Dixie* (New York: E. P. Dutton, 1948), pp. 116-117; *Memphis Appeal*, 9 May 1862; *The Argus* (Memphis), 13 May, 2 June 1862.

[24] *Memphis Avalanche*, 6 June 1862.

THE BATTLE OF THE RAMS 215

was better to fight now before the two sunk at Plum Point Bend rejoined the Federal fleet, and the Ellet rams, although seen, had been taken as some sort of transport.

The swashbuckling Jeff Thompson would have enjoyed the coming battle, jousting with the enemy while white handkerchiefs, fluttering on the shore, cheered him on. But Thompson's Missourians got along poorly with the gunboat men and they had been withdrawn from the fleet. Last-minute efforts to get them back on board failed, so General Thompson watched the battle on horseback from the bluffs and the Confederate fleet headed into action without their sharpshooters.[25]

Upstream on board *Benton* the boatswain piped all hands to quarters. The ironclads raised anchor, and, with *Carondelet* nearest the Tennessee shore, formed a single line of battle across the river. Davis, like Foote, did not like to fight downstream. His captains had found that the rapid current plus awkward steering qualities of their boats made it impossible for them to back upstream, and if badly hit, the ironclads could not be backed out of range. Their steering and speed were not helped by cypress logs lashed at the water line after Plum Point Bend for protection against the Confederate rams. Accordingly, Davis came down the river stern first and very slowly, prepared for any injury.[26]

His caution gave Montgomery a chance. The vulnerable sterns with only two guns apiece offered tempting targets. But the Confederates, still over a mile away, stopped to shoot; they did not charge in to ram. At 5:30 the four Confederates in the van opened fire with their bow guns. *Benton* replied and soon firing became general on both sides, four Confederate 64-pounders against ten Union 32-pounders, two on each of the five ironclads. However, the range was great, the gunnery was poor, and neither side suffered any damage.[27]

For about twenty minutes the two fleets drifted indecisively, each under a pall of smoke from their own guns. At this juncture two black sidewheelers came up fast from the Federal rear. They were the rams *Queen of the West* and *Monarch* under the command of Colonel Ellet and his brother. Ellet had not been informed of the presence of Montgomery's fleet at Memphis and had not expected a battle here. Early that morning the ram fleet had dropped down the river, and *Queen* was just mooring

[25] Knox, *Camp-Fire and Cotton Field*, p. 179.

[26] Foote to Secretary Welles, 20 March, Thompson to Beauregard, 13 May, Walke to Davis, 6 June 1862, *Official Records*, 22: p. 697, 23: pp. 57, 122-123; account of pilot of *Carondelet* in *Daily Democrat* (St. Louis), 10 June 1862, A. W. Ellet said later that the ironclads remained at anchor. 'Ellet and His Steam-Rams at Memphis,' *Battles and Leaders of the Civil War*, I, 459.

[27] Account of Captain J. Hart in LaBree, *Confederate Soldier*, p. 403; Foote to Navy Department, 7 March 1862, *Official Records*, 22: p. 665; *Memphis Appeal*, 9 June 1862.

in the shelter of the great cottonwoods on the Arkansas shore when the first Confederate cannon boomed down around Hopefield Point. Finding a fight, Ellet lost no time getting into it. To his brother on *Monarch* behind, Ellet shouted, 'Round out and follow me! Now is our chance!' *Monarch* followed, but the rest of his ram fleet did not. Of two nearby, one backed full into the bank and broke her rudder when her officers got confused in the excitement, and the other held back and came up only when the shooting was over.[28]

Queen, gathering momentum, steamed out into the broad Mississippi. Ellet rejoiced. Standing on the hurricane deck and waving his hat, he was wildly cheered by the ironclad crews as his *Queen*, steam hissing from her pipes and smoke rolling from her stacks, sailed through their line, her two great wheels whirling up clouds of spray, her prow half buried under water, plowing a furrow which rolled the width of the river. She plunged into and through a wall of acrid smoke that had formed in the still air.[29]

Ellet was not tempted to stop to shoot; he had no guns, only his carbine-carrying sharpshooters whose opportunity would come at close quarters. Unlike the ironclads he had no second thoughts about the dangers of down-river attack. The current boosted his speed, and speed was what he wanted. Waving to his brother coming on hard behind him to attack another boat, Ellet headed straight for the Confederate ram, *Lovell*.[30]

The Confederate soon realized the intent of this strange steamer and the two boats came on head and head. *Lovell* got off a shot from her bow gun, but the grape and canister were lost in the water. At the last minute she swerved when a Federal sharpshooter sent a ball through the head of her captain. *Queen* hit her fairly on the beam, and with a grinding roar of splintering timbers, the vessel was cut almost in two; her chimneys swung over *Queen* at a ludicrous angle. Everything loose about *Queen*—tables, pantry ware, and half-eaten breakfast—was tossed about and broken by the shock. Similar debris from *Lovell* cluttered the forward deck of *Queen*. For a minute the two boats stuck fast, the momentum of *Queen* carrying her and her victim forward. When *Queen* managed to back away, there opposite Beale Street before the crowds on shore *Lovell* sank, taking sixty-eight of her crew of eighty-six down with her.[31]

[28] Ibid.; Ellet, 'Ellet and His Steam-Rams at Memphis,' p. 456; Ellet to Mary, 6 June, to Stanton, 8, 11 June 1862, testimony on *Lancaster*, 9 June, Ellet Papers.
[29] Coffin, *My Days and Nights on the Battlefield* (Boston, 1887), pp. 299-300; *New York Times*, 17 June 1862; Ellet to Ellie, 6 June, to Stanton, 11 June 1862, Ellet Papers.
[30] Ellet to Stanton, 11 June 1862, ibid.
[31] Ibid.; 'Incidents of the naval engagement at Memphis, June 6, 1862,' ibid.; *Memphis Avalanche*, 8 June 1862; account of Lt. W. F. Warren in Crandall, *History of the Ram Fleet*, p. 80.

THE BATTLE OF THE RAMS

Before *Queen* could recover headway, two other Confederates were on her. In the melee one of her wheels was disabled, her tiller rope was broken, and Ellet was hit in the knee by a Confederate pistol ball when he came out from the pilothouse for a better view of the action. All this happened within seven or eight minutes of leaving her mooring. *Queen* worked herself to the Arkansas shore with only one wheel and without a rudder.[32]

Monarch, alone now, was charged by her intended victims. With Captain Dryden standing at the wheel alongside Pilot Collins she was handled with fine judgment and slipped between two of her attackers, one grazing her stern and the other missing by only twenty feet. Jets of smoke and flame came from the loopholes of *Monarch*'s sharpshooters forcing the Confederate gunners to abandon their guns and the pilots to lose control of their boats. They collided with each other. With one of her opponents disabled *Monarch* swept around in a tight curve and with only the bite of the paddle wheel keeping her from lying down on her side hit the other, *Beauregard,* a little forward of the wheelhouse. At the same time a shell from one of the Federal ironclads disabled her machinery and the Confederates waved surrender from the deck.[33]

Since the danger of ramming had now passed, the ironclads cut loose their cypress girdles and, turning 'one slow length around,' closed the range. They found good targets among the disorganized Confederate gunboats. Gunner Dwyer of *Benton*'s No. 2 bow gun with his third shot cut the head out of the steam drum of *Little Rebel*. Many of her crew were scalded. A broadside from the same ironclad hit another Confederate, setting her on fire. The burning gunboat drifted down the river toward President's Island; 'flames burst through the upper works, the boilers heated to redness, hissed and smoked and burst at last, enveloping ships, flames and all in a momentary mist' until the magazine blew up.[34]

It was all over by 7:00 A.M. Montgomery's fleet was put out of action; only one of the Confederate gunboats, *Van Dorn,* escaped. Two or three wild shots had landed in Memphis streets, one taking off a corner of an

---

[32] Ellet to Stanton, 11 June, C. R. Ellet to 'Grandma,' 9 June 1862, Ellet Papers.

[33] A. W. Ellet to Ellet, 6 June 1862, 'List of crew of *Monarch* on 6 June,' ibid.; account of J. Hart in La Bree, *Confederate Soldier,* p. 403; Jeff Thompson to General Beauregard, 9 June 1862, *Official Records,* 10: p. 913; account of Lt. W. F. Warren in Crandall, *History of the Ram Fleet,* pp. 80-81. Milligan, 'The Federal Fresh-Water Navy,' p. 243, believes that *Monarch* probably struck *Lovell* a second time before she sank. Unlike the navy at the time, Gerald N. Capers, *The Biography of a River Town: Memphis, Its Heroic Age* (Chapel Hill: University of North Carolina Press, 1939), p. 149, credits the Federal rams with the devastation but mistakenly calls them 'steel rams' and implies that the ironclad fleet had 'an inestimable advantage in having the current with it.'

[34] *Cincinnati Commercial,* 9 June 1862, quoted in Moore, *Rebellion Record,* V, 180; Davis to Secretary Welles, 6 June 1862, *Official Records,* 23: pp. 119-120; A. W. Ellet to Ellet, 6 June 1862 Ellet Papers; *Memphis Avalanche,* 13 June 1862.

icehouse at Front and Jefferson, but there were no casualties ashore. The unfinished ironclad ram being built at Memphis was left burning on the stocks.

The Confederate telegraph operator at Memphis left a hastily scribbled note: 'to any Lincolnite successor . . . if you will come out on land we'll whip you like hell.'[35] In a sense he was right; Federal success at Memphis helped counter grim news from the eastern front.

On Monday, 9 June 1862, the front pages of the *New York Times* carried a three-column casualty list from McClellan's Peninsular Campaign in Virginia. But the other three columns gloried in the victory at Memphis.

General Jeff Thompson gathered a few of his men and commandeered the first train south to Grenada, Mississippi, Commodore Montgomery lived to fight against Farragut at Mobile Bay, and Memphis prospered in the cotton trade under Federal occupation. Captain Davis made admiral within a month, and, later on, so did Captains Stembel of *Cincinnati*, Kilty of *Mound City*, and Walke of *Carondelet*. Colonel Ellet, the only serious Federal casualty, died of blood poisoning two weeks later as his boat neared the landing at Cairo. Ironically his rams were soon put under Navy control, armored and gunned, and *Queen* was the only one ever again to fight, as intended, by ramming. But at Memphis Ellet's two little boats, the skirmishers, without guns and without armor, broke up the fight when the ironclads dallied. It was most irregular; but it worked.

[35] *Cincinnati Commercial*, 9 June 1862, quoted in *Rebellion Record*, V, 181.

The Iron Sea Elephants

BY WALTER MILLIS

EVERY schoolboy is familiar with the name and fame of Ericsson's *Monitor*, and most of them are under the erroneous impression that she was the first steam-driven, ironclad man-of-war and the direct progenitor of all the mighty steel fleets which subsequently filled the waters of the world. But it is curious how few, whether schoolboys or even naval officers, know anything at all about the Civil War monitor fleet of which she was actually the prototype. Some time ago, having occasion to look into the history of these odd and interesting ships, I was surprised to find how scattered and fragmentary is the information on them in the standard naval works. While the following notes are drawn mainly from secondary sources, they may be of some value as bringing together in one place a brief account of a curious type which also constituted the bulk of the world's first important ironclad fleet developed to meet combat conditions.

While chiefly of antiquarian interest, it is an account not wholly without contemporary significance. In many respects, the story of the Civil War monitors is not unlike that of the vast carrier and landing-craft fleets produced during the recent war. The monitors, like the great sea-air combinations of 1941-1945, were the products of a sudden and dire necessity operating on a ground already fertile with new ideas and experiments. Evoked to meet certain special problems, they rapidly expanded in size and power until it seemed that they would dominate the seas. As with the recent carrier types, the greatest of them were not completed until the war was ending and there was no further chance of testing their battle value. *Miantonomoh*, visiting Europe in 1866, was as formidable a portent as was *Franklin D. Roosevelt* in Mediterranean waters in 1947. Then a few years later the times and technology had changed and the monitors were no more than clumsy anachronisms. Whether the parallel will carry so far again, no one can say, but the possibility is at least instructive.

The Civil War broke out at a time when steam was fully established as a motive power, when the Paixhans shell gun had clearly doomed the wooden warship, when iron armor was known to be the only practicable answer, and when even the turret mounting had received considerable attention, but when no one had as yet combined all these factors into a satisfactory solution for the problems of naval design. There was, however, no dearth of plans and proposals. The Confederate Secretary of the Navy, Stephen R. Mallory, was prompt to realize that ironclad ships offered the South its one chance of breaking the blockade which the North could otherwise impose with its overwhelming superiority in wooden vessels; and as early as June 1861 he was energetically pressing the conversion of *Merrimac* into the ironclad *Virginia*.[1] The Federal ironclad board, authorized by the act of 3 August 1861, and appointed five days later, brought in its report on 16 September. In that brief space it had examined no less than seventeen proposals, and it bravely recommended the adoption of three of them.

The ships undertaken as a result of this report were the rail-plated wooden gunboat *Galena* (C. S. Bushnell & Co., New Haven), the wood and iron frigate *New Ironsides* (Merrick & Sons, Philadelphia), and the odd steam battery with revolving turret designed by John Ericsson. Initially, it is to be noted, this last was never regarded as anything but a coastal craft, offering great possibilities for the special requirements of the war against the Confederacy but in no sense an answer to the sea-going ironclads that had appeared in the French and British navies. *New Ironsides* might fulfill that function; as to *Monitor*, the board frankly reported that 'we are somewhat apprehensive that her properties for sea are not such as a sea-going vessel should possess. But she may be moved from one place to another on the coast in smooth water.'[2]

The Ericsson design, with its light draft, heavy caliber guns, and its solution for the problem of maneuverability in narrow waters by 'maneuvering the guns instead of the ship,' similarly impressed the Secretary of the Navy, Gideon Welles. 'The nautical qualities of the vessel,' as he later explained, were not a 'governing object'; she was 'adapted to the shallow waters of our coasts and harbors, few of which are accessible to vessels of great magnitude,' and that was what was wanted.[3] *Monitor* was put in hand; meanwhile, the Navy Department, already projecting

---

[1] James Phinney Baxter 3d, *The Introduction of the Ironclad Warship* (1933), pp. 224, 229. Cited as "Baxter."

[2] Frank M. Bennett, *The Steam Navy of the United States* (1896), pp. 264-272, gives the full text of the report. Cited as "Bennett."

[3] *Annual Report of the Secretary of the Navy*, 1862.

a fleet of no less than twenty ironclads, developed a design of its own along somewhat similar lines. By the end of November it had completed specifications for a class rather larger than *Monitor,* likewise of comparatively light draft and low freeboard (3 feet), but mounting two turrets instead of one. These were to be 'Coles cupolas,' following the design already developed by Captain Cowper Coles of the Royal Navy rather than the more primitive Ericsson system.[4] The Navy was asking $12 million for the contemplated fleet. However, the appropriation bill was delayed, and did not pass until 20 February 1862, barely a fortnight before *Monitor* made her spectacular and historic appearance in Hampton Roads.

It is unnecessary to rehearse the well-worn story of the Battle of Hampton Roads, 8 and 9 March 1862. But its effect, as everyone knows, was enormous. Four days after the action John Lenthall, Chief of the Bureau of Construction and Repair, was urging Welles to go ahead with the Navy's projected double-turrets; he was also urging the grander vision of ocean-going ironclads—a fleet of 'first class invincible ocean ships' to keep 'command of the open sea.'[5] But it was the coastal war which came first, and *Monitor's* success had swept the field in favor of the Ericsson design. On 31 March, three weeks after the battle, Ericsson received contracts for six more of the type, while four additional ships of the same class were ordered from other builders. These were the ten *Passaics,* which were to see more service, first and last, than any others of the monitor fleet. Ericsson, pleased with the success of the name he had given to his first product, labelled his sextette *Impenetrable, Penetrator, Paradox, Gauntlet, Palladium,* and *Agitator;* fortunately, the Navy Department disapproved and with better taste designated the ten ships *Passaic, Montauk, Catskill, Patapsco, Lehigh, Sangamon* (later renamed *Jason*), *Camanche,*[6] *Nahant, Nantucket,* and *Weehawken.*

On 19 March, ten days after the battle, the Department recommended that the wooden frigate *Roanoke* (a sister ship to *Merrimac* and present at Hampton Roads when the latter emerged for her onslaught) should be

---

[4] Baxter, pp. 274, 275-278, Appendix F. The Coles cupola was carried on a ring of iron rollers under the bottom edge of the turret rather than on the single central spindle which sustained the whole weight of Ericsson's turret whenever it was keyed up for training. Coles's design also contemplated sinking the base of the turret with its training mechanism behind a 'glacis' of fixed armor, comparable to the later barbette. There is a drawing in Baxter, p. 188.

[5] Baxter, pp. 303, 305.

[6] *Camanche* had a curious career. The contract was awarded to the San Francisco firm of Donahue, Ryan & Secor, but the parts were actually fabricated by the Secor firm in Jersey City. Her engines were cannibalized to repair *Weehawken* when the latter broke down on the Carolina coast. Ultimately the completed parts were shipped out around Cape Horn in the hold of a sailing vessel; the latter unfortunately sank at her dock in San Francisco with the disassembled *Camanche* still on board. The parts were later recovered, but the monitor was not reassembled and completed until 1865. Bennett, pp. 339-340.

razeed, armored, and provided with center-line turrets.[7] On 25 March a contract was given to Charles W. Whitney of New York for *Keokuk,* an ill-fated experiment springing from one of the designs which had been unsuccessfully submitted to the ironclad board in the preceding fall. Her armor was of alternate strips of wood and iron; her two 11-inch guns were carried in two armored 'towers.' Each of these was a fixed conical structure with three gun-ports—center-line, starboard, and port—through any one of which the piece could be trained.[8] The Department pressed on. A contract was awarded to George W. Quintard of New York for the big double-turret monitor *Onondaga,* while four more double-turrets were ordered from Navy yards. These—*Miantonomoh, Monadnock, Agamenticus* (later renamed *Terror*), and *Tonawanda* (later *Amphitrite*) were destined to live long in name if not, exactly, in fact. They were the products of the Navy's own program of November; but Hampton Roads materially modified their design. The Coles cupolas were abandoned in favor of Ericsson turrets, each mounting two 15-inch guns; although unlike the Ericsson monitors, which were built of iron with wood introduced only as backing for the side armor, these were wooden vessels.

These seventeen vessels, plus the three of the original program, represented a very extensive building policy. Still the Navy did not stop. The growing fleet of western river 'tinclads' was still under Army control, but the Navy sensed the probable need for a heavier type for use on the lower Mississippi or along the coast; and on 27 May it ordered from various inland boatbuilders four double-turret, monitor-type vessels to the design of James B. Eads. These—*Winnebago, Chickasaw, Kickapoo,* and *Milwaukee* —were interesting ships. Their decks were crowned into a turtle-back; they had quadruple screws driven from two main engine shafts, and the Eads 'disappearing' turret.[9] Though the turret itself did not disappear, the guns were mounted on a steam-operated elevator which dropped them to the lower deck, where they were loaded from protected handling rooms, then hoisted and run out through ports defended by automatic, steam-operated shutters. It seems a much more modern and ingenious design than Ericsson's, and Mobile Bay would appear to prove that it worked.[10]

[7] Baxter, p. 305. These were to have been Coles turrets, but, according to Bennett, the Ericsson system was finally adopted. One result was that the keel proved too weak to carry the weight concentrated on the spindles. When the turrets were keyed up for training they threatened to 'force out the bottom.' There is a spirited lithograph of *Roanoke* with her three Ericsson turrets in the collection of the New York Historical Society.

[8] Bennett, p. 348. A drawing in the collection of the New York Historical Society clearly shows the arrangement.

[9] Bennett, p. 347-348.

[10] The system is described in a pamphlet in the New York Public Library, *Eads Revolving Steam*

The Navy Department had still larger plans. On 3 July a contract was given to W. H. Webb of New York for *Dunderberg*, a large sea-going 'ironclad frigate ram' of the broadside type.[11] And on 28 July Ericsson received contracts for two giant single-turret monitors, *Puritan* and *Dictator*. Bennett gives the displacement as 4,438 tons;[12] of massive size and large fuel capacity, these were intended as ocean-going vessels. The monitor type, evolved expressly to meet the special needs of coastal warfare against an enemy without sea-power, was growing with success into altogether more ambitious forms.

Nevertheless, the coastal war was still the important thing. In September orders were given to various builders for nine more Ericsson monitors of less grandiose dimensions. *Canonicus, Catawba, Oneonta, Mahopac, Manhattan, Tecumseh, Saugus, Manayunk* (later *Ajax*), and *Tippecanoe* (later *Wyandotte*) were somewhat enlarged and improved versions of the *Passaics*. Thus, within six months after Hampton Roads, the government had ordered, in addition to the western river flotilla, no less than thirty-three coastal or ocean-going ironclads. Thirty of them—ten *Passaics, Onondaga*, four *Miantonomohs*, four *Winnebagos*, two *Dictators*, and nine of the *Canonicus* class—were on the monitor principle. Considering the paucity of experience available, these were bold decisions—like many of those which had to be taken during the recent war—and in the meantime, unfortunately, the experience had begun to come in.

Monitor's initial victory had perhaps blinded the Navy Department, and had certainly blinded both Ericsson and the public, to the fact that she had her defects. She had given her people a tough time getting to Hampton Roads under tow from New York. They ran into heavy weather, and *Monitor* quickly revealed that, however solid her defenses against Confederate shot, she was very weak in her defenses against the sea. Chief Engineer Alban C. Stimers, who had supervised her construction as representative of the Navy Department and had come along as observer and adviser, enthusiastically reported her 'the finest sea boat I was ever in.' But this must have been the verdict of love, since she had nearly killed him both by drowning and asphyxiation. Her executive officer, Lieutenant S. Dana Greene, took a darker and more accurate view. 'I do not,' he severely reported, 'consider this steamer a sea-going vessel.' The motion

---

Turret (Washington, 1864). Eads' article in *Battles and Leaders of the Civil War*, I, 343, says that the Navy allowed him to place only one of these turrets on each of two of the ships—*Chickasaw* and *Milwaukee*—the others to be on the proven Ericsson system. If the Eads turrets failed, they were to be replaced with Ericssons. There is a good view of *Kickapoo* in *The Photographic History of the Civil War*, VI, 321.

[11] Bennett, p. 350.
[12] Bennett, p. 343.

was easy enough ('she is buoyant but not very lively') but she lacked power to go against wind and sea and was nearly swamped by the torrents of water that poured through her inadequately protected deck openings as she wallowed virtually submerged through the seas. Even Stimers had to admit that 'it is only the man who has studied the philosophical laws of floatation and stability who feels exactly comfortable in her during a gale of wind.'[13] As Greene afterward remembered it:

> The berth deck hatch leaked in spite of all we could do and the water came down under the turret like a waterfall. It would strike the pilot house and go over the turret in beautiful curves, and it came through the narrow eye-holes of the pilot house with such force as to knock the helmsman completely round from the wheel. The waves also broke over the blower-pipes [temporary trunks erected over the holes in the deck which served in action as air intakes and smoke vents] and the water came down them in such quantities that the belts of the blower-engines slipped and the [main] engines consequently stopped for lack of artificial draught.[14]

Simultaneously the engine-room filled with gas and fumes. The devoted Stimers, together with *Monitor's* engineer, First Assistant Isaac Newton, were dragged out 'more dead than alive' and had to be laid out on the turret top, where the fresh air happily revived them. With the pumps failing for lack of steam, only a lucky moderation of the weather saved the ship from foundering.

Her famous action suggested that her military no less than her seakeeping qualities left something to be desired. Her 11-inch smoothbores, which had made no very critical impression on *Merrimac's* armor, seemed too weak for their task. Owing to the arrangement of her heavy port stoppers only one gun could be run out at a time (a little appreciated fact which vitiates all the many drawings showing her with both guns firing together) and the service was slow.[15] The conning tower in the bow was a nuisance; it rendered ahead fire impossible and when the speaking tubes failed it left the captain cut off from communication with his guns. Lines painted on the deck in order to indicate the position of the turret in relation to the ship were soon obliterated; consequently, when the conning tower did manage to report the enemy's bearing those in the turret had no way of knowing where the bearing was. All they could do was to run out a gun and start revolving until the enemy appeared in the sights; and even this was difficult, as the turret proved hard to start and almost equally hard to stop.[16]

---

[13] *Official Records of the Union and Confederate Navies in the War of the Rebellion*, Series I, VII, 26, 27, 170. Cited as 'ONR.'

[14] *Battles and Leaders of the Civil War*, I, 720-721. Cited as '*Battles*.'

[15] ONR, VII, 411.

[16] *Battles*, I, 721. Even Stimers, the engineer, who took over the job when Acting Master L. N.

Soon after the action the rail-plated *Galena* with her tumble-home sides joined the squadron; and on 15 May she and *Monitor*, now under the command of Lieutenant William N. Jeffers, who had replaced the wounded Worden, were sent up the James to try the forts at Drewry's Bluff. The Stevens brothers' armored gunboat *Naugatuck*, which was never accepted by the Navy, also went along under the command of a Revenue Marine officer.[17] *Naugatuck* burst her one gun and no more was heard of her. *Galena* was badly holed; she suffered casualties from fragments of her own iron flung about inside the ship, and though she remained in service throughout the war and was in Farragut's line at Mobile Bay, she was put down as a failure as an ironclad.[18] *Monitor* survived well enough, but Jeffers stated his view of her with some asperity. Hampton Roads, he observed, had 'caused an exaggerated confidence to be entertained by the public in the powers of the *Monitor*, which it was not good policy to check. I, however, feel that I owe it to you, sir, to put on record my deliberate opinion.' It was not high; partly, perhaps, because the awkward location of the conning tower had forced him to take station in the turret-top hatchway, protected only by 'barricades of hammocks' from the lively fire of the Confederate riflemen on the bank. Jeffers, a somewhat corpulent man,[19] was acutely aware of the 'inconvenience' of this arrangement.

There were other failings. Not only did the conning tower preclude ahead fire, but when a gun was fired due aft the blast effect on the boilers under the after deck was 'very great'; as a result, the practicable field of fire seemed to be only about 220° out of the intended 360°. Ventilation was a grisly failure. Under the southern sun the temperature reached 140° in the turret, while below the combination of powder smoke, boiler fumes, heat, and stench was insupportable.[20] Jeffers made the further observation, later well borne out, that while the type could run by any existing coastal forts, it lacked the weight and rapidity of fire necessary to reduce them.[21]

Stodder was disabled, found the turret hard to manage. Stimers, incidentally, had served for a time as chief engineer of *Merrimac* when, as a graceful steam frigate, she still 'sailed under an honorable flag.' ONR, VII, 27.

[17] Bennett, pp. 314-315.

[18] ONR, VII, 357-358.

[19] *Photographic History of the Civil War*, VI, 153.

[20] Another feature of the monitors not always understood was the fact that the turret roofs were open grids or gratings of railway iron; the turrets themselves thus served as exhaust ventilating trunks and were the main reliance for keeping the under-deck areas habitable. But they must have been traps for the southern sun as well as for rain. The monitors quickly learned to spread awnings over their turret tops and iron decks. In the photographs these awnings lend a kind of gala or at least summer-resort air to these queer ships, but they must have been grim necessities.

[21] ONR, VII, 410-413.

Some of these lessons were applied in the ten *Passaics* which were now coming on. They were given round armored conning towers centered over the turrets (this was done by carrying the central spindle up to the roof level and mounting the conning tower in a fixed position upon it), standing funnels, armored a third of the way up, and standing air intake pipes. And Secretary Welles insisted on 15-inch guns. The monster new weapons were ready and tested by October, but when it came to mounting them it was found that the gun-ports of the new ships were too small to receive the muzzles. According to West's life of Welles, there was doubt as to whether this was due to an error in calculation or to the stubbornness of Ericsson, a testy and irascible genius who could admit no flaws in his designs. He had, at all events, devised a 'muzzle box' to confine the blast and permit the guns to be fired inside the turret.[22] The *Passaics* were finally armed with one 15-inch arranged on this system and one 11-inch (in some an 8-inch Parrott rifle) on the normal plan. But the somewhat larger *Canonicus* class, ordered in September, were designed for two 15-inch, and the Navy insisted that they should fire with protruding muzzles.

On 26 August the ponderous broadside ship, *New Ironsides,* reached Hampton Roads. Slab-sided and flat-topped, she was not a thing of beauty; and though she was greatly admired at the time, she had her own peculiarities. In deference to sailing ship requirements (she was designed to carry a full bark rig) the armored conning tower had been placed abaft the large, squat funnel, thus severely reducing what little visibility was afforded by the slits. She had been sent down, however, without waiting for her spars. Her captain begged to have them, as he found that while he could get a maximum of seven knots out of her under steam she would not steer at a speed above five or six; and he believed that without her sails she would be unmanageable in heavy weather.[23]

But at all events, the ironclad fleet was beginning to take shape. As winter approached, the *Passaics* were coming to completion. The first of them, *Passaic* herself, had a dangerous trip from New York under tow, and had to be sent to the Washington Navy Yard for boiler repairs. Mr. Lincoln visited her there with much interest;[24] while the Navy Depart-

---

[22] Richard S. West, Jr., *Gideon Welles: Lincoln's Navy Department* (1943), p. 222. Cited as 'West.' Baxter implies that the internal firing arrangement was deliberately adopted to overcome the difficulties experienced with the slow and ponderous port-stoppers. West says that Ericsson held that enlarging the ports would unduly weaken the turret wall. *The Photographic History of the Civil War* gives a view of *Catskill* (VI, 173) in which the muzzle box can be dimly seen.

[23] *Report of the Secretary of the Navy in Relation to Armored Vessels* (1864), p. 30. Cited as '*Armored Vessels.*'

[24] West, p. 224.

ment, anxious to utilize the squadron for the attack on Charleston, hurried on the rest. As the year 1862 ran out, the southward procession began. *New Ironsides* was despatched as flagship. On 29 December *Monitor*, now under Commander J. P. Bankhead, and *Passaic*, under Captain Percival Drayton, left Hampton Roads, each, as usual, under tow. Off Hatteras they ran into a southwest gale; and by nightfall on 30 December *Monitor* was laboring heavily, with her people fighting another desperate battle against the incoming water. Bankhead thought that the violent pounding of the projecting armor belt or 'upper vessel' must have torn it loose from the lower hull, an idea which started a fierce controversy between Ericsson and the Navy. Wherever it was coming from, the rising water in due course put out their fires, and the game was up. About 11:00 P.M. they made signal of distress. Boats from her consort succeeded, by heroic seamanship, in getting a majority of the crew off the floundering, submerged raft; but when she finally went under in the darkness and the gale she took sixteen of her officers and men with her.[25]

Passaic made it, but by a narrow margin. The builders had neglected to clean out her bilges, and the pumps and limber-holes clogged; she also pounded her armor belt very heavily. Drayton thought that this feature, together with the opening around the base of the turret, would 'prevent these vessels from ever being safe at sea.' However, John Rodgers, coming down a little later in *Weehawken* and encountering all the same troubles, boldly cast off his tow-line and was able to ride the gale alone without too much difficulty. He also suspected the 'upper vessel' (he had thoroughly calked his hatches and turret base) but he thought that safety for the type was simply a question of building enough strength into it.[26]

On 4 January 1863, Worden, now recovered from his wound, arrived at Beaufort in *Montauk,* and in due course *Patapsco, Nantucket, Nahant,* and *Catskill* joined. Admiral Du Pont made some preliminary tests both of the monitors and their 15-inch guns by sending them against Fort McAllister on the Ogeechee River; the results were encouraging, although various minor troubles developed and a new difficulty appeared. The laminated armor was held together by heavy bolts, and under the impact of enemy shot these sheared off their nuts and flung them about the interior with deadly effect. In some of the ships the danger was easily countered, however, by lining the turrets and conning towers with sheet iron.[27]

By 7 April 1863, Du Pont felt ready for the great attempt on Charles-

[25] Bennett, p. 333; ONR, VII, 345-348.
[26] ONR, VIII, 342, 372; also in *Armored Vessels.*
[27] West, p. 229.

ton. At noon that day he weighed and stood in against Sumter with *Weehawken* leading, followed by *Passaic, Montauk, Patapsco, New Ironsides* (flag), *Catskill, Nantucket, Nahant,* and Whitney's *Keokuk*—with her 'striped' armor and fixed gun-towers—bringing up the rear. It was the first major test of the new ironclad fleet. As they came up to Sumter the leading monitors found the way blocked with channel obstructions and the line was thrown into 'some confusion.' The lumbering *New Ironsides* had to anchor twice to avoid going aground; she became, 'in a measure, entangled with the monitors' and was finally forced by her deep draft to take station on the fringes of the battle, too far away to do much. But the monitors stood and slugged it out with the fort at closer quarters from 3 to about 4:30, when Du Pont made signal to withdraw because of the state of the tide and his desire to clear the channel before dark. The mighty 15-inch guns had made no very noticeable impression on Sumter, but neither had the concentrated fire of the fort appeared to make much impression on the monitors. *Keokuk's* armor proved a flat failure; her upper works were riddled and she was holed so badly at the waterline that she sank later in the night. But nobody minded much about her, and Du Pont withdrew intending to renew the action next day.

But then the monitor captains came aboard to report. Though it turned out that they had suffered but a single fatality (a man killed in the conning tower of *Nahant* by a flying fragment of armor broken from the inner wall) four of the seven monitors had been, in the admiral's somewhat gloomy view, 'wholly or partially disabled.' The top of *Passaic's* conning tower had been almost knocked off and her turret had jammed for a time. *Nahant's* turret jammed. The slides of *Patapsco's* rifled gun were smashed when a shot struck at the turret base. *Nantucket* blew the bolts off her muzzle-box with the first round; after the third the port-stopper jammed and the gun was out of action. Most of this damage was of a temporary nature, but Du Pont was not an engineer and he was far from ironworks, machine shops or anything approaching the repair facilities of the modern navy. He gave it up; the action was not renewed.[28]

It was a stunning reverse after all the high hopes that had been pinned on the armorclads, and it precipitated a storm of controversy over the soundness of the monitor design and the Navy's building policies. Secretary Welles and the Department refused to be swayed by it. As a result of the monitors' experiences at sea Ericsson was forced reluctantly to reduce the projecting armor belt in the *Canonicus* class, but the building went forward. Then on 17 June John Rodgers took *Weehawken* into Was-

[28] *Battles,* IV, 39; *Armored Vessels,* pp. 55-74.

saw Sound to meet the formidable new Confederate ironclad *Atlanta*. *Weehawken* fired only five rounds, getting four hits which drove her adversary aground and to ignominious surrender in the space of fifteen minutes. *Nahant,* acting in support, never had a chance to get into action.[29] Secretary Welles, who had insisted on the 15-inch gun, felt himself fully justified.

On 6 July Du Pont was replaced by John A. Dahlgren, who had a better understanding of the machine age and a greater confidence in the monitor type. The Army had meanwhile been called in against Charleston, and the combined forces settled down to a slow siege of the port. In a series of actions throughout the summer and fall the monitors (reinforced by *Lehigh* in August) won no single spectacular victory, but they proved themselves tough and useful little ships, valuable not only against the forts and in support of infantry ashore but even as blockaders.[30] Dahlgren calculated that from his assumption of command up to 7 September his eight monitors fired over 3,500 rounds, taking 1,030 hits in return without serious disablement.[31] He acquired a high regard for his 'shot-proofs.'

Meanwhile *Roanoke, Merrimac's* sister frigate which had been cut down and given three center-line turrets, arrived at Hampton Roads in July on her trial trip. While this design was actually more prophetic than were the monitors, *Roanoke* herself was a failure. Her captain reported that she rolled so heavily and dangerously as to be useless as a sea-going ship, while her draft was prohibitive for coastal service.[32] She was sent back to New York to serve out the war in the harmless duty of protecting the city's merchants from their own fears of Confederate raiders. The Navy returned to the monitor system, and toward the end of the year put in hand in various Navy yards a new class of four ocean-going battleship monitors—giant developments of the original idea, at least suggestive, in their own way, of the *Midway* class of giant 'battle carriers' which were likewise begun too late to see any fighting. 'These,' as Bennett puts it, 'were big vessels (5,660 tons displacement) with big names—*Quinsigamond, Passaconaway, Kalamazoo,* and *Shackamaxon.*' With wooden hulls, like the *Miantonomohs,* they were to have not only two turrets but two funnels as well. With their 15-inch guns, they were said to 'surpass in defensive and offensive power any vessels which have yet been constructed here or in Eu-

---

[29] *Annual Report of the Secretary of the Navy,* 1863; Bennett, pp. 378-379.
[30] *Armored Vessels,* pp. 579-588. Dahlgren's report is also in Frank Moore, ed., *The Rebellion Record,* X, 186.
[31] *Armored Vessels,* p. 584; Bennett, p. 382.
[32] *Armored Vessels,* p. 49.

rope,' and were clearly not designed merely to fight the Confederates.[33]

For the war still in progress, the Navy also ordered in this same year, 1863, the twenty light-draft, single-turret monitors of the *Yazoo* class, mounting one gun and intended to work up the shallower inlets and creeks. They were a complete fiasco. All were put in hand at the same time; unhappily, when the first was launched it was found that owing to various mistakes and miscalculations she possessed what one writer delicately describes as 'negative buoyancy,' and it was then too late to do much about the others.[34] Some were made to float by removing the turret armor, leaving the gun wholly unprotected, but in that state their military value was obviously slight.[35]

Early in 1864 the enlarged *Passaics* of the *Canonicus* class began to go into service, and the big double-turret *Onondaga* appeared. *Onondaga* together with three of the *Canonicus* class—*Tecumseh, Saugus,* and *Canonicus* herself—and the captured ironclad *Atlanta* were stationed in the James to coöperate in Grant's operations against Richmond. They effectively blocked the river against a sortie by the Confederate squadron (including the second *Virginia* ironclad) but they were not boldly used and made no great names for themselves. Then in May Farragut wrote urgently from the Gulf, reporting the formidable characteristics of the ironclad ram *Tennessee* which the Confederates were fitting out in Mobile Bay and which threatened to reduce his unarmored squadrons to matchwood. 'I therefore deeply regret,' he observed, 'that the Department has not been able to give us *one* of the many ironclads that are off Charleston and in the Mississippi.'[36] The Department's answer was to rush two of the double-turret Eads monitors—*Chickasaw* and *Winnebago*—from the Mississippi, to detach *Tecumseh* from the James and to send her with her sister ship *Manhattan* to the Gulf.

Thus reinforced, Farragut stood in early on the morning of 5 August 1864 against the Mobile Bay forts and *Tennessee,* the latter commanded by the same Franklin Buchanan who had opened the ironclad war in the conning tower of *Merrimac.* Farragut advanced in two lines ahead, with his four monitors, led by *Tecumseh,* in the starboard line, nearest to Fort Morgan and a little ahead of the wooden ships in the port line. As *Tecumseh* came up with the fort, she fired each of her 15-inch guns and then reloaded to be ready for *Tennessee.* Shortly afterward, forging ahead into

---

[33] Bennett, p. 400.

[34] West, p. 242.

[35] *Photographic History of the Civil War,* VI, 177, shows one in this condition.

[36] Charles B. Boynton, *History of the Navy During the Rebellion* (1867), II, 531. Cited as 'Boynton.'

the bay, she struck on a Confederate mine; she was seen to lurch heavily forward and slide straight to the bottom, her screw racing momentarily in the air as she disappeared. Ninety-two men and officers were lost with her. Farragut may or may not have 'damned the torpedoes'; at all events, he drove the rest of the squadron ahead through the confusion and closed with the bravely charging *Tennessee*. It took nearly an hour to batter her into surrender, a task in which most of the ships participated but in which the remaining monitors did the heavy work. And in these three ships not a single man was even injured.

In the summer of 1864 the four wooden-hulled, double-turret *Miantonomohs*—the products of the Navy Department's original program, advanced even before *Monitor* had been completed—at last began to come upon the scene. Built without the projecting armor belts, they were successful sea boats; and there is a dashing report of *Monadnock* in heavy weather, with her deck virtually submerged and the angry seas 'curling well up the turrets' and flinging their spray across the tops. Admiral Porter thought her 'the best monitor afloat' and was sure that she could 'safely and expeditiously go anywhere.'[37] But obviously everything had to be tightly calked under such conditions. *Tecumseh's* disaster was not the only reminder of the dangerously small reserves of buoyancy which the type possessed. In December 1863, *Weehawken* suddenly and rather mysteriously foundered while lying at anchor off Charleston, perhaps because of a failure to close the forward hatch against a rising swell; and in the same harbor a year later (January 1865) *Patapsco* drifted down on a Confederate mine and sank with equal suddenness.[38]

The more powerful later ships were coming to completion, but so was the war—a circumstance again suggesting the experience of the recent conflict. The monitors' last chance for important service was in the bombardments of Fort Fisher, December 1864 and January 1865. *Canonicus* and *Saugus* were withdrawn from the James for this duty; *Mahopac* of the same class and *Monadnock* were sent along and the veteran *New Ironsides* was brought up. Ericsson's massive single-turret *Dictator* was also ordered to the scene, but her heavy propeller shaft destroyed its bearings before she had gone twenty miles and she had to turn back.[39] *Canonicus, Saugus, Mahopac,* and *Monadnock*, standing inshore of the wooden fleet, did the heavy work of the bombardments; as with Iwo Jima, however, the fort still had to be taken the hard way, with naked infantry. In March 1865

[37] ONR, XI, 67.
[38] Bennett, pp. 382, 498.
[39] Bennett, p. 344.

Milwaukee, one of the Eads monitors, was mined and lost in the headwaters of Mobile Bay; this was the last combat experience of the Civil War monitor fleet.

It was, however, by no means their last appearance in history. The Civil War ended with the American people under the exhilarating impression that they possessed the most powerful navy in the world. The monitors, beginning as mere coastal floating batteries, had sprouted 15-inch guns, more powerful than those carried in the ships of any other nation, and had grown to ocean-going tonnages and cruising radii. Their enthusiasts compared the French and British ironclad types most unfavorably to these mighty developments of an unconventional 'Yankee notion,' and saw the latter sweeping the seas for the American flag. Other powers had something of the same idea; and it seems probable that the existence of the monitor fleet assisted in dissuading Britain from intervention and in eliminating the French from Mexico.

Indeed, when properly calked the monitors could, like the modern submarine, keep the sea well enough. To prove it, *Monadnock* was sent out to the Pacific Coast over the long and dangerous route around South America, while *Miantonomoh* in 1866 carried Assistant Secretary Gustavus V. Fox across the Atlantic and back on a ceremonial visit to Russia.[40] Perhaps the monitors were actually rather closer to the submarine idea than to that of the later battleships, of which they are so often supposed to have been the progenitors. To keep the bulk of the ship under water in order to reduce target area and vulnerability was a major aim of their designers.[41] Like the elephant, which was said to swim virtually submerged, drawing air through its uplifted trunk, the monitors were expected to wallow through rather than over the ocean seas, breathing in through their standing air trunks and out through their grated turret tops. There is more than a fanciful resemblance between the rounded heads of their air intakes and the 'snorkel' heads of the post-war submarines; and the Reverend Dr. Boynton was being complimentary when he described them as 'iron sea elephants.'[42]

The Europeans may have looked thoughtful when they saw *Miantonomoh's* huge gun muzzles peering from their massive turrets as she lay at anchor in their harbors.[43] But the monitors had an obvious defect.

---

[40] Bennett, pp. 589-592.

[41] The Stevens gunboat *Naugatuck* was provided with water ballast tanks to reduce her freeboard in action, and a similar installation in the *Yazoo* class was one source of its calamities. West, p. 241.

[42] Boynton, I, 183.

[43] Bennett, p. 345, gives a photograph of *Miantonomoh* lying in an unnamed European port. It gives a good idea of the type, with its peacetime arrangement of boats and flying bridges.

Though they could keep the sea, they could not possibly fight on it. They dared not train their turrets or even open their gun-ports in heavy weather. Until the problem of mounting heavy guns and armor on sea-fighting as well as sea-keeping ships could be solved, there was no doubt a certain logic in these ocean-going floating batteries, sufficiently invulnerable to force their way past the high seas fleets of the time in order to carry a war to the enemy coast. But the development of a satisfactory high-freeboard battleship was bound to end their usefulness; this was the problem on which the European designers were engaged, and the semi-submerged monitor type made little direct contribution to its solution.

Dunderberg, the powerful broadside 'frigate ram' ordered in the summer of 1862, was closer to the actual line of development and many thought her the best of all the Civil War designs. She was not finished, however, until the end of the war, too late to see service. The government turned her back to her builders who sold her to France. Under the name *Rochambeau* she long served in that navy, exercising an influence on French designers which was traceable for years in the exaggerated ram bows and tumble-home sides of their ships.[44] Of the monitors, at least one other crossed the Atlantic—*Onondaga,* also sold to France—while two more made the voyage around South America. These were *Catawba* and *Oneonta,* surreptitiously sold to Peru.[45]

Unfortunately for the monitor enthusiasts, the American taxpayer was losing interest in naval expansion. The four giant *Quinsigamonds* were not quite complete when the war ended; they were incontinently broken up on the stocks.[46] Of Ericsson's two big single-turrets, *Puritan* was first redesigned for two turrets on the insistence of the Navy Department and then left unfinished. *Dictator,* which broke down on the way to Fort Fisher, did not receive her new bearings in time to fight. She was recommissioned during the *Virginius* crisis with Spain in 1874 and got as far as Key West, but was scrapped a few years later. *New Ironsides* was accidentally destroyed by fire, in 1866, while lying at her dock. The three surviving *Winnebagos* were scrapped in 1874. *Saugus* was disposed of in 1891. But that still left five remaining members of the *Canonicus* class and the eight surviving *Passaics* on the Navy list.

In the meanwhile, the unfinished *Puritan* and the four *Miantonomohs* had been pursuing their weird subsequent career. Congress would appropriate no money for new ships, so the ingenious expedient was adopt-

[44] Bennett, pp. 348-354.
[45] Bennett, p. 627.
[46] Bennett, p. 400.

ed of 'repairing' these five. The 'repairs' consisted in breaking them up and building five new vessels around the old names. The business dragged on through various changes of design over a period of some twenty years, with the results finally emerging in the mid-'90's, just in time to lumber ineffectively through the Spanish-American War. The new *Puritan, Miantonomoh, Monadnock, Terror* (ex-*Agamenticus*), and *Amphitrite* (ex-*Tonawanda*) bore only slight resemblance to the originals. They were still recognizably monitors, but they had new turrets and modern rifles; all save *Miantonomoh* had steel superstructures and light caliber batteries between the turrets; they were equipped with comfortable wooden pilot-houses, and only the curses of the crews which had to suffer their discomforts and inefficiencies recalled the ships whose names they bore.[47]

When war came in 1898, however, the thirteen survivors of the *Canonicus* and *Passaic* classes were still virtually in their original condition, 15-inch smoothbores, 'grasshopper' engines[48] and all the rest. Their speed can scarcely have increased with the years and their laminated wrought-iron armor would not have withstood a contemporary shell of even modest caliber; but the Navy Department solemnly brought them forth, manned them with naval militia and set them to patrolling the harbors. A photograph of *Nahant* in the hands of the New York State Naval Militia shows her looking much as she must have done in the great days of the campaign against Charleston, except that a conical wooden penthouse surmounts her turret, with a kind of dormer window peering forward through which, presumably, the ship was conned.[49] Not long after the war she and the last of her consorts were disposed of.

The monitors had their many failings, but hardly as many as one might have expected of so untried and hastily developed a design. As the event proved, they did not swim in the main stream of naval progress, but they did the job for which they were intended under the conditions which obtained, and it is hard to say more for any naval type. Their primary mission, after all, was to counter Confederate Secretary Mallory's shrewd policy of using the new ironclad principle as a means of breaking the Federal supremacy at sea, and that mission they brilliantly performed. Like the giant sea-air fleets of the recent war, they also proved themselves pow-

---

[47] Bennett gives the history of all these ships; the dates of disposal are taken from his table in Appendix B.

[48] The Ericsson bell-crank engines deserve a paper to themselves. *Monitor* had a single cylinder casting, divided into two working cylinders by a steam-tight partition in the center, laid horizontally and athwartship. The two piston-rods, projecting to port and starboard, worked through a system of cranks and shafts on the single crank of the main shaft. While the Ericsson design seems quaint, there was a real reason for it—to keep the weights low and the machinery protected under the waterline.

[49] *Harper's Pictorial History of the War with Spain*, pp. 119, 214.

erful coadjutors in the blockade and against enemy coastal defenses; and if the future did not belong to them, neither can one be too sure that it belongs to the tremendous 'battle carriers' of today. The 'iron sea elephants' were the world's first real 'engineer' ships and they constituted its first true steam-and-iron navy. It seems a bit unfortunate that some of their names could not have been better remembered in the huge fleets developed for the second World War.

RECAPITULATION

The Federal ironclad fleet, 1861-1865, omitting the western river flotillas.

1861

New Ironsides	Broadside ship	Burned, 15 Dec. 1866
Galena	"	
Monitor	Single-turret	Lost, 30 Dec. 1862

1862

Passaic	Single-turret	
Montauk	"	
Catskill	"	
Patapsco	"	Mined, 5 Jan. 1865
Lehigh	"	
Sangamon (Jason)	"	
Camanche	"	Assembled in San Francisco
Nantucket	"	
Nahant	"	
Weehawken	"	Lost, 6 Dec. 1863
Keokuk	'Tower' ship	Sunk, 7 April 1863
Roanoke	Sea-going turret	
Onondaga	Double-turret	Sold to France
Miantonomoh	"	'Repaired'
Monadnock	"	"
Agamenticus (Terror)	"	"
Tonawanda (Amphitrite)	"	"
Winnebago	Eads double-turret	
Chickasaw	"	
Milwaukee	"	Mined, 28 Mar. 1865
Kickapoo	"	
Dunderberg	Broadside ram	Sold to France

Dictator	Single-turret	
Puritan	"	Redesigned; 'repaired'
Canonicus	Single-turret	
Catawba	"	Sold to Peru
Oneonta	"	"
Mahopac	"	
Manhattan	"	
Tecumseh	"	Mined, 5 Aug. 1864
Manayunk (Ajax)	"	
Saugus	"	
Tippecanoe (Wyandotte)	"	

1863

Quinsigamond	Double-turret	Unfinished
Passaconaway	"	"
Kalamazoo	"	"
Shackamaxon	"	"
20 *Yazoo* class	Single-turret, light draft	Failures

Subtracting the *Yazoos*, this is a total of 40 sea-going or coastal ironclads. Of these, 4 (*Galena, New Ironsides, Keokuk,* and *Dunderberg*) were broadside ships; 1 (*Roanoke*) was a high-freeboard turret, and 35 were of the monitor type. Of these 35 Civil War monitors only 3 were lost in action (*Tecumseh, Patapsco,* and *Milwaukee*) and 2 more (*Monitor* and *Weehawken*) by accident. None was ever seriously disabled by gunfire; indeed, in the whole course of the war only one man appears to have been killed by gunfire in the monitor fleet, though many were drowned in their sudden sinkings.

The 4 *Quinsigamonds* were never finished; *Onondaga, Catawba,* and *Oneonta* were sold abroad, leaving 23 monitors on the list. Five were 'repaired'; the 3 *Winnebagos* were sold in 1874; *Dictator* in 1883, and *Saugus* in 1891. The remaining 13 were still in existence at the time of the Spanish-American War. They were scrapped soon afterward.

VI

Varied Fare

Fur Seal Hunting in the South Atlantic *by A. Alfred Mattsson*	239
Campeche Days *by Fred Hunt*	253
The Tradition of the St. Elmo's Fire *by George G. Carey*	267
The Travels of *Tilikum* *by W. Gillies Ross*	277

Some men followed the sea for trade, others sought whales, or seals, or fish. Some sailed for the sake of voyaging—to see distant lands or beguiling islands. Whatever the reason, they experienced the sea's changing moods, and occasionally spectacular natural phenomena.

Fur Seal Hunting in the South Atlantic

BY A. ALFRED MATTSSON

FUR sealing, as I knew it, was carried on from the west coast until about the year 1900. I had no part in the west coast sealing, but the hunting there led to the discovery of fur seals in South American waters in the following manner.

The great seal rookery on the Pribylov Islands in the Bering Sea came to the United States with the purchase of Alaska in 1867. At that time an estimated herd of seals, numbering 2,500,000, used to find their way to the rookery during mating season (June to September). To protect the herd and preserve the yearly increase, the government decided to follow the course the Russian government had used, which was to lease the rookery to responsible parties who would take mostly unproductive seals (young bulls and batchelor seals).

The rookery was leased to the Alaska Commercial Company from 1870 to 1890 for an annual rental of $55,000, plus a royalty of $2.62 for each skin taken. In the twenty years 1,977,377 skins were taken, paying the United States government $6,020,152, almost the cost of Alaska, which was $7,200,000 in gold.

But that was by no means the total number of seals taken from the herd. A number of vessels were engaged in Pelagic sealing, that is, hunting in open water, and were making raids on the rookery whenever chance offered a safe getaway. I don't know when shotguns were first used in seal hunting, maybe in the late seventies or early eighties, but in 1886 the United States closed the Bering Sea to all vessels using shotguns to hunt seals. A number of vessels which ventured in there were seized and confiscated and the resulting claims finally brought about a meeting between the four nations concerned—the United States, Canada, Russia, and Japan—to settle the matter.

The tribunal was held in Paris in 1893. The United States, as owner of the rookery, claimed that since the seal herd returned every year to the rookery it was domesticated and not a herd of wild animals, and therefore our government had the right to close the Bering Sea for their protection. The other three nations claimed freedom of the seas, but did concede ownership rights and agreed upon a closed zone of sixty-mile radius around the rookery, and so the matter was settled.

The following year, 1894, was a banner year for open water sealing, the combined fleets taking a catch of 140,000 skins. The demand for sealskins was great and the fleet of vessels sailing out of Victoria, British Columbia, needed more men and ships to carry on the business. Some of the skippers were sent east to Nova Scotia in off season to pick up fishing schooners and sail them around the Horn to Victoria, British Columbia. These vessels discovered fur seals along the South American coast from the River Plate down to the Horn.

I don't know how many vessels were sent around to Victoria, perhaps five or six. They surely had old sealers on board, as ordinary seafaring men would not know the difference between fur seals and small sea-lions in the water.

Now there had been a number of Nova Scotians, Cape Bretoners, and Newfoundlanders sealing out west. When word got around that a new sealing ground had been found, some of these men returned east and got capital interested in Halifax, and the result was that one or two vessels were fitted out to go sealing in South America in 1900. They must have done well, because next year one or two more were sent out and some of them wintered in Port Stanley, Falkland Islands, the nearest British port to the sealing grounds outside the River Plate. In 1903 a fleet of eleven schooners left Halifax for the sealing grounds.

Now in the closing days of December 1903 I was in a ship that was wrecked on the West Falkland Islands.[1] We found a sheep ranch not far from the spot where we landed and stayed at the ranch a few days, until the coasting schooner came along and took us in to Port Stanley on the East Falklands, the only port on the islands that I know of. We arrived there on New Year's Day 1904 and found the sealing fleet of eleven schooners shipping their skins to England. Four of them were new and painted white; the rest were black, but all were very trim and yacht-like, of about 100 tons, 100 feet long—typical Lunenburg fishing schooners

---

[1] The Falkland Islands are located some three hundred miles east of the Magellan Straits. They were discovered by Captain John Davis in 1592 and settled by the British in 1832, Stanley Harbor being used as a naval base. No trees can be found on the islands, only grassy moorland and high rocky cliffs suitable for sheep raising, which seems to be the main occupation of the people there. The population is about three thousand, Port Stanley having the lion's share of sixteen hundred in 1904. There are geese in abundance to be found all over the islands all the year around. So plentiful are they, in fact, that the government pays a bounty of ten shillings per hundred 'goosebeaks' to save grass for the sheep. Many a hundred geese were killed that year, not for the bounty but for roasting and eating purposes.

of forty years ago. Besides the sealing fleet there were four square-riggers in more or less dismasted state, having had a go at rounding Cape Stiff and getting the worst of it. There were also a British cruiser and a destroyer in port for the holiday.

Now take the bluejackets on shore leave. Mix them up with the sealers and ships' crews. Then add a generous splash of New Year's holiday spirits, and you have a fine dish for a shipwrecked crew, and we enjoyed it immensely.

One of the new sealing schooners had lost two of her boats in a fog on the sealing grounds and I got the chance to go in her as boat-steerer, which I did. Later we heard that the two boats had made their way to land somewhere in Argentina.

The seal hunting season in the southern hemisphere begins in late September or early October. From then on there are two months of good hunting, 'til mid-December when seals become scarce on the grounds. At that time their mating season begins, lasting about three months (December to March). The seals go to their rookeries along the coast and the sealers make for port to ship their skins, Port Stanley in this case. It was there we found them on New Year's Day, 1904.

In late February the sealers would up anchor and one by one leave for the grounds. The distance being from 700 to 1,100 miles, it usually took about two weeks. We were one of the last to leave and were delayed some more when, a few days out, the vessel, running before the wind in a medium breeze, dipped the mainboom in one of the long rollers and before the helmsman could straighten her out jibed her big mainsail over, breaking her mainboom in two places. Now it's quite a job to find room on a 100-foot vessel for a 75-foot spar when you have nine sealing boats on board. The boats are 19 feet long by 4½ feet beam, double-enders that look like small life-boats and they *are very good sea boats*. They can't be nested like dories so they are placed on edge, three to a side on the main deck, one on each side of the mainmast, and the ninth tipped against the cabin aft. All of them are, of course, lashed securely. These boats had to be moved around so as to have one side of the deck clear for repairing the boom. Well, the job was done in a day and a half, but being a new vessel with no spare spars, the boom had to be shortened and we could only set a double reefed mainsail after that.

In due time we got to the grounds and one late afternoon a man aloft shouted, 'Dogsleeper to windward!' The captain eased the vessel gently up into the wind, a boat was lowered, and the second mate who was on watch took his gun and a couple of shells, hopped into the bow of the boat, and with his boat-steerer and another man doing the rowing brought the seal back with him after one shot. The second mate was quarter-breed Siwash, a man mountain weighing two hundred and seventy pounds, yet quick as a cat on his feet and the best shot in the fleet. Later that evening we saw two travellers crossing our bow, so the captain 'hove to' under ground sails. We were 'on the grounds.' The hunters were loading fresh shells and cleaning the guns; the boat-steerers were filling waterbreakers and seeing to the boat gear; and the cabin boy was getting the lunch boxes ready for the morning. The boxes would have half a loaf of bread, one can of corned beef, one can of salmon, half a pie, and some cookies and hard biscuit. On Sundays we would have lunch tongue instead of Willie (corned beef).

We had breakfast at 3:30 in the morning, lowering the boats just at daybreak. A light wind was blowing and the sea had gone down some. When there is wind, the boats will go out under sail in berths, the lee boat running to leeward a couple of miles and the rest half a mile apart and always behind, as seals can smell a boat as far as they can see one. If a leeward boat lowers his sail after seal, the windward boats will wait for him, usually only a few minutes. He either gets his seal or he doesn't. If many seals are found the hunting becomes general and the boats get spread apart and soon one finds himself out of sight of everything. Then one must be sure that he has a good bearing on the vessel. On calm days the boats can hunt every which way. If much shooting is heard in one direction and nothing is seen where one is going, it is better to edge over that way. One may have better luck.

Now, that first day we had only gone a little while to leeward when the hunter took down his jib and motioned to me to help get the sail in as quietly as possible, saying there were two sleepers ahead. He was a young Newfoundlander, a first year man himself, but he had a half season's experience which I hadn't. When going up on seal, sleepers or any kind, both men stand up pushing on the oars, but getting close the boat-steerer takes his pushing board and sits down, which gives him better control. The hunter probably wanted to train me to stand up for he didn't mention the board. Well, we got very close and my knees were knocking with excitement. The hunter was ready to shoot when a small wave slapped the bow of the boat and both seals went under in a flash. 'Keep your oars out of the water!' was the command. In a few seconds the seals came up, one on each side of the boat. He fired once at each side and missed both of them. He picked up his other gun and watched, swinging his gun from side to side and I stood looking goggle-eyed all around. After a while we saw the seals breaking out of the water like porpoise away ahead. We chased them but saw no more of them. I got some fatherly advice about pushing a boat into a wave when going up on a sleeper and such. Later we got two or three seals that day and some of the boats had eight or ten.

The easiest seal to get is a sleeper of course. There are four different degrees of soundness. The dogsleeper is the soundest sleeper of all. He is found in stormy weather, a young seal all by himself that gets tired and goes to sleep with his back just awash and his flippers hanging, looking dead. Only his nose comes up to breathe once in a while. They all sleep with nose to windward, so the boat must be pushed up to them from the leeward. One watches his chance and shoots for the back of the head.

The next best is a jughandle. He sleeps on his side with the hind flippers curled up in the air towards his head and one fore flipper laid over them and the other fore flipper hanging straight down usually. His head and neck lie straight along the water. He looks just like a jughandle from a distance. One pushes up on him and picks the side where the back of his head is. The throat shot is not so good.

Next comes the breaster. He sleeps with his flippers crossed, not tight on his chest but up in the air, making the shape of a squat O. His head and part of his body hang down. He is only half asleep, so be careful. If he is shot in the breast and not killed, he will go down, his lungs will fill with water and he will drown. Some hunters shoot in the flipper joint to make him come up and jump around and perhaps allow a better shot later.

The finner is next. He is only half asleep. With his one fore flipper sticking up in the air and head and body down, one has only the flipper joint to shoot at. If left alone awhile he might curl up into a jughandle, but one does not waste time when among seals.

It often happens that a big bunch of sleepers are found, five or six or seven. Six is the most I've ever seen together. The old experienced hunters will 'double up' with the first gun; that is, they will place the boat is such a position that two seals will be close together and in line. Then they will hit the first seal in the head and the second across the back as he turns to go down, all within a fraction of a second. If the second shot is well placed across the small of the back, it will paralyze the hind flippers, making the seal jump around frantically. The other seals usually go straight down and straight up again. One may 'nose' at the dead one, making a good target. The others will hang around the crippled seal; then you gaff the dead ones and go after the others. With luck, if the water is smooth, one is sure of the cripple and of one or two more. But such shooting is not done by a green hunter with a greener boat-steerer. *We* never got more than one or two out of a bunch.

Sealing is not all sleepers, however. One has to go after anything one sees, such as travellers and moochers. Moochers go along slowly as if they were looking for a soft spot to sleep on, and present a good target if taken unawares. Travellers go in one direction at a good rate of speed, looking for bait no doubt. For effective shooting one must get within one hundred feet of the moving seal. A small sleeper can be killed at one hundred and fifty to two hundred feet, but big ones are tough.

The guns used are 'Parker' hammerless, 32-inch, double-barrelled 12-gauge. Brass shells are used so they can be reloaded. The usual load is three and a quarter drams of black powder and twenty-one buck shot. Some hunters use four drams of powder and twenty-eight shot, claiming seven more chances; but such a load fills the shell right up to the top and often, when one barrel is fired, the shot will jar the wadding loose in the other shell and the twenty-eight shot will run out of the barrel, leaving the shell blank. To fix that, pour a box of wadding into a can of paint oil, drain off the oil and let the wadding dry. Thus prepared, it holds very well, but the gun will kick like a steer and if it is easy on the triggers both barrels will go off—'wow'!

The hardest work of all is chasing seal among a school of porpoise. They not only go faster, but they won't hold their direction long. They go down; one can see them under water a little way and one gets the gun ready; then one can't see them at all, and a minute later they may reappear dead astern going the other way. So one earns one's salt getting seal that way. Also, travellers, if heavy seals, will sink very quickly if killed broadside of the boat. Even with a 17-foot gaff (carried in every boat) one will lose a few by sinking; especially if the boat is heavy with seal so that it can't be turned easily.

It's best to start skinning when you get five aboard, unless there are so many seals around that you can't stop. One boat had twenty-nine aboard one day. The skipper paddled to the schooner, unloaded, went out again and got eight or ten more. Skinning in a boat is done on a skinning board, a piece of canvas tacked on two pieces of wood reaching across the gunnels, just like a small stretcher, with two end pieces to hold the board flat. First cut off his whiskers; rip down his belly, chin to tail; cut round his flippers front and back with the sticking knife. Then, with the skinning knife, which is curved like a scimitar, start from the chin, cut down toward his tail, holding the freed skin in the left hand, like peeling a log, and leaving a fair amount of blubber on the skin to hold the salt.

The skins are salted in the hold every night. Every inch of the blubber side of the skin is rubbed carefully with salt, placed flat, and covered with more salt. The next skin, treated likewise, goes on top and so forth until the catch is all salted.

If the daily catch is good, the captain will keep the vessel 'hove to' on the same spot. If the catch gets scant, he will ask every boat, 'Did you see many travellers and what direction did they go?' He will then follow in the night the seal so as to keep in touch with them. Once in a while he does not catch up or over shoots. Then the boats may have a day or two without much luck.

Travelling seal instinctively hunt for bait, schools of small sardine-like fish on which they feed. If we row two or three hours without a sign of a seal, we watch flying birds. They hunt bait too. We follow them and soon may see a flock wildly flying around. They are in a bait sure. A bait can be seen a mile or more away, showing purple against the blue or green of the sea. We get closer. There is something black in it—seals! We edge to leeward, then push up to it; make sure of the first shot and get in two or three more if we can; pick up the dead one, reload, and get after the cripples.

Sometimes we may find a whale or two in a bait, as well as seals, and sea-lions, porpoise, turtles, and birds of all kinds feeding off the same bait. We must then approach carefully to try to make our kill on the edge of the bait and gaff him quickly. The other seals, if any, will get on the other side of the whale where we can't get them, except by rowing around the whale, only to find ourselves still on the wrong side. Don't go right into the bait. The whale might come up under the boat, which happens sometimes even outside the bait. The whale will slide through the bait, belly up with mouth open, and do a slow barrel roll, and then repeat— all very quietly and peacefully.

If a swordfish should appear on the scene, look out for trouble. There may be a killer whale around also as they usually hunt together. The swordfish jabs the whale from underneath, driving him up to the surface. The killer then jumps in the air and turns and drives his sharp boney backfin into the whale, cutting him into ribbons. Thus attacked, the whale will break blindly full length out of the water, dripping gore and blubber, and the best thing for puny man and his little sealing boat is to get away from there quick.

In foggy weather the hunt goes on just the same, except the boats don't leave the vessel before daylight as they do in clear weather. Every boat has a fine little spirit compass fastened to the thwart in front of the boat-steerer. It is his job to keep a good bearing on the vessel at all times. The captain keeps the vessel 'hove to' all day and keeps the foghorn going. The bomb gun is fired once an hour by the cook, whose job it is to load and fire it on the hour. The gun is a small muzzle loader weighing one hundred pounds. He loads it on deck, using a milk tin full of powder and paper and rags for wadding. Then he hoists it up in the fore-staysail boom lift some eight feet above deck and fires it with a red-hot poker. It can be heard perhaps five or six miles in calm weather and both men in the boats listen for it to check their bearings, usually keeping within sound of it all day. But if one should run into a bunch of seals, one forgets everything but the hunt and often gets out of sound of the gun.

The biggest danger in fog is a tide-rip. One may be five miles from the vessel, chasing a seal into a tide-rip. In calm weather this does not appear to be any different from the rest of the sea, except by a slight ripple at the very edge of it. Yet it may carry one four or five miles an hour away from the bearings if he is not careful. Usually there is a string of birds sitting along the edge of it, also, there and here a bunch of seaweed and other debris. In the heat of the chase, however, one misses things like that and sometimes finds himself out of sound of the gun when darkness falls. We once got back to the schooner at 1 A.M. having passed her some five miles to windward and gone some two miles beyond, when it breezed up, clearing the fog, and we could see a flare at her main truck. That's what a tide-rip can do to you.

Sometimes people will ask, 'Is sealing very dangerous?' I should like to say that it is no more dangerous than any other seafaring trade. Sometimes a boat may get lost in a fog or even get lost by other accidental means, but that happens on the fishing banks just as often. A man may get washed overboard in a storm from any ship. But at times a drowning occurs that could be prevented. Take, for example, the incident of one of our young boat-steerers. He was on the morning watch with his hunter at the wheel, and, being on the lookout, he went to take the sidelights down at daybreak. He got the windward light down first; then went to leeward outside the shrouds. The fore-sail must have given a hard slap just as he got the light out of the screen, breaking his hand hold; and the heavy light, weighing some forty to fifty pounds, carried him down and under and sad to say not even his hunter, the man at the wheel, saw him go. Had he gone up on the *inboard* side of the lee shrouds, he would not fallen overboard. Still, I have read about somebody drowning in a bathtub.

That season, with eleven schooners on the grounds, it was not unusual to find ourselves within sight of one or two or them, and we often visited on board for a few minutes. There is always hot coffee in the galley for such a visit. While swapping the latest sealing news and praising the cook's pie, we are pointed out the bunk of someone we know well. After tying the victim's blankets in knots and hiding his pillow in the chain locker, we blithely bid the skipper and cook goodby and hop into our boat—to find her half full of water! The cabin boy has pulled the plug out and put it back again with a match along the side, causing a slow leak. Well, we had our fun and so did they and playing pranks doesn't hurt anybody.

We had a Newfoundlander aboard, the complaining long-suffering kind, but not above playing a trick if the chance offered. Once he went aboard another vessel, had his coffee and pie, found a friend's bunk and spiked his mattress to the under side of the deck. Then he got into his boat, hoisted his sail, and went sealing again. After a while his hands got cold so he stooped down to get his mittens from the bottom of the boat, only to find them carefully nailed down right through the planking.

While making a passage, the boys used to play a game called 'leather breeches.' The fore-sail halyards were coiled up on the bow of a boat and the man who was 'it' stuck his head in the coil, the rest of the men standing around. One of them would slap the victim sharply where his pants were tightest. He would have to pick out the man who did it, or stay 'it' until he did. A fine game in cold weather—everybody kept warm.

In late April and early May a storm is likely to keep the boats from sealing four or five days at a time. One may get a few clear, warm days only to find that the storm has gotten him out of touch with the seals; and, after hunting by day and cruising from one end of the grounds to the other by night with the catch getting smaller every day, another storm will come up to keep the boats on board a week maybe. Then it is the end of the season and the schooners will leave the grounds. Those heading for Halifax and home will call at some Brazilian port on the way to ship their skins.

Our vessel and another headed for Port Stanley, Falkland Islands, to lay up for the winter. Upon arriving in port, the first job to do was to get our catch of skins ready for shipping to England. All sealing vessels bring their barrels 'knocked down,' carefully marked and stowed in the hold. Two men are set to work coopering. The rest set to work on skins.

The old salt is shaken off, fresh salt is rubbed in, and each skin is rolled up into a small tight roll. These rolls are then tightly packed into the barrels with plenty of salt all around them, the barrels holding between twenty to forty skins.

After the skins were shipped there was not much to do except to go ashore whenever anybody felt like it. A new mainboom was made during the winter from a ship's yard, of which there seemed to be a good supply stored along the shore, no doubt from the many hulks anchored all over the harbor.

After four months lay up we were all glad to leave port in early September for the sealing grounds, reaching there a bit earlier than usual and finding very few seals. We got only a hundred the first three weeks and no doubt the catch of the eleven schooners the year before had something to do with the scarcity. The captain, talking it over with the hunters, decided to raid a rookery along the coast of Uruguay. The largest rookery there is 'Lobo's Island,' off the mouth of the River Plate, belonging to Uruguay and having a coast-guard station. Raiding that was out of the question, but to the north some eighty miles were two smaller rookeries, 'Castillo Chico' and 'Castillo Grande'; and there we found ourselves at daybreak one fine morning. The rocks were a half mile offshore in a shallow bight of the coastline. To the northeast there was a high promontory; to the south, some seven miles away, a rocky point with a lighthouse on it.

The day was fine, almost calm, and there were plenty of seals on the rocks. We got two hundred skins that day and everyone was happy making for open sea that night. The hunters skinned by lantern light; the mates and boat-steerers salted in the hold. No sleep that night. Shells had to be loaded for the morrow; and daybreak found us at the rocks again. The weather was still fine, but the seals had been pretty well cleaned out. We got only a few over a hundred, but still it made a good day's work and a happy crew going to sea that night.

The third morning found us at the rocks again. A long swell was running and the sky was a hazy gray. We had barely got to the rocks in the boats when one of the boats got caught in a breaking swell, smashed against the rock and stove·in pretty badly. The three men managed to climb onto the rocks after swimming around some. They even pulled the boat up with them, but they lost the guns, shells, and the rest of the boat gear.

When hunting seals around a rookery, three men are needed in a boat: two on the oars and the hunter tending to his guns and to gaffing the dead seals. I was pulling in the mate's boat that day and he drove his boat into the rock, but got the men off and their boat too. We started for the vessel which was lying a short distance off, towing the boat full of water. We saw the cabin boy run up the rigging and wave the flag. That means, come on board quick! All boats started for the vessel, arriving there ahead of us. We looked around and saw the revenue cutter rounding the lighthouse point to the south of us. We hustled on board. All sails were set, boats lashed down, and we started to beat it out to sea. The wind was blowing straight in, so, because of the coastline, we could not go on the starboard tack. We had to take port tack, which would take us across the cutter's bow. She had us bottled up for fair. Some of the boats brought four seals on board. We had no time to skin them, so they were dumped whole into the hold and covered with salt.

When about three miles off, the cutter fired a shot overhead. The captain, at the wheel, paid no attention. A few minutes later another shot came across our bows. Still no attention from the skipper. A third shot came, dead ahead and very close, but the skipper kept her on her course. When less than half a mile away, a fourth shot came whistling at us. It must have gone between the spars, for everybody felt the wind of it. The captain then brought her up in the wind, waiting. While all this shooting was going on, I wondered how long he intended to ignore the shots of the cutter, knowing full well that he could not get away. Later it came to me that he wanted to get outside the three-mile limit, and he did just that before he hove to.

The cutter came alongside and ordered our captain to come on board. He sent one of the hunters instead and told him to say we were in looking for water, as our water was bad. A few minutes later the hunter came back, accompanied by an officer and two marines armed to the teeth with orders to send half the crew aboard the cutter. The officer and marines took charge of our schooner and we were thus officially seized by Uruguay.

Seven boat-steerers and one hunter went aboard the cutter. She was steel built, about two hundred feet long, and had a three-inch swivel gun mounted on her fore-deck. On boarding her, we were told to go aft and sit down. There was a big hawser grating at the round of her stern. We coiled the hawser, making a comfortable rest for our backs, and sat on the grating. A package of tobacco and cigarette papers were given to each man and there we sat the whole day, smoking, singing, and swapping lies, while the cutter headed for Montevideo with the vessel following under shortened sail.

At seven that night the cutter tied up at a small coast-guard station within the River Plate, some fifteen miles from Montevideo. It was named 'Flores Island,' no doubt because of the profusion of wild flowers growing there. We were given soup and rolls for our evening meal and *it was good!* We had had nothing since breakfast at 3 A.M. that day. We spent the night on the grating, talking most of the time, and at daylight the vessel hove in sight. The captain had taken his time, no doubt wanting to make his freedom last as long as possible. The cutter backed out and took her in tow for Montevideo, where she was anchored some two hundred yards from the Custom House in the inner harbor.

We were put back aboard the vessel and had a good breakfast in the forecastle, where we found a note from the cook. It told us to say, when questioned, that we had been in looking for fresh water, as our water in the tanks was very bad. In the meantime, a lot of 'Gold Braid' had come aboard with interpreters. We were taken one by one to the cabin for questioning. Everybody had the same story—'Bad water.' A sample of water was taken from our tanks for analysis and was found very bad. A guard of four *marineros* and an officer were left on board and here we laid up for seven months and a half, the guard changing morning and night and bringing us a tub of fresh drinking water daily from ashore.

Our water really was bad. Port Stanley has no public water supply and every house uses rain water; of which there is plenty. Most of the houses are of corrugated iron construction with tanks at each corner to catch rainwater. The sealing schooners, on the way out of the port, would anchor at Sparrow Cove, about half way through the narrow entrance to the harbor. A small creek of fresh water runs into that cove. The sealing boats would be sent up along the creek, filled with fresh water and rowed out to the schooner, where the water was emptied into the tanks. That winter, 1904, was, perhaps, a bad one, for numerous dead sheep were floating down the creek when we filled our tanks.

The first two months in Montevideo we were all confined to the vessel. Although covered with salt, the four dead seals that were dumped into the hold the morning we were seized had rotted. The whole ship smelled like a glue works and white maggots were crawling all over. They had to be gotten rid of somehow, but how? The hatches were sealed, so one rainy night when the guard was huddled under a boat on deck, the two mates crawled from the cabin to the store-room and thence to the hold. They cut up the seal carcasses, put the pieces in bags, dragged them back the same way, and dumped them overboard. I don't know how they got by the officer. He usually stayed in the cabin all the time. Well, those bags would float out with the tide and come right back again on the next incoming tide, and for a week that went on until they finally disappeared.

It was now midsummer and pretty warm, so we got permission to go swimming around the vessel, and a month later we could go ashore on the promise not to leave the country. Five of the boys did leave and nothing was done about it. One or two court decisions had been passed. Each one had been appealed by the ship's lawyer and we were now waiting for the supreme court to act on our case. The decision came sometime in late June. The schooner was confiscated; the captain was in for three years, the mates one year each, and the crew six months. Having been there over seven months we were free to go and were sent home as consul's passengers. The time we spent in Montevideo was made very pleasant by the courteous and considerate treatment we received from all officials and civilians we came in contact with. We were treated more like paying guests than captives.

In the meantime, an international lawyer was sent to Montevideo from Liverpool, Nova Scotia. He cleared the vessel of all charges and made a few on our behalf—illegal seizure outside the three-mile limit and holding the vessel in port over seven months without a specific law on the books covering such a seizure. The schooner's owners, having furnished our provisions all the time we spent in Montevideo, then presented a claim for damages amounting to $60,000.

After seven years of diplomatic stalling the claim was paid. Each crew member that could be found received a share based on the estimated average catch for that year, 1905. Sealers are not paid a monthly wage. They are paid for the skins they catch in their own boat. And so ends my sealing trip.

Campeche Days

BY FRED HUNT

PERHAPS the Pensacola red snapper fleet of world war days was neither as picturesque as it then seemed to an inland youth meeting salt water for the first time, nor as it now seems to one who views it in memory, but one thing is certain. That is this: in the late 'teens it was the only big American deep-sea fishing fleet using all-sail vessels exclusively. In the early twenties the chugging bulgine began to befoul the clean Campeche horizon with its scrawling black trails; and by the end of the decade there were but few Pensacolamen left whose in'ards were not retching with greasy power plants.[1]

During the period under consideration, 1915-1919, there were thirty-five schooners in the Pensacola fleet fishing on Campeche Bank, down off the northern coast of Yucatan.[2] This, of course, did not include the small inshore craft, known locally as Chingamarings, or simply Chings, fishing within a day's sail of port. These small fry, incidentally, already had power.

The offshore schooners were owned by two big fish concerns, E. E. Saunders and Company and the Warren Fish Company. They ranged in size from less than 50 to over 100 tons and in length from around 70 to more than 100 feet.[3] Most of them had been built in New England shipyards, and had been 'sold South' after they had been driven hard for some years in the North Atlantic fisheries. The rest, with a few strays, had been built around Pensacola.

Most of the smacks had been constructed around the first decade of the century, with many exceptions.[4] The oldest was the *Amy Wixen,* 47 tons, 67 feet, built in Boothbay, Maine, in 1870. Other oldsters included three launched in 1887: the *Cavalier,* 50 tons, built in Glencove, New

---
[1] 'Bulgine' was often used on the Gulf for 'engine.'
[2] Galveston had a fleet of about six big schooners also fishing on Campeche.
[3] References are to gross tonnage and registered length.
[4] Gulf fishermen used 'fishing schooner' and 'smack' synonymously.

York; the *Louise F. Harper,* 62 tons, built at Harkers Island, North Carolina, and the *Caldwell H. Colt,* 64 tons, built at Greenpoint, New York.

The *Colt* was a doughty veteran that differed sharply from other vessels in the fleet, what with her straight stem, her bowsprit that steeved upward at an angle to the sheer and her rakish masts. She had the only skipper's state-room to be found in any Pensacola fisherman. She was an ugly duckling all right, but I forgave her looks when she was pointed out to me as originally one of the few New York pilot boats that rode out safely the tragic gale which smashed that fleet of able vessels off Sandy Hook shortly after she was commissioned.[5] Even when I knew her, and she was thirty-five years old then, she had the reputation of being an able vessel.

The Yankee-built schooners in the Pensacola fleet were, with few exceptions, of the clipper-bowed *Fredonia* model that prevailed in the New England fleet at the turn of the century. There were two or three round-bowed vessels, and about the same number of knockabouts. One of these knockabouts, the *Virginia,* an Essex-built vessel of 106 tons launched in 1910, was the longest schooner in the port, 102 feet. The largest fisherman sailing out of Pensacola was the *Yakima,* 108.5 tons, 96.6 feet, built in Essex in 1902.

The Florida-built schooners were clipper-bowed. They averaged slightly smaller than their Northern sisters; had more sheer and more flaring lines forward. With their fuller curves, they had something of the appearance of the Biloxi schooners, except that they had more freeboard and were less squatty in looks.

Up to 1920, none of these vessels had any means of propulsion save wind and canvas. A few of the larger ones had small gasoline engines, located on deck to starboard of the foremast, to heave up anchor and to hoist sail.

As to rig, these vessels were all orthodox two-masted fishing schooners. About the only variation was in topmasts and light sails. The smaller ones were bald-headed and carried only four lowers, mainsail, fore-sail, jumbo and jib.[6] The larger ones carried two topmasts and, in addition to their four lowers, jib topsails and fisherman staysails. Those in the middle brackets carried a main topmast and their only light weather canvas was a fisherman's staysail. All three classes, of course, carried storm trysails to bend on in place of the mainsail when it began to blow hard.

The deck layout varied little, if any. Starting from forward and going

---

[5] The famous blizzard of March 1888. A dozen pilot boats out of New York were wrecked. For the full account, see Charles Edward Russell, *From Sandy Hook to 62,* pp. 199-223. For the story of the *Caldwell H. Colt,* pp. 216-222.

[6] 'Jumbo,' of course, refers to the fore-stay sail.

aft, one found, in order, the windlass, fore-mast, forecastle companion, fore hatch, mainmast, after hatch, cabin and wheel box. The Northern-built schooners usually had a break just forward of the mainmast to form a poop deck; something the Southern schooners lacked.

The layout below decks also followed orthodox fisherman practice. The forecastle was forward, with upper and lower bunk tiers on each side of the triangular table, and after end of which was braced by the butt of the fore-mast. In the after part of the forecastle was the galley, from which a door led aft to the fish hold. This had ice boxes on each side, four to six to a side depending on the size of the vessel, with a passageway between. Aft was the cabin, usually with only two bunks on each side; sometimes with a thwartwise bunk under the companionway. Aft in the overhang was the open storage locker for spare lines, fishing gear and the like. Light sails were usually carried in the forepeak when not in use.

The skipper always slept in the forward bunk on the starboard side of the cabin; and the mate in the forward bunk on the port side. The cook slept, as a rule, in the lower after bunk on the port side of the forecastle. The rest of the bunks went to the men who first slung their bags into them; although there was a sort of unwritten law that the more experienced men should sleep aft. The bunks had no springs and no mattresses. Some fishermen carried mattresses in their seabags, but most of them were content with a couple of blankets spread out on the bare bunk boards in bad weather or on deck in fine weather.

The men who manned this fleet were largely Yankee fishermen, with some Southerners, some Nova Scotians, and a sprinkling of other seafaring nationalities, mostly Scandinavians. Three or four of the schooners were manned exclusivel by Italians; but the majority had polyglot crews.

The private lives of Pensacola snapper fishermen in the late 'teens would have been an interesting field for a sociologist. A number of the skippers had wives, children and homes, and lived a normal domestic life between trips. The fore-mast hands, with very few exceptions, had no domestic ties. They worked hard, bore hardships and risked their lives to earn a few dollars which they threw away on riotous living. It was not uncommon for a fisherman to be begging drinks forty-eight hours after he had been paid off a $75 share.

Fishing was on a share basis. After the 'trip' was weighed out and the gross value of the catch had been compiled, the fish house deducted thirty-five to forty per cent as the vessel's share, depending on the age and condition of the schooner.[7] From the balance was deducted the expenses of the trip, including food, bait, ice and fuel for the shipmate range. The amount that remained was split into as many shares as there were men, plus one. That is, if there were ten men, the net was split eleven ways. The skipper, the mate and the cook each got a share and a third.[8] All the rest of the crew got a share each. Meanwhile the fish house kicked back to the skipper a percentage of the vessel's share as a bonus.[9]

When the gross profits failed to equal the expenses, the trip was called a 'broker.' In that case the fish house made up the deficit, and the crew got nothing save that each man was given, as a sort of consolation, a ten-pound snapper. In theory he could peddle this for a dollar or so. In practice — well, before he could reach the residential district and start peddling his fish, he would have to pass a number of saloons where former shipmates were roistering!

It was the usual practice for all hands save the mate, the cook and one or two regulars who went with the same skipper time after time, to quit a vessel as soon as she paid off after a trip. Hence the skipper was generally faced with the problem of shipping almost an entire new crew each time. Although Pensacola fishermen of the time of which I write were pretty hard to drag away from certain hangouts on Palafox Street, there was a standardized procedure which could always be resorted to with confidence.

After stores and ice and bait were aboard, the skipper would hire a one-horse dray and drive up in front of the Green Front.[10] There he would load a couple of barrels of beer into it, and perhaps several quarts of liquor.[11] The skipper would then perch himself on the seat beside the driver, and the dray could move slowly down Palafox Street, which leads to the water front. By the time the vehicle had covered the few blocks to the piers, there would be a ragged queue of fishermen rolling along boisterously in its wake.

The dray would rattle out onto the long wharf and fetch up alongside the schooner. Ready hands would help the skipper lower the purchases to the decks. He would then swing down from the wharf to his vessel, look up at the expectant grinning faces, crook an arm and call out, 'Come aboard, boys.'

[7] 'Trip' is used to mean 'catch' by fishermen.
[8] 'Mate' of a fishing schooner is usually called 'first hand.'
[9] The skipper's bonus was generally understood to be twenty per cent of the vessel's share.
[10] The Green Front was a favorite bar for fishermen.
[11] The liquor would be purchased on the store bill.

They would swarm over the rail as if drawn by a magnet; and the barrels would be broached, sometimes openly on deck, sometimes in a cabin, and a roaring wassail would ensue. At the end of an hour or so, with the beer about half gone, the skipper could clamp a stopper on it, and start shipping his crew.

'No more booze until I get my gang together,' he would say.

The business of shipping a man was simple. The skipper would merely slap him on the shoulder and say something like this: 'Get your bag, Bill, and make a trip with me, High-line trip sure, this time.'[12]

Bill would be thinking something like this: 'I wouldn't ship in this louse-bound hooker with this Hoosier if I was starving to death.[13] But I'll throw my bag aboard so I can get some more gin; and then, when he casts off, I'll grab my bag and hop back on the dock again.'

But he would actually say, 'Sure, skipper,' and run down the dock and get his bag from the last schooner he sailed in and lug it aboard. Very often when Bill came to again he'd be lying in the scuppers, the vessel would be well offshore, and he'd wonder how he ever came to ship in this 'bleedin' mud-scow.'

After the skipper had shipped the required number of men he'd shoo the rest ashore, let go his lines and, with a chugging launch alongside, pull out into the stream, hoisting the fore-sail as he went. Well away from the dock and with the fore-sail and jumbo on her, he'd drop his towline and head down the harbor.

The chances are, however, that he would not proceed to sea directly. Instead, he'd drop his hook in the outer harbor, lower sail and lay there overnight, until the liquor was gone and his crew had begun to show some signs of sobering up sufficiently to heave up, hoist sail and head out the harbor.

On several schooners in which I sailed the crew refused to hoist the mainsail after lying overnight in the outer harbor, but insisted on the skipper letting some of them taking a dory back to town and pawn seaboots or oilskins or some other of their meager possessions to get more liquor. 'Jes' enough, skipper, ter straighten us out so's we can get that big mains'l on her,' they pleaded. On their return another orgy ensued and it was hours later before the mainsail started up the mast. It was, however, almost an inflexible rule that the schooner would be dry as a spar yard when she headed offshore.[14]

[12] 'High line' is the fisherman's way of saying 'best' or 'biggest.'
[13] 'Hoosier' is the Gulf fisherman's term for landlubber.
[14] 'Dry as a spar yard' is fishermanese for 'dry' or 'thirsty.'

With some of the gang sprawled about the deck helpless from drink and most of the others still weak and jittery, the first day out was something of a nightmare. Often only three or four men were able to stand a watch during the first night. By the end of the second day, however, heads had cleared, tough hides had sweated out the alcohol, regular watches had been set and the cook was serving regular meals. The two-day wassail was definitely at an end, and from now on it was a grim, relentless fight with wood, canvas and cordage against wind and weather; a fight against time; against dwindling stores, softening bait, melting ice; a fight to fill those big boxes.

Campeche Bank is roughly four hundred and fifty miles from Pensacola, steering a little West of South, and it extends north from the northern coast of Yucatan for one hundred miles. A fair passage one way was from three to five days, although six or eight days was not uncommon.

All hands save the skipper and the cook stood a trick. When watches were set, the mate took the first wheel and the rest of the gang followed in the order in which they bunked around the vessel, clockwise, from his berth. This system gave each man an hour and a half at the wheel day and night. In fine weather only the helmsman was on deck; in bad weather an extra man stood a lookout.

The helmsman would call the skipper only if the weather took a turn for the worse. When beating to windward at night the helmsman would tack ship by himself, unless it was blowing too hard. He would simply put the wheel down, run forward and cast off the lee jib sheet, make the tail rope fast to the lee shrouds, thus backing the jumbo and forcing the vessel's head around; and then, when the schooner had crossed to the other tack, he'd let go the tail rope, jump across the deck to the new lee side and sheet home the jib.[15] He had to step lively, because if he let the jib fill, he couldn't sheet it unless the air was very light. All in all, it is not a hard job to tack a 100-foot, 100-ton schooner alone when she is under only four lowers and it is not blowing too briskly. The helmsman could flatten in the main and force sheets by merely luffing a bit. Incidentally the jumbo sheet of a Gulf fisherman is never touched. It is made fast closehauled and left alone.

As to navigation: the skipper used dead reckoning exclusively save for taking meridian sights for latitude. I heard that there were a few chronometers in the fishing fleet, but I was never shipmate with one. There must have been some fairly competent navigators sailing out of

---

[15] 'Tail rope' is a short line made fast to the after end of the fore-staysail boom for the express purpose of backing the jumbo.

Pensacola; but I do know that some of those with whom I sailed had only a limited knowledge of celestial navigation. One high-line skipper got so mad at me when I insisted that the sun was 'round like a ball' instead of 'round like a plate,' as he contended, that he ordered me off his schooner the minute he paid me my share of the second trip I made with him.

Despite their shortcomings in regard to scientific navigation, those Pensacola fishing skippers seldom made a bad landfall. I have seen Pensacola Light show up dead over the end of the bowsprit after a five hundred mile zig-zagging passage to windward during which no sights for longitude were taken.

On a passage to or from the Banks no work was done save the ordinary routine of taking a wheel twice each twenty-four hours, taking in the mainsail and jib when the squalls got too boisterous and standing a night watch in bad weather. Only repairs necessary to the ship's safety, such as sewing up a rent in a sail or splicing a line, were made by fishermen. The rest of the time was spent in sleeping, eating, reading and yarn spinning.

The day before the schooner was scheduled to get soundings on the northern edge of Campeche Bank, the men would overhaul their gear.[16] This consists of a single hand line to which is attached an ordinary deep-sea kidney-shaped fishing lead with two hooks. The men fish from the windward rail of the schooner while the vessel is under the bank rig, that is, single-reefed mainsail, fore-sail and jumbo. The fish are caught on the bottom in fifteen to seventy fathoms. Bait is usually pickled skipjacks. When bait runs short sometimes it can be 'pieced out' by mixing a little shark meat with it: that is, a piece of regular bait and a piece of shark are placed on each hook. Straight shark meat is practically worthless as bait. Porgies are sometimes mixed with bait, also.

Once on the Banks, no time is lost, and fishing starts immediately. Fish start coming over the rail the minute the skipper has put his vessel 'on fish.'

Life on the Banks can be most easily depicted, perhaps, by taking a single day, chronologically. The work on Campeche begins when the sun shows its first chord above the eastern horizon and ends when its last thin rim disappears below the horizon in the west.

As the sun creeps up out of the east it finds the vessel lying at anchor, with the mainsail set.[17] The cook comes out of the forecastle companion, strides aft and sings out, 'Come and get it.'

[16] A schooner would 'get soundings,' i.e., her headline would reach bottom, shortly after crossing the hundred-fathom curve on the northern edge of the Banks.

[17] If the weather was threatening, the mainsail would be lowered for the night. When it was left set, often a fisherman's crew found several flying fish, that had presumably struck the mainsail, on deck at daylight.

The sleeping crew, instantly awake, spring up from their bunks, or more likely from their blankets spread around deck if the weather is fine, and pile down into the forecastle for their sunrise 'mug-up.'[18] After gulping down hot coffee and some doughnuts or a piece of pie, they hurry on deck.

Now comes a daily ritual. Each man goes to his regular fishing station and takes his position sitting on the rail, facing inward, of course, elbows on knees, chin in cupped hands. And since a Gulf fisherman has no plumbing facilities, there they sit like so many pelicans perched on a drifting spar. The peculiar aspect of the situation is that no man attempts dismounting from the rail until the skipper, sitting solemnly at his regular fishing station abreast the wheel box, makes the first move. Once the master has completed his part of the ritual, the rest of the hands are soon off the rail and ready for the day's work.

The fore-sail goes up, the anchor is broken out and catted and the jumbo is hoisted. The mainsail is slacked off about right for reaching and the boom tackle is clapped on the big boom to prevent it from slatting.

With the vessel underway now and the skipper at the wheel the rest of the hands place their baitboards at their regular fishing stations along the windward rail, get their lines and start slicing up a supply of skipjacks taken from the bait barrel lashed near the mainmast.

While the vessel is standing off on a short slant, one has time to observe how the men dress for fishing in fine weather. They are wearing undershirts, canvas fishing aprons belted about with marlin and either dungarees, or merely shorts. They are barefooted. When the winter northers come, they will wear flannel shirts and, in bad weather, oilers and southwesters and rubber boots.

The skipper's station is abreast the wheel, the mate, or first hand, is just abaft the main rigging; the cook's station is abreast the forecastle companion; the man presumed to be the best fisherman aboard is aft of the skipper on the quarter, and the rest of the gang are strung along the rail at intervals of about six feet.

After standing off for a few minutes, the skipper rolls the wheel down and calls out, 'Fore-sheet!'

The man fishing just forward of the main rigging, who is known as the 'Fore-sheet man,' drops his bait knife, whirls about and casts the fore-

---

[18] 'Spring' is used advisedly, for fishermen worked on the share basis so that every fish a man caught augmented not only the net profits of the trip but his own individual share. Few of the Gulf fishermen soldiered on the job.

sheet off the cleat. The vessel shoots up into the wind; and while she still has considerable way on, the mate steps up on the rail just abaft the main rigging, whirls the sounding lead around his head and lets it fly. It bullets forward past the fore-rigging and splashes into the sea well forward of the bowsprit, perhaps sixteen fathoms from the mate. The lead sinks as the schooner ranges forward, losing way; and, if the mate has nicely calculated, the lead will touch bottom directly under his hand, the line taut.

He sings out the depth and then waits a few seconds to see if he gets a bite on the baited hook on the lead line. After he hauls in the lead he glances at its soap-filled hollow end and sings out what sort of bottom he brought up, 'Brown sand and dead coral, skipper.'

As soon as the schooner has lost most of her way, all hands drop their leads over the rail and their lines run down.

As the smack, even though hove to now, still ranges forward at a snail's pace and makes a little leeway, the lines lead out to windward and a little aft. The men, of course, are all fishing from the windward rail. To avoid fouling, each man drops his lead just 'under' the line of the man forward of him, that is, in the apex of the angle made by this shipmate's line and the side of the schooner.

As soon as his line stops running out, each fisherman pulls it in a few feet so that the bait will not lie on the bottom; and then he stands relaxed at his fishing station; slightly bent over the rail, perhaps with his left hand resting on it, and holds his line sensitively between the forefinger and the thumb of his right hand.

The whole art of catching fish in this manner lies in the ability to distinguish a bite from a slight tremor of the line caused by the surface wave motion—an art which is not perfected in a week or a month or maybe a year.

Due to the line being very slack, what with the forward and leeward drift of the vessel, perhaps fifty or sixty fathoms would be out to fish in a depth of thirty fathoms. With three hundred or four hundred feet of line out, a big fish could give the hook a forceful jerk and yet only a slight tremor would be transmitted along the slack line. Hence the difficulty in distinguishing a bite from the constant trembling of the line caused by wave motion.

Once the bite is felt, it is now just a matter of jerking sharply with the right hand and then hauling the line in hand-over-hand until the fish is over the rail. The fishermen, of course, wear rubber nippers to protect their hands. In good fishing a man frequently brings them over the rail in pairs; in poor fishing he is lucky to get them one at a time.

As the fish begin to come in, the skipper, sitting on the wheel box, watches the row of fishermen with a judicial eye. If, as it happens in rare cases, each man comes up with a pair of big ones, he'll drop the anchor and let the fore-sail and jumbo run down. If the fishing is good, but not quite that good, he'll simply toss out a buoy to mark the spot so he can find it again when he drifts off in half an hour or so. In most instances, however, he merely puts the wheel in the becket, thus leaving the vessel to hove to without any attention, and takes a line himself and fishes along with the rest of the gang until the pickings begin getting slim, or the 'spot is fished out,' usually a matter of half an hour or so during which a few hundred pounds—twenty or thirty fish, maybe—are picked up.[19]

Then the skipper goes back to the wheel, puts it up and calls out, 'Fore-sheet!' The fore-sheet man sheets home, the sails fill and the vessel swings off to try another spot a few hundred yards away.

After the morning 'mug up,' the gang gets in a couple hours' fishing before breakfast. There is another break around ten-thirty o'clock for the mid-morning 'mug up.' Dinner comes at noon, with a mid-afternoon 'mug up,' supper at five o'clock and a final 'mug up' just before turning in at night.

While on the subject of eating, it might be well to interpolate here that food aboard a Gulf fisherman leaves nothing that even a searfaring man can find to growl about. In quality and quantity, it is comparable with the meals served in a prosperous American farmhouse to a threshing machine crew. The smackmen realize that any given trip might turn out to be a 'broker,' with their net profits confined to the food stowed away; and so they see to it that the cook goes the limit in storing up. With seventy thousand pounds of ice in the hold, there is no refrigeration problem; and about the only thing that differs from what they could get ashore is canned milk instead of fresh. A whole side of beef is carried aboard; but even with the ice they see fit to salt the remnants of this down by about the end of the second week.

About the third week out, when much of the food has lost something of its 'freshness' despite the ice, fish begin to make their appearance on the forecastle table. When fish begin to pall along toward the end of the trip, the cook sometimes takes a big fifteen-pound snapper, cuts out the lips and cheeks and serves them as delicacies after throwing the rest away.

[19] Skippers often remained on the wheel box if fishing was pretty thin. A big umbrella, usually advertising the wares of some ship chandler five hundred miles to the northwa d, protected them from the sun. Cooks fished only between their galley duties. The becket is a light line with which the wheel is lashed.

The cook's 'Come and get it, boys!' is the signal for a mad dash from the rail for the forecastle, the men wiping their hands on their aprons and tossing the latter over their shoulders as they pile pell-mell down the companionway. Crowded in between the triangular table and the bunk tiers, naked from the waist up, with beads of sweat rolling off their noses and chins and dropping into their heaping plates, they wolf down their grub as fast as possible to escape the intense heat below. Sweltering is a nice word for a Campecheman's forecastle in summertime.

This digression on food over, we'll return now to the back-breaking business at the rail. When fish are first caught they are tossed in the lee scuppers for the time being. At the end of half an hour or so, depending on the intensity of the sun, they are forked down into the hold where the first hand ices them down in the big boxes, layers of cracked ice alternating with layers of fish. When the box is broken out two or three weeks later it will be a frozen solid mass of fish and ice. The fish are not cleaned aboard.

Supper over and the end of the long day fast approaching, there will be around twenty-five hundred pounds of fish iced down, if the fishing has run about average. As the sun slides down behind the rim of the sea the fishermen along the rail watch its final chord turn green and disappear.[20]

'Reel up, boys,' the skipper sings out, and the tired men do up their gear and throw it, with their baitboards and aprons in the gurry pen.[21] They take in the jumbo and fore-sail, let go the anchor, parcel the cable at the hawsepipe and go down into the cabin for their final—and fourth—'mug up' of the day before turning in.

And so it goes, day after day, from sun-up to sun-down, until the 'trip is made.' If this trip is about average there will be from thirty to forty thousand pounds in the boxes before they give her the jib for home. The bulk of the catch will be red snappers, running from two or three to twelve or sixteen pounds, and the rest will be groupers, running a little heavier. Perhaps there will be half a dozen warsaws, running upwards of one hundred pounds each.

Such a trip should be made in twenty-two to twenty-four days, ten of which were in passage-making; and each man would share about $75.

Sharks were a bit of a bother in fishing on Campeche Bank. A man would be hauling in a fine twelve-pound snapper when he would sud-

---

[20] If one watches a sunset at sea, the final thin chord of the sun appears to turn vivid green, due to eye fatigue, just before it drops out of sight.
[21] 'Gurry pen' is a small enclosure just forward of the cabin trunk used for stowing baitboards; and sometimes fish are thrown into it temporarily.

denly feel a hard jerk, and after that the fish would come up more easily. When he got it on the rail he would find that only the head remained — the rest had provided a meal for a shark.

Occasionally a man, taking a quick glimpse into the depths to see if he had hooked a snapper or a grouper, would see a huge gray shape swimming around and around his fish. This, of course, would be a shark; and then it was a race between the man and shark. By speeding up his hand-over-hand movement, the man could win easily enough provided that he did not, in his hurry, miss the line with the groove of one of his nippers. If he did that, the wet line would slide through his wet palm, the fish would stop momentarily, and the shark, nine times out of ten, would win.[22]

Weather on Campeche and on the passages was usually fine. The exceptions were the fresh 'northers' in winter and the sudden dangerous squalls in summer. Sometimes these squalls marked the beginning of a stiff blow that would last a day or two. Of course, from July through October the Campeche skipper must watch the glass for signs of hurricane.

The big able schooners were rarely worried by the 'northers,' even in passage-making. Usually they carried through them under a storm trysail, fore-sail and jumbo, although a tough one might necessitate heaving to under the fore-sail.

Summer squalls were humored according to their strength and the ableness of the vessel and the daring of the skipper. Under fishing rig, the skipper would hang on to his mainsail as long as he dared, as it took a lot of time and beef to hoist it again. With the skipper himself on the wheel box expertly gauging the strength of the squall and with men standing by the main halliards ready to lower away at his signal, I have been in the big *Yakima*, the *Clara G. Silva*, the *Ida S. Brooks* and a number of others when they took some stiff dustings without lowering their mainsails. Many times, however, this big rag had to come in when a squall struck. Certain skippers prided themselves on carrying the mainsail longer than their brothers.

Of course, when making a passage, the jib, jib topsail and fisherman's staysail came in at the first sign of a nearing squall. Incidentally, no Gulf schooners carried gaff-topsails. I was told that this was because the fast-rising squalls did not allow time to take them in.

A big able schooner like the *Yakima* or the *Rena A. Percy* or the *Fishhawk*, could take care of herself, given sea room, in about anything the

---

[22] Four times out of five, perhaps, the shark cut the fish off just behind the gills; sometimes, however, he bungles the job.

Gulf had to offer when she was hove to under a reefed fore-sail.[23] Snugged down to this, you could put the wheel in the becket, go below and forget about the weather. That is, you could laugh at about anything save a hurricane; but that is a different story, and a long one and one that has been the obituary of many a stout-hearted man and many a fine vessel on the Gulf of Mexico.

Snapper fishing on Campeche was a hard life, but a colorful one and devoid of neither risk or thrills. Something was always taking place to break the routine. I remember, for instance, that time in the *Ariola* when we went ashore on Alacran Reef on Christmas Eve and spent the holiday with the Mexican family tending the light there. The day after Christmas, when we headed back for the Banks, we found out that somebody—we suspected the skipper and mate—had practically cleaned out our remaining stores and had traded them to the hungry Mexicans for a case of *ginebra*.[24] We had to set sail for home at once, of course; and during the five-day passage we lived on fish and coffee and bread; but so expert was the cook that we scarcely minded the sameness in his cuisine.

I remember a trip on another vessel when there was much loose talk of filling her up with guano on Alacran and heading somewhere north of Hatteras and selling the cargo for fertilizer.[25] Half-way across the Gulf, the skipper got cold feet and reneged, suddenly announcing his intention to 'make a trip of fish.' Most of the gang bluntly refused to either stand watch or fish; and the skipper took the wheel himself and swore he'd make the 'trip' if he had to stand all wheels and catch all fish. Losing interest in the guano plan, the gang then conceived the idea of running into Tampa for a grand carousal. About this time the cook came out of the forecastle bellowing that the water tanks were dry. He blamed the skipper for failing to refill them before sailing, the skipper blamed the mate and the mate said that it was the cook's job. I now suspect that one of the gang, disgusted with the mess, drained the tanks into the bilges, thinking that this would force us back to Pensacola. The skipper proposed to continue the trip melting ice for cooking and drinking purposes; but the gang protested that the ice water was brackish. The sullen com-

---

[23] The *Fish-hawk*, built in Quincy, Massachusetts, in 1902, was an unorthodox type for a Gulf fisherman. A big 91-tonner, she had a spoon-bow and a tiny pinched-in transom stern. Her spoon-bow and her outside ballast caused her to pound and have such a jerky motion in the short Gulf seas that men could not sleep in her forecastle. The outside balance was removed, easing her motion. With tremendous beam for her length (24.4 feet to 86.2 feet) she was reputed to be 'stiff as a church.'

[24] 'Ginebra' was a brand of Mexican gin.

[25] Alacran Reef, 22° 18′ N, 89° 40′ W, is 'The Alacranes' on which William Dampier, the pirate, grounded in a small ketch just before he joined the buccaneers. Guano was the result of birds leaving their deposits on the islands probably for hundreds of years.

promise resulted in running several hundred miles to Port St. Joe to refill our tanks. We then made a halfhearted trip to the inshore banks trying to pick up enough fish to pay expenses, and, of course, made a 'broker.'

I remember another time hilariously heading seaward with a bevy of painted chorus girls, from some cheap road show, lolling about our decks. That trip probably would have made Campeche history had not the towing launch wisely insisted on taking our maudlin companions aboard and hustling them back to town.

Occasionally when we put to sea a dozen spring chickens would be perched mysteriously around the bunks in the forecastle. The cook would serve them a couple days later and no questions would be asked.

I remember making port on 25 November 1918, after we had been keeping a careful watch for German submarines, only to find that the war had been over for two weeks.[26] Our first question when the tow boat took our line was, 'Who won?'

Yes, they were a picturesque, hard-drinking, hard-fighting rough gang, those men who manned the all-sail snapper fleet in the lusty days of its glory, but something fine could be found in even the roughest of them. Take Big P. for instance, a great hulk of a man whose fall from aloft in a Grand Banker years before had left him slow of speech and slower of thought. It was only with deep concentration that he could tell time or make change.

But, when he saw me fishing at the rail in a bitter norther shivering with cold and my thin shoes soaked with sprindrift, he slipped down into the cabin, kicked off his boots and came back on deck in stocking feet. A few minutes later he turned to me and said, 'Go below, bye, and get me boots. I can't wear em; they make me feet sweat, B'Jesus.'

If consideration for others is the test of a gentleman, I consider that dull ox-witted giant to be the finest gentleman I have ever met.

Perhaps that breed of men died out with the ships that bred them. With the twenties came the introduction of auxiliary power, and by the end of that decade thirty of the forty big schooners in the Pensacola fleet had engines.

---

[26] In so far as we know, no German submarine came into the Gulf during the First World War; but we were on the alert constantly for them, especially after the U-boat had appeared off Cape Cod in the summer of 1918.

The Tradition of the St. Elmo's Fire

BY GEORGE G. CAREY

WITH the passing of the wind ship, many of the great superstitions and beliefs of the old sea dogs have disappeared from tradition. To the sailor, whose life was by definition a lonely one, some of nature's odd forms and shapes became premonitions from another world, spirits from elsewhere returned to make or break his voyage at will. The fog looming in the offing emerged as the Flying Dutchman on his eternal voyage. Sea monsters and mermaids were not uncommon to the imaginative mind of the seafarer, and the devil's own hand was said to have been seen arising from the deep on gloomy days. To the sailor each of these fantastic sights had its own meaning, sometimes fair, sometimes foul, but no one tradition is so embedded in the bowels of maritime history as the St. Elmo's fire. As long as men have ploughed the seas the incredible sight of this ghostly flame has hung itself in the rigging of ships much to the amazement of all its spectators. Appearing in various numbers and sizes it has given to the keen mind of the mariner a theme for improvisation, and at certain times, worship. He has seen in this phenomenon the body of Christ, or the Holy Spirit, the revenants of Castor and Pollux as benefactors, or the soul of a defunct comrade returned to warn of some approaching danger.

The confusion of names applied to the light itself runs the gamut from classical references to such common terminology as 'Corbie's Aunt'; to list only a few of the variants: Helena, The Dioscuri, St. Elme, St. Anselmo, Santelmo, St. Erme, St. Clair, St. Nicholas, St. Peter, Corpusant, Cuerpo Santo, Fermie's Fire, Zeelicht, Vree vurren, The Peaceable Fires.[1]

It is not my purpose here to track down each of the names to uncover its source; however, several of the more important are worth looking into. Castor and Pollux, and St. Elmo are the names most commonly used to designate the fire. The former, obviously classical, stems from the voyage of the Argonauts in search of the Golden Fleece. Diodorus writing about 65 B.C. explains it:

[1] For complete listings see: F. S. Bassett, *Legends and Superstitions of the Sea and Sailors* (New York, 1885), p. 319; H. Gaidoz and E. Rolland, 'Le feu Saint-Elme,' *Mélusine*, II (1884-1885), 112-113.

But there came a great storm and the chieftains had given up hope of being saved, when Orpheus, they say, who was the only one on shipboard who had ever been initiated in the mysteries of the deities of Samothrace, offered to these deities the prayers for their salvation. And immediately the wind died down and two stars fell over the heads of the Dioscuri [Castor and Pollox] and the whole company was amazed at the marvel which had taken place and concluded that they had been rescued from the perils by an act of Providence of the Gods.[2]

In his *Classical Dictionary* Anthon elaborates upon the ancient belief that one light seen on a vessel was certain doom, while two habitually brought about favorable weather. Helen, the offspring of Leda (meaning darkness) and Tyndaeus (light) is the same as Silen (moon) and usually carries with it evil overtones, whereas Castor (the adorner) and Pollux (lightful) had more pleasant connotations; consequently the twins were often invoked by sailors in times of peril.[3] The single light, or Helen, was feared above all else on the seas.

The name St. Elmo presents a problem, however, for several answers have been offered for its origin. One source says that St. Elmo is St. Erasmus, seen in early art with a lighted taper over his head, or another saint by the same name who was an early Christian martyr 'usually invoked by Mediterranean mariners.'[4] A somewhat more reasonable explanation claims the fire is the spirit of Pedro Gonzales Telmo, a Spanish priest who died at sea and was canonized in 1254.[5]

It is interesting to note that St. Elmo's fire is not listed as such in Stith Thompson's *Motif Index of Folk Literature*. There is a reference, however, to the Will-of-the-Wisp (F 491) or a light seen over marshy places. In many areas people still believe marsh fire to be the souls of the dead. On the island of Batz, near France, the inhabitants, on seeing the flame over the water, batten down their hatches, or windows as the case may be. If anyone wanders too close to the specter, he is liable to come under its evil spell.

The history of St. Elmo's fire gives us a depth of perception, not only into the mind of the mariner and his beliefs, but also into the way a tradition adapts itself to a particular place or religion. The classical Castor and Pollux become, for the Christian seafarer, the Holy Spirit or the saving grace of a saint manifested in a fiery form. The sign of imminent death, when seen over houses or wigwams,[6] on the sea develops into a weather

---

[2] Diodorus, *Diodorus of Sicily*, trans. C. H. Oldfather (Cambridge, 1934), II, 477-478.

[3] C. Anthon, *Classical Dictionary* (New York, 1843), p. 314.

[4] Bassett, *Legends*, pp. 319-320.

[5] Gaidoz and Rolland, 'Le feu Saint-Elme,' p. 117.

[6] John Josselyn, 'Two Voyages to New England,' *Collections of the Massachusetts Historical Society* (Cambridge, 1883), III, iii, 300.

THE TRADITION OF ST. ELMO'S FIRE

omen. Classical writers and sailors often thought the lights were stars; Statius writing about A.D. 100 calls Castor and Pollux stars of dawn.[7] Horace alluded to them in his *Odes* as 'Helen's brothers, stars by the sailors blest.'[8]

Pliny, who was deeply interested in all natural phenomena, gave considerable space to a discussion of the weird fire and claimed to have seen it himself on a certain occasion:

> I have seen during the night watch of soldiers, a luminous appearance like a star, attached to the javelins on the ramparts. They also settle on the yard arm and other parts of the ship while sailing, producing a kind of vocal sound like birds flitting about. When they occur singly they are mischievous, so as even to sink the vessels, and if they strike on the lower part of the keel, setting them on fire. When there are two of them they are auspicious, and are thought to predict a prosperous voyage, as it is said they drive away that dreadful and terrific meteor named Helena. On this dreadful account their efficacy is ascribed to Castor and Pollux and they are invoked as gods.[9]

Lucian, another classical scholar, alludes to the experiences of certain mariners whose ship was saved from a formidable shore by the advent of the fires.[10] Moreover, Maximus of Tyre personally tells us 'vidi autem in summa navis parte Castores stellas, lucidas, quae navem in tempestate dirigebant.'[11] The Roman playwright, Seneca, referred to 'des étoiles qui se posent sur la voile d'un vaisseau.' When these stars appeared the mariners knew that Castor and Pollux had come to their rescue, for 'la tempête se brise de ce moment et que les vents faiblissent.'[12]

The Bible affirms that the Apostle Paul sailed on an Alexandrian ship named the 'Dioscuri'; titled such, no doubt, to protect sailors from evil.[13] This practice of giving lofty names to ships was later disregarded and thought to bring only bad luck. About A.D. 45, Plutarch declared that those traveling with the Greek warrior, Lysander, 'affirmed that the stars of Castor and Pollux were seen on each side of Lysander's ship [and] . . . shining about the helm. . . .'[14]

During the Dark Ages, little traveling was done, and what was, was seldom recorded. Fletcher S. Bassett does give the relation of a voyage to

---

[7] Statius, *The Silvae of Statius,* trans. D. A. Slater (Oxford, 1908), p. 159.
[8] Horace, *The Complete Works of Horace,* trans. 'various hands' (London, 1945), I, 4.
[9] Pliny, *The Natural History of Pliny,* trans. J. Bostock (London, 1885), I, 64-65.
[10] Lucian, *The Complete Works of Lucian of Samosata,* trans. H. W. and F. G. Fowler (Oxford, 1905), IV, 36.
[11] Maximus, 'Dissertationes,' *Theophrasti Characteres Marcus Antonius Epictetus. Simplicius. Cebes Maximus Tyrius* (Paris).
[12] Sénèque, *Questions Naturelles,* trans. P. Oltramare (Paris, 1929), I, 29.
[13] *The Complete Bible,* trans. Smith and Goodspeed (Chicago, 1951), III, 141.
[14] Plutarch, *Plutarch's Lives,* trans. John Dryden, ed. A. H. Clough (New York, 1940), p. 531.

the Middle East around A.D. 850, indicating that the explorer saw the flame in the form of a luminous bird at the top of the mast. The apparition quelled the heavy seas.[15] With the arrival of the Age of Exploration the seas once more became populated and references to St. Elmo's fire reappear on the pages of literature as well as in ships' logs. Columbus on his second voyage to the New World encountered the omen when 'on Saturday at night the body of St. Elmo was seen with seven lighted candles on the round top and there followed mighty rains and frightful thunders.'[16] The report goes on to point out that the sailors sang several litanies and offered up prayers to the spirit which they believed would work in their favor.

In the year 1519 Magellan made his famous trip around the world. A man named Pigafetta kept a journal of the voyage and gave several indications that they had seen the light:

> In stormy weather we frequently saw what is called the corpo santo, or St. Elme. On one very dark night it appeared to us like a flambeau on the summit of a large tree and thus remained for the space of two hours which was a matter of great consolation to us during the tempest.[17]
>
> ... the said saint appeared in the form of a light lighted at the top of the mast, and remained there near two hours and a half which comforted us greatly, for we were in tears, only expecting the hour of perishing; and when the holy light was going away from us it gave out so great a brilliancy, in the eyes of each, that we were near a quarter of an hour like blinded people calling out for mercy. For without any doubt nobody hoped to escape from the storm. It is noted that all and as many times as that light, which represents the said St. Anselme shows itself and descends upon a vessel which is in a storm at sea that vessel is never lost. Immediately that this light had departed the sea grew calmer, ...[18]

In the narration of a voyage to Brazil in 1540, Nienhoff renders to the light the name of 'Peaceable Fires.' He attempts to explain the fiery presences by saying they are vapors forced by the winds from the land. Once upon the water the violent agitation of the air lights them and they burn until their elements are consumed. He does not hesitate to mention, however, that the seamen believe them a lucky omen.[19]

A Dutch traveler of the same period experiences the mysterious sight on board his ship when 'the same night we saw upon the maine yarde, and in many other places a certaine signe, which the Portugalles call Corpo

---

[15] Bassett, *Legends*, pp. 304-305.

[16] F. Colon, 'The History of the Life and Actions of Admiral Christopher Colon,' *Pinkerton's Voyages* (London, 1812), XII, 58.

[17] *The First Voyage Around the World by Magellan*, trans. Lord Stanley (London, 1874), p. 42.

[18] Pigafetta, 'Pigafetta's Voyage Around the World,' *Pinkerton's Voyages* (London, 1812), II, 309.

[19] H. Nienhoff, 'Voyages and Travels into Brazil,' *Pinkerton's Voyages* (London, 1812), XIV, 698-699.

Santo ... when they first perceived it, the maister or chief boatswaine whistleth everyman to salute it was a Salve, Corpor Santo and a misericordia and with a very great cry....'[20]

A report from a learned English gentleman, Sir Humphrey Gilbert, en route to America about 1583, recalls the classical notion of Castor and Pollux. 'We had also upon our mainyard an apparition of a little fire by night, which the seamen do call Castor and Pollux. But we had only one which they take to be an evil sign of more tempest; ...'[21]

Yet another explorer in the sixteenth century claims he saw the fire about the size of a small candle pasted in the rigging of the ship. The crew, upon seeing what they thought was a spirit, immediately went to their knees in token of worship, and a priest on board threw relics into the sea as a sacrifice. The writer, himself, appears not to have been overly impressed by the sight, and when he returned home received what he felt was a more logical explanation of the event.[22]

Somewhat later (1639) a letter from Peru states that the light appeared in three distinct flames which moved from mast to mast, being correctly saluted in each new location by everyone aboard, thus assuring the safe passage.[23]

Dampier on his voyage of about the same time, averred that he had 'heard some ignorant seamen discoursing how they have seen the St. Elmo creep, or as they say, travel about in the scuppers, telling many dismal stories that hap'ned at such times, but I never did see one stir out of the place where it first was fixed, except upon the deck where every sea washeth it about.'[24]

Meanwhile, John Josselyn, the gossipy naturalist, saw the fire 'about the bigness of a great candle' which settled on the mainmast 'about 8 of the clock at night.' It is, says Josselyn, 'commonly thought to be a spirit.'[25]

The fiery specters infected the more literary minds of the times, and more than once we find suggestions of the St. Elmo's light in the 'belles lettres.' It is not hard to see how the concept of a spirit in flaming dress could work its way into some of the wild fantasies written in the sixteenth and seventeeth centuries. Much of the literary output was riddled with

---

[20] A. C. Burnell and P. A. Tiele, *The Voyage of John Huyghen Van Linschoten to the Indies* (London, 1885), II, 238.
[21] E. J. Paine, *Voyages of Elizabethian Seamen* (Oxford, 1900), pp. 46-47.
[22] R. Tomson, 'Voyage,' *The Principle Voyages, Trafiques and Discoveries of the English Nation*, ed. R. Hakluyt (Glasgow, 1904), IX, 345-346.
[23] Bassett, *Legends*, p. 309.
[24] Quoted in: Bassett, *Legends*, p. 310.
[25] Josselyn, 'Two Voyages,' p. 218.

fairies, elves, and witches, not to mention other monstrous Providences. Consequently one is not surprised to find Shakespeare using Ariel as the luminous shade:

> I boarded the king's ship; now on the beak,
> Now in the waist, the deck, in every cabin,
> I flamed amazement; sometimes I'd divide
> And burn in many places: on the topmast,
> The yards and bowsprit, would I flame distinctly . . .[26]

Douce, a later critic, explains Shakespeare's reference as a meteor or 'little blaze of fire' which appears on board ships, and has been known 'to lead people to suicide by drowning.'[27]

Bacon alludes to the light as 'St. Ermyn who never appears but after a storm.'[28] In Ariosto's *Orlando Furioso*, however, at the very height of the gale, when 'every hope was passed,' the crew saw 'the splendor of Saint Ermo's light' and the storm 'ceased to roar.'[29]

Erasmus mentions the dreaded sight in a colloquy entitled, appropriately, *The Shipwreck*. Here the flame takes up a position very near one of the crew; the worst of all possible signs according to the author.[30]

The Anatomy of Melancholy includes St. Elmo's fire under the chapter headed 'Spirits.' The seventeenth-century work claims the nautical lights take the form of stars, and mariners see them following a storm.[31] Camoens, an earlier poet, believes the ghostly fires to be simply a holy light seen in times of heavy weather at sea.[32]

An interesting personal account can be found in Forbin's memoirs of about 1700, when:

> . . . in the night-time, a very black cloud was formed on a sudden, which was accompanied with terrible thunder and lightning. For fear of a great storm I caused the sails to be furl'd. There came above thirty St. Elmos (the meteor which we call Will and a Wisp) about the ship, and one in particular on the Fane of the Mainmast, which was a foot and a half in height, I sent a sailor up to fetch it down. When the fellow got up to it, he said it made a noise like the Hiss of Gunpowder that is fired when it is wet. I ordered him to take off the Fane and come down; but as soon as he had taken it off, the Fire quitted it and pitch'd upon the top of the

---

[26] William Shakespeare, *The Complete Works of Shakespeare*, ed. H. Craig (New York, 1951), p. 1252; or see: *The Tempest*, I, ii, 196-200.

[27] F. Douce, *Illustrations of Shakespeare and Ancient Manners* (London, 1807), I, 3-4.

[28] F. Bacon, *The Works of Francis Bacon* (Boston, 1870), XIII, 358.

[29] L. Ariosto, *Orlando Furioso*, trans. John Hoole (London, 1783), V, 388-390.

[30] Erasmus, *The Colloquies of Erasmus*, trans. N. Bailey, ed. Rev. E. Johnson (London, 1878), pp. 275-276.

[31] R. Burton, *The Anatomy of Melancholy* (London, 1904), I, 217.

[32] Luiz de Camoes, *The Lusiad of Luiz de Camoes*, trans. L. Bacon (New York, 1950), p. 179.

mast where it stayed a long while till by degrees it spent itself. Tho' we so much dreaded a storm, we had nothing but a heavy Shower of Raine....[33]

The Count had a similar experience later with a flame-like substance which appeared on the horizon: the crew became terrified and refused to lower the sails, fearing the sign of the meteor had doomed them.[34]

Another intriguing account, of 1709, records the fiery presence aboard a merchantman. The sailors howled at the specter until it finally dissolved, whereupon they rejoiced in their victory over the ill omen.[35]

An eighteenth-century German belief has it that the candle-like flames are the souls of dead comrades. If the spirits ascend the mast, fair wind will follow; if they descend, beware of a gale.[36] Other sources of the period try to explain the phenomenon as either phosphorescent marine insects scooped up into the air, or rarified sulphurous elements in the atmosphere.[37]

The creative writers of the nineteenth century made fair game of the tradition. In his novel, a Frenchman named Corbière tells the story of a man who chased the 'Corpusant' up the mast in an effort to capture it. Warned by the crew that this soul of a drowned sailor should be ignored, he nevertheless persisted. When he was about to gain possession of the elusive flame, one of the sailors made the sign of the cross. The flame disappeared at once.[38]

Melville's *Moby Dick* incorporates the flame into a vivid description with infernal overtones. A trinity of bluish flames string themselves out along the yardarm:

> To sailors, oaths are household words; they will swear in the trance of calm, and in the teeth of tempest; they will imprecate curses from the topsail-yard-arms when most they teter over to a seething sea; but in all my voyagings, seldom have I heard a common oath when God's burning finger has been laid on the ship; ...
> While this palidness was burning aloft, few words were heard from the enchanted crew; who in one thick cluster stood on the forecastle, all their eyes gleaming in the pale phosphorescence, like a far away constellation of stars.[39]

Richard Dana indicates that he has made acquaintance with the 'corpusants.'

> When we got down we found all hands looking aloft, and there, directly over where

[33] C. Forbin, *Memoirs of the Count de Forbin*, trans. R. Hoole (London, 1731), I, 336.
[34] Forbin, *Memoirs*, II, 46.
[35] 'Lettres edifiantes,' *Mélusine*, II (1884-1885), 282.
[36] R. Basset, 'Le feu Saint-Elme,' *Mélusine*, II (1884-1885), 256.
[37] F. S. Bassett, *Legends*, p. 312-313.
[38] Quoted in: Gaidoz and Rolland, 'Le feu Saint-Elme,' pp. 116-117.
[39] Herman Melville, *Moby Dick* (New York, 1952), p. 498.

we had been standing upon the main-top-gallant-mast-head, was a ball of light, which the sailors name a corpusant (corpus sancti), and which the mate called out to us to look at. They were all watching it carefully, for the sailors have a notion that if the corpusant rises in the rigging, it is a sign of fair weather, but if it comes lower down, there will be a storm.[40]

On this occasion, however, only a heavy thunderstorm followed the descent of the flame.

A report from late nineteenth-century Greece calls the fires 'telonias,' maintaining they are spirits whose progress towards heaven has been impeded by evil demons, and they must wander about as haunting flames for a limited period of time. Sailors use various incantations to ward off the intruders: prayers, incense, and gun reports. If a pig is on board the seamen pull his tail so that his squeals may drive off the fires. The luminous forms always forbode bad weather.[41]

About 1880 Sébillot found the belief current in various parts of France. In Brittany sailors thought the light signified the imminent death of a crew member. Around Nice the cabin boy is always the first to spy the fire. The belief held that if the fires ignited on the mast all would be saved, but should the flames descend into the sea all would be lost.[42]

Gregor found a similar tradition in northern Scotland in 1884 where the fishermen believe that once they had seen 'Jack's Lantern' they will never see land again. Here too the seamen think the specters are revenants of former comrades.[43]

As recently as 1950 I heard a story emanating from Rhode Island which concerns St. Elmo's fire. The crew of a vessel named *Viola* had seen the fire on the previous voyage. When the ship put out again one of the crew decided to heed the prognostication and stayed ashore. The vessel went down with all hands.

This article by no means pretends to contain a complete survey of all the references made to St. Elmo's fire. Bassett's chapter on the light,[44] although more inclusive, is much less informative in its source material. The data presented does, I hope, give a more lucid insight into the growth of such a tradition and how different ages have reacted to the electrical phenomenon.

I might just point out here that science, as early as the mid-nineteenth

---

[40] Richard H. Dana, *Two Years Before the Mast* (New York, 1924), p. 340.
[41] N. G. Politis, 'Le feu Saint-Elme,' *Mélusine*, II (1884-1885), 118.
[42] P. Sébillot, *Le Folk-lore Des Pêcheurs* (Paris, 1901), pp. 210-211.
[43] W. Gregor, 'Some Folk-lore of the Sea,' *Journal of Folklore*, IV (1884), 7.
[44] F. S. Bassett, *Legends*, pp. 302-320.

century, had proved that the hobgoblin of the mariner's existence was no more than an overabundance of electricity in the atmosphere. Once ignited by the chafing of the rigging, the flames would naturally adhere to anything metallic, thus the iron of the spars and yardarms became likely targets for the fitful fires. If touched, the greatest harm the fiery tongues can deliver is to give the meddler an unpleasant shock.

The belief offers two possible gauges for divining weather. First, and foremost, is the number of lights seen. Two usually mean fair, one foul; obviously a hand-me-down from the Roman times. In only one case, to my knowledge, is this arrangement reversed completely. A traveler of 1600, calling the fires 'St. Germain,' explains the resultant evil from the fact that demons are never seen alone, always in pairs.[45] The second weather indication results from the flame's movement on the spar. If the body of fire begins to ascend the mast, good; if it descends, start taking in canvas!

In practically every account discussed, St. Elmo arrives before, or at the height of the blow. It is gratifying to note that the only two who claim that the fire follows the storm (Burton and Bacon) are not mariners, and undoubtedly have their knowledge secondhand.

The St. Elmo history illustrates well the workings of folklore in a culture. The ancients never questioned the meaning of Castor and Pollux when they shone on the sails. The learnèd not only wrote about the phenomenon, but believed in the omen implicitly. In the sixteenth and seventeenth centuries much of the thought rested on Divine Providences and their influences over the lives of men. Therefore such things as ghostly lights, phantom ships, and odd natural occurrences were taken by all but the skeptic as meaningful signs. In the eighteenth century the picture changed. The Age of Reason introduced a new approach to natural science. No longer was Pliny so revered, when men began to look more closely into nature's organisms to ascertain their honest functions. The fire of St. Elmo ceased to be explained as the Holy Spirit and beckoned science to give it a 'raison d'être.' Thus such explanations as luminous plankton and sulphuric vapor began to frequent the printed page.

With the advent of the nineteenth century the learnèd men spurned the once valid superstitions concerning the Corpusants and left them to the gullible minds of the peasant and more primitive peoples. In the environment of the uneducated, superstitious fishermen and sailors passed on memories of the shimmering specter.

How prevalent the superstition concerning St. Elmo's fire is today is

[45] Gaidoz and Rolland, 'Le feu Staint-Elme,' p. 116.

a matter for conjecture. Stories about the light undoubtedly still exist, but no worthwhile maritime collecting has been done to augment this statement. That the once renowned St. Elmo still hisses among the smoke stacks of the ocean-going liner seems only an incongruous thought. We can imagine that today's seamen would think it merely a malfunction of the engine, at best, and lay below to watch the current film.

Helen Creighton has an interesting chapter on fire ships in her book, *Bluenose Ghosts*.[46] It seems logical that these current stories about fiery specters are no more than large editions of St. Elmo's light. In practically every instance they predict foul weather. 'The Palatine Ship,' not infrequently seen off Block Island, in the nineteenth century became a symbol for heavy blows. So the 'Teazer,' often seen today in the Maritime Provinces, has come to represent the same thing.

If the St. Elmo tradition, as presented here, is still in circulation, it has concealed itself well from the collector. It is doubtful that the belief will ever see the light, unless some hardy soul takes it upon himself to do some earnest work in sea lore. To date little has been done.

[46] See: Helen Creighton, *Bluenose Ghosts* (Toronto, 1957).

The Travels of Tilikum

BY W. GILLIES ROSS

THE Nootkan dugout canoe, *Tilikum*, was built on Vancouver Island, probably in about 1870. This small craft, scarcely thirty feet in water-line length, left Victoria, British Columbia, in May 1901, crossed in turn the Pacific, Indian and Atlantic oceans, and arrived at Margate, England, in September 1904. After vicissitudes and hard knocks she returned to Victoria and for twenty-five years rested in a park full of totem poles, a fate which most deep-sea vessels have been fortunate enough to avoid. Inured though she was to hard treatment, *Tilikum* evidently found this last burden too great, for in 1965 she moved from Thunderbird Park to a new, possibly final, resting place in the Maritime Museum of British Columbia.

The master of this dauntless craft during her world cruise was Captain J. C. Voss, veteran of many trading and sealing voyages in the Pacific Ocean and Bering Sea, a man short in stature but brimming over with confidence and eager for adventure. His first companion, Winnipeg-born journalist Norman Luxton, was a novice at sea but made up for it in enthusiasm. As for the idea, neither man was willing to admit having conceived it, Voss declaring the idea Luxton's and Luxton insisting that he had been persuaded into it by Voss.

Throughout the 40,000 miles of this ocean cruise, *Tilikum* was admired by crowds everywhere. They paid to see her on exhibit. They gathered on beaches to watch Voss bring her through crashing breakers to demonstrate the use of his sea anchor. They thronged the water fronts to watch her depart, and followed her to sea in steamers and small boats. In Australia, New Zealand, and South Africa, she logged more than 1,400 miles by train, the first (and likely the last) ocean-going ship to visit dozens of inland towns. On reaching Johannesburg, elevation 5,764 feet, she established the high-altitude record for deep-sea sailing vessels.

The three-year cruise of *Tilikum*, however, occupied only a fraction of her life, which must now approach the century mark. Some attention

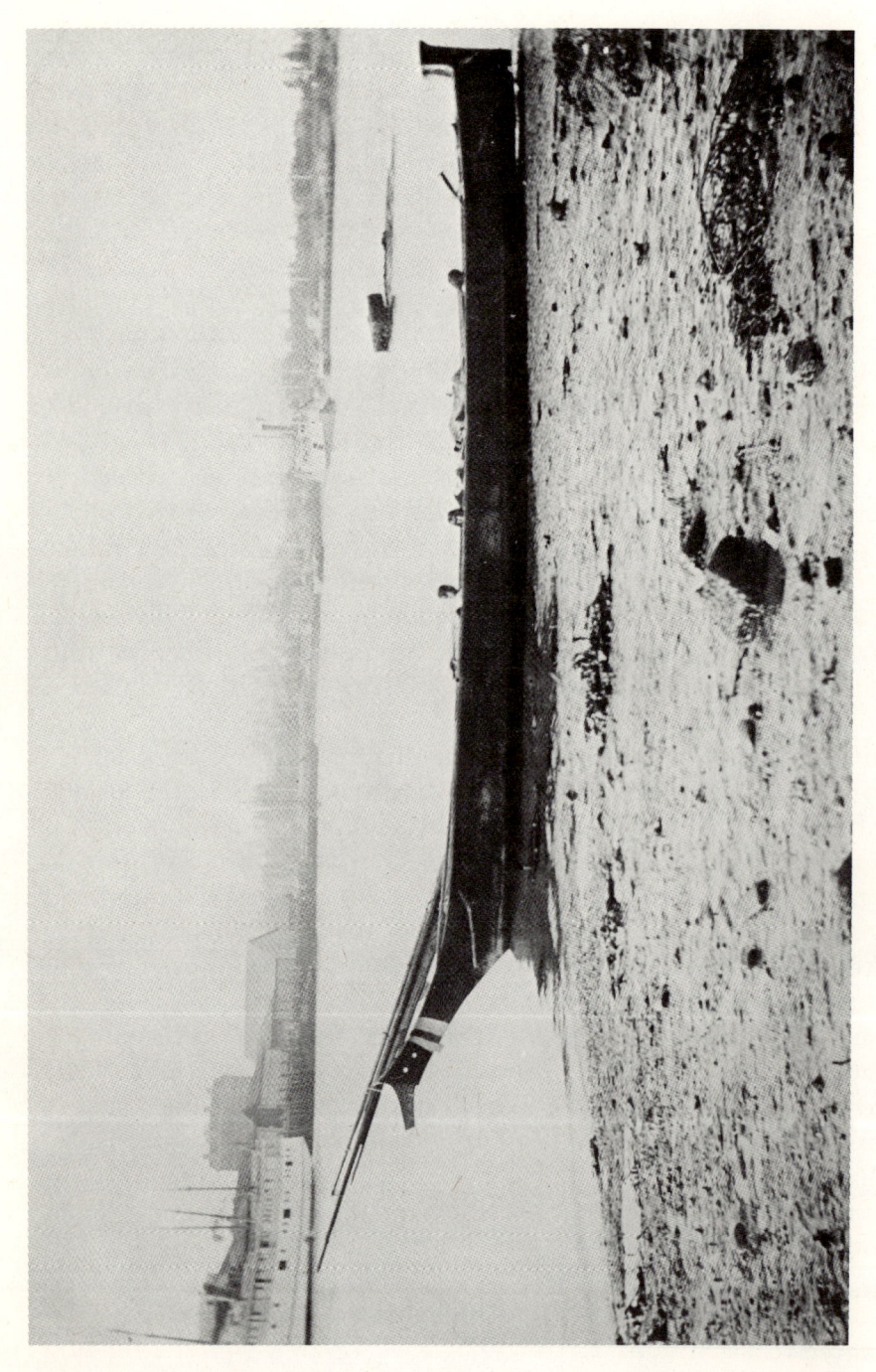

A Nootkan dugout canoe, said to be *Tilikum*, immediately before Voss and Volmers modified her into a decked, schooner-rigged, ocean cruiser

Courtesy Provincial Archives, Victoria, British Columbia

ought, therefore, to be given to her travels after the completion of her voyage in England, where Voss abandoned her to her own devices and himself departed in search of other adventures in South America and Japan.

Tilikum *Takes Shape*

Among the West Coast Indians the time-honored method of making a light and seaworthy canoe was to start by felling a red cedar tree of about five feet in diameter and trimming it to the desired length. They then planed off the top third of the log, traced out a plan, and pointed up the ends. To hollow out the interior they split off wedges of wood inside the hull, working downwards in this way to within a few inches of the bottom. To smooth out the inside they used an adze, and sometimes fire. When the hull had assumed its hollow, pointed shape, they increased its beam by spreading out the sides. This they did by filling the hull with water into which they dropped red-hot stones until steam was produced. Mats over the top kept the steam within the hull. As the wood gradually became more supple they tapped in spreaders to push out the sides. Later, when the wood was dry, they inserted permanent thwarts. At this point the canoe was essentially complete. It only remained to knock out knots, plug the holes, flatten the bottom, smooth the exterior, fasten the headboard and sternpost, and apply a mixture of seal oil and ochre.

The result was a roomy vessel, suitable for coastal traveling, fishing, sealing, and even the hunting of whales. The Nootkan canoe was buoyant enough in bow and stern to lift nicely to approaching waves, and the high freeboard was effective in reasonable weather conditions in keeping the sea where it was wanted—on the outside of the hull. Early explorers often saw such canoes on long, coasting voyages.

With due respect to the qualities and achievements of these dugout canoes, it must however be added that they were essentially good-weather, coastal craft, neither intended for nor suited to extended deep-sea cruising. They were open and without keels, and could not withstand heavy weather. Nor did they customarily possess a more economical means of propulsion than the muscle power of several paddlers. Voss could have invited a team of Nootka paddlers along but he could not have stored enough food for them, and furthermore, with paddlers along both sides he could not have decked the vessel.

When Voss found the canoe on the east coast of Vancouver Island she was lying on her side on a beach. A quick examination convinced him that the craft was solid and large enough to carry provisions and equipment for two men on a long trip. He addressed himself to the Indian owner, who had suddenly appeared, sensing a sale. As Voss recalled the transaction, 'business is business, and with the aid of my flask I secured the canoe for a reasonable price.' The Indian, delighted by the sale of the boat, and stimulated by the Old Rye which had accompanied the deal, presented Voss with the skull of his father, the maker of the canoe. The skull of the deceased shipwright traveled around the world with *Tilikum* —glorious last rites. Later, in a ceremony involving the sacrifice of a bottle of wine, Voss bestowed the name *Tilikum,* which means 'friend' in the language of the Chinook Indians of Oregon.

The plan to circumnavigate the world in a small boat was devised by Voss and Luxton in 1901. Three years before, Joshua Slocum, Nova Scotia-born but a United States citizen by naturalization, had completed the first solo voyage around the world in his yawl *Spray*. The desire to equal *Spray's* voyage with a smaller boat involved perhaps some sense of geographical and national rivalry and, no doubt, the prospect of gain as well, for such achievements, then as now, could be turned to financial advantage. Luxton promised Voss $2,500 and half of any income from the book he intended to write.

In terms of over-all length there was little difference between the two boats. *Tilikum,* with her long headboard, measured thirty-eight feet, a foot or two longer than *Spray*. In most other respects, however, they were vastly different. *Spray* was broad in beam, roomy on deck and below, and had a gross tonnage of twelve. *Tilikum,* on the other hand, measured only three tons gross and was a much narrower boat, with less freeboard, little deck space, and virtually no room below. Of the two boats *Tilikum* was unquestionably inferior for a long ocean cruise.

For the ocean voyage Voss had to modify *Tilikum* from a simple dugout hull without keel, decking or masts, to a decked, sailing craft that could endure rough seas, carry sufficient provisions, and be tolerably comfortable. It was a large order, and Voss enlisted the help of Harry Vollmers, who owned a small-boat works on Galiano Island, British Columbia.

The first job was to strengthen the hull: red cedar has a tendency to split. Vollmers laid a strong keelson inside the boat, bolted to it an eight-inch wooden keel, and fastened oak frames inside the hull at two-foot intervals. For stability he secured 300 pounds of lead to the keel and put a half ton of ballast beneath the floor boards. The hull was now strong enough to withstand the force of waves and stable enough to offset the pressure of the wind on the 230 square feet of sail.

After raising the gunwales and decking the canoe they set up three masts guyed by wire shrouds and stays. The fore- and mainmasts were gaff rigged and the mizzen carried a jib-headed sail. There was one foresail. All the sails were made at Galiano Island, cut out of six-ounce canvas by Mr. Vollmers and sewed by his wife. Amidships they constructed a small cabin, five by eight feet in area and rising about two feet above deck level. Behind it a cockpit constituted the operational heart of the vessel —the steering position and the place from which all sails could be raised, trimmed and lowered. Inside the cabin there was little space. One bunk accommodated a man of average size, the supposition being that, while sailing, the second man would be at the tiller. In port, Voss slept on top of the locker opposite the bunk, a platform only fourteen inches wide. A passageway of only ten inches separated the bunk from the locker, and the mainmast may have occupied some of this space.

Luxton had left Voss to obtain a suitable boat for the circumnavigation. His reaction, on being confronted with an Indian dugout canoe, is not recorded. But probably he took kindly to the idea, for Luxton was all his life a great admirer of Indian folklore and handicraft. Certainly he was quick to appreciate the novelty of such a craft, as was Voss, who remarked, 'It struck me at once that if we could make our proposed voyage in an Indian canoe we would not alone make a world's record for the smallest vessel but also the only canoe that had circumnavigated the globe.'

Voss was pleased with the modifications to *Tilikum*. In a letter to a friend in San Francisco he wrote:

Having finished her, and having stood on my head, lain on my back and looked down on her from the nearest tree, I am forced to the conclusion that I have never seen anything of her size so moulded and proportioned.

This admiration was not universal, however. Weston Martyr, the yachting writer, saw *Tilikum* later in Cape Town and remarked to Voss in a guarded statement that she was a 'queer looking boat.' Others, more outspoken, called the craft 'ridiculous.' Captain Sainty of the barque *Port Sonachon*, which later spoke *Tilikum* near the Azores, described her as a 'dainty-looking little lady' but added that she 'looked a very frail craft to have buffeted the gales of three oceans.' A Sydney beachcomber considered *Tilikum* too 'tottlish.' If opinions on the appearance of *Tilikum* were mixed, opinions on her chances of survival were not. Landlubbers and seamen alike were confident that the boat would not survive a heavy sea.

Tilikum's World Cruise

Early in the morning of 21 May 1901 the narrow, schooner-rigged vessel left Oak Bay, near Victoria, and headed into the Strait of Juan de Fuca. Voss felt that a period of adjustment for boat and crew was needed, and whenever weather threatened he took shelter in some convenient bay. The first night was spent just west of Race Rocks, the next five in Port San Juan, the seventh in a cove near the Cape Beale light, and the next nine in Dodges Cove. In this way, sixteen days passed before *Tilikum* pointed her prow into the Pacific and let the coast fall away astern. Ahead lay a voyage of over three years, the long way round, to England.

In fair weather and fresh breezes *Tilikum* sailed well, once covering as much as 177 miles in twenty-four hours. There were also calm periods when the boat drifted aimlessly while food and fresh water dwindled. During one such calm in the Atlantic doldrums they sighted a large sailing ship a few miles away in the same predicament. Voss and his mate did what the other crew could not: they rowed their vessel over to visit. By the time the wind came up their visit had lasted two days.

When they encountered gales *Tilikum* simply hove to, the Voss-designed sea anchor holding the bow into the waves and reducing the boat's drift to leeward, and the men went below to rest—if two men can be said to rest in the middle of a storm on a small boat, with a bunk and a half between them.

Tilikum demonstrated a remarkable adaptability to the needs of the moment. Once, when driven onto a lee shore in Australia, she rode gracefully through huge breakers with the aid of her sea anchor, and then, after grounding in a vulnerable position at the entrance to a lagoon, she hoisted all sails and bumped her way over the bar into safe water. In Sydney, incensed by the notion of paying harbor and pilotage dues of £2–10 merely to sail out, Voss left the city by train, taking *Tilikum* along as baggage, and put her back into salt water at Newcastle. The most serious incident of the voyage was the loss of Louis Begent, a Tasmanian seaman who had replaced Luxton at Samoa. He and the ship's compass were washed overboard by a breaking wave some 1,200 miles from Sydney, and never seen again. The double loss made navigation difficult, but *Tilikum* reached her destination.

Tilikum suffered more on land than she did at sea. At Melbourne a crane hook broke and dropped her to the ground, opening a network of splits up to two inches wide in the hull. Voss sued the carrier company and stayed in Melbourne several months to obtain a settlement. Then, with steel strips, bolts, caulking, a new keel, and some fresh paint, *Tilikum* returned to salt water at Geelong and continued the cruise.

Later, having survived a train trip from Durban to Pretoria she had her Indian figurehead kicked to pieces by a horse. There were some who credited the horse with a good deal of critical judgment in undertaking this piece of destruction.

If many were skeptical of *Tilikum* there was one, at least, who showed unreasonable faith. A short, plump lady paid her way into an exhibition of *Tilikum* at Manley Park, Sydney. Voss discovered her seated in the cockpit and showing signs of impatience. 'When is she going to start?' she demanded. Voss's explanation that the boat, propped up as she was in a tent, was not about to start anywhere, was rejected. 'I paid you sixpence for a boat ride and I'm going to have it,' she insisted, and Voss endured a stream of vocal abuse that must have made a force nine wind seem mild by comparison.

'Two's company but three's a crowd' was amply demonstrated on board *Tilikum*. Voss and the canoe struck up a solid friendship that seemed to operate against a succession of mates. Luxton left at Samoa, and when he later encountered Voss in Australia he would not be lured back to his berth on *Tilikum*, claiming that he had received a warning from a reliable fortuneteller.

Begent was of little use after his loss at sea.

A man engaged at Newcastle was continually seasick, and could not continue past Melbourne. The same thing happened to a man at Geelong, who decided to leave after a trial run out of harbor and back.

The Seamen's Home at Melbourne sent Voss a fellow who was dead drunk. He came to at sea and proved an excellent seaman while sober, which was until the next port, Adelaide. Voss then signed on Ed Donner, the 'Tattooed Man of Australia,' who stuck it out until Dunedin, after which a man named MacDonald came on board as far as Christchurch. Next came H. Buckridge, just back from Scott's first Antarctic expedition. He lasted until Auckland and there announced that he would get a boat and sail her to England himself. He would have done better to stay with Voss, for his four-ton yawl *Keora*, was later lost off the New Zealand coast.

An Irishman, the Reverend Mr. Russell, who for some undisclosed reason went by the name of MacMillan in New Zealand, joined Voss until East London, South Africa, and was there replaced by a Canadian named Cairns. Finally, at Cape Town, Voss and *Tilikum* received on board Mr. E. Harrison, eleventh and last in the long series of mates. He was suffering from consumption.

On 2 September 1904, *Tilikum* sailed into a tumultuous welcome at Margate, England, her arrival in sharp contrast to the quiet departure from Oak Bay three years, three months and ten days before. In the words of Voss, the crowd

> ... started cheering, and kept it up till I made the *Tilikum* fast alongside of a fishing schooner called the *Sunbeam*. When I got on shore the people were standing all round the wharf to receive me. It was almost impossible for me to get through the mass of people. Everyone wanted to shake me by the hand and congratulate me on my successful voyage. All at once I felt myself going up in the air and the next moment dropped in a carriage and taken to a hotel where champagne was opened, bottle after bottle, and that ended the voyage of the *Tilikum*.

That, however, did not end the voyage of *Tilikum*. Driven, one might say, by the desire to complete the circumnavigation of the world and to see once more the mist-shrouded coastal mountains of British Columbia, *Tilikum* spent the next quarter century in a homeward quest, during which she suffered harder knocks than the Pacific, Indian and Atlantic oceans had been able to deliver, and came closer to destruction than she ever had under the hands of Captain Voss and his eleven mates.

For Voss himself the voyage was indeed over. It only remained to wind it up with exhibition of his marvelous canoe and a lecture tour through England and Scotland. The latter was arranged with the help of the polar explorer, Ernest Shackleton, who had once been an attentive listener at a public lecture given by Voss and his mate Buckridge in Wellington, New Zealand.

Shackleton profited by his association with Voss, for twelve years later he and his men were marooned on Elephant Island in the Antarctic Ocean, having lost their ship *Endurance* in the polar pack ice. His decision to attempt to cross 800 miles of wintry seas in a twenty-seven-foot whaleboat to get help at South Georgia was no doubt influenced by the experience of Captain Voss, who had always emphasized that in rough seas a small boat well handled is as safe as a large one.

English Interlude

For two years *Tilikum* remained in the Navy and Marine Exhibition, Earl's Court, London. Voss had hoped that she could be permanently interred in the British Museum, but this was not to pass, and when she was discharged from Earl's Court she appears to have been more or less cast aside, the novelty of her achievement having worn off.

The end of the three-year ocean voyage at Margate, England, in 1904, and the beginning of hard times for *Tilikum*
From Illustrated London News, 10 September 1904

In 1906 *Tilikum* was discovered in a Thames-side factory yard by a Mr. H. Ingersoll. He acquired the boat and made arrangements to install an engine in a machine shop eight miles away. It is clear from the events which followed that *Tilikum,* paddled by British Columbia Indians across coastal fishing grounds, and sailed by a master mariner across three oceans, was unwilling to accept the indignity of a foul-smelling engine.

Two draft horses moved the boat out of the factory yard and down the road on an iron-wheeled cradle. Everything went smoothly until the contraption reached the right-angle turn into the machine shop, where the ensuing maneuvers and the growing crowd of onlookers caused an impressive traffic jam. When at last the boat had been turned and there seemed to be no obstacles to a successful transit of the gate, the horses decided not to go in. They were unhitched and a crowd of well-wishers replaced them. With a chain tackle they moved *Tilikum* forward a few feet, but a small incline proved a barrier. A Panhard automobile was then hitched on. At the peak of its effort, straining all forty horsepower, the chain parted and the car shot arrow-like into a wall. Another automotive attempt with a manila rope was successful, and the boat moved into the shop, where a thirty-five-horsepower, single-cylinder engine was duly installed.

Ingersoll had also requested an enlargement of the cabin, some rigging alterations, and general repairs. In September 1906 the boat was ready to be launched, and the shop employees were given a holiday. Two horses towed the cradle and boat out. The freshly painted hull was gleaming white. Masts and other gear were stowed neatly on deck, and the anchor hung from the bow in preparation of the launch nearby at Putney. Two girls sat on the cabin top. It was a gala occasion.

The contraption moved along at moderate speed, narrowly missed a ditch, and then stopped when a wheel came off. The wheel was replaced, but as the cradle started down a hill its brakes gave out. Blocks had to be jammed under the wheels from time to time, so that the descent was made in a series of jumps. On Putney High Street, not far from the launching place, a wheel disintegrated. Motorists were confronted by the unfamiliar obstacle of an Indian dugout canoe mounted on wheels and drawn by two horses, stuck in the main thoroughfare. They had no technique for dealing with it. A crowd dragged the rig on three wheels the remaining distance and pushed it into the water. A rising tide lifted *Tilikum* off and she began to sink. The splits so successfully supplied by the crane operator in Melbourne had lost their caulking. In some haste the boat was beached for repairs.

Three months later Ingersoll and two others sailed *Tilikum* through London to the Thames estuary, an eventful trip that makes the worst rounding of the Horn appear commonplace. There was no end of trouble. The headboard broke off in a collision, and was replaced by a bowsprit. The masts had the impudence to quarrel with the Blackfriars Bridge and came out a little shorter, but it was not of great consequence because soon after *Tilikum* collided with a barge and broke the fore- and mainmasts clean off. Ingersoll set up a jury rig. Repeated engine failures caused many embarrassing moments. Once *Tilikum* drifted into a fleet of boats and fouled a number of moorings. On another occasion she was

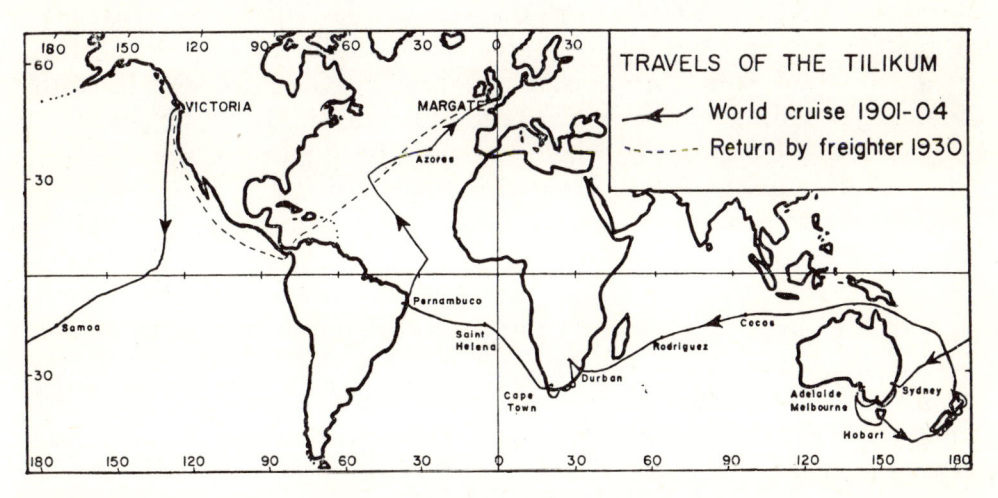

TRAVELS OF THE TILIKUM
⟵ World cruise 1901-04
------ Return by freighter 1930

blown ashore and had to be towed off. Near Gravesend she dragged anchor during futile attempts to start the engine, and broke her bowsprit against another boat. She dragged again at Hole Haven and again at Havengore Creek. On the odd occasion when the engine did work the propeller seemed always to catch the dinghy painter and wind it into hopeless snarls. One gets the impression that the engine was somewhat less than a success. With assistance from a fisherman and from several motorboats which gave tows, *Tilikum* made her way to Pin Mill on the River Orwell and sagged onto the mud as the tide ebbed. At this point one of the crew, with admirable coordination, dropped an open can of gasoline and a lighted Primus stove simultaneously into the cabin. As flames erupted through the cabin door the crew shot out of the fore hatch. The fire was extinguished with mud and water.

Ingersoll made two more 'cruises' in *Tilikum,* and in 1908 she was still at Pin Mill. A photograph of 1911 shows her at Canvey Island in the Thames estuary, moored, but evidently not in sailing trim. She has a slight list to port and is without booms, gaffs or sails. The bowsprit is gone; probably it was never replaced after the Thames trip. Who owned the boat at this time is unrecorded. It appears that during the next thirteen years the condition of *Tilikum* became steadily worse. A photograph of 1924 shows her as a derelict on the mud flats at Gains Creek, Canvey Island, without masts and in very bad shape.

Tilikum *Returns*

In 1926, H. T. Barnes of Victoria, a good friend of Captain Voss up to his death in 1922, received word that *Tilikum* lay abandoned at Canvey Island. In response to a notice placed by Barnes in an English yachting magazine the Ryeford brothers, members of the Greenwich Yacht Club, identified themselves as owners of the hulk and subsequently agreed to donate it to the City of Victoria in order to have it set up as a permanent, free exhibit. In 1930 the Furness Lines agreed to ship home what remained of *Tilikum,* and the Port of London Authority generously waived the usual loading charges.

And so *Tilikum,* veteran of paddle, sail, train, crane, horse, automobile, and her own and faulty engine, added another means of conveyance to her list and made the voyage home on board the freighter *Pacific Ranger* via the freshly cut Panama Canal—which would surely have tempted Voss had it existed in 1904. In late June 1930, the crated hull was unloaded at the Rithet Consolidated dock in Victoria. *Tilikum* had completed her world circumnavigation.

None of the warmth rightfully accorded a triumphant native son was evident. *Tilikum,* battered and exhausted by her travels, stood neglected on the pier while the city Chamber of Commerce debated where to put three tons of boat. Not until 7 August could the newspapers report that the hull, after painting and repairs, had been with ceremony set up outside the Crystal Gardens swimming pool. There she remained for several years, under a sign that identified her incorrectly as the 'Old Tillicum.'

By 1936 her condition, through neglect, was pitiful. Captain Alexander MacDonald, veteran of twenty-six trips around the Horn and a staunch member of the Thermopylae Club, an organization of retired seafarers, led a crusade to raise $200 for the necessary restoration. The result of his newspaper articles and public lectures was the collection of only $90, but Victor Jacobsen, a shipwright of the old school, began the restoration just the same. Captain Voss's daughter, Mrs. B. F. Kuhn of Portland, Oregon, visited Victoria, reminisced about the departure of her father thirty-six years before, and was photographed beside *Tilikum*, the sight of which brought tears to her eyes.

The location of the vessel outside Crystal Gardens had dissatisfied many persons, and in 1940 she was transferred to nearby Thunderbird Park and set up among the totem poles, under a protecting roof. But there was no protecting fence, and in no time at all souvenir hunters and that curious breed of people who feel obliged to initial all available surfaces were damaging the craft. In 1943 Justice Sydney Smith of the British Columbia Supreme Court emphasized the value of *Tilikum* as a historical document in an address to the British Columbia Historical Society, and said, 'Now it is being scrawled over by people with little weight and less manners. It should be better looked after.' The Thermopylae Club implored government action but the government held that a fence around *Tilikum* would prevent a true and proper appreciation of the objet d'art. By 1944 the rudder had gone and the tongue of the figurehead had been removed. 'Vandals Wrecking *Tilikum*' was the headline of an item in the *Vancouver Sun*. Finally a few dollars were collected to provide a railing around the boat.

With the security of a railing *Tilikum* suffered less from vandalism, but the elements of weather continued their relentless deterioration. The faithful members of the Thermopylae Club came again to the boat's aid when, in 1958, dry rot was discovered in the hull. Three short dummy masts, hollow to permit air to circulate through the hull, were erected and the vessel got a coat of paint.

In March 1965, *Tilikum* unobtrusively took her departure from Thunderbird Park on a low-bed trailer truck for the newly founded Maritime Museum of British Columbia. The move had been authorized by the Provincial Museum, custodians of Thunderbird Park, but it gave rise to a full gale of controversy. According to one 'Rebel' Mowat, a Victoria bus-tour driver, the city owned the boat and had not been consulted about the move. He threatened to press charges of theft or piracy against the Victoria Van and Storage Company, which had carried *Tilikum* to her new quarters. But the city prosecutor declared it impossible to press a charge of theft until ownership of the vessel was proved. There followed a frantic search of city records, newspaper files, and private memoirs, in an attempt to learn more of the details of the 1930 transaction whereby *Tilikum* had returned to Victoria. The *Victoria Daily Times* contained the headline, 'Legal Squall Hits *Tilikum;* Rebel at the Helm.'

Seizing the occasion of public interest, Mowat obtained the support of hundreds of sympathizers in his 'Keep-*Tilikum*-Free' campaign. When the Ryeford brothers had donated the boat in 1930 they had specified that she should be exhibited free—and now the Maritime Museum intended to charge admission! Here was a clear breach of promise. Mrs. Kuhn wrote from Oregon to protest the 'commercialization' of her father's boat. Frank Calder, an Indian member of the British Columbia legislature, declared that Indians of the province regarded *Tilikum* as a form of Indian art and favored 'free display of such items.' 'Rebel' Mowat gathered 1,286 signatures on his petition of protest and prepared to present it to the owner of the boat, whoever the owner might prove to be.

When at last an examination of the private papers of a deceased commissioner of the Victoria Visitors' Bureau revealed that *Tilikum* had been given to the City of Victoria, 'Rebel' Mowat presented his petition to the city council. The council, seeking to dodge the issue, claimed that the boat really belonged to the Victoria Visitors' Bureau. Meantime, the curator of the Maritime Museum came forward to announce that *Tilikum* was secure in the Museum and unlikely to be moved anywhere else. And as the *Victoria Daily Times* reporter observed of the brick wall that had been torn down to permit the entrance of the boat into the Museum, and then bricked up again, 'the mortar is hard and dry.'

The mortar remained hard and dry as the issue resolved itself. Public feeling subsided when it became clear that the city council, the Visitors' Bureau, the Provincial Museum, and the old salts of the Thermopylae Club were solidly united in favor of *Tilikum*'s new quarters, admission or not. And there the matter stands. *Tilikum* remains in the Maritime Museum—at least for the present. One wonders uneasily what may happen when the new British Columbia Centennial Museum is opened in a year or two.

Captain Voss brought his venturesome voyages to a close in 1922, when he died in California. Norman Luxton, his companion across the Pacific in 1901, died in Banff, Alberta, in 1962. But *Tilikum* has outlasted both, surviving the challenge of storms, defective cranes, exhibitions, low bridges, apathy, souvenir hunters, petitions and dry rot, to remain a powerful tribute to the workmanship of West Coast Indians and the superb navigation of Captain Voss.

NOTES ON SOURCES

The Venturesome Voyages of Captain Voss (Yokohama: Herald Press, 1913) contains Voss's delightful firsthand account of the world cruise in *Tilikum*. A more recent edition is still available (London: Rupert Hart-Davis, 1955). A typescript copy of the original manuscript written by Voss, somewhat saltier in language than the book and different occasionally in context, exists in the Public Archives of British Columbia, Victoria. Most of the quotations above are taken either from the manuscript or the book.

Newspapers have provided additional details on the world cruise. Scattered bits of information have been obtained from: the *Newcastle Chronicle;* the *Australasian;* the *Argus;* the *Sydney Herald;* the *Hobart Mercury;* and the *Launceston Examiner*. For the period since *Tilikum*'s return to Victoria several West Coast newspapers have been essential sources of information. Among these are: the *Vancouver Sun;* the *Vancouver Province;* the *Victoria Colonist;* the *Victoria Times;* the *Islander;* the *Vancouver Observer;* and the *Pacific Tribune*.

Articles or short items have appeared in a number of magazines, including: the *Yachting and Boating Monthly;* the *Yachting Monthly;* the *Spray; Illustrated London News; Skipper; Vision; Escape; MacLean's; British Columbia Digest*.

Appendix

Notes about the Contributors 295
Sources of Articles 297
Neptune's Editors and Advisory Board 299

The Contributors

Mrs. B. C. Baker, widow of Captain Baker of the bark *William H. Besse,* died over half a century ago. The late Dr. Harold Bowditch edited her reminiscences.

Alexander Crosby Brown, a newspaperman of Newport News, Virginia, has been an editorial adviser and frequent contributor to *The American Neptune* since its inception.

David Cabot of Westerly, Rhode Island, was an undergraduate at Harvard and an enthusiastic small boat sailor when he wrote this article.

George G. Carey, a folklorist who has written three books, presently holds a professorship at the University of Massachusetts.

Joanna C. Colcord, sister of Lincoln, as a child sailed with her parents on a square-rigger to China.

Lincoln Colcord, "the sage of Searsport," inspired the founding of *The American Neptune* and took an active interest in it throughout his life.

Sheldon H. Harris, a social science professor at the New Bedford Institute of Technology, is deeply interested in the colorful maritime history of that port.

R. C. Holmes, a Trinity House Pilot for the Port of Plymouth, England, wrote as a hobby. He was killed in 1956 when he fell between a cutter and a quay.

Llewellyn Howland was an irrepressible writer and yacht designer.

Fred Hunt, a native of Alabama, was a reporter on the *Quincy Patriot-Ledger* for many years until his death.

Henry C. Kittredge, author of three books on Cape Cod, wrote this article after he retired to Barnstable, Massachusetts, as Rector Emeritus of St. Paul's School.

George MacBeath was Curator of Canadian History at the New Brunswick Museum in 1957.

A. Alfred Mattsson was a Norwegian sailor who swallowed the anchor and settled down in Salem, Massachusetts, as a clock repair man.

James M. Merrill, a graduate of the Merchant Marine Academy and World War II naval officer, is professor of history at Whittier College.

Walter Millis, a journalist and historian, and author of several books, edited *The Forrestal Diaries*.

Samuel Eliot Morison, America's most eminent maritime historian, was the only president of *The American Neptune, Inc.*

Lee Nathaniel Newcomer, professor of history at Wisconsin State University when he wrote this paper, is the author of several books and articles.

Wallace B. Ordway was a farmer and student of local history in West Newbury, Massachusetts, whose family had grown sage for generations.

W. Gillies Ross, a geographer, has done about 10,000 miles of ocean sailing and made an unsuccessful attempt to sail the Northwest Passage from west to east.

William G. Saltonstall, former headmaster of Phillips Exeter Academy and Peace Corps director, is an enthusiastic sailor.

William B. Sturtevant was an old sailor who enjoyed reminiscing about his seagoing career.

Dr. William Allen Wilbur was the son of Captain John P. Wilbur, one of the two brothers in this intimate and touching incident.

Sources of Articles

The articles in this book were reprinted from the following issues of *The American Neptune*:

A Boy's First Day at Sea in the Bark *Belle of Oregon*—1886
                              Vol. I, no. 1 (January 1941)

Domestic Life on American Sailing Ships
                              Vol. II, no. 3 (July 1942)

The Meeting of the Ships *Dauntless* and *Thomas Dana* off Cape Horn
                              Vol. VII, no. 1 (January 1947)

Reminiscences of a Voyage in the Bark *William H. Besse*
                              Vol. VI, no. 2 (April 1946)

The Dry Salvages and the Thacher Shipwreck
                              Vol. XXV, no. 4 (October 1965)

The Disorderly Voyage of the Brig *Betsy*
                              Vol. III, no. 1 (January 1943)

"Just Ease Her When She Pitches"
                              Vol. XV, no. 4 (October 1955)

The Battle of Priest's Cove
                              Vol. X, no. 4 (October 1950)

The Merrimac River Gundalow and Gundalowmen
                              Vol. X, no. 4 (October 1950)

The Boston Packets
                              Vol. XXIV, no. 2 (April 1964)

Enchanted Voyage
                              Vol. VII, no. 3 (July 1947)

The New England Double Enders
                              Vol. XII, no. 2 (April 1952)

Johnny Woodboat
                              Vol. XVII, no. 1 (January 1957)

Murder at Sea
                              Vol. XVI, no. 3 (July 1956)

Mutiny on *Junior*

    Vol. XXI, no. 2 (April 1961)

A Tidal Wave at Huanillos, Chile, in 1877

    Vol. I, no. 2 (April 1941)

Men, Monotony, and Mouldy Beans

    Vol. XVI, no. 1 (January 1956)

The Battle of the Rams

    Vol. XXV, no. 2 (April 1965)

The Iron Sea Elephants

    Vol. X, no. 1 (January 1950)

Fur Seal Hunting in the South Atlantic

    Vol. II, no. 2 (April 1942)

Campeche Days

    Vol. II, no. 3 (July 1942)

The Tradition of the St. Elmo's Fire

    Vol. XXIII, no. 1 (January 1963)

The Travels of *Tilikum*

    Vol. XXVIII, no. 1 (January 1968)

Neptune's *Editors and Advisory Board*

Managing Editor

Walter Muir Whitehill, 1941–1950
Ernest S. Dodge, 1951–1968
Philip C. F. Smith, 1969–

Editors

M. V. Brewington, 1941
Alexander C. Brown, 1946
Howard I. Chapelle, 1941–1965
Lincoln Colcord, 1941–1948

Ernest S. Dodge, 1969
Storer B. Lunt, 1951
Samuel Eliot Morison, 1942
Vernon D. Tate, 1941

Walter Muir Whitehill, 1951

Editorial Advisory Board

Robert G. Albion, 1941
William A. Baker, 1952
Charles F. Batchelder, 1967
Alexander C. Brown, 1941–1946
Lloyd A. Brown, 1941–1966
Edward G. Brownlee, 1942
Robert H. Burgess, 1966
Lionel Casson, 1954
Charles D. Childs, 1941
Edward Strong Clark, 1941–1952
William Bell Clark, 1941–1969
Griffith Baily Coale, 1941–1950
Edward L. Cochrane, 1949–1960
Charles H. P. Copeland, 1952–1964
John Philips Cranwell, 1941–1952

Carl C. Cutler, 1941–1966
Ernest S. Dodge, 1941–1951
Elwin M. Eldredge, 1941–1959
E. M. Eller, 1959
Robert E. Farlow, 1941
Arthur D. Fay, 1966–1971
E. Kenneth Haviland, 1971
John B. Heffernan, 1951
John R. Herbert, 1946
Francis Lee Higginson, Jr., 1959
F. W. Howay, 1941–1944
Harold A. Innis, 1941–1942
S. W. Jackman, 1965
L. W. Jenkins, 1941–1961
John Haskell Kemble, 1941

Editorial Advisory Board (Continued)

Russell W. Knight, 1969
Dudley W. Knox, 1941–1960
W. Kaye Lamb, 1941
Augustus P. Loring, Jr., 1944–1952
Francis B. Lothrop, 1959
A. R. M. Lower, 1941–1943
John Lyman, 1942
Edward Lynan, 1947–1950
John W. McElroy, 1941
Arthur Pierce Middleton, 1948
C. Bradford Mitchell, 1955
Charles S. Morgan, 1941
Samuel Eliot Morison, 1941–1942
Cedric Ridgely-Nevitt, 1941
Harry Shaw Newman, 1952–1966
Richard Orr, 1941–1943
Alfred W. Paine, 1941–1944
Stanley Pargellis, 1951–1968

W. J. Lewis Parker, 1951
James Duncan Phillips, 1943–1954
Critchell Rimington, 1952
Bryant K. Rogers, 1941–1952
Erik A. R. Ronnberg, Jr., 1971
Henry Rusk, 1941–1952
R. A. Skelton, 1951–1971
Harold S. Sniffen, 1966
W. P. Stephens, 1941–1947
Herbert L. Stone, 1941–1959
Charles G. Summersell, 1946
D. Foster Taylor, 1941–1969
Frank A. Taylor, 1941
Giles M. S. Tod, 1962
William H. Tripp, 1941–1960
Charles M. Wright, 1941–1944
Lawrence C. Wroth, 1941–1971